GOD IN OUR TIME

*Arguments for the Existence of a Creator
in this Scientific Age*

Frederik H. Jonker

ATHENA PRESS
LONDON

GOD IN OUR TIME: *Arguments for the Existence of a Creator in this Scientific Age*
Copyright © Frederik H. Jonker 2004

All Rights Reserved

No part of this book may be reproduced in any form
by photocopying or by any electronic or mechanical means,
including information storage or retrieval systems,
without permission in writing from both the copyright
owner and the publisher of this book.

ISBN 1 931456 12 7

First Published 2004 by
ATHENA PRESS
Queen's House, 2 Holly Road
Twickenham TW1 4EG
United Kingdom

Printed for Athena Press

Margot & Family.

I hope the book may give you something to think about. Thanks again for your time and support during our recent visit to San Diego. We loved it (and you)

Frits

GOD IN OUR TIME

*Arguments for the Existence of a Creator
in this Scientific Age*

This book is dedicated to my children, Johannes and Anneke, and my grandchildren, Marijke and Lukas

ACKNOWLEDGEMENTS

I wish to acknowledge my indebtedness to the many people who commented on the early drafts of this book. Their advice and encouragement have been of great help in completing it.

In particular, I want to mention the thorough review of the various chapters by the Reverend Douglas Hallman. His insight and knowledge of both the religious and scientific aspects of the various arguments have greatly helped me in clarifying my own thoughts.

I also want to express my appreciation to Dr. Peter Morris, Alan Keates, and Dan Decaire who read early drafts of the book. Their comments greatly assisted me in continuing to scrutinize the literature for new insights and understanding.

It is a great pleasure to also thank my wife, Barbara, for the various reviews of the text, the wording, the spelling, the punctuation, etc. Also, her patience to put up with my preoccupation, at various times, was and is greatly appreciated.

Lastly, I want to thank the congregation and the ministers, Reverends Gerald Brown, Randall MacKenzie and Judith Bowman of Trinity United Church in Beamsville, Ontario, who have over the years patiently listened to my attempts at clarifying the thoughts expressed in this book.

Science without religion is lame, religion without science is blind. I wish to know how God created the world… the rest are details.

Albert Einstein

We all believe in our hearts,
and confess with our mouth,
that there is a single,
and simple
spiritual being,
whom we call God.
eternal
incomprehensible
invisible
unchangeable
infinite
almighty
completely wise
just
and good
and the overflowing source
of all good.

We know him by two means.

First by the creation, preservation and government of the universe,
since the universe is before our eyes,
like a beautiful book,
in which all creatures,
great and small,
are as letters,
to make us ponder
the invisible things of God,
his eternal power
and his divinity.

Second, he makes himself known to us more openly by his holy and divine Word.

Confessio Belgico
By Guido de Bres in 1567

Contents

Acknowledgements   v

Part A – Relevant Scientific Findings

I   Introduction   19

II   Some Recent Discoveries and Theories Affecting our Understanding of Ourselves and the Universe Around Us   29
- IIa   Introduction   29
- IIb   New Scientific Discoveries and Theories   30
- IIc   Some Notable Features of the Laws of Nature   64

III   Creation – Where Do We Come From?   80
- IIIa   Introduction   80
- IIIb   The Creation of the Universe   81
- IIIc   The Creation of Life   94
- IIId   The Creation of Human Beings   104
- IIIe   The Mousetrap Versus the Wagon or Evolutionists Versus Creationists   126

IV   Our Long-Term Future According to Science   147
- IVa   The Future of Human Life on Earth   147
- IVb   The Future of Human Life in the Solar System   154

		IVc	Are We Alone in the Universe?	161
		IVd	The Search for Extraterrestrial Life	168

V	The Human Being		173
	Va	Introduction	173
	Vb	Cells – the Building Blocks of Human Life	175
	Vc	The Human Immune System	186
	Vd	The Formation of the Human Body	192
	Ve	Cloning and Stem Cell Research	195
	Vf	The Central Nervous System	198
	Vg	The Human Mind, Consciousness and Intelligence	208
		A Mechanical, Material and Physical Machine?	217
		The Body/Mind Connection	220
		Body/Mind – Nonlocal in Space and Time	225
		The Nonlocality of Mind and Consciousness	228
		The Reality of the Physical World	229
	Vh	The Interconnectedness of All Nature – The Collective Unconscious	230

VI	Materialism Versus Spiritualism – Determinism Versus Free Will	241

Part B – Religious Beliefs and Concepts

VII	Religious Beliefs Through the Ages	259
VIII	The Emergence of God, the Creator	273
	VIIIa God, the Creator, in Hinduism	273

	VIIIb	God, the Creator, in Judaism, Christianity and Islam	279
	VIIIc	Jesus, the Long-Awaited Messenger of God	298
IX		God as Revealed in Phenomena We Cannot Perceive with Our Five Senses	308
	IXa	Introduction	308
	IXb	The Effect of Religion and Prayer on Health	311
	IXc	Out-of-Body Experiences and Near-Death Experiences	327
	IXd	Mystical Experiences	340
	IXe	Parapsychological Phenomena	344
X		God as Revealed in the Creation and Preservation of the Universe	351
	Xa	Introduction	351
	Xb	The First Level of Certainty	357
	Xc	The Second Level of Certainty	374
	Xd	Conclusions	390
XI		The Meaning of Life – Where Are We Going?	397
	XIa	Introduction	397
	XIb	Who Are We?	398
	XIc	Why Are We Here?	401
	XId	The Meaning of Life and Our Importance in the Scheme of Things	402
	XIe	Our Responsibilities and Tasks During Life on Earth	404
	XIf	What Is Our Final Destiny?	407

| XII | When and How Does God Act or Interact in Creation? | 410 |

Appendix I – Some Basic Physics 422

Bibliography 442

Index 452

Illustrations

Figure

2.1	The Magnetic Field Between Two Poles of a Bar Magnet	50
2.2	The Koch Curve, an Example of a Fractal Shape	59
3.1	The History of the Universe and the Rise of Humankind	92
3.2	The Earliest Date Life Could Have Developed	93
3.3	Two Models of the Emergence of Homo sapiens across the Continents	107
3.4	Milestones in the Development of our Civilization over the last 10,000 years	119
5.1	A Schematic Cross Section of a Cell	176
5.2	Schematic Presentation of the Replication of a DNA Molecule	178
5.3	A Simplified Diagram of the Operation of the Human Immune System	190
5.4	Schematic Presentation of the Central Nervous System	201
5.5	Schematic Presentation of a Nerve Cell or Neuron	202

5.6	A Schematic Presentation of the Synaptic Gap Between Neurons	205
5.7	The Interpersonal and External Lines of Communications in Era I	219
5.8	The Interpersonal and External Lines of Communications in Era II	224
5.9	The Interpersonal and External Lines of Communications in Era III	233
7.1	The Emergence of the Early Civilizations and the Birth of the Major World Religions	267
8.1	The Fertile Crescent	285
8.2	The Historical Record of the Hebrews from Abraham to the Birth of Christ	297
12.1	Places Where God's Direct Intervention May Be Discerned	420
A.1	The Geocentric Concept of the Universe in the Middle Ages	425
A.2	The Classical Model of the Atomic Structure of Hydrogen, Helium and Carbon	428

Graphs

Va	Various Aspects of the Human Psyche	210
Vb	Major Functions of the Human Psyche	226

Tables

VIIa	Chronology of the Religious and Ceremonial Developments	268
Xa	The Areas in Nature Where We See a Creator's Presence Most Clearly	393

Part A
Relevant Scientific Findings

Chapter I
INTRODUCTION

In the last three or four decades, scientific discoveries and technological advances have been made at, what seems to be, an ever-increasing pace. As a result, many people feel that they have not been able to keep up with these developments, and that they have been left behind, even to the extent that they feel alienated from this new world. This is especially true of anything that has to do with electronics and computers. Children, even of preschool age, are learning how to operate these machines. Not only do they seem to enjoy operating them, but also many are becoming addicted to their use, especially computer games; at the same time, many adults are fascinated and addicted to surfing the Internet. All this is happening while a large percentage of the world's population has no clear idea of what a computer is or what it can do. Certainly, this will be true for many of the grandparents of the children who take computers and the Internet for granted. The older generation grew up in an age when computers, if they did exist at all, were too complicated to operate and too expensive to own. Sometimes, it is hard to believe that it is only fifty-five years ago that the then president of IBM publicly stated that he could only see the need for three computers in the whole of the United States.

It is probably safe to assume that there are developments in the pipeline now which will cause the same drastic changes in the way we do things as the computer, the Internet, the CD, the TV, etc. have done to this generation; and this present generation will probably feel just as left behind as some of their grandparents do now. At the same time, discoveries are continually being made in other fields than computer technology such as physics, medicine, genetics and communications, to name just a few discoveries that will have lasting effects on the human condition of the future. Hand in hand with this go the changes that are taking place in moral values and in attitudes to such relatively new areas as cloning, abortion, euthanasia, genetic selection, homosexual marriages, and a host of other issues.

Also, in pure science, discoveries have been made and theories are being promulgated that seem to go counter to our most basic instincts. Such findings as the quantum theory, the theory of relativity, the uncertainty principle, the postulation of the existence of antimatter, etc. are difficult to grasp for the uninitiated. Nevertheless, these theories and discoveries will shape our lives and the lives of our children and grandchildren; they may even threaten the continued existence of the human race and our planet.

One area of research that has a more direct and immediate influence on our everyday life concerns the human psyche, the human make-up. There are an ever-increasing number of books being written by medical doctors, psychologists and psychiatrists, about the close connection between our body, our mind, our soul and our subconscious; they all show how this interaction can be used to affect the healing of the body and the mind, and how it affects our understanding of the interconnectedness of all living things.

In the beginning of this scientific age, almost all discoveries tended to decrease the importance of humankind and to diminish the need for God as the Creator and Sustainer of the universe. First there was the discovery by Copernicus (1473–1543) that the Earth, and therefore humankind, was not the center of the universe, followed later by the discovery of Newton (1643–1727) that the universe operated on a fixed set of mechanical laws, which was followed a century or more later by Darwin's (1809–1882) theory of evolution which relegated humans to the position of glorified animals. All these developments made many people feel that God was no longer needed and that humankind could forge its own destiny. Unfortunately, with God out of the way, the value system we once had, or at least tried to follow, went out of the window as well. Certainly, some of these theories, discoveries and technical achievements have had a great influence for the better on the human condition of many people. But hunger and poverty, for which we have all the means at our disposal for their complete elimination, are still as prevalent as they were decades ago. To eliminate them, all we need to do is to muster the political will. Clearly, all the material and human resources are in place to eliminate these scourges that have plagued a very large part of human society from its very beginning. Unfortunately for those caught in these conditions, our scientific efforts and objectives are directed to more glamorous goals than the elimination of hunger and poverty. For instance, if we are really trying to do the best for *all* humankind, why is it that we spend billions of dollars on research to fight illnesses that affect only a very small part of the world's population, when the same amount of money spent on fighting malnutrition would have a much greater effect on the general well-being of all the world's people?

Some of the most discouraging things that have happened in the last decades are the continuing waves of atrocities on a national scale that seem to continue to wash over the world of today. After the "Rape of Nanking", the

"Killing Fields" of Cambodia and the Holocaust, we now have had to add to this list the atrocities committed recently in the former Yugoslavia and in Central Africa. The truly discouraging thing about these outbreaks of inhuman behavior is that they are crimes often committed by some of the best educated people using the most modern inventions. Also, crime and violence on the local level seem to be on the increase and seem to thrive under the new condition of world peace or, at least, in a world that for the first time in memory is not threatened by a major world conflict. For instance, the democratization of Russia, in itself a splendid thing, appears to be going very slowly: the only thing that seems to be expanding rapidly there is crime and, especially, organized international crime. All of this has left many people wondering how, under these new conditions and with these new discoveries, we are going to take control of where this civilization is going and steer the world in a direction that will ensure a brighter and more equitable future for all of humankind.

Also, in an immense universe where time is measured in billions of years, and which contains stars and galaxies by the billions, a good many people begin to wonder about their place and importance in the scheme of things, both at the level of the individual and that of the human species. The question is whether we, who once thought of ourselves as the center of the universe, are here by pure accident, or are we created for a special purpose? If so, what is this purpose? Are we just the accidental merging of a great number of complicated molecules, or are we an essential part of an overall plan? If so, who made this plan? What is that overall plan and what is humankind's role in it and, probably even more important, what is our own personal role in it? These are the eternal questions people have been asking themselves ever since humans obtained the capacity to reason and became conscious of the world around them.

This book is an attempt to place these questions in the context of recent scientific discoveries and postmodern thought. From what we see around us, we might well conclude that God has disappeared from the scene. Did not science tell us years ago that God was not needed any longer to explain the creation of the universe? Today, few people would agree with this anymore. Many of the latest advances in the fields of science, medicine, and psychology seem to indicate that God was very much there at the time of creation and that God is very much here today. One might say that science has shown that it is not possible to explain the existence and operation of the universe, and the existence of human life, without bringing in the idea of a Creator who planned it this way. Someone went so far as to say that science is a much better way to God than religion. So this book is about the evidence we see all around us that there is a Creator or Guiding Intelligence at work, not only in the creation but also in the maintenance of the universe.

Christian doctrine has always maintained that God can be found in two basically different ways. The first way is through God's own revelation through the scriptures, through visions and through mystical experiences. The second way we can discover God's existence is through divine disclosure in nature. As Guido de Bres expressed it in 1567: "The universe is before our eyes as a beautiful book to make us ponder the invisible things of God." The difference is that, in the latter case, the God we encounter is the Creator of the Universe and not necessarily the God of the Christian religion. Muslims can, with equal justification, call this God "Allah", and Hindus can well equate this God with "Brahman".

The results of some recent research in the reasons why

people believe in a Creator God are published in Michael Shermer's[1] book, *How We Believe*. The three main reasons given by the more than a thousand people interviewed were as follows:

- Arguments based on good design, natural beauty, perfection, and complexity of the world or the universe. (28.6 per cent)
- The experience of God in everyday life – a feeling that God is in us. (20.6 per cent)
- Belief in a Creator God gives meaning and purpose to life. (10.3 per cent)

The same survey showed that people who do *not* believe in God do so because they cannot find any proof of God's existence (37.9 per cent).

It is the objective of this book to show that there is overwhelming evidence that God does exist and that good design, natural beauty, perfection, and complexity are evident all over nature.

Of course, there are many books and articles written which reject the arguments I will be using in the following pages. Some of the writers use the same scientific data but interpret it in a different way to prove exactly the opposite. It is for the reader, then, to decide which interpretation is more persuasive.

This book is divided into two parts. In the first part, A, I will describe my understanding of the latest scientific discoveries and theories and how I believe they impact on our belief in a Creator or Guiding Intelligence. Some sections of these first chapters may prove somewhat difficult to follow for readers who have forgotten most of what they were taught in school in their science classes. For this reason, I have summarized our present understanding of physics and of the workings of both the macro and micro cosmos in Appendix I at the end of the book. However, most of the arguments used can be followed without having a profound understanding of the underlying scientific details. Chapter II presents some recent discoveries and theories which have a direct impact on the arguments for the existence of a Creator God. This is followed by Chapter III which gives a brief history of the universe as we see it today in the light of our most recent discoveries. This takes us to the creation of life in its most general form and from there to the creation of human life in particular. Today, it is impossible to write about this subject without touching upon the controversy between those who believe that the universe and all life was created by a Creator God, and those who believe that the world is a product of pure chance when the right molecules came together under the right circumstances and conditions.

Chapter IV deals with what science tells us about the probable future of the universe and the future of human life. It includes a section on the question whether there is intelligent life elsewhere in the cosmos, or whether we are alone in this incredibly large universe. The chapter closes with a brief description of the efforts that are being made today to detect whether there is such extraterrestrial life out there among the billions of stars and galaxies.

In Chapter V, a description is presented of the latest findings that touch upon our human existence: how our mind and body function; how we are slowly developing new ideas about the capacity of our mind and consciousness to influence the world around us; and how we may be interconnected with all creation through a universal consciousness.

This first section of the book closes with a description of one of the major controversies in the world today; the controversy between people who believe that we are created by God with a free will to choose between good and evil, and those who believe that we are here purely by chance and that our existence is governed entirely by chemical and physical processes. If the latter is true, it essentially means that we have no free will and that the course of our life is set in stone at the outset.

Chapter VII, the first chapter of Section B, contains a brief description of how the idea of a deity, who has a direct influence on the lives of people, emerged through the ages, starting with the early mother and fertility goddesses and ending with the idea of a Creator who created and sustains the universe.

This is followed in Chapter VIII by a short description of the concept of God, the Creator, in Hinduism, Judaism, and Christianity. (The Muslim concept of God, the Creator, has not been included because it is in many ways the same as that of Judaism and Christianity.) The chapter closes with a description of how, in the Christian religion, this further developed into the Father/Mother figure of God the Creator and Sustainer of life, and who is so close to all people that he/she can be approached by every person through prayer.

Chapter IX deals with the phenomena which cannot be perceived by our five senses, including prayer and its effectiveness. It contains a section on the healing effects the practice of religion can have on the general well-being of people who believe in God. It also includes a description of the Out-of-Body and Near-Death Experiences many people have had.

This is followed by Chapter X in which the various arguments for the existence of a Guiding Intelligence or Creator are summarized. The arguments are assembled according to my evaluation of the level of certainty that these arguments are valid. This, of course, is a highly subjective selection and others may give a different weight to the validity of the various arguments. However, I believe that *all the arguments taken together* present overwhelming evidence for the existence of a Guiding Intelligence or Creator in the creation and continuing operation of the universe.

Chapter XI deals with what a belief in God and, in particular, a belief in the God of the Christian religion means in terms of the importance of the human being in the scheme of things and what I believe our final destiny will be.

In the last chapter, I try to define the occasions when God most clearly interacted with creation. We believe that this started with the act of creation some fifteen billion years ago. It was probably not until 11.5 billion years later with the creation of the first life forms that God became more intimately involved in the path that led eventually to the emergence of conscious human beings. Of course, as Christians we believe that involvement became even more intimate 2,000 years ago with the birth of Jesus Christ, who is believed to be the Son of God.

In writing a book of this type, inevitably there arises the question of the relationship between religion and science. Over the years this relationship has not always been a harmonious one; in fact, they have often found themselves in opposing camps, sometimes for good reason. It must be remembered, however, that both science and religion find their basis in a faith or trust they both accept without proof. Science is based on the faith or understanding that we live in a rational world that can be understood by the human intellect. While religion is based on the faith that there is a Rational Being who put this rational universe together, and that we can learn more about this Creator by observing and discovering the wonders behind that creation. This book then tries to look at the most recent discoveries and look at them as the work of a Guiding Intelligence or Creator.

The book has been written from the perspective of one who believes that God has revealed him/herself most clearly to the Western world through his Son, Jesus Christ. This is not to say that there may not be other valid revelations of God in other forms to other people, in particular to those in the Eastern world.

NOTES

Note on the use of inclusive language

It has always been recognized that God is spirit and therefore neither male nor female. Recently, it has been increasingly recognized that using only male terms for God limits our understanding of the qualities of God, which include many attributes more readily associated with the female gender. Since I find it difficult to refer to God as "it", I have used the male and female pronouns in alternate chapters.

Note on the use of designations for dates in ancient times

Wherever appropriate I have used the designations B.C.E. (before common era) and C.E. (common era) instead of the older designation B.C. and A.D.

[1]Shermer, Michael, *How We Believe, The Search for God in an Age of Science*, W. H. Freeman & Co, New York, 1999.

Chapter II
SOME RECENT DISCOVERIES AND THEORIES AFFECTING OUR UNDERSTANDING OF OURSELVES AND THE UNIVERSE AROUND US

IIa   Introduction

As stated in the introduction, the purpose of this book is to evaluate the possibility that the creation of the universe was not an accidental occurrence; but there was a Creative Spirit at work in its creation and that this Spirit is still active in the world today. The second objective is to get a better insight into the position we humans occupy in this universe. From a purely scientific point of view, that position has changed over the years from being central to the creation and existence of the entire cosmos, to something much lower, if not completely insignificant. However, as we shall see later, some of the latest theories and discoveries have put humankind back again into its original position as central to the creation of the universe. Of course, from a religious point of view, that position has never changed. Humankind was, and is, simply considered to be the main reason for the existence of the cosmos and is thought to be the culmination of the entire creation process.

This chapter consists of three sections. The first section contains a brief description of the recent scientific findings which are affecting our understanding of the nature of creation and our position in it. In the second section some of the notable features of the laws which govern the operation of the universe, as we understand them today, are examined in some detail.

IIb   New Scientific Discoveries and Theories

SOME OF THE LATEST SCIENTIFIC DISCOVERIES AND THEORIES WHICH ARE HAVING A PROFOUND EFFECT ON HOW WE PERCEIVE THE WORLD TODAY

In the last century, and especially in the last half, research in most branches of science has increased exponentially. More research papers are being published today in one year than were previously published in decades. This research is being carried out not only in government-sponsored research institutes but also in many large industrial enterprises. The research effort in industry is generally aimed at developing better products, while the work in government institutions and universities tends to be dedicated more to fundamental research. It is this pure, fundamental research into the basic understanding of how both the microcosm and the macrocosm function that has led to some very fascinating discoveries and interesting theories. Some of these discoveries were made after someone developed a theory and set out to prove that theory by experimentation; while, in other cases, a discovery was made and then a theory was developed to explain the observed facts. Many of these recent discoveries appear very strange and seem to go very much against our intuitive understanding of how things work or ought to work. As Niels Bohr, a Danish physicist, expressed it, "If you have no problem understanding these theories then most likely you have not understood them."

The first laws I want to mention are the first and the second law of thermodynamics. They were first formulated in the late 1800s, and they have had such a profound influence on our understanding of the final destiny of the universe that it is impossible to understand what follows without a brief introduction to the basic ideas behind these laws.

The first law is also called the law of the "conservation of energy". It simply states that you cannot destroy energy; you can change it into different forms of energy, but you cannot destroy it. For instance, if we burn wood or coal, we do nothing else but convert the energy contained in that piece of wood or lump of coal into the energy that heats a home or bakes a cake, plus the energy contained in the smoke and the ashes: all together they add up to exactly the same amount of energy contained in the original fuel source.

The second law states that everything on Earth, and in the universe, moves always from order to disorder and on to greater disorder (entropy). There seems to be a number of standard examples used to explain this theory. The first concerns a bottle filled with perfume. If you take the stopper out of the bottle, the perfume spreads and disperses throughout the room. There is no way you or anyone else can put this perfume back into the flask. It has gone from a highly ordered state in the bottle to a highly disordered state dispersed in the room. In making this perfume and putting it into the bottle, energy was spent that cannot be recovered in any useful form and is, therefore, effectively lost forever. The same goes for a cup or plate that has been dropped on the ground and has been shattered into small pieces. There is no way that the broken pieces can reassemble themselves into a cup or a plate without expending further energy. The energy that went into the manufacturing of the plate has gone into some useless pieces of crockery, and into some equally useless forms of energy such as heat that has dissipated in the surrounding air and cannot be retrieved. Thus, the energy used in manufacturing it can never be recovered in any useful form and it is, therefore, lost forever.

One of the apparent exceptions to this general increase

in disorder is the creation and maintenance of life. Cells, which are the building blocks of all life, are the most astonishing complicated assembly of *highly organized* systems, and they are continually being formed from a *highly disorganized* assortment of molecules. The apparent contradiction disappears when a clause is added to this general law which states that this law is true only for systems that are isolated or closed. The fact is that our Earth is not an isolated system and our living cells continually absorb energy from outside our Earth in the form of sunlight. This continuous energy input makes it possible for complicated cells to be continually formed from disorganized molecules. When this source of energy is exhausted, as it eventually will be, the second law of thermodynamics will be valid for the living cells on Earth as well.

On the scale of everyday life, the fact that we are constantly converting useable energy into useless energy is not such a calamity since there is, at least at present, an adequate supply of materials and energy to heat our houses and to make more perfume, plates or cups. However, on the much larger scale of stars and galaxies, this theory has rather disastrous consequences. All stars convert their mass into radiant energy which is mostly used in heating the vast space around them and is therefore lost as useful energy. Eventually, after a very long time, all mass will have been converted and every star will become a "dead" star. The only thing it will have accomplished in the long run is to have raised the average temperature of the space surrounding it and, since the distance between stars and galaxies is so large, all the energy of all the stars and galaxies will only have been able to raise the average temperature of the universe by a very small amount. So, eventually, if the universe is found to be in a steady state with no additional matter somehow being created, the whole universe will end up cluttered with dead stars, and the average temperature of the space between these stars will have increased only slightly. This so-called "heat death" of the cosmos will put a definite end to the universe as we know it. Most people do not worry about this too much at this point in time since the date that this will happen, if nothing else interferes with the development of the universe in the meantime, is some billions of years away. This theory does, however, influence the thinking of philosophers and people who reflect on the meaning of life and our place in it, in that it posits a well-defined end to the existence of the universe and by implication will also put an end to all human activity. As we will see later, there is one possible route of escape from this fate of the universe, and that is if the Big Bang is followed by an infinite series of Big Crunches and Big Bangs. However, this does little for the continuation of human life as we know it since it would be annihilated at each Big Crunch (see Chapter III).

The second set of the theories I want to mention is Einstein's theories of relativity. They were first formulated by Albert Einstein in the early 1900s and they caused a revolution in our thinking about mass, energy, gravity, time and space. Einstein formulated his first theory, the special theory of relativity, in 1905 and this was followed in 1915 by the general theory of relativity. In the special theory of relativity, he proposed that we should look at the universe around us as operating, not in a three-dimensional space, but in four dimensions with time being considered the fourth dimension. The position of any object in the universe can be described by three distances along the three axes of elementary mathematics: the x, or horizontal axis; the y, or vertical axis and the z, or depth axis. If the object moves, it will cause these values to change. So, at any given point in time we can locate ourselves using these three coordinates. For instance, we can make an appointment to meet someone at such and such a time and at such and such a place. In this example, we still use three space dimensions for a given time. Einstein's theory proposed that time and space were actually inseparably linked together in a four-dimensional geometry which he called "space-time". For most, if not all people, a four-dimensional space is difficult to visualize, but it can easily be manipulated with the help of mathematics.

In the early 1900s, it was thought that light needed a medium through which it could propagate in the same way as sound moves through air. It was therefore assumed that the space around the Earth was filled with a mysterious matter called "ether" through which light could travel. When it was proven that the speed of light was not affected by the existence or nonexistence of ether, Einstein contended that it did not exist and was not needed as a medium through which light could move. In fact, it became clear that light could move in a vacuum.

Later, he postulated that the speed of light was one of the true constants of nature and that it did not depend upon the speed of the observer. No matter how fast an observer moved in the same or in the opposite direction as the beam of light, the observer would measure the same velocity of light.

Normally, the relative speeds between two objects moving in the same direction is the difference between the two speeds, and the relative speed between objects traveling in opposite directions is the sum of the two speeds. For instance, for a person in a car moving beside a railway track in the same direction as the train and at the same speed, the train appears to be standing still. In such circumstances, the relative speed between the train and the car is zero; but if the passenger looks out of the window on the other side of the car, he sees that the car is moving at great speed relative to the trees on the side of the road. Not so for light. No matter how fast we are moving in the direction of the light source, the speed of light we measure always remains the

SOME RECENT DISCOVERIES AND THEORIES

same. Similarly, if we are moving in the same direction as the light beam, no matter how fast we move, we can never catch up to it and we will always measure the same speed of light.

When Einstein first published his laws of relativity, people found it difficult to accept them. The consequences of it were even more at odds with what was considered to be the natural and proper way for nature to act. For instance, in applying Einstein's equations, it was found that when a body in motion approaches the speed of light, all kinds of weird and wonderful things happen. For one thing, time slows down. It does not *appear* to slow down, it actually does slow down. When a person who has been riding a fast moving rocket in space returns to Earth, he is actually younger than the person who has remained stationary on our planet. For low speeds this effect is so small that it can be ignored; however, it becomes really significant if the person travels through space at a speed that approaches the speed of light. For instance, for a person traveling at a speed of 100 kilometers per hour *less* than the speed of light, a day in his rocket is equivalent to four years on Earth. This would be a fine solution for people who want to prolong life as long as possible. Unfortunately, they would have the inconvenience of having to travel through space at a speed close to 300,000 km/sec. and, in addition, the cost of getting up to that speed would be astronomical indeed, even if it were possible to reach that speed. An interesting side effect on this limit to the speed of light is that the closer we get to the speed of light, the closer we get to observing things that have just happened. For instance, as we look out into space, we are actually looking back in time. The star or galaxy we are observing is not the star or galaxy as it is now, but as what it was hundreds of millions of years ago when the light we see left the star or galaxy.

The special theory of relativity produces other strange results in addition to prolonging life in a fast-moving rocket. First, it was found that objects traveling near the speed of light appear to the observer on the ground to become compressed in the direction of their movement, and thus appear to become smaller and smaller as the speed increases. However, the people in the rocket do not see anything extraordinary, since their speed relative to the rocket is nil.

The second strange effect is that objects, traveling near the speed of light, gain in mass. This is one of the reasons why we can never exceed the speed of light. The closer the object we are accelerating gets to that speed, the more massive the object becomes and the more energy is needed to keep accelerating it. The explanation of this strange phenomenon is that the object absorbs more and more energy from the accelerating force. This simple observation led Einstein to one of the best known and most fundamental laws of nature, namely that mass and energy are equivalent, and that mass can be converted into energy and vice versa ($E=Mc^2$). The conversion factor he found was the square of the speed of light. Since this is a very large number, it follows that a very small bit of matter can be converted into a very large amount of energy. This is the principle on which the atomic bomb operates and, more beneficially to humankind, it also is the principle on which atomic power plants operate. To get an idea of the large amount of energy generated by a small amount of matter, it is useful to compare the amount of fuel burned in a conventional thermal station, which is measured in tons of coal per hour, with the fuel consumption in a nuclear station that can be measured in ounces per day.

All his life, Einstein was looking for the theory that would explain everything which is happening in the universe from the microcosm to the macrocosm. This naturally led him to think about that mysterious force that we all experience every second of our lives – gravity. In true

Einstein fashion, the inspiration for his theory about gravity came from observing what was happening around him. It is said that when he saw a man climbing a church steeple, he started to imagine what this man would feel if he fell from that height. His conclusion was that whatever else the man might feel, he would not experience the force of gravity. During his descent he would accelerate through space at the rate of 10 m/sec^2 and he would be weightless. If, at the last moment before he fell from the steeple, he had grasped a piece of lead from the church roof, he would be able to let go of that piece of lead and it would stay with him and descend at exactly the same rate as the unfortunate steeple climber himself.

For us today, it is somewhat easier to experience what Einstein could only imagine by going up and down in a fast-moving elevator. At the beginning of the trip going up, when the elevator is accelerating in the upward direction, we have a feeling of being squashed down; on the other hand, when we are going down and the elevator is accelerating in the downward direction, we have a feeling of being lifted up. If the elevator cables were ever to break, the elevator would go in a free fall and the passengers would find themselves weightless and floating in space. This, of course, would come to a very abrupt end when the elevator hits the bottom of the shaft, and the almost instant deceleration from its final speed to zero would have a disastrous effect on the unlucky passengers. Fortunately, most elevators, after the initial acceleration or deceleration, reach a cruising speed and from then on the passengers experience nothing out of the ordinary.

The genius of Einstein was that out of these simple observations and thought processes, he came up with a completely new theory about gravity and space, the so-called general theory of relativity. He argued that we feel something like gravity only when we are accelerated through space. Therefore, all gravity must be the result of acceleration and, in fact, he argued, gravity and acceleration are equivalent. He then went on to say that, since acceleration is the rate of change in velocity, which is a measure of the distance traveled over a certain period of time, gravity must be a geometric concept. He then came up with the idea that the space around each source of mass was warped by that mass, and the larger the mass the greater the warping. Any object in that warped space would describe a trajectory of the least resistance in that space. So, if the Moon orbits around the Earth, it must be because the Moon is moving in a four-dimensional path of least resistance in a curved or warped space around the Earth – much like a roulette ball moves around the roulette wheel. Therefore, what looks like the force of gravity, pulling the planets in orbits around the Sun, is actually not a force at all but an effect of a particular space-time configuration. When Einstein first started to talk about curved space-time, he left a lot of people far behind, as he did when he started talking about four-dimensional space. We simply cannot imagine what any four-dimensional space is like. However, there is no problem in expressing curved four-dimensional space in mathematical terms. Despite all this, mostly for the sake of convenience, scientists continue to talk about the force of gravity as a real force and they continue to calculate its effects on all objects, great and small, on that basis.

One other, equally strange, result of Einstein's theory of relativity is that the presence of a large mass does not only curve space, it also slows down time. So, if you want to live long you should take up residence as close as you can to a very large mass. Since the gravitational pull depends on the distance between the two objects, time for a person on top of a mountain goes faster than for someone at sea level. Fortunately, the difference is very small and is very difficult to measure, otherwise a lot of people might want to live in

Holland in the polders which are mostly below sea level. As unconventional and unbelievable at first as all these theories may appear, they have repeatedly been validated by experiments.

The next theory, which drastically changed our perception of the world around us, is called the quantum theory. It has such startling consequences that someone called it the most surprising and counter-intuitive discovery of the century (George Ellis[1] in *Before the Beginning of Time*), or as Brian Silver[2] wrote in *The Ascent of Science*:

> It can be said of quantum mechanics that we are thankful, impressed, but, in the still of the night, profoundly uneasy, because quantum theory presents us with paradoxes more puzzling than the questions it solves.

A further example of the difficulty to understand quantum mechanics is the fact that two of the foremost scientists involved in its early formulation, Albert Einstein and Niels Bohr, never could agree on its interpretation. Each felt so strongly about their particular interpretation of the meaning of this theory that, although they were close friends at one time, they would not even talk to each other towards the end of their lives.

Basically, this new theory started with Niels Bohr. Before the quantum theory came to be accepted, the general picture of the atom was that of a mini-solar system with a massive central core and lighter electrons orbiting around this core at, relatively speaking, very large distances. Furthermore, it was believed that this atomic mini-solar system was subject to the same forces as its much larger macro system. Bohr began to question the validity of this picture of the atomic world when he found that if he applied the "classical" laws to the atomic structure, the electrons would not be able to maintain their orbit but would almost instantly crash into the core of the atom. Of course, if this were true, the world could not exist as it does and we would not be here. Bohr argued that since we are very much here, the original theory and model was obviously not correct.

Bohr then came up with the theory that electrons could only move around the nucleus in a number of fixed orbits, and that they could move only from one fixed orbit to another. For instance, if the atom absorbs energy, the electrons will move to higher orbits in, what were later called, quantum leaps. When the atom gives off energy, the electrons will move in quantum leaps to lower orbits. At a certain point, the electron will have reached its lowest orbit around its nucleus and it will not be able to give off any additional energy.

The intriguing point about this theory is that these quantum jumps from one energy level to another appear to be instantaneous, and no one has ever been able to figure out where the electron is during its jump from one location to another – it simply appears to have no existence in-between. Also, there seems to be no reason why, in an atom with several electrons, one particular electron would move and not another. At best, it can be said that, on receiving a given amount of energy, the average energy level of all the electrons in the atom increases, and if the atom gives off energy then the average energy level of the electrons decreases. In other words, there is no deterministic cause and effect – there is only a probability that one electron will move and not the other.

Niels Bohr,[3] in one of his publications in which he discussed this lack of cause and effect in a similar experiment, put it this way:

> If we look at a group of particles arriving at point B from a source at point A, we can correctly calculate *possibilities and*

patterns of what we find at point B, but that is all. We cannot even say for sure that the particles detected at point B were the same ones that were emitted from point A and we certainly cannot say what path they took to get there. We can't even know what arrived at B. We show tracks of particles on our screens. But what they really are is uncertain.

How much more uncertain can you be about anything? This is, of course, a far cry from classical physics in which every cause had a well-defined, always the same, invariable effect.

The second quantum phenomenon that is of interest is the fact that light can have the property of both a particle and a wave. Moreover, as a particle it can be in two places at the same time. The typical experimental set-up, which led to the discovery of this strange phenomenon, is somewhat as follows: a light source is placed in front of a solid barrier with one small hole in it. Behind this a second barrier is placed with two small holes and behind that a photographic plate is used to record the arrival of the light. Without going into detail, it was found that a photon of light emitted from the light source and proceeding through the first hole could go through both of the two holes in the second barrier at the same time. Even stranger, the light that left the light source as a photon particle traveled through space as a wave and arrived at the photographic plate again as a photon particle. This strange behavior of a photon of light turned out not to be limited to photons only. Later experiments have shown the same strange behavior for electrons (1987) and even atoms (1990). They all were found to be able to be two things at the same time, and to be able to be in two places at the same time. The thing to remember is that these are not some crazy ideas of an unbalanced mind, but hard facts proven and demonstrated time and time again in laboratories across the world.

More recently, the view has been expressed that light,

and matter as well, cannot be described by simple wave or particle models. In fact they are something else entirely; more sophisticated than either, and not fully capable of description by current concepts.(Charles Wynn and Anita Wiggins in *The Five Biggest Ideas in Science*[4]) For our purpose, we will continue to use the dual model of waves and particles to describe light and matter; surely the fact that they can be both is difficult enough to understand.

The third quantum phenomenon I want to touch upon, and which has had a profound influence on our understanding of our place in the universe, is called Heisenberg's uncertainty principle. It states that it is not possible to measure two properties of a subatomic particle, such as an electron, at the same time, because the very fact of observation changes what we observe. It is not just that we cannot measure the two properties simultaneously, but the fact seems to be that a subatomic particle cannot have these two properties at the same time. For instance, if we know where a particle is located, we cannot know what it is doing, and if we know what the particle is doing we cannot know where it is located. The fact that there is an observer present looking at it changes the state of the particle. This is somewhat similar to the situation when I want to take a picture of my grandchildren. The point is that as soon as they see that I want to take their picture (record their state) they change their appearance, the one makes a face and the other makes a grab for the camera. The fact that I am trying to record their state immediately changes that state.

These findings have resulted in some revolutionary statements by a number of scientists. John Gribben[5] writes: "On this picture, everything in the universe only exists because *we* are looking at it." John Wheeler[6] expresses it this way: "The entire universe only exists because someone is watching it; everything right back to the Big Bang, some fifteen billion years ago, remained undefined until it was noticed." Of course, the last statement begs the question what kind of creature qualifies as being alert and conscious enough to notice that it, and the universe around it, exists. Eugene Wigner[7] answered that question by stating that it is the conscious mind which determines that which is observed. According to him, this places humans firmly back into a central position in the universe. Because of the importance of these conclusions, which place humankind in the central position again, I am quoting below a few other scientists who have come to the same, or similar, conclusions.

Colin A. Ronan[8] in *The Natural History of the Universe* raises the enthralling question whether the ability of humankind to observe and understand the universe has an effect on its reality. Similarly, Shimon Malin,[9] in his book *Nature Loves to Hide*, asks almost the same question: "Do physics and quantum mechanics have anything to say in regard to our place in the universe?" He answers the question as follows: "Unexpectedly, the answer is yes – the role of the observer in quantum mechanics suggests a paradigm shift regarding the question of our place in the universe." Unfortunately, he leaves it at that and does not define what that paradigm shift is. Amit Goswami[10] in *The Self-Aware Universe* puts it even more strongly when he writes that meaning in the universe arises only when sentient beings observe it, which leads him to claim that: "We are the center of the universe because we are its meaning."

Paul Davies[11] suggests in *The Cosmic Blueprint* that our presence in the universe represents a fundamental rather than an incidental feature of existence which gives us a deep and satisfying basis for human dignity.

Bishop George Berkeley[12] phrased it as early as the mid-1700s as follows:

> All the choirs of heaven and furniture of Earth, in a word, all those bodies which compose the mighty frame of the

> world, have not any substance without the mind... So long as they are not actually perceived by me or do not exist in my mind, or that of any other created spirit, they must either have no existence at all, or else subsist in the mind of some Eternal Spirit.

Richard Tarna[13] writes in *Passions of the Western Mind*:

> In this understanding, the world cannot be said to possess any features in principle prior to interpretation. The world does not exist as a thing-in-itself, independent of interpretation; rather, it comes into being only in and through interpretation.

These surely are some of the most astonishing statements ever made by scientists in this scientific age, especially considering the fact that, in the recent history of science, humans had been dethroned from being the center of the universe to that of insignificant specs in the vastness of space.

As was mentioned before, Einstein and Bohr, towards the end of their lives, violently disagreed about the interpretation of these quantum theories. According to Einstein, these theories displaced the clear cause and effect principle of classical science; to him this meant that these new theories must be incomplete. He believed that the universe had to be objective and deterministic, and the underlying processes should be totally causal and independent of the observer. This led to his famous statement that God does not play dice with his creation. Einstein believed that there must be an as yet undiscovered phenomenon beneath the surface of quantum mechanics that, when discovered, would account for the strange behavior of the quantum world.

This nonacceptance of the quantum theories, despite the fact that he had been one of its originators, isolated Einstein from the mainstream of science in his later years. Although he was revered for his early work, he was at the same time pitied by many scientists for his inability to accept the new quantum science. Despite this, it was Einstein again who, in cooperation with two of his students, originated the idea for an experiment that was to disprove the validity of the quantum theory. While Einstein and his students originated the idea, it was a British physicist, J. S. Bell, who worked out the mathematics, and it was a French physicist, Alain Aspect, who finally carried out the experiment in 1982 which had exactly the opposite effect of what Einstein and his collaborators had anticipated. In the experiment a pair of particles, which were created at the same time, were separated. It was then found that if one of the properties of one of the particles was changed, the other particle would instantly react and change as well, regardless how far apart they were. This all happened without any visible means of contact or communication between the two. In the actual experiment, Alain Aspect split correlated pairs of photons, fired them in opposite directions and then changed the condition of one of the photons; he found that this caused an instantaneous change in the twin photon no matter where it was located. In fact, the two acted as if they had never been separated. More recently (early 2001), the experiment has been duplicated by using beryllium ions as reported by David Wineland at the National Institute of Standards and Technology (see *Discover Magazine*, July 2001). Wineland called it "some spooky action at a distance". Of course, this violates Einstein's theory that nothing can exceed the speed of light. In some ways, it is comparable with the experiences of Siamese twins who have been separated at birth. It has been said that if one twin experiences pain or pleasure, the other twin feels the same sensation at the same time no matter where he is located in relation to the other.

This is the second time we have encountered something happening instantaneously and thus exceeding the speed of light. The first was the quantum jump by an electron from one orbit to another, something which happens over very small subatomic distances. This time, however, the distance can be very large and at our scale of existence. In his book, *Science and Philosophy*, Derek Gjertsen[14] writes:

> The fact that something can influence something else without any connection, and can do that instantaneously, changes our perception of what is possible in the mind/consciousness/prayer field entirely.

The phenomenon that something can act instantaneously is considered to be a *nonlocal* reaction. It is nonlocal in the sense that location is not a factor in the reaction. Considering these experimental results, Gribben[15] is going as far as to say, "If you want to believe in a real world you cannot do so without accepting nonlocality; if on the other hand you want to believe that no form of communication can exceed the speed of light, you cannot have a real world independent of the observer." This is strong stuff! What happened to science telling us that telepathy was scientifically impossible? A quantum physicist by the name of David Bohm,[16] in an effort to explain this phenomenon, has developed the idea that each particle is associated with an invisible, undetectable pilot wave which operates in a quantum field. This quantum field, like the fields of gravity and electromagnetism, permeates all of space-time. Also, unlike other fields, it exerts no force on particles. Essentially, it is a wave of undecaying information. It binds the entire universe together into what Bohm liked to call "a seamless unbroken wholeness" in which every particle in the universe is connected by the quantum potential to every other particle. As a simple allegory, Bohm used the example of the shadow of a dancer which is thrown on two screens on opposite sides of a stage by spotlights. As the dancer moves about the stage, each of the shadows changes. An observer who can only see the shadows would come to the conclusion that, while the shadows move differently, they nevertheless interact with each other in some mysterious way in both time and space. To the observer their movements involve action at a distance between two unconnected dancers and is therefore nonlocal.

The last of the quantum phenomenon, I want to mention, is the idea that some particles seem to know in advance what experiment is going to be made and they react as if they know what another particle is going to do. Again, this startling discovery was made when light photons were sent through two slits. One photon seemed to know where another photon was going to go. The results of this two-split experiment cut away at the very basis of our understanding of the universe. How does the photon know where to go? As Brian Silver wrote: "This is very difficult to understand. So difficult that no one has been able to explain it." John Gribben goes even further when he writes:

> The behavior of the photon in a certain experiment is changed by how we are going to look at them, even when we have not yet made up our own minds about how we are going to look at them. The whole universe seems to know in advance, what experiment an individual human being is going to carry out, perhaps on a mountain top in Chile some tens of years from now.

So what has happened to the objection of science against precognition?

Recently, someone has formulated a theory that would "sort of" explain all these mysteries of the world of quantum mechanics. It was originally put forward by John Cramer[17] in 1986, but his work was not fully recognized until 1993. The theory is based on the fact that almost all the equations describing the behavior of *subatomic particles* have two solutions: one going forward in time and one going backward in time. This is somewhat similar to us using the square root of a number that also has two solutions: a positive one and a negative one. For instance, the square root of +4 is normally given as +2; however, the solution of –2 is equally valid because –2 squared also amounts to +4. And, just as we seldom use the minus solution of a square root, so science has always ignored the backward-in-time solution to the mathematical equations describing the behavior of subatomic particles.

What Cramer has done is to bring this backward-in-time solution to bear in solving some of the mysteries of quantum mechanics. It is somewhat difficult to explain, but it goes something like this. Assume that an electron is vibrating and sending "information" waves both in a forward-in-time direction and in a backward-in-time direction. When this information wave hits the next electron it causes it to send a similar information wave in the two time directions. The information wave going backwards in time "arrives" at the first electron exactly at the same time it was sending its original wave; consequently, it knows all about the state of the other electron when it is (was) sending its information wave. So, there it is – instantaneous transmission of information across space. Note that distance in this theory does not matter, as the second electron could just as well have been situated across the country, because the time required for the first wave to reach the next electron is exactly the same as for the returning wave, going backward in time, to reach the sending electron. Thus the sending electron always knows what the second electron is doing regardless of the distance between them. To get the essence of this theory, all you have to do is to accept the idea of time moving backwards.

The authors of this theory are quick to point out, however, that this theory only works on the subatomic level; that is, for particles smaller than 9.10^{-28} grams. On the macro level of our existence, we still have to operate on the principle that effect follows cause in a forward moving time frame. Thus, this theory does not take away from us our free will which is generally considered to be one of the most important attributes of the human being. No doubt, other theories explaining the quantum phenomena will eventually come forward, but here is one that, at least mathematically speaking, makes sense. As a normal human being, who can only move forward in time, the explanation may seem unreal; but then all the quantum phenomena go counter to what we intuitively feel to be right and appropriate.

Before leaving the world of relativity and quantum mechanics, it may be well to emphasize again how these theories have changed the perception of the importance of humans in the operation of the universe. David Darling[18] describes it in a somewhat lyrical way in his book *Deep Time* as follows:

> Suddenly, inescapably, humanity stood in the glare of two brilliant spotlights. That of quantum mechanics, with its strange insistence that reality sprang from observership. And that of the new, anthropic cosmology, with its complementary message: the existence of intelligence was somehow directly linked to the structure and state of the universe…
>
> So it was that physicists and astronomers of the late twentieth century found the universe looking back intently at them. Looking as if to say, You are what is important. You are the reason and the cause of all that is here.

Certainly, this is a big difference from the previous assertions that humans were just an accidental by-product of the evolutionary process.

The next theory which is having a profound effect on how we look at nature has been developed by Rupert Sheldrake[19] and others. *The Rebirth of Nature, Science and God* by Rupert Sheldrake postulates that the universe is filled with "fields of influence" similar to the magnetic field between the two poles of a magnet. You probably recall the experiment in school which showed how iron filings arranged themselves in neat lines between these two poles, and if you changed the position of the poles how, as if by magic, the filings arranged themselves along lines consistent with the new position of the poles (see Figure 2.1).

These lines are the physical evidence that there are fields of influence generated by the poles of the magnet that are not normally discernible by our five senses. However, it is the presence of these magnetic fields that make it possible to generate electrical energy in a generator and to change electrical energy into rotating energy in an electrical motor. In a similar way there exists a magnetic field between the North and South Pole of our Earth. It is this magnetic field that aligns the needle in a compass in a north-south direction and thus makes it possible for us to orient ourselves when we are lost.

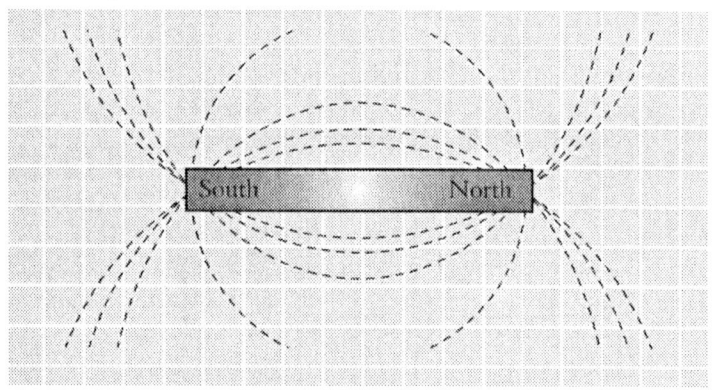

FIGURE 2.1
The Magnetic Field Between Two Poles of a Bar Magnet

All these fields can be measured and quantified, and their existence is obviously of great benefit to us. However, the fields Sheldrake is talking about are nonmaterial and their existence cannot be confirmed by measurements. One way to visualize these fields of influence is by observing the movements of a flock of birds, a school of fish or a herd of reindeer. When, for no apparent reason, they suddenly change direction, they do so in perfect unison without bumping into each other, and they are turning far too fast to do it just by watching their neighbor or by responding to ordinary sensory information. Also, there seems to be no leader in any of these tight groups of animals which gives the direction in which they are supposed to move. In fact, it looks as if all the fish or birds are connected by invisible strings that makes all of them move instantly in the same direction. It is easy to imagine that their uniform movement is the result of a field of influence to which they all are sensitive and which makes it possible for them to move in this extraordinary fashion.

Another example of a field of influence operating in the animal world may be the uncanny ability of some pets, such as cats and dogs, to find their owners at a new location thousands of miles away from where they were lost or abandoned. Sheldrake is continuing his research into the existence of these fields of influence by examining the sense of being stared at that some people have when they are being observed from a distance. Over 18,000 trials have been conducted so far, and the odds against this effect being due to chance is something in the order of 1,000 to 1.

Sheldrake takes the theory of fields of influence a step further by postulating the existence of several different fields: in social organization they are called social fields; in the organization of mental activity they are called mental fields; and in the area of developmental biology they are called *morpho genetic or form-giving fields*. These latter fields are envisaged as giving shape and movement to everything existing in the universe, from the minute particles of the microcosm to humans and even to the gigantic galaxies of the macrocosm. One of the prime examples where these form-giving fields may be active is in the embryonic development of our offspring. It is thought that the presence of these fields may explain how, after conception, the original cells start to split into millions of new and different cells, and how these different cells are produced in the right quantity and how they all find their proper location in the emerging body. How does the liver cell know how to get to the place where the liver is being formed, or how does the toenail cell know how to get to the end of the foot which is being formed (see also Chapter V). This is surely one of the most baffling phenomenon in all of creation.

The existence of these form-giving fields acting as channels or blueprints, or even as formative principles, may provide some insight into how we are formed and created, always keeping in mind that these fields are nonmaterial. If these fields exist, and if they are actually interacting with the human body, and if they are nonmaterial, then they must be of a spiritual nature. Sheldrake believes that each person inherits his or her own fields of influence in the same way she or he inherit genes. The intriguing thing is that, if they are inherited, then they must be created by the very thing which they are forming. So, Sheldrake believes that these form-giving fields are the repositories of what might be described as genetic habits, and are in fact the carriers of memories. Also, he believes that these form-giving fields connect us to other humans and even to animals which is close to what Jung calls the "collective unconscious" (see Chapter V). He expands this further by suggesting that there is such a thing as a collective memory or a *morphic resonance* whereby each kind of thing has a collective

SOME RECENT DISCOVERIES AND THEORIES

memory. This resonance, he believes, is behind the fact that ideas and inventions occur often in different places in the world at the same time, such as happen quite frequently in art, fashion design, and in science and technology. Also, it is thought to be responsible for the fact that it appears to be easier to learn what other people have already learned. Consequently, he thinks that morphic resonance could lead to accelerated learning and more effective educational methods.

The introduction of these form-giving fields adds another dimension to our understanding of the nature of the real world. Up to this point, the only building block of the real world was energy which was convertible into matter. We now may have to add another building block which directs where the energy and matter are going to be placed in the universe. Thus, nature now is thought to consist of the material world of matter and energy, and the nonmaterial or spiritual world of form-giving fields. Sheldrake goes as far as to intimate that the Word and Spirit of God work through or are expressed through these form-giving fields.

Recently, a new dimension has been added to this subject with the suggestion that all subatomic particles such as electrons, protons and neutrons may be regarded as a bunching up of fields or even the interaction between fields. It is postulated that when two fields interact, they do so instantaneously and at a single point in time. If this is true, it makes fields the real substantive stuff of the universe, and matter simply becomes the manifestation of fields. Of course, this makes the universe even less substantive than we had thought up to now. Time will probably tell how durable these concepts are. For the present, we will simply take it as yet another unproved theory that may, at some time in the future, provide us with a better and deeper insight into the operation of the universe. Sheldrake himself believes that morphic resonance, etc. may eventually be explained in terms of the nonlocality of quantum mechanics.

The last new theory I want to mention is of a different nature altogether. It is not a part of physics, nor of mathematics, although it involves both. I am referring to the "Chaos Theory" which has grown over the years to become a separate science. It has a number of aspects that touch upon everyday life and is a useful tool in explaining some of the mysteries of nature. The name "Chaos" is probably a misnomer, but it has stuck and is used to cover a number of seemingly quite different subjects. As far as I can see there are two different parts to it. The first part is probably best known as the "Butterfly Effect", while the second part might be referred to as "Order in Chaos", or "Order in Disorder".

The Butterfly Effect is so named after the "tongue-in-cheek" theory that the small disturbance of the air caused by the flapping of the wings of a butterfly in Beijing can lead to greater and greater disturbances of the air around the world and can eventually cause a hurricane in Florida. In other words, very small changes in initial conditions in faraway places can have large effects on conditions far removed from the place of the original disturbance. A more mundane example may be the man who cuts himself shaving; thereby missing the bus that goes every ten minutes to the train station; thereby missing the train that goes every hour; thereby missing the plane that goes only once a day; and thereby missing the deadline for the delivery of an important proposal; thereby eventually causing the demise of his company.

The development of this new science went hand in hand with the development of computers. It was only when it became possible to do tedious calculations at great speed, and with much greater accuracy, that it was found that

SOME RECENT DISCOVERIES AND THEORIES

certain processes, which seemed to be quite regular under most assumptions, could become very irregular as a result of very small changes in some of the initial conditions. To stay with the weather for a moment: as soon as it became possible to make mathematical models of the weather, and thereby make better weather predictions, it was found that very small changes in the initial assumptions could cause very large changes in the weather predicted for even a few days later. The problem, of course, is that there are many factors which affect the weather, and the discovery that small changes in the initial conditions of any one of these could cause these large changes made the forecasting of the weather even more difficult. The result, as we all know too well, is that, even today, with all the new techniques and large computers, the weather prediction for even three or four days ahead is often not very accurate.

Another example of this sort of instability or randomness was found when scientists started to make projections of the world population or, for that matter, how many fish a fish tank could hold. Obviously, the population in any given year is equal to the population of the year before, plus the people who were born, and minus the people who died during that year. Both the birth rate and the death rate depend on a number of factors such as the average age of the population, the availability of food, etc. Since there is clearly a limit on how many people the Earth can support, or how many fish can survive in a fish tank, the equation used to calculate future population levels must include a factor that causes growth to decrease with increasing density of population. It was always assumed that for each set of factors used, the population would eventually settle down to a steady level, and this was actually confirmed by using simple assumptions regarding the rate of growth and the factors applied to limit the growth. However, when computers were used to investigate what would happen under a much wider range of assumptions, it was found, to the surprise of the investigators, that under certain conditions the final population would fluctuate wildly and would never settle down to a steady level. The astounding thing was that the system would change from a steady state to a chaotic state as a result of very small changes in the initial conditions or assumptions. Barbara Brown Taylor[20] in her book *The Luminous Web* takes it one step further when she writes:

> Whatever language you prefer, the apparent truth is that we belong to a web of creation in which nothing, absolutely nothing is inconsequential – nothing can even be *rounded off* without changing the whole gorgeous geometry of the universe.

To a certain extent, this Chaos Theory undermined the belief that, given time, science would be able to predict such occurrences as hurricanes, floods, earthquakes, droughts, etc.; in general, anything that has to do with weather. We now realize that we can never know the initial conditions of these systems accurately enough to predict the state of these systems in the future.

When these principles are applied to evolution, and in particular to the effect of small mutations on future generations, it shows how even a small change in genetic make-up can result in very large changes in the species some generations later. This, coupled with the fact that we can never know all the properties of subatomic particles at the same time, makes a mockery of the belief that we live in a deterministic universe, and that we could predict the future course of events if we had enough basic data and knew the initial conditions with sufficient accuracy. On the contrary, it would seem that our, and the world's, future is not cast in stone but that through our own free will we can influence not only our own future but that of the world as well.

The second interesting aspect of Chaos Theory is the idea that there is order in what appears to be chaos. For instance, many chaotic phenomena exhibit a very regular pattern of recurrences. The classic example is the case of an irregular coastline. Seen from a spaceship, a coastline, say that of Alaska, appears to be smooth; however, when we look at the same coastline from an airplane the coast appears to be ragged with many coastal inlets. If we then observe this coastline from a small beach, the immediate surroundings may appear quite smooth again; if we go to a smaller level yet, we may find the same roughness we observed previously; however, if we go to the size of the sand grain we find it smooth again, but if we use a microscope on the sand grain we see that its surface is rough with lots of knobs and pits, etc. The pattern seems to repeat itself over and over again, and so this phenomenon is generally known as "self-similarity over scale changes".

Another example is the blood circulation system in our body. From a picture of the whole blood circulating system it appears chaotic; there is no evident regularity. However, looking at it closely, it becomes obvious that, from the aorta to the capillaries, the blood vessels divide and branch out in very similar patterns. This pattern holds true even when the blood vessels become so narrow that blood cells have to slide through a vein in single file. In the end, I am told, there is no cell in the body that is farther removed from a blood cell than the distance of three or four cells. Again, the same pattern repeats itself over and over again.

These patterns of repetition are referred to as "fractals". It appears that not only our bodies, but also nature in general, are filled with these fractals. The branches and leaves of a tree, snow flakes, etc. are all examples of fractals. One of the more interesting problems associated with these fractals arose when attempts were made to measure the circumference of irregular shapes. The most irregular shape is probably that of the coastline of a land mass. Modern atlases will probably give you a figure for the length of the coastline of a country. However, whatever the figure is, it is wrong. The figure is very large if not infinite. The length one is given depends entirely on the scale by which it is measured. Measured from an airplane, the coast appears relatively smooth and the measured figure is relatively small; measured by walking around every small irregularity gives a much larger figure; and measuring it with a ruler gives yet a larger figure, and so on.

A simple example of this is the so-called "Koch" curve. It is very easily constructed at home with a piece of paper and a pencil. It starts off with a triangle: on each of the sides a smaller triangle is constructed (see Figure 2.2). The intriguing property of this drawing is that, while the surface area covered by the figure never even reaches the area of the circle which passes through the points of the triangle, the circumference becomes *infinite* if one continues with the process ad infinitum.

One of the standard examples of another type of chaos is typified by the smoke rising from a burning cigarette. At first, the smoke rises in a straight column, but then for an unknown reason it suddenly starts to swirl around and the movement of the smoke becomes completely chaotic. Another example that everyone is familiar with is the traffic on a busy highway. The traffic will move smoothly until suddenly it slows down and at times it may come to a complete halt. Later it starts to move again and you are looking for a traffic accident that may have caused the stoppage, but you find no such thing. For an observer, in a plane above, the movement of the traffic is completely chaotic – stopping and starting completely at random for no apparent reason. In all these chaotic and random events there is a certain order underlying the disorder. It appears that there exists in nature a hidden unity or a common underlying form.

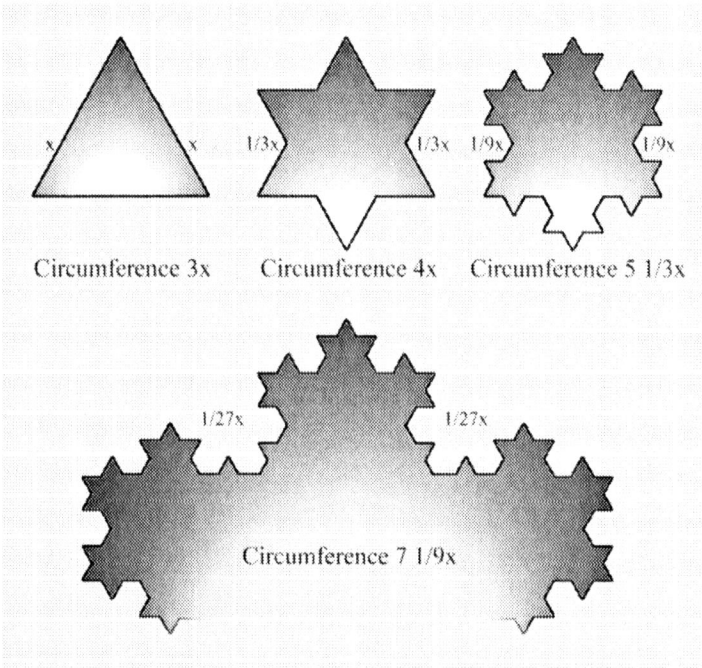

On the side of each equilateral triangle erect another equilateral triangle and so forth. The circumference increases every time this procedure is repeated and will approach infinity if the procedure is continued ad infinitum. At the same time, the area enclosed by the figure will never increase beyond that enclosed by the circle which touches the three points of the original triangle.

Figure 2.2
The Koch Curve – an Example of a Fractal Shape

Thus it can be said in a nutshell that:

- There is a law of nature that says everything on Earth and in the universe is eventually going to end up in complete uniformity; consequently, no life will be able to exist anywhere.
- Energy and matter are interchangeable.
- Time can slow down and time can go backwards.
- Space and time make a fourth dimension in a space-time continuum.
- This space-time is warped or curved by the proximity of mass.
- Some particles can be two things at the same time and can be at two places at the same time.
- An observer changes the properties he is measuring simply by the act of looking at it.
- Without observers there may be no reality.
- Changes in one particle can be instantaneously transmitted to another particle even though there is no connection between them.
- The same cause does not always have the same effect; at best, there is only a *probability* that a certain cause will have a certain effect.
- Some phenomena we will never be able to predict because we cannot ever know the initial conditions with enough accuracy.
- Some particles seem to know in advance what an observer is going to do in the future.
- There seem to be nonmaterial fields that shape our bodies and many other things in nature.
- There seems to exist a hidden unity in some of nature's chaotic and random events and processes.
- Humans are the center of the universe because they are its meaning.

If one can accept some or all of the apparently "crazy" findings, surely one can accept some of the miracles and the paranormal phenomena that have been reported since the beginning of time. The second quantum phenomenon even seems to put our very existence in question. If the act of observing can change things, how sure are we that what we observe is really there – maybe it is all an illusion. Some scientists go even so far as to consider that all particles may be nothing else but thought objects. Contradictory as this may seem to be to all that we experience daily, there are many people who believe this to be true. And, of course, it is one of the basic tenets of the Hindu religion that life is an illusion.

In addition to these sometimes very strange and unbelievable theories about the behavior of atomic particles, there are a number of other ideas that are being discussed which all deal with the nature of our universe. Some of these ideas are far-out indeed; they provide the occasion for science fiction writers to exercise their imagination and provide us with a wide range of narratives and accounts of extraterrestrial adventures.

First, there is the theory that we live in a universe that has many more dimensions than our simple four-dimensional concept of three dimensions of space and one of time. I suppose Einstein initiated this thought when he began talking about curved, four-dimensional space as producing the same effect as the gravitational force. Some theories postulate that our universe started off as twenty-dimensional space and then split up into two: our four-dimensional and a very much smaller twenty-dimensional space that reduced itself to the size of subatomic particles. Of course, additional dimensions, beyond the four we experience, are impossible to envisage, although it is easy enough to play with them mathematically.

Secondly, there is the concept that there exist other

universes in space, all created at roughly the same time as ours. In other words, it is suggested that we live in one universe amongst many others. Some of these universes are thought to be connected with each other through what are called "worm holes". Of course, the existence of these other universes will be very hard to prove, unless someone manages to creep through one of these worm holes and tells us what it is like to live in another universe. Even, if these other universes exist, the likelihood of a living entity being able to survive the trip through the worm hole appears to be very unlikely indeed.

A third hypothesis has been called the "many-world" theory. The basic idea behind this theory seems to be that every time the universe is faced with a choice at the quantum level, the entire universe is split into as many copies of itself as it takes to carry out every option. As anyone can see, the problem with this theory is that it requires the existence of billions of universes to coexist since every universe is splitting every second in more and more universes. On the human scale, this would mean that, for instance, there is another universe in which no life of any type ever developed, and another universe with life but where the dinosaurs were not wiped out, and yet another universe where there is some type of life but not human life, etc. ad infinitum. Strange as this may seem to us who are not involved in scientific research, there are still scientists who support this theory as being the best one to explain the weird and wonderful happenings in the quantum world. Someone has even calculated that if this theory were true, there would be at least 10^{100} universes out there. That is more than there are atoms in the entire known universe. Based on this, I believe that we can safely discard this theory as somewhat unrealistic, to say the least.

Before closing this section, it may be well to remind ourselves that practically all we have discussed in this chapter is conjecture. There are certain facts we think we have established, and science has woven around these facts theories that put these facts in context. If later, other facts show up that do not fit into this theory, the theory is changed or the theory is expanded. For instance, Newton's laws of motion were for 300 years considered to be valid throughout the universe, but the discoveries of the last century have shown that this is not true for the subatomic world of electrons and quarks. So, new theories were developed in which Newton's laws could be accommodated but only as a special case valid for large bodies in the macrocosm. The simple standard model of an atom consisting of a nucleus and electrons, although universally accepted, is nothing more than a model that fits the facts as far as we know them. Other facts may come to light later that do not fit this model; in which case we will have to abandon it. As said before, the simple fact is that no one has ever seen a nucleus or an electron.

Even the measurements and facts we think we have established beyond doubt could easily be proven wrong if it is ever found that there are other, at present unknown, forces at work which have influenced these measurements. Probably, three of the most elementary assumptions we all make is that the workings of the universe, on both the macro and micro level, are understandable by human beings; that the laws governing the operation of the universe are fixed and do not change with time, and that these laws are the same here as well as in the remotest galaxy. If we ever find out that this is not so, we are in deep trouble as far as our understanding of the universe is concerned. All this, to remind us that we should not take all these theories too seriously because tomorrow they might have to be changed.

IIc Some Notable Features of the Laws of Nature

In the previous section, we mentioned that four forces acting together determine the entire operation of the cosmos, both on the microcosmic and the macrocosmic level. For the uninitiated it seems almost unbelievable that the movements of all stars, of all galaxies and of all atomic and subatomic particles can be described by the interaction of four basic forces. On the other hand, scientists, starting with Einstein, have tried for years to put together one theory that would explain everything – "The Unified Theory" or "The Theory of Everything". One of the supporters of the recently formulated superstring hypothesis, Michio Kaku, believes that this theory at least has the potential to lead to the formulation of such a unified theory. Others hold that such a theory simply does not exist and that the search for it is a waste of time.

The four forces of nature have such amazing properties that they make us wonder if they are here just by pure chance, or if there was some higher intelligence at work in their formulation. The four forces that govern the operation of the entire universe are respectively: the force of gravity, the electromagnetic force and the strong and weak nuclear forces – together, they rule the universe.

The first force, gravity, is one we are all very familiar with. It can do us great harm: for instance, when we take a fall from any height it will cause broken bones or worse. At the same time, it makes it possible for us to walk on the surface of the Earth that is round and spins at a considerable speed around its axis. Without the force of gravity holding us back, we would be flung into space by the centrifugal force of the rotating Earth. It is the gravitational force that holds the Earth and the other satellites in place circling around the Sun, and the same force governs the motion of

SOME RECENT DISCOVERIES AND THEORIES

all the stars and galaxies. It will eventually determine whether the universe will keep expanding or whether the universe will eventually contract back into a point of infinite temperature and infinite density.

The second force that most of us are familiar with is the electromagnetic force which makes it possible for motors, generators, computers, radios, and televisions to operate. In its most basic form, this force holds the atom together; without it, the negatively charged electron would collide with the positively charged nucleus. The gravitational and the electromagnetic forces both act over large distances; they both diminish in strength as the square of the distances between the two objects.

On the other hand, the third and fourth forces operate only over the very small, subatomic distances. The strong nuclear force holds the nucleus of the atom together against the repulsion of the electromagnetic force that is interacting between its protons. The weak force, which is much smaller than the strong force, acts within the nucleus and controls the decay of radioactive material. These forces vary greatly in strength and in range as shown on the following table:

	Strong Force	Electromagnetic	Weak Force	Gravity
Relative strength	1	10^{-2}	10^{-13}	10^{-36}
Range in meters	10^{-12}	infinite	10^{-18}	Infinite

It is somewhat surprising to see that the force of gravity is by far the weakest among the four and that the electromagnetic force is so strong (10^{34} times the force of gravity), while both act theoretically over an infinite range. Scientists have often wondered about the significance of this large difference (a 10 followed by 34 zeros) but so far no explanation has been forthcoming.

Together, the four forces and the constants in the laws, which regulate the interaction of these forces, are called the laws of nature. There are a number of other remarkable features of these laws of nature, including the following.

First, all of these forces appear to be the same throughout the universe. In other words, the laws that govern our daily lives appear to be exactly the same as the laws that govern not only the behavior of galaxies billions of light years away, but also the atomic particles and electrons that are so small that they can only be imagined. Also, the chemical elements, and the reactions amongst them, produce the same chemical compounds on these faraway galaxies as they do here on Earth.

The second amazing thing about these laws of nature is that they do not change with time, location or physical circumstances. Thus the laws, which created the first subatomic particles under temperatures and pressures that were unimaginably high at the very first moment after the Big Bang, are exactly the same as those which govern our existence on this planet under much more normal conditions. This is truly astonishing considering that almost everything in the universe is subject to change. The stars, which were originally thought to be stationary, turn out to be moving at great speeds within their galaxy. Each galaxy itself moves at equally great speeds in the direction of the outer edges of the universe. The Sun changes daily by giving off large amounts of energy, making life on Earth possible. The Earth itself is subject to constant change through erosion, earthquakes, floods, hurricanes, etc. Except for these few laws of nature, everything in the universe appears to be subject to change. If we ever discover that they were different in the past or find evidence that they may change in the future, almost all that we think we

SOME RECENT DISCOVERIES AND THEORIES

know about the universe, its history and its destiny, would have to be changed, probably in a most essential way. An appropriate analogy in the field of chess might be if someone in charge of maintaining the chess rules decided that from now on the rules of the game would be changed. Suddenly, all the textbooks and all the strategies so painfully learned over the centuries would have to be revised.

The third astonishing property of these laws of nature is their simplicity. Consider for a moment the best-known law of them all – Einstein's law governing the relationship between matter and energy. If anyone had ever thought about this relationship before Einstein, they would probably have imagined a very complicated formula with lots of other variables such as temperatures and pressures. Instead, here is Einstein with a law that could not possibly be any simpler – $E=MC^2$. Energy is equal to matter multiplied by the square of the speed of light. This simple law governs almost everything that is happening in the universe: it makes it possible for the Sun to produce prodigious amounts of energy simply by converting a small amount of matter into radiant energy. The very minute part of this energy that reaches the Earth provides us with enough energy to make things grow on our planet and for us to exist. This law does not even have a constant in the metric system other than the square of the speed of light. What could be simpler?

Or consider the law describing the gravitational force acting on two objects with a mass of M and m respectively, and placed at a distance of d from each other: it simply states that the force is equal to the multiple of the two masses, divided by the square of the distance, and multiplied by the gravitational constant – $g.m.M/d^2$.

The simplicity of these laws governing our universe has led to an interesting criterion for judging proposed new laws and theories. This criterion states that if the proposed law is not simple, or lacks a certain amount of beauty, it is probably not correct. In effect, what we are saying is that if you believe in a guiding intelligence in the creation of the universe, then it just seems logical to expect simple laws with finely tuned constants governing the operation of that universe. A creation which was put together without any thought, and in which everything is ruled by chance, would very unlikely have these simple laws and finely tuned constants. In a recent book that I have quoted before, *Before the Beginning of Time, Cosmology Explained*, by George Ellis,[21] the author has listed what he believes are proper criteria for the selection of a satisfactory theory from among many alternatives. The primary candidates for such criteria he lists as:

- Simplicity – we should choose the simplest possible theory that can accommodate the facts (Occam's razor).
- Beauty – on the face of it a very subjective criterion, but there is a remarkably good consensus about it in many cases. For instance, one admires the beauty of the cosmos, how it behaves from the tiniest particle to the largest galaxy.
- Prediction and verifiability – the ability to confirm the theory by a mixture of observations and tests. For instance, the bending of light by the Sun was predicted by Einstein and was only years later confirmed by observation.
- Overall explanatory power and unity of explanation – in particular, congruence with the rest of our current body of knowledge. For instance, the quantum theory is a very odd kind of theory, but it is generally accepted because of its explanatory power.

It appears that many scientists have actually used the criterion of mathematical beauty in the development of their theories. They believe that the best scientific explanations must also be aesthetically pleasing. Without this requirement, a great many discoveries would not have been made. Of course, mathematical beauty could never be the sole criterion but it obviously helped some scientists to feel that they were on the right track. Sir James Jean, the famous British scientist, was so impressed by this that he once exclaimed that God must be a mathematician. In the same vein, other scientists have written:

> The search for beautiful equations lies at the heart of fundamental physics. The unreasonable effectiveness of mathematics in uncovering the structures of the physical world is a kind of hint of the presence of a Creator given to us creatures who are made in the divine image.
>
> Eugene Wigner[22]
>
> There is something absolute and God given about mathematical truth.
>
> Roger Penrose
>
> Why is mathematics so surprisingly effective in describing the physical world.
>
> *Scientific American*, August 1998

Also, in addition to this surprising effectiveness of mathematics, one may well ask where the mathematical capability of humankind came from. John Maddox[23] in his book *What Remains to Be Discovered* writes:

> In any case, what is the biological basis for the capacity of the human mind to practice mathematics? On the face of things, there can be little in the past history of Homo sapiens to prompt the evolution by natural selection of such a facility.

One of the more interesting aspects of nature is the fact that, in addition to the four basic forces, there are slightly more than a dozen constants that appear in the laws that describe the interaction between the various elements of nature. These constants, which are called the fundamental constants of nature, include the numbers that represent the well-known gravitational constant, the charge of an electron, the strength of the weak and the strong nuclear force, the velocity of light, the mass of an electron and a proton, and a few others.

The interesting thing about these constants is that it appears that they must have exactly the value they actually have for the universe to emerge and for life and consciousness to evolve. Computer simulations have shown that the slightest change in any of them completely eliminates the possibility of the universe to form and for life to emerge. In his book, *The Secret Melody*, Trinh Xuan Thuan,[24] makes the following statement:

> Life as we know it would not have the slightest chance of emerging in any universe that was the slightest bit different from our own. All the model universes would be sterile and devoid of consciousness. The numerical parameters do not suffer any modification. If we slightly increase the parameter that controls the intensity of the strong nuclear force, protons could no longer exist in a free state. They would combine with other protons and neutrons to form heavy nuclei. Without hydrogen, we could say goodbye to water and life. Stars could form, but they would speedily burn themselves out in the absence of hydrogen fuel.

Others have come up with similar statements, all to the effect that variations of even one part per million would have produced universes in which the development of galaxies, stars and planets would have been impossible. The question then is: "Why is this universe so fine-tuned as to make life possible?"

The fact that the slightest deviation in the value of these constants makes life impossible has, I believe, a profound, if not decisive, implication about the creation of the universe. There are basically only two ways that creation could have happened: either it was an incredibly lucky coincidence or it was planned by an Intelligent Designer. Looking at these four laws and the dozen or so constants, it is very hard to imagine how the universe could have evolved by itself, with exactly the right value of these constants. To illustrate the problem, consider the following two examples from everyday life. First, there is the example of a carburetor: anyone who has ever tinkered with one knows from bitter experience that there are two or three settings of controls that have to be exactly right for the engine to function. If you ever take one apart, you had better mark the settings of these controls or you will spend a long time adjusting them to make the machine work. Similarly, if you want to bake a cake, you had better get the ingredients right; then heat the oven to the right temperature and cook the cake for the right duration or it will not rise, or if it does it will collapse when it is taken out of the oven. In both cases we are dealing with only two independent variables that have to be just right. In the case of the universe, there are more than a dozen variables and they have to be exactly right within one hundredth of a percentage point. Surely the appearance in nature of the exact values of these constants did not come about by pure chance.

To overcome this perceived dilemma some scientists who cannot accept the idea of a Intelligent Designer have come up with the idea that every time nature has to make a choice it generates two parallel universes – one going in one direction and the other one going in the opposite direction. Applying this theory, to arriving at the precise values of the constants of nature, translates into trying out billions of parallel universes all with slightly different values of these constants. Some of these universes would collapse immediately; others would dissipate into thin air; some would come to a stable existence but without the possibility that any life would emerge. They would simply continue to exist side by side with our own universe. This process would go on until the constants were just right for life to emerge. Presumably, when this point is reached, the creation of further universes would stop. Ridiculous as this may seem at first glance, there are a large number of scientists who believe that this was how we finally arrived at the laws of nature and at the exact value of the universal constants. But then again, quantum mechanics appears often equally unreal (see also page 39 of this chapter).

Even if we accept this argument for a moment, one might well ask what is it in nature that kept creating different universes with different values for these constants without a set objective. If nature's goal was to create a universe where the emergence of life and consciousness was a possibility, then we might ask who or what was behind this drive and who set this objective. I believe that in either case we end by postulating the existence of a Guiding Intelligence who was (and is still) involved in the fine-tuning of the universe. One way, the final set of values is part of a grand design; the other way, these values are finally arrived at after a long period of trial and error by someone or something guiding and adjusting the setting of these constants of nature until they are just right. Barrow and Tippler[25] put it this way in their book, *The Anthropic Cosmological Principle*:

> As yet, we have no explanation for the precise numerical value taken by these unchanging dimensionless numbers. They are not subject to evolution or selection by any known natural or unnatural mechanism. The fortuitous

nature of many of these numerical values is a mystery that cries out for a solution.

A side effect of the theory of parallel universes is that it would do away with our free will, because every time we have to make a choice two universes are created: one with us going to the left at the intersection, and one going to the right, with us living blissfully in both universes, unaware of the fact that we never made the choice but went in both directions. To my mind this argument of parallel universes goes against everything we believe in. Common sense, I believe, tells us that this is a no go. It certainly does not meet any of the criteria for beauty and simplicity which George Ellis mentioned in *Before the Beginning of Time*.

The writer of *The Secret Melody* argues that the rejection of the parallel universes does not necessarily imply the acceptance of the idea of a Master Designer behind the creation of the universe. Most scientists believe that something very special happened at 10^{-43} seconds after the Big Bang. At that time the universe was only 10^{-33} centimeters across and the temperatures and pressures were such that the normal laws of nature did not apply. They believe that it was a quantum fluctuation that caused the Big Bang and the subsequent creation of the first particles. These people believe that it is not necessary to think in terms of a first cause or Divine Initiator. For myself, I cannot follow that argument; there are simply too many unanswered questions remaining such as: where do they think these quantum fluctuations came from? Are they not just as much part of the nature of the universe as any of the other laws? If we assume, that the universe had its beginning at the Big Bang, when all the elements together with time and space were created at the same time, then it is clear that neither quantum fluctuations nor any other law of nature could have been responsible for the start of the universe. In *Deep Time*, David Darling,[26] I believe, hit the nail on its head when he wrote:

> Wherever the universe came from, before it could emerge there had to be guiding principles, pre-existing natural laws. But where did these laws come from? And in any case, how can a law exist disembodied and outside of time?

Similarly, James S. Trefil[27] wrote in his book *The Moment of Creation*:

> Very well, we agree that the universe exists because of the laws of physics. But who created these laws?... Who made the laws of logic? My message, then, to those who feel that science is overstepping its bounds when it probes that early universe, is simple: don't worry. No matter how far the boundaries are pushed back, there will always be room for religious faith and religious interpretation of the physical world. For myself, I feel much more comfortable with the concept of a God who is clever enough to devise the laws of physics that make the existence of our marvelous universe inevitable than I do with the old-fashioned God who made it all laboriously, piece by piece.

At the end of his book Trinh Xuan Thuan[28] admits that, if he had to guess, he would be prepared to bet on the existence of a supreme being. He writes:

> For myself, I am prepared to bet on the existence of a supreme being. The hypothesis of a multiplicity of imaginary, unverifiable universes violates my sense of simplicity and economy... I find the hypothesis of innumerable universes, all inaccessible to observation, to be rather unwarranted. And, besides, I like to have free will... Finally, betting on chance implies nonsense and despair. Why not, then, bet rather on sense and hope.

Freeman Dyson,[29] one of the founders of quantum

SOME RECENT DISCOVERIES AND THEORIES

electrodynamics, in the "Disturbing the Universe" writes:

> I do not claim that the architecture of the universe proves the existence of God. I claim only that the architecture of the universe is consistent with the hypothesis that mind plays an essential role in its functioning.

Fred Hoyle,[30] as quoted by Derek Gjertsen, said:

> I do not believe that any scientist who examined the evidence would fail to draw the inference that the laws of nuclear physics have been deliberately designed with regard to the consequences they produce in stars.

Vera Kistrakowsky, a physicist at the Massachusetts Institute of Technology, writes:

> The exquisite order displayed by our scientific understanding of the physical world calls for the divine.
>
> *Discover Magazine*, November 2000

Even scientists who cannot accept the existence of a Creator find it difficult to completely distance themselves from a superior mind or spirit being involved in the creation of the universe. Brian Silver,[31] who confesses that he does not believe in the existence of God, nevertheless makes statements like this in his book, *The Ascent of Science*:

> The anthropic principle is fascinating, unprovable, and unlikely. The principle always seems to me to be a substitution for the religious belief in the special creation of man.
>
> I am not suggesting that there was a guiding hand, but we do not understand the mechanism by which the host of elementary particles turned out to be like the standardized product of a production line.
>
> It must be admitted, even by all those with whom I

share disbelief, that at present by far and away the most likely hypothesis is that Zeus rules.

Several times in the preceding pages, reference was made to the anthropic principle – anthropic meaning of humankind. That term was first used by the British cosmologist Brandon Carter in 1974; however, the implied principle goes back as far as 1957 when Robert Dicke first voiced the opinion that we simply cannot talk of luck that the constants have exactly the right values to make it possible for life to develop.

There are a number of these anthropic principles, the best known are the Weak Anthropic Principle (WAP) and the Strong Anthropic Principle (SAP). These principles are stated in many different forms. The weak anthropic principle states that the simple fact of our existence limits the possible number of values of the constants of nature that we need to consider. The strong anthropic principle goes one step further and states that the universe must have those properties that will allow life to develop within it at some stage in its history. The presence of life is required in order that the universe model makes sense. The universe must be such as to admit the creation of observers in it at some stage.

Lastly, there is what is called the Participatory Anthropic Principle which states simply that things cannot be said to exist until they are observed. The observer is necessary to bring the universe into being. John Wheeler puts it even more strongly when he states that a universe in which life could not develop would never have come into being. The central point of these anthropic principles is that there is a life-giving factor at the center of the whole machinery and design of the universe. And also, that the chances that this life-giving factor was created by accident are so small that the intervention of a Creator is necessary to alter the odds in favor of it happening.

All these considerations led Nobel laureate Charles Townes to write as quoted in *Newsweek* of July 20, 1998:

> The present discoveries in cosmology reveal a universe that fits religious views specifically that somehow intelligence must have been involved in the laws of the universe.

Finally, Ken Croswell[32] in *Planet Quest* even seems to burst forth in poetic language when he writes:

> Is it mere coincidence that the universe happens to possess just those properties which allow part of it to be alive? Some people say yes; it was simply good luck that the universe was born with the particular characteristics that it has. Others say no; our universe is only one of many universes, each with different properties, and we naturally inhabit one of the few planets that has a mild climate. Still others, of a more spiritual persuasion, see the universe's remarkable offspring as a sign that an intelligent creator wrote a tremendous symphony whose melodies the stars, galaxies, and planets now play with beauty and precision, and we living beings are one of the fortunate resulting chords, perhaps the climatic chord in that symphony's greatest movement. Whatever the case, and vast and complex though the universe is, its most astonishing features are two of the simplest; it exists, and so do we.

On this note we finish our quick run through some of the latest discoveries of science that are influencing our thinking about the nature of our universe. Some think that these findings are simply stages in the ongoing development of our understanding of nature and that further discoveries will lift the veil on mysteries that remain unsolved. Others, including the writer, believe that these findings are a clear indication of the involvement of an Intelligent Designer in the creation of the universe.

One final note about the nature of God's involvement in the creation of the universe and the exact value of the fifteen constants of nature. Someone wrote recently that he could not see God fiddling with the value of these constants until they had just the right values for the creation of a stable universe. In some ways, this is rather a naïve evaluation of God's creative powers. If God was able to create the universe out of nothing, then he surely would be able to know beforehand what these values should be. I am sure that, sometime in the future when the capacity of computers has increased sufficiently, we ourselves will be able to build a model of the universe that will eventually produce the exact value of these constants.

NOTES

[1] Ellis, George, *Before the Beginning of Time, Cosmology Explained*, Boyars/Bowerdean, London, 1993, p.104.

[2] Silver, Brian L., *The Ascent of Science*, Oxford University Press, New York, Oxford, 1998.

[3] Bohr, Niels, *Atomic Theory And The Description of Nature*, Cambridge University Press, 1934.

[4] Wynn, Charles and Wiggins, Anita, *The Five Biggest Ideas in Science*, John Wiley and Sons, New York, 1993.

[5] Gribben, John, *Schroder's Kittens and the Search for Reality*, Little, Brown and Co., Boston, 1995, p.142.

[6] Wheeler, John A, quoted in *Schroder's Kittens*, p.142.

[7] Wigner, Eugene, *Symmetries and Reflections*, Indiana University Press, Bloomington, 1967.

[8] Ronan, Colin A., *The Natural History of the Universe, From the Big Bang to the End of Time*, Macmillan Publishing Company, New York, 1991.

[9] Malin, Shimon, *Nature Loves to Hide, Quantum Physics and the Nature of Reality, A Western Perspective*, Oxford University Press, New York, 2001.

[10] Goswami, Amit, *The Self-Aware Universe, How Consciousness Creates the Material World*, G. P. Putnam & Sons, New York, 1993.

[11] Davies, Paul, *The Cosmic Blue Print*, Simon and Schuster, New York, 1988, p.203.

[12] Berkeley, Bishop George, 1685–1753, *Treatise Concerning the Principles of Human Knowledge*, 1709.

[13] Tarna, Richard, *Passions of the Western Mind, Understanding the Ideas that Have Shaped our Worldview*, Ballantine Books, New York, 1991, p.397.

[14] Gjertsen, Derek, *Science and Philosophy, Past and Present*, Penguin Books, New York, 1989.
[15] Gribben, John, *Schroder's Kittens*, pp.140, 142.
[16] Bohm, David, quoted in *Schroder's Kittens*, p.159.
[17] Cramer, John G., *Review of Modern Physics*, Vol. 58, 1986, p.647.
[18] Darling, David, *Deep Time*, Delacorte Press, Bantam, Doubleday, Dell, New York, 1989, p.115.
[19] Sheldrake, Rupert, *The Rebirth of Nature, Science and God*, Bantam Books, New York, 1991.
[20] Brown Taylor, Barbara, *The Luminous Web, Essays on Science and Religion*, Cowley Publications, Boston, 2000.
[21] Ellis, George, op. cit.
[22] Wigner, Eugene, *Symmetries and Reflections*.
[23] Maddox, John, *What Remains to Be Discovered*, The Free Press, Simon and Schuster, New York, 1998, p.312.
[24] Thuan Trinh Xuan, *The Secret Melody, and Man Created the Universe*, Oxford University Press, New York, 1995, p.229.
[25] Barrow, John and Tippler, Frank J., *The Anthropic Cosmological Principle*, Clarendon Press Oxford University Press, Oxford, 1986, p.31.
[26] Darling, David, see note 17.
[27] Trefil, James S., *The Moment of Creation – Big Bang Physics*, Charles Scribner and Sons, New York, 1983, pp.222–223.
[28] Thuan, Trinh Xuan, see note 23.
[29] Dyson, Freeman, *Disturbing the Universe*, Harper and Row, New York, 1979, p.250.
[30] Hoyle, Fred, quoted in *Science and Philosophy*.
[31] Silver, Brian, see note 2.
[32] Crosswell, Ken, *Planet Quest, The Epic Discovery of Alien Solar Systems*, Harcourt Brace & Co, 1998, p.247.

Chapter III
CREATION – WHERE DO WE COME FROM?

IIIa   Introduction

Before going into detail about the creation of the universe in general, and the creation of human life in particular, it should be mentioned that there are basically two diametrically opposed views about that creation. The first view is that espoused by the Creationists who believe that God created all of the universe in six days as described in the first chapter of the Bible. According to this view, the world was created fairly recently, say 6,000 to 10,000 years ago, and humans are the culmination of that creation: in fact, humans are the reason that the whole universe was created in the first place.

Of course, there are many other creation stories, such as those of the First Nations in North America and the Mayans of Central America. The latter is described in great detail in the *Popol Vuh, The Sacred Book of the Ancient Quiche Maya*[1] which contains such familiar language as:

> There was nothing standing; only the calm water, the placid sea, alone and tranquil. Nothing existed... Thus they spoke. Let the emptiness be filled! Let the water recede and make a void, let the Earth appear and become solid. Let there be light, let there be dawn in the sky and on the Earth! There shall be neither glory nor grandeur in our creation and formation until the human being is made, man is formed. So they spoke.

An alternative view to that of the Creationists was most clearly enunciated by Charles Darwin[2] in 1859 in his book, *The Origin of the Species*. According to this theory humans evolved over billions of years from single cell creatures through the agencies of natural selection and random mutation. According to this evolutionary theory, the human being is just one life form out of a very large number of others; life developed purely by accident and humans are basically nothing else but intelligent animals with no special significance and with no special place in the universe.

As mentioned before, it is the purpose of this book to show that there are clear indications that there is a Guiding Spirit or Intelligence at work in the universe which guided the emergence of conscious human beings from the most basic particles and that, therefore, we are not here by chance but as the result of a well worked out plan.

Thus, while I reject the main thrust of the creationist argument, I do believe that the creation story, as told in the first chapter of Genesis, has an important message for humankind. This message is that we are created in the image of God with a free will to choose between good and evil and with the ability to create things, not create things out of nothing like God can, but nevertheless create things using our God-given intelligence.

IIIb The Creation of the Universe

Probably one of the oldest questions humans have asked themselves, since they became conscious of their surroundings, is where do we come from and where are we going. The very earliest civilizations we know about studied the night sky and came to the conclusion that the Earth was the center of the universe and that the Sun, the Moon and all the other constellations in the sky neatly circled around the Earth. This gave them a sense of importance which unfortunately has been taken away, bit by bit, by the discoveries of the last four or five centuries which clearly show that the Earth is not the center of the universe and is not even the center of our solar system.

Some of these early civilizations even developed their understanding of the movement of the celestial bodies to the extent that they were able to predict eclipses of the Sun and Moon. Of course, they were very much intimidated by the apparent vastness of the sky and by what appeared to be the influence of the Sun and Moon on their daily existence. As a result, they started to assign godlike qualities to some of the more readily identifiable cosmic appearances – starting initially with the Sun and Moon and later to some of the other planets such as Venus, which was named the god of love and Mars, which became the god of war. Having only the naked eye to guide them, and lacking the necessary equipment to measure the movement of the celestial bodies, the geocentric view of the universe remained unchanged for millennia. It is only in the last four or five centuries that our ideas have changed and we have removed the Earth, and with it humans, from the center of the universe, a place it had occupied for all these millennia.

So, how do today's scientists think this universe of ours came into being? Surprisingly, modern scientific thinking about the creation of the universe tends to follow along the same sequence as that described in the Bible. The Bible simply states, "In the beginning, when God created the universe, the Earth was formless and desolate." – the latest scientific thinking supports this description.

Today, most scientists believe that some fifteen billion years ago, all that existed was concentrated in a single point. Scientists will argue that this single point contained an infinite amount of energy and matter at infinitely high temperatures and pressures. When this point became unstable and exploded the universe was on its way. In other words, creation started from practically nothing with a very large explosion, the so-called Big Bang. With the Big Bang came the creation of energy and matter, in the form of the most fundamental building blocks (particles) of the atom and the establishment of the laws of nature which govern the behavior of these particles. We may well ask with David Darling[3] in *Deep Time*, where did these laws of nature come from? And how could a law exist disembodied and outside of time?

In any case, since we believe that time and space were also created at that time, it is in principle impossible to determine scientifically what there was before the Big Bang occurred. In more scientific terms, $t=0$ is inaccessible to scientific scrutiny; it appears as a singularity to which the laws of physics do not apply.

Obviously there had to be more than just a point of energy in the time before the Big Bang for events to unfold as they did. Not only that, but the density of that early universe had to be just right; it appears that a slightly denser universe would have collapsed on itself, while a slightly less dense universe would have flown apart without ever producing stars and galaxies. One may ask, who or what set this density at just the right value?

As indicated before, we believe that before the Big Bang there was no time and no space. The adherents of the major religions would probably want to add that, outside of time and space, God was there. For most of us it is difficult to imagine a condition when there was no time and no space and no matter – only a void. Maybe this comes closest to the Hindu concept of Nirvana, where the individual becomes one with Brahma in rest and nothingness. In our own tradition, Augustine, as early as the fourth century, concluded that time itself had been created at the moment of creation. He suggested that creation was not an event in time, but that time was created along with the world.

In any case, it is now believed that after the Big Bang, which hurled the newly formed particles into outer space, there was a very rapid expansion of the mini-universe, the so-called 'inflationary epoch'. Using this theory, it is speculated that there may be galaxies so far removed from us that their light has not even reached us yet. In fact, we may never see or hear of such galaxies for thousands of years to come.

The initial subatomic particles, which were formed at the time of the Big Bang, eventually arranged themselves to form atoms of helium and hydrogen, the most basic and simplest atoms in the universe. At present, this is thought to have occurred some 500,000 years after the Big Bang (see Figure 3.1). After some time, these atoms formed clouds of gas which later condensed to form stars. These stars in their turn began to condense in large groups called galaxies; this is thought to have occurred around a billion years after the Big Bang. After some time, these galaxies themselves began to form large clusters mostly at immense distances from the initial point of departure.

With the Hubble telescope we can actually see back some twelve billion years in the past; that is, we believe that the clouds of gas and dust we observe are located at a distance of twelve billion light years away from us. Since it took twelve billion light years for the light from these clouds to reach the telescope, we actually see what the condition of these clouds was twelve billion years ago. And, as long as we are limited by the speed of light, we can never find out what their condition is today.

Today, we know that these clusters and galaxies are moving at great speeds into the further and further reaches of the universe. It was the discovery that the universe is expanding, and probably always has been expanding, that led cosmologists to conclude that the cosmos must have started from a single point. From this single point, a primordial explosion started the universe on its way. All this, of course, is based on the assumption that the rules guiding this expansion of the universe were the same during all these billions of years. If they were different at any time during this period, the initial condition of the universe could be entirely different from what we now believe to be the case. Fortunately, the confirmation of the existence of a uniform background radiation, which was predicted on the basis of theoretical considerations, has led to the almost uniform acceptance of the theory that the universe started with the explosion of a point of infinite temperature and infinite pressure. Recently (summer 2000), an ultra-sensitive telescope, hung from a helium balloon and circling the Antarctic for ten days, is said to have provided data which showed what the universe was like fourteen billion years ago, one billion years after the Big Bang. The data also provided what the press release called "Fantastic Confirmation" of the Big Bang theory. A full report on this experiment is not yet available (*Globe and Mail*, September 2000).

In a book by Gregg Easterbrook[4] entitled *Beside Still Waters: Searching for Meaning in an Age of Doubt* he makes some interesting observations about this Big Bang theory. He writes:

> For sheer extravagant implausibility, nothing in theology or metaphysics can hold a candle to the Big Bang. Surely, if this description of the cosmic genesis came from the Bible or the Koran rather than from our institutions of technology, it would be treated as a preposterous myth.

The Big Bang theory is not the only way to explain the existence and formation of the universe. There is the "Steady State" theory which theorizes that the universe is infinite and that new matter is continually being created to fill the spaces left by the receding galaxies. Scientists supporting this approach still need to explain the origin of this new matter that is continuously being created according to this theory. This hypothesis, of course, does away with the requirement for a specific beginning of the universe. The adherents to this theory believe that the universe has always been there and will always be there in exactly the same form. According to this theory, there is no need to posit the involvement of a Guiding Intelligence in the creation of the universe. It simply was always there. In the last decade or so, this theory has lost ground mainly because the Big Bang theory explains a lot of things about the universe that the Steady State theory cannot do, such as the uniform background radiation mentioned before.

The rate of expansion of the universe must of necessity decrease with time due to the gravitational pull that the galaxies exert on each other. This pull tries to overcome the outward force exerted on them resulting from the momentum of the original explosion. There are basically three possibilities about the relative strength of these two forces. The first possibility is that the gravitational force will eventually overcome the outward force; as a consequence, the universe will eventually stop expanding and then collapse on itself and end up in a "Big Crunch". Some people argue that, ultimately, this could result in the reappearance of the single point of infinite energy and infinite temperatures and pressures. If this were to happen, one can speculate that this single point would become unstable again and the whole scenario would repeat itself, and this could go on ad infinitum.

The second possibility is that the expansionary force will continue to exceed the strength of the gravitational pull and the universe will continue to expand. Since there is only so much matter and energy to go around, the end result would be that life would eventually become impossible as matter and energy become too thinly spread throughout the universe.

The third possibility is that the two forces will become perfectly balanced at some time in the future and that the expansion will come to a gradual halt. For this to happen, the universe must have a critical density counting all matter in the universe. Because of the immense distances between the stars and galaxies, this critical density is very small. At present, it is thought to be in the order of 10 milligrams of matter in a volume equivalent to that of our Earth! Most scientists seem to think that we are actually in, or approaching, this equilibrium state. The problem is, however, that there is not nearly enough visible matter in the universe to reach this critical density. Depending on what is included in the count, there appears to exist only about one to ten per cent of the matter in the universe necessary to reach this equilibrium.

However, there is some evidence that there is far more matter in the universe than can be accounted for by the known galaxies. This matter, which is invisible to the eye, and has therefore been called "dark matter", may be distributed throughout the universe in an entirely different way than visible matter. It may even be made of entirely different particles than visible matter. The paper, which reported on the experiment with the ultra-sensitive telescope over the Antarctic, also mentioned that they found that only five to ten per cent of all matter in the universe is ordinary matter, and that as much as twenty-five per cent is what is known as *dark matter* and seventy per cent is *dark energy*, what the reporter called "weird stuff".

For most people, the concept of the formation of the universe out of nothing is quite difficult to grasp. This is especially so for those people who do not believe in a Guiding Spirit, or a God, who orchestrated the creation of the universe according to a pre-ordained plan. In my earlier book,[5] *Good News for Today, We Are not Alone*, I suggested that people who have difficulty with the concept of "creation out of nothing" might think of it as the taking of a loan to build a house. First, there is nothing, no money, no house, but only the concept in one's mind of owning a house. Then there is the visit to the bank and a loan is negotiated. With this loan it is now possible to build a home, to raise a family, etc. So, out of nothing grew a house (positive) and a loan (negative), together they add up to nothing, but the loan allows the family to have a home in which to live. Similarly, it is quite possible that if we add up all the positive matter and all the negative matter in the universe, the total will add up to a grand zero. In fact, the physicist, Edward Tayon has calculated that if we count gravity as a negative in the ledger and sum up all matter and energy the result is actually zero (Timothy Ferris[6] in *The Whole Shebang*).

It is now believed that the stars and most galaxies were formed relatively soon after the Big Bang. Apparently, our own galaxy was a relatively late arrival and was not formed until late in this process; at present the best guess is that this took place some five billion years after the start of the universe or ten billion years ago. The formation of our solar system is thought to have taken another 5.5 billion years and to have happened some 4.5 billion years ago.

Continuing with the life of a star, as we envisage it today, we see that once a star becomes dense enough, it will start to convert its mass into radiant energy which is emitted into the space around it. It is this radiant energy from our star, the Sun, which makes life on Earth possible. However, no matter how large the available matter is in the star, eventually it will run out of fuel and the star will explode or implode. It is only during these last stages in the life of a star that the pressures and temperatures are high enough to allow the formation of the heavier elements, such as carbon, from the helium and hydrogen atoms. As can be seen from Figure A.2 in Appendix I, a carbon atom can potentially be formed by the merging of three helium atoms. Apparently, the merging of three helium atoms is extremely rare and it takes a very finely tuned process to make carbon out of helium and hydrogen. Without this fine-tuning there would not be enough carbon to meet the needs of carbon-based life; thus, without this fine-tuning we would not be here. Fred Hoyle is often quoted as having said that nothing had shaken his atheism as much as the discovery of this finely tuned process. As he wrote in the *Cal Tech* alumni magazine:

> A common sense interpretation of the facts suggests that a super intellect has monkeyed with physics, as well as with chemistry and biology, and that there are no blind forces worth speaking about in nature. The numbers one calculates from the facts seem to me to be so overwhelming as to put this conclusion almost beyond question.

In any case, it is during the final stages of the star's existence, when the star explodes, that these heavier elements are spewed forth in prodigious amounts into the universe. This explosion shows up on our telescopes as strong points of light called "super novae". Of course, what we actually observe is what happened millions, if not billions, of years ago.

It is now understood that it was the arrival of these carbon atoms on our planet that made it possible for carbon-based life to develop here. Thus you might say that we exist courtesy of faraway stars that exploded some billions of years ago. Piers Bizony,[7] in his book *Rivers of March, Searching for the Cosmic Origin of Life,* makes the statement:

The atoms which constitute the elements of our body were created not on our own Sun but by other stars long since dead. They are not our atoms. They do not belong to us, or to our bodies. They are just passing through. Every moment of our lives we exhale carbon dioxide. The atoms in that gas will have existed for five billion years or more and they will exist for billions of years after we are gone.

The fact that carbon atoms cannot be formed in our solar system, but become available only on Earth through dying stars located at great distances from our solar system, creates some interesting consequences for the timing of the appearance of carbon-based life on Earth and elsewhere in the universe.

If we assume that our solar system is typical of others in the universe, and if we also assume that we are, at present, halfway through the life of our solar system, we get the following scenario. The first time carbon atoms could have become available anywhere in the universe occurred something like eight to ten billion years after the formation of the first star. At present, this is thought to have occurred some 0.5 billion years after the Big Bang. If we further assume that our Earth is typical of other planets and that it takes about four billion years for life to develop after the arrival of these first carbon atoms, we get the picture that life could not have possibly started anywhere in the universe until between 2.5 (15.0 minus 0.5, 8.0 and 4.0) to 0.5 (15.0 minus 0.5, 10.0 and 4.0) billion years ago. From these figures we must subtract the time it must have taken for these carbon atoms to reach a suitable planet; this further substantially reduces the time available for life to develop (see Figure 3.2). Of course, these times depend entirely on how representative our galaxy is of the other billions of galaxies in the universe. But if it were, it would seem to indicate that *our universe must be as old as it is and as big it is* for life to have had a chance to develop anywhere in that universe. Thus, it now appears that the existence of all this space and all these stars was simply a prerequisite for carbon-based life to have a chance to develop.

In closing this section on the creation of the universe, it is necessary to note that eventually science may be able to explain how the universe began but it will never be able to explain *why* the universe was created. For that, we must leave the realm of science and think in terms of philosophy and religion. John Wheeler,[8] an American physicist, expressed it this way: "Why is there something rather than nothing? The answer is that there is no answer, just a question."

Table IIIa: *Events Leading to the Creation of the Universe*

Event	Years Ago	Years After the Big Bang
Big Bang	15,000,000,000	0
First atoms were formed	14,999,500,000	500,000
First stars were born	14,500,000,000	500,000,000
First galaxies were formed	14,000,000,000	1,000,000,000
Start of our galaxy	10,000,000,000	5,000,000,000
Explosion of the first star	6,500,000,000	8,500,000,000
Start of our solar system	4,500,000,000	10,500,000,000
First microscopic life	3,500,000,000	11,500,000,000
First mammals	300,000,000	14,700,000,000
First human type life	1,800,000	14,998,200,000
Emergence of Cro-Magnon	40,000	14,999,960,000
Emergence of modern humans	10,000	14,999,990,000
Today	0	15,000,000,000

CREATION – WHERE DO WE COME FROM?

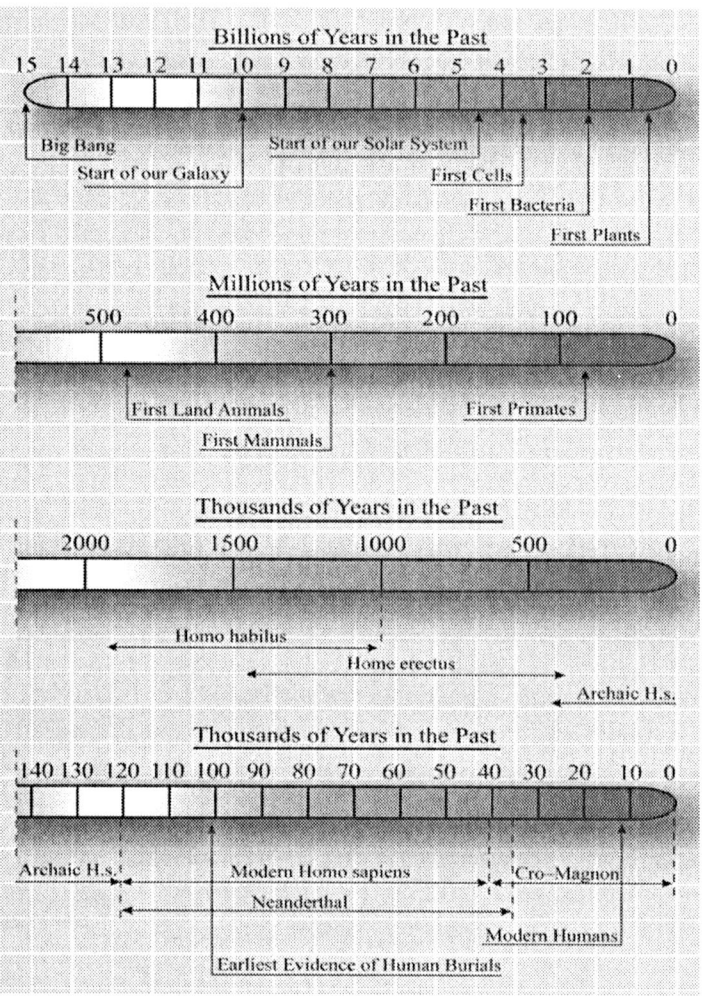

Figure 3.1
The History of the Universe and the Rise of Humankind

CREATION — WHERE DO WE COME FROM?

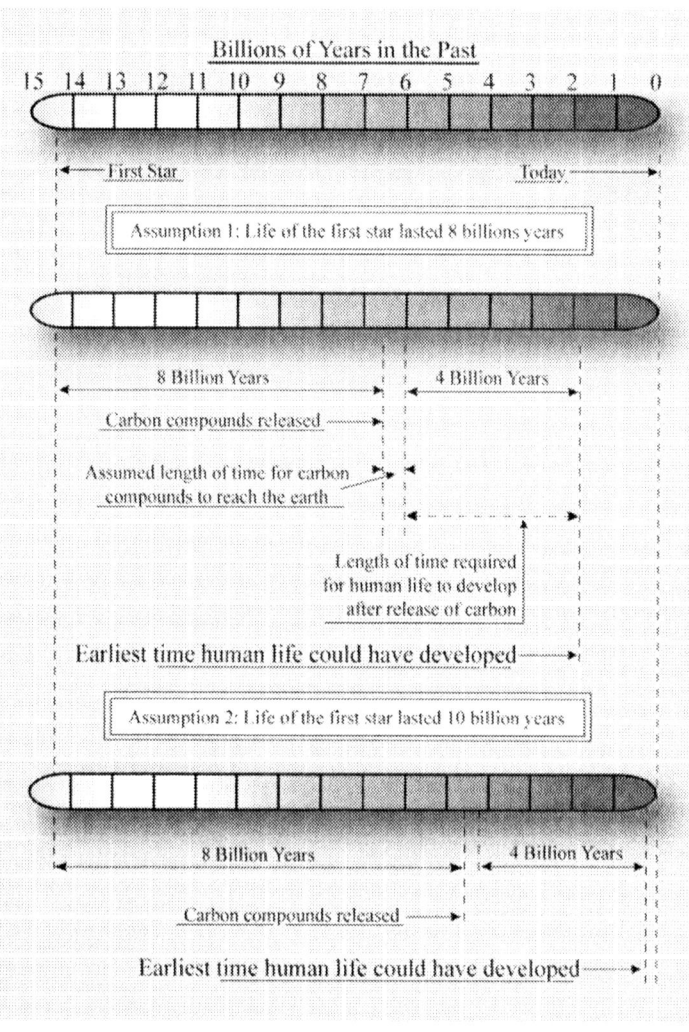

Figure 3.2:
The Earliest Date Human Life Could Have Developed Using Two Different Assumptions Concerning the Death of the First Star

IIIc   The Creation of Life

If we accept the latest scientific thinking, the sequence of events that led eventually to the beginning of life on Earth is as shown in Figures 3.1 and 3.2. We believe, as was pointed out in the previous section, that the universe came into being some 15 billion years ago. It was not until 10.5 billion years later that our solar system made its appearance; that is "only" 4.5 billion years ago. The first signs of life on Earth appeared in the form of single-cell creatures; these are thought to have shown up "shortly" thereafter, about 3.5 to 3.8 billion years ago. In other words, life on Earth appeared first when the universe had already existed for over 11 billion years, or stated differently, the first signs of life on Earth did not appear until the last quarter of the existence of the universe.

Before continuing with the story of how life began, it may be useful to consider for a moment what we actually mean when we are talking about living things. Where is the boundary between inanimate entities such as crystals and rocks and the animate world of plants and animals?

It is generally agreed that there are three characteristics of behavior which are found only in living things – they are:

- self-reproduction – the capacity to reproduce and make copies of itself;
- mutation – the capacity to make small changes in the reproduced copies of oneself; without that capacity, the first cells would have stayed forever the same and no further development would have occurred; and
- metabolism – the capacity to absorb and process food and convert the chemicals in the food into the building blocks of which living things are made.

The division between living and inanimate things is not

always as clear as may have been thought at first: for instance, some crystals have the capacity to self-reproduce, but do not mutate or metabolize.

It is believed that the very first single cells were formed under very special circumstances. Conditions had to be just right for the creation of the large molecules that are part of every cell. For that to happen, there had to be enough of the basic elements of these molecules around at exactly the right temperature. These conditions apparently existed in the estuaries of some of the rivers in the warmer climates on Earth some 3.5 to 3.8 billion years ago.

Some years ago, it was discovered that there exists an abundance of life near some deep-sea hot water vents located so deep in the ocean that no sunlight can penetrate there. Some scientists have speculated that the first forms of life could well have been formed in these locations. At this point in time, this is pure speculation and, even if true, does not really answer the question of how life began. The only real significance of these finds is that it proves that life does not necessarily need the energy from the Sun to flourish. Apparently, this energy could equally well be supplied from the heat and chemical energy contained in the center of our planet.

The creation of these first living cells is, without doubt, one of the highlights in the history of the Earth and probably of the universe: it has been the subject of intense study and speculation. The main question scientists have been trying to answer is "Was the creation of living cells a product of chance or was it the result of a natural process of cause and effect that could be duplicated in a laboratory?" So far, this question has not been answered, although a graduate student, Stanley Miller, at the University of Chicago, caused quite a stir in 1953 when it appeared that he had been able to do so. He sent sparks (to represent thunderstorms) through a mixture of water, steam, ammonia, methane and hydrogen. The result was that after a comparatively short time he had created a thick concentration of amino acids that are indeed some of the important building blocks of a living cell. In the end, however, the experiment only proved that it is relatively easy to make amino acids from the basic elements. This, however, is a far cry from creating a self-reproducing, mutating, and metabolizing living cell, a cell that contains complicated DNA molecules that carry all the genetic information necessary for the propagation of the organism. Later on, we will consider whether this process, which led to the creation of living things, could have occurred in any one of the billion stars that make up our own galaxy or even in the billions of other galaxies that seem to be part of our universe.

The attempt to create life synthetically in a laboratory tube created a tremendous amount of interest not only in the scientific press but also in the popular media. In the wake of this initial success, many scientists tried to expand on the findings of Stanley Miller. The result of this research, however, has been disappointing. In the end, all that this research has shown is how unbelievably complex this most basic form of life is. The following quote is taken from *Darwin's Black Box* by Michael Behe[9] attributed to Klaus Dose:

> More than thirty years of experimentation on the origins of life in the fields of chemical and molecular evolution have led to a better perception of the immensity of the problem of the origin of life on Earth rather than its solution. At present, all discussion on principal theories and experiments in the field either end in stalemate or in a confession of ignorance... Scientists working on the origin of life deserve a lot of credit: they have attacked the problem by experimentation and calculation as scientists should. And, although, the experiments have not turned

out as many hoped, through their efforts we now have a clear idea of the staggering difficulties that would face an origin of life by natural chemical processes.

Today, the origin of life remains one of the most profound mysteries of the world. First, there is the mystery of the creation of the first cells without a nucleus, and then there is the equally mysterious change from these single cells with no nucleus to the living cells that have a nucleus and that contain sufficient numbers of DNA and RNA molecules to make replication of these cells possible. Added to this, one may well ask, as Harold Franklin[10] did in his book, *The Way of the Cell*, "Since it takes a cell to make a cell, how did cells arise before there were cells". One might add to that the question: What evolutionary driving force was there in nature to make the move from a bunch of lifeless molecules to living things? And where did this driving force come from? Certainly, it cannot have been a material force governed by the forces in atoms and subatomic particles. In the end, therefore, we must, I believe, conclude that this driving force was of a spiritual nature.

With the introduction of DNA, an entirely new entity made its appearance in the evolutionary process. Up to this point, there had been only the interaction of energy and matter that governed the way the universe was evolving; now, however, a new basic building block was added in the form of *information* stored in the coils of the DNA and RNA molecules. From this point on, it is this information and the changes in this information that will decide how nature will evolve. Of course, the sudden appearance, as it were out of nowhere, of this new building block is an utter mystery.

There are a number of philosophical attitudes that one can take regarding the origin of DNA and RNA and, ultimately, the appearance of life. They can be stated briefly as follows:

- It was a miracle.
- It was a stupendously improbable accident.
- It was an inevitable consequence of the workings of physics and chemistry given the right conditions.
- It was a purposeful act of a Guiding Intelligence: the whole universe was formed so that life and ultimately human life could develop.

In considering these options, one must take into account the conditions that must exist so that life can eventually become possible. Some of these are listed below; undoubtedly, there are many more:

- There must be an abundant supply of chemicals that make up the raw materials of living things such as carbon, hydrogen and oxygen. However, the amount of free oxygen in the atmosphere must not exceed 25 per cent nor dip below 15 per cent. In the first case, everything will burn; in the second case, nothing will burn.
- There must be no risk of contamination by other chemicals that are poisonous, such as methane and ammonia that are both found in great abundance on some of the planets.
- Living things can only exist within a very narrow band of temperatures. This means, in our case, that the Earth must be at exactly the right distance from the Sun, and probably that it must spin on its axis at a certain speed so that all parts of the Earth are more or less evenly exposed to sunlight.
- Life requires a constant supply of energy that in our case is supplied by the Sun; if that energy supply ever dries up, life on Earth will become impossible.
- The force of gravity must be strong enough to restrain

the atmosphere from evaporating into space. At the same time, it must be weak enough so that we can move about easily on the face of the Earth.
- For life to exist requires a layer of ozone above the atmosphere to prevent the Sun's deadly ultraviolet radiation from reaching the surface of the Earth.
- Lately, another requirement has been added. For a solar system to be inhabitable it must have a number of much larger planets, like our Saturn and Jupiter, circling the center star in outer orbits. These large planets absorb the comets and asteroids that would otherwise plunge into the planets in the inner orbits and make continued life on those planets impossible.
- And, finally, as we have seen before, all the other constants of the laws of nature must be exactly right for life to be possible.

This is rather a formidable list of conditions that must be fulfilled for life, even its most simple form, to have started and continue to exist. We will come back to this later when we consider the possibility of life existing on planets of other stars.

There is one other way that life could possibly have arrived on this Earth and that is by seeding from other life-bearing stars in outer space. Some scientists, including Fred Hoyle, maintain that this is a reasonable proposition. But it is difficult to see how a living cell could survive a long journey under the intense radiation it would encounter in its travels through space. Recently, however, it has been shown that some spores and microbes might be able to survive this journey through space. Even if true, it does not really solve the problem of creation; the question has simply shifted to how life began on this other, faraway, planet. The same Fred Hoyle argued that the spontaneous generation of life was as improbable as the spontaneous assembly of a fully functional Boeing 747 aircraft by a whirlwind sweeping through a junkyard.

Most scientists agree that the possibility of life emerging by pure accident is extremely remote. Paul Davies[11] in his latest book *The Fifth Miracle* writes:

> There are at least ten billion billion stars in the observable universe. But the number, gigantic as it may appear to us, is nevertheless trivially small compared with the gigantic odds against the random assembly of even a single protein molecule.

It is now thought that the first single cells appeared about one billion years after the formation of the solar system, or 3.5 billion years ago. These single cells dominated life for some 2.5 billion years. This is a very long time of stagnation, especially considering that it took only one billion years to progress from this single cell to fully conscious human beings. One may well ask what rekindled the force that made nature go the next step and generate more complex cells resulting in more complex forms of life.

It was not until about 750 million years ago that the first multicelled organisms appeared. After this very slow development from single to multicelled organisms, there was a sudden explosion of life forms around 570 to 500 million years ago. Recent geological explorations have shown that during this time representatives of all major animal groups suddenly appeared on the scene. Consequently, this is often referred to as the Cambrian Explosion. One of the more mysterious forms of life that appeared at this time was the Ediacaran that represents some life form between that of a single cell and an animal.

During most of this time, the land mass was still as barren and sterile as it had been when formed some three billion years earlier. The first hard-shelled organisms appeared around 550 million years ago, and the first real fish some 150 million years later. This first life on land was probably in the form of plants, but apparently animal life in the form of spiders, millipedes, scorpions and insects followed fairly quickly thereafter. Insects in particular have done well for themselves: today, 320 million years since their first appearance, insects still constitute 75 per cent of all living species. Among them is the infamous cockroach that seemed to have survived in its present form for all of these 320 million years. It is no wonder that an insect which has survived this long is difficult to get rid of once it has decided that your kitchen is an ideal place to raise a family for a couple of generations.

The first animals with vertebrae developed from the fish in the sea and their skeletons have been dated 300 million years ago. They eventually developed into a wide variety of animals including mammals and the large dinosaurs. The latter roamed the Earth for millions of years but were suddenly wiped out about sixty-five million years ago. The sudden extinction of the dinosaurs has always been one of the world's great mysteries. What could possibly have caused this sudden disappearance of not only the dinosaurs but also of some 60 to 70 per cent of all living species? It is now generally accepted that the cause of this sudden demise was the impact of a ten-kilometer-sized asteroid which hit the sea just off the coast of the Yucatan Peninsula of Mexico at an estimated speed of 90,000 km/hour. The impact of such a large asteroid would have had disastrous effects on the continued existence of all plants and animals. First of all, it would have generated a monstrous "tidal wave" which could have been hundreds of meters high. In all the low-lying areas around the crash site, and probably around the world, this wave would have caused death and destruction. Secondly, it would have created a very strong superheated windstorm causing fires all around the globe. But the most devastating effect would have come from the material that would have been spewed into the air in the form of dust created from the disintegration of the asteroid and the Earth immediately below the impact zone. It has been estimated that this cloud of dust would have circled the Earth for years and would have been so thick that it would have prevented sunlight from reaching the Earth, thereby making the growth of almost all vegetation impossible. The large animals, such as dinosaurs, which directly or indirectly consumed prodigious amounts of vegetable matter each day, would have, of course, been the hardest hit and could not have survived the years without adequate vegetation.

The intriguing question is, can such a catastrophic event happen again? It is clear that even today, with all our technology, we could not survive such a disaster. The answer, I believe, is yes since there has been no basic change in the make-up of our solar system in the intervening time that would prevent something similar from happening again, but the chance that this will happen is extremely small. After all, this happened sixty-five million years ago. More recently, it has been found that there were a number of other occasions during the Earth's history when large percentages of all species were obliterated. The largest one apparently occurred some 250 million years ago and is thought to have wiped out 96 per cent of all species. Others seem to have occurred 440, 360 and 210 million years ago. Scientists, who have tried to determine the cause of the disappearances of these species, over relatively short periods of time, believe that in most cases the cause was not the impact of a meteor or asteroid but changes in climate. These changes in climate caused some types of life to disappear while others became prominent among the survivors. The species that disappeared were typically the larger animals, with requirements for large amounts of food, while the ones that survived were generally the smaller animals with much smaller appetites.

While the dinosaurs and other large animals were wiped out by these catastrophes, enough of the smaller mammals generally survived to guarantee the continued development of the animal world. This further, and one might say, renewed evolution resulted about fifty to thirty-five million years ago in the emerging of the first primates. With their appearance, the stage is set for the eventual entry on the world stage of our forefathers some one to two million years ago.

That we cannot completely forget about the threat to human life imposed by asteroids or comets colliding with our planet Earth is clear from the fact that in 1989 a 1,000-meter asteroid was discovered only after it had crossed the Earth's orbit at a location where the Earth had been only six hours earlier. Similarly, it is reported that in May 1996 a same-sized asteroid was first discovered only four days before it sped across the Earth's orbit, ultimately missing our planet by only four hours (*Perils of a Restless Planet, Scientific Perspectives on Natural Disasters* by Ernest Zebrowski Jr.[12]). Also, as recently as March 1998, it was reported that a large asteroid is heading in our direction and is expected to pass the Earth at a distance of some 50 to 100,000 kilometers some time in March 2028.

In 1991 NASA estimated that there are 1,000 to 4,000 asteroids of a size greater than half a mile across which cross the Earth's path; if this sized asteroid were ever to actually hit the Earth it would inflict enormous damage.

While there is undoubtedly some chance that a catastrophe of this type could happen at any time in the future, there are, I believe, many other far more immediate dangers to the continuance of life on Earth for us to worry about, such as: atomic accidents in nuclear plants which could make life impossible in large areas of the Earth; pollution which could have cumulative effects on the climate that could result in the same types of disasters as those which wiped out large percentages of all living species in the past; and, more recently, we have to add to this the uncontrolled genetic manipulation of plants and animals which could generate new strains of viruses for which there are no antibodies.

In looking at the chain of evolution that eventually led to the emergence of fully conscious human beings, it is impossible not to realize how unique Homo sapiens is among the million of other creatures that were created in this evolutionary process. As Stephen Gould[13] wrote in *Rock of Ages*:

> Homo sapiens may be the brainiest species of all, but we represent only a tiny twig, grown but yesterday on a single branch of a really arborescent bush of life. Homo sapiens is a single species among 200 species of primates on a branch of some 4,000 species of mammals; on a limb of nearly 40,000 species of vertebrates; on a bough of animals dominated by more than a 100,000 described species of insects; on a trunk of millions of bacteria; etc.

No matter how we look at this, it is obvious that humans are at the top of the evolutionary tree. Even if there was enough time left on Earth for further evolutionary advances, the fact is that humankind, through genetic manipulation, is interfering with the natural flow of evolution which will forever mask what nature would have created over time by itself.

IIId   The Creation of Human Beings

We closed the last section with the appearance of the first primates some thirty to fifty million years ago. At first, these primates were small tree-dwelling animals, but over the years they developed to something akin to our present-day monkeys and apes. One of the distinctive characteristics of these animals was that they had opposable thumbs which, once they started to walk on their hind legs, gave them great advantages over the other animals in that they could hold things in their hands such as sticks and make implements to help them in their hunt for food. All of this would not have been of much use to them if it had not been accompanied by a growing intelligence which allowed the early human species to outwit the much stronger and faster predators that surrounded them. As someone wrote: "Without intelligence, man is just a walking meal, just waiting to be eaten" (Matthew Alper[14] in *The God Part of the Brain*).

The development or evolution from primates to fully conscious human beings went, according to the latest archeological discoveries, as shown on Figure 3.1. The first in the line of succession was Homo habilus (dexterous man); he walked upright and lived between 1.8 and 1.0 million years ago in Central Africa. Next came Homo erectus (erect man); he lived somewhere between 1.6 and 0.3 million years ago. Apparently, he was the first to leave home and spread out from Africa into Europe and Asia. The next in this chain was Homo sapiens (wise man). He appears in two versions: the so-called archaic Homo sapiens lived from approximately 400,000 years to 120,000 years ago. At this date there occurred a split and two different, large-brained ancestors appeared on the scene: the modern Homo sapiens and the Neanderthals. The modern Homo sapiens, generally referred to as Cro-Magnon, after a cave in Southern France where their first remains were found, reached Europe about 40,000 years ago. For some reason which is not entirely clear at this time, the Neanderthals died out around 35,000 years ago, so that the Cro-Magnon people and the Neanderthals lived side by side, at least in Europe, for about 5,000 years.

At present, there are two different lines of thought about how Homo sapiens arrived at roughly the same time in

Africa, Europe, and Asia (see Figure 3.3). In the first model, named the multiregional model, Homo habilis evolved into Homo erectus 1,700,000 years ago and spread from Africa to Europe and Asia. During the next million years or so, there was a continuous interchange between the species in the three continents so that eventually the genetic make-up of the new, evolving Homo sapiens was the same in the three continents, and Homo sapiens appeared in all three continents at approximately the same time.

In the second model, called the "Out-of-Africa Model", Homo erectus also spread out over the three continents, but the various species had very little contact with each other after their emigration from Africa, resulting in very little genetic interchange. According to this model, it was only in Africa that Homo erectus evolved into Homo sapiens. This new species then spread out from Africa to Europe and Asia completely replacing the existing populations of Homo erectus in these locations. Thus, according to this theory, there was a distinct creation of Homo sapiens *in one place* and not simultaneously in many places. For this reason the model has also been called "Noah's Ark" and the "Garden of Eden" model. As Richard Leaky[15] writes in his latest book, *The Origin of Humankind*, "I suspect that modern Homo sapiens arose as a distinct evolutionary event somewhere in Africa."

In recent years, it has become more and more recognized that our most immediate ancestors, the modern Homo sapiens, were not just a better-adapted ape, but that they were, in many ways, fundamentally different from their predecessors, the archaic Homo sapiens. As Ian Tattersall[16] writes in *Becoming Human, Evolution and Human Uniqueness*:

> With the arrival of behaviorally modern Homo sapiens, a totally unprecedented entity had appeared on Earth. For

CREATION – WHERE DO WE COME FROM?

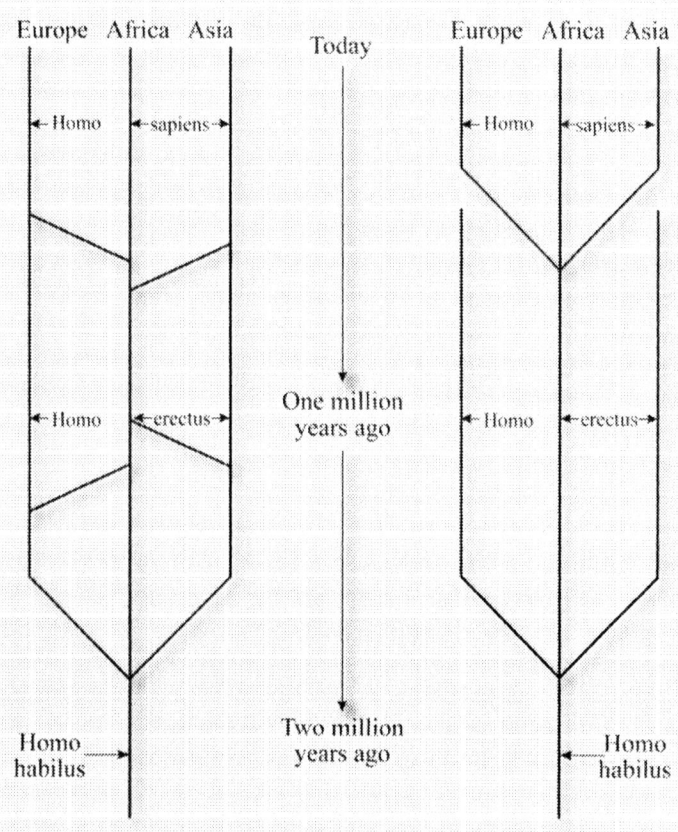

Figure 3.3
*Two Models of the Emergence of Homo sapiens
Across the Continents*

the first time since the adoption of upright walking – or perhaps stone tool making – a new kind of hominid was around of which it could not be said that it merely did what its predecessors had done, only a little bit better, or even a little bit different. Homo sapiens is not simply an improved version of its ancestors – *it is a new concept, qualitatively distinct from them in significant if limited respects.* (author's italics)

It was these early humans who, some 30,000 years ago, painted the beautiful pictures found in caves in North Africa and Europe.

The latest "Out-of-Africa" model has been given support from an unexpected source – molecular genetics. Douglas Wallace and Allen Wilson wrote a paper in the January 1987 issue of *Nature* in which they presented what they called a "Mitochondrial Eve Hypothesis". According to this theory, all modern humans can trace their genetic ancestry to one female who lived in Africa, perhaps 150,000 years ago. The authors of this hypothesis scrutinized the genetic material called mitochondria that occurs in tiny organelles within a human cell. Apparently, when the egg of the mother and the sperm of the father merge, the only mitochondria that becomes part of the newly formed embryo comes from the egg of the mother. Thus mitochondria DNA is inherited only through the maternal line (see also Chapter V).

The authors found that all the samples of the mitochondrial DNA analyzed so far from living human populations are remarkably similar to one another, indicating a common recent origin. With the Multiregional Model one would expect the mitochondrial DNA of people from different places around the globe to have mitochondrial DNA from both very ancient and more recent origin. With the Out-of-Africa Model, on the other hand, one would expect this DNA to be of recent origin only. Of the thousands of people tested around the world, no such ancient mitochondrial DNA was found. All appear to be of "recent" origin. The implication is that these modern newcomers from Africa completely replaced ancient populations everywhere, starting some 150,000 years ago. If this hypothesis continues to be supported by new evidence, it would appear that modern science points to the creation of the first humans at one particular point in time and at one place, thus *making humans a distinct creation*, essentially different and distinct from their forefathers, the primates. Using the same mitochondrial DNA procedure, Bryan Sykes[17], professor of genetics at Oxford University, made an exhaustive study of the mitochondrial DNA of people across the world. His investigations confirmed the findings of Wallace and Wilson that all six billion people in the world today can trace their ancestry back to this one woman living in Africa some 150,000 years ago. He further found that these ancestors started to spread out of Africa into the Middle East about 100,000 years ago. Apparently, it was not until 50,000 years later that they actually entered Europe. One of the reasons for this hold-up may well have been the presence of the Neanderthalers who are thought to have occupied much of Europe at that time.

In a recent article (August 22, 1998) in the *Globe and Mail* by Gwynne Dyer the writer makes the following statements:

> In the 1980s, it was still generally believed that primitive human beings had migrated out of Africa between one and two million years ago, settled all over Eurasia and there evolved into the various races of humanity. Now it is all but certain that we are a much more recent and closely knit species that evolved in Africa less than 200,000 years ago and moved out into the rest of the world no longer than 100,000 years ago... Even Scots and Japanese are closer to

each other than adjacent African groups... There were twenty-seven differences between Homo sapiens and Neanderthals in 379 base-pair strip of DNA, whereas the world's entire human population differs by only eight pairs along this strip. It indicates that Neanderthals had nothing to do with our history.

To put this sequence of events in some perspective, the following illustration may be helpful. Visitors from outer space 130,000 years ago would have noted nothing special about our human ancestors. They would probably have been most impressed by the ability of beavers to construct dams; by the uncanny ability of bowerbirds to weave the most intricate nests from twigs; or by the highly structured societies of the bees and the ants. If, however, the same aliens had returned 100,000 years later, around 30,000 years ago, they would have found an entirely different scene. They would have encountered the first truly human beings and there would have been no doubt in their minds who the dominant creature was. They would have found people living in social groupings making tools, painting pictures, making statues, and hunting much larger animals with tools such as bows and arrows, spears, harpoons, etc. They would have found people communicating with each other through a spoken language entirely different from the grunts and squeals of the animals.

In the evolution of human beings from the primates, the most decisive development was the development of the brain. Sometimes we find it difficult to imagine how an eye or an ear could have developed through a step-by-step evolution. However, this is nothing compared to the evolution of the brain. Recent research on the brain has shown roughly how the brain works. It is literally mind-boggling to think how this three-pound clump of gelatin-like material can control all our functions and store all our memories. It now appears that the human brain is composed of some 100 billion nerve cells, each one being able to connect with between 1,000 and 6,000 other nerve cells. This allows the brain to make 100 trillion connections at any given time – that is, 100,000,000,000,000 or 10^{+14} connections. The mechanism by which these interconnections are made is truly astonishing, but it is this complexity that allows us to experience things, to remember things, to study things, etc. (see also Chapter V).

From the anthropological records of skulls, it appears that the capacity of the human brain has steadily increased with the emergence of the modern human being from the earliest homo types. For instance, the earliest human-like creature had a brain capacity of 500 cm^3; whereas Homo habilus had a brain capacity of around 800 cm^3 that increased to 1,000 cm^3 in Homo erectus. Today, that volume has further increased to 1,350 cm^3 in modern humans.

Of course, humans are not the only ones that have brains; we only have larger ones than our most recent ancestors. For instance, the DNA of a chimpanzee is almost identical to that of a human, but the size of its brain is only one-quarter of that of a human. So, in the first instance, it is not the make-up of our genetic material that makes the difference between animals and human beings; rather, it is the size of our brain which is decisive. However, even the brain of the most primitive animal is a work of art without comparison in this world. For instance, I am always intrigued by butterflies. They must have a very small brain, but even with these minute brains they can find their way from the Canadian North to the same location in Mexico every season, despite the fact that it is another generation of butterflies which makes the return flight. Just think of it: somewhere in that tiny brain must be encoded a complete travel plan with sufficient details to allow the butterfly to find its way over distances of thousands of kilometers. The complexity of even that little brain and the amount of information stored in that little space must be phenomenal. What is more, this tiny brain must have a retrieval system which allows it to call up the right information at the right time. This is what a brain can do that is perhaps a million times smaller than ours. Truly amazing! Chet Raymo[18] in *Skeptics and Believers* is similarly impressed by the incredible journey of the red knot. Apparently this tiny bird makes the trip from Northern Canada to the tip of South America every year. He writes:

> Nothing in my religious training is more wondrous to me than the flight of the juvenile red knot from Northern Canada to Tierra del Fuego, a journey whose map is contained in the red knot's DNA. Such real-world mysteries inspire in me awe far more than the so-called miracles on display in the Cathedral of Turin. In the red knot's story, we catch a glimpse of God who never lifts his hand from his work and who leads everything to the purpose for which it was created.

The interesting thing about the human brain is that a large part of it has lain dormant for hundreds of thousands of years. In his book *The Evolution of Consciousness* the author, Robert Ornstein,[19] writes:

> This is the central mystery of the mind. It is difficult to see why we are so advanced relative to our near ancestors. We aren't just slightly better chimps and it is difficult on reflection to figure out why. The brain seems to have increased in size before all the organized societies' cooperation and languages would have any call for such development... Why be able to fly to the Moon when no one has even understood how to make iron; why have a brain able to work with micro processors when all it was used for was the crude hammering of the first few stone tools?

CREATION – WHERE DO WE COME FROM?

Similarly, David Darling[20] writes in *Deep Time*:

> The human brain, in size and structure, had reached its ultimate state of development perhaps 100,000 years earlier. A man or woman of the twentieth century, for all their cultural sophistication, has no more intellectual potential than their counterpart who painted on cave walls.

It is difficult to see how a process of natural selection and random mutations could possibly have led to the creation of a brain size that had no immediate benefit for the survival of the species, and that was not fully utilized until a hundred thousand years later. It would seem that the creation of such an unnecessarily large brain, at such an early date, indicates an amount of planning and foresight that cannot possibly be attributed to random mutations.

Part of the puzzle of this large, unused brain is its capacity to do mathematics. First of all, there is the question of the origin of mathematics itself. Where did it come from? Is it a human invention? The astounding thing is that relatively simple mathematical equations are able to describe a wide range of natural processes that govern the operation of the universe (see also Chapter IId). The fact that this is so would seem to indicate that it is not simply a human invention but was built into nature. The question then is, who put it there? The only answer that makes any sense is that whoever created the universe also created mathematics at the same time and used it as one of the building blocks of creation. So, I believe that both the prematurely large brain and the fact that mathematics plays such a large role in the operation of the universe clearly point to the involvement of a Guiding Intelligence in the creation of the universe.

Somewhere in the development of the brain, consciousness and mind must have been created. Again, like in so many instances, it is difficult to see how consciousness and mind could have developed accidentally. For people who do not believe in the involvement of a Guiding Intelligence in creation, the emergence of consciousness and mind is simply an accidental occurrence. For instance, adherents of this theory believe that if life should be accidentally destroyed back to the level of single cell organisms, the re-emergence of consciousness and mind would be highly unlikely. The mystery is that consciousness and mind are nonmaterial things and it is hard to believe that material objects could create nonmaterial entities just by accident.

The emergence of consciousness and mind is believed to be one of the prerequisites for the emergence of that other factor which was decisive in the development of humans from animals – the ability to speak and the ability to use language. Apparently, it is something that is inherent in the human species alone. Maybe the closest anything in the animal world comes to our language and speech skills is the communication abilities of honeybees. They seem to be able to indicate to each other, in some most complicated manner, where there is a good supply of nectar to be found. In fact, most animals seem to have some ability to communicate with each other in one way or another. However, there appears to be nothing resembling the speech capabilities of humankind. It is presently estimated that the human ability to express itself in a language which was understood by clan members developed some 50,000 years ago. In this regard, it is interesting to note that the most primitive tribes, which have not had any contact with other societies for over 40,000 years, such as the inhabitants of central New Guinea and the aborigines of Australia, and were, until recently, living in the Stone Age, nevertheless have astonishing sophisticated spoken languages, more complicated, in some instances, than English or even Chinese.

It is clear that language capability is something we are born with; it appears to be an essential part of our human make-up. How else can we explain the ease with which young children start making coherent sentences at a very early age, including the use of the present, past and future tenses. Also, children the world over, regardless of the type of language, seem to develop this capability at about the same rate and at the same age. It is interesting to note that deaf children, who are taught sign language, develop language capability at about the same rate as normal children.

The other intriguing thing about languages is that there appears to be no in-betweens. In other words, there appears to be no simple language somewhere in-between the most advanced animal utterances and the language of humans. Surely, no matter how primitive these "in-between" languages might have been, even a very limited amount of speech would have given that species a great advantage over its competitors. So why didn't the evolution process generate such an "in-between" language? I believe that this language capability, that is not found anywhere in the animal world, is a clear indication that humans are a very special creation, entirely distinct and separate from the animal world.

It has been speculated that humans may have a special voice and language organ that is lacking in the other animals. This would explain a great number of puzzling things about language and speech, such as why all languages have similar grammatical rules.

It appears that the average human uses something in the order of 45,000 words; considering that we must have learned most of these words in the first fifteen years of our lives, we must have learned more than 3,000 words per year or eight new words every day of our lives. Another interesting aspect of this is that the basic number of words needed for effective communication is only between 500 and 600 words. If this number is sufficient for our everyday needs, why then do we have a brain large enough to accommodate this additional capacity for words?

It is difficult to pinpoint when language and speech developed. It probably has something to do with the size of the human brain. In any case, researchers believe that 35,000 years ago language was well developed. As indicated by the appearance of art objects, and the first signs of long-distance trade and commerce, it was around this time that a sudden surge in technological innovations seem to have occurred. It is generally agreed that the practice of trade and commerce is only possible if there is an effective way to communicate through the spoken or written word.

The earliest recorded *written* languages, those of the Sumerians and Egyptians, were typically modern, complex languages. They first appeared some 5,500 years ago. Therefore, in between 50,000 and 5,000 years ago, humans developed the capacity to speak, to reason and to write down their thoughts, and thus freely communicate with others wherever they might be located. Thus, the first steps were taken that were eventually to lead to the establishment of the first civilized societies in the history of the human race. Before this could happen however, another key development had to take place – the emergence of agriculture.

The first signs in the archeological record of the deliberate planting of seeds and the harvesting of the resulting crops appear some 40,000 years ago. However, it is believed that this was practiced mainly as a substitute for and in addition to their normal hunting and gathering diet. It was not until about 10,000 years ago that agriculture and husbandry began to be practiced as the sole means of food supply. The importance of this event is not only that it caused the permanent settlement of people in groups and small villages but it also, for the first time in history, provided people with time to do something other than struggle for their livelihood. People were able to pursue such things as making pottery and working metal during the time when the crops were growing. Metallurgy, which was first practiced approximately 7,000 years ago, allowed people to make farm implements, household articles and, of course, weapons. Except for the latter, these inventions made life much easier for our distant ancestors and gave them even more time to pursue other interests. It is interesting to note that it was the soft metals such as copper, tin and bronze which first appeared, and only after 3,500 years did iron make its first appearance (see Figure 3.4).

The next development of great importance was the invention of the wheel. It first appeared on the scene only some 5,500 years ago. From our perspective, it seems that these developments followed each other in a logical sequence. However, this was not always the case. For example, the Mayans in Central America had a great civilization, but they never developed the wheel nor did they ever invent metallurgy. Yet, they built their magnificent pyramids and worship centers without the aid of these two elements we consider today to be essential in the building of such large structures. The Mayans also lacked the help of horses which had been domesticated in Europe and the Middle East some 4,000 years earlier. Actually, it was the conquistadors from Spain who introduced the first horses to the Americas.

So, what we might call a "civilized society" appeared for the first time around 8,000 and 10,000 years ago. The first of these civilizations emerged in Mesopotamia (what is now Iraq) along the banks of the Tigris and Euphrates rivers; later in Egypt in the Nile Valley; in India in the Indus Valley; and in China in the valley of the Yellow River. It is interesting to note that these first civilizations all developed along rivers or in river valleys.

In Europe, the early stages of civilization did not so much develop in the river valleys but in city states mostly located on the seacoasts, such as Athens in Greece and later Rome in Italy. From there, civilization eventually spread to the northern part of Europe and Africa.

Sometimes we think that, once humans with large brains and with language capability arrived on the scene, the further development to our modern scientific age would automatically follow. Nothing could be further from the truth. There are many examples of people who split off from the mainstream civilizations on the Europe, Middle East, and China axis that did not follow the same path of development. The first example is the tribes in New Guinea and Australia which I mentioned before. It is thought that they became separated from the main axis some 40,000 years ago and, although they have the same intellectual capacity as modern man, they did not develop agriculture on any large scale. They remained hunters all this time and consequently they did not progress much beyond the Stone Age.

The other group of people who also split off from the main axis, about the same time, became the first inhabitants of the Americas. The North American Indians developed some fairly advanced societies such as that of the Hopi, Pueblo and Anasazi Indians. They practiced a fairly sophisticated type of agriculture, but they did not develop much beyond the Stone Age either. Further south, the Aztecs in Mexico and the Mayans in Mexico and Central America built up fairly sophisticated agricultural systems. Unfortunately, the Aztec civilization came to an abrupt end with the arrival of the Spaniards. The Mayans even developed a script and progressed in astronomy to the extent that they could predict Sun and Moon eclipses. For some unknown reason their civilization disappeared

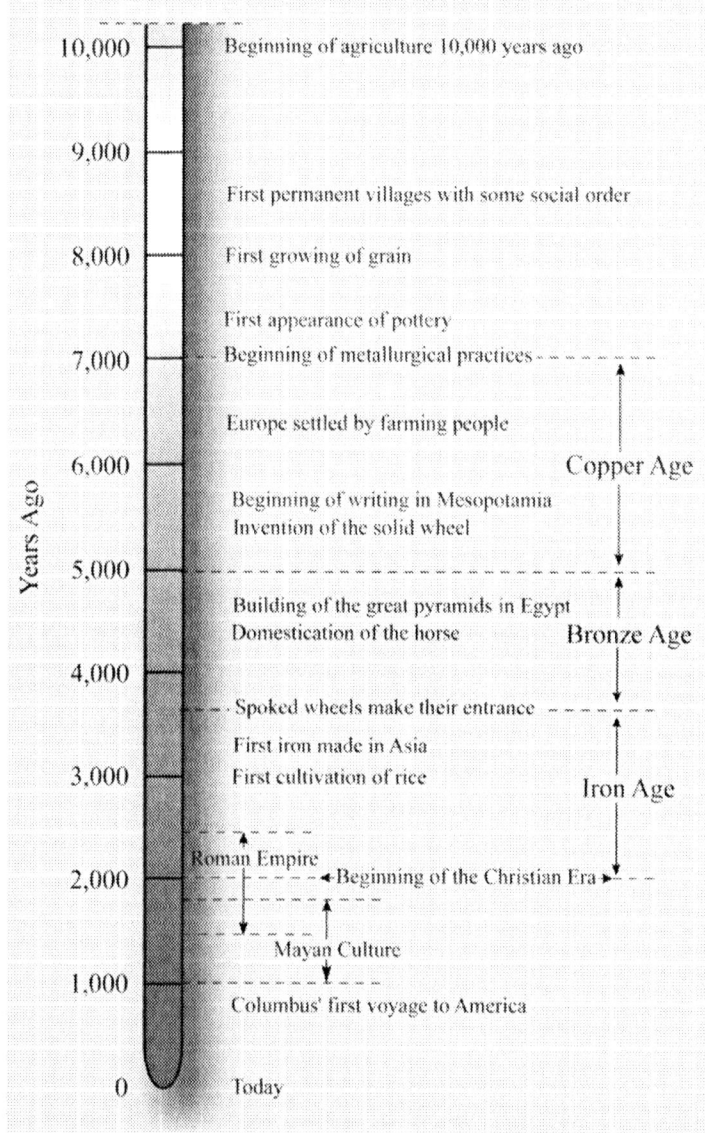

Figure 3.4
Milestones in the Development of our Civilization over the last 10,000 Years

suddenly around 1300 C.E., just before the arrival of the first Europeans. Going further south, the Incas in Peru built a society based on agriculture with very sophisticated irrigation systems. They were able to perform certain complicated medical operations; for example, in museums in Lima there are skulls showing round holes where brain tumors were removed. The edges of these holes show that the bone grew after the operation; thus the patient must have lived for some time afterwards. They also had a very good communication system stretching from Chile to North Peru. Unfortunately, their civilization disappeared almost overnight with the colonization by the Spaniards.

It is possible that, given time, these people would have developed more advanced civilizations. The point is, however, that these people were almost exactly like us in intellectual and language capacity, but somewhere along the road their development stagnated. One could ask, could they ever have broken out of that impasse and developed somewhat along the lines of our society? That is, of course, difficult to say. In any case, these examples show that the development of a scientific society like ours does not automatically occur, even when all the building blocks are in place. Thus, if our civilization were ever destroyed, it is not at all certain that, even given enough time, a similar society would ever develop again.

In this context, it may be interesting to mention again the fate that befell the dinosaurs. At the time of their demise, there were literally hundreds of different types of dinosaurs. Not just large ones but also small ones, and not just land animals but also birds. So, it is reasonable to assume that their appearance on the scene was not just a fluke of nature but a natural evolution from smaller animals. Yet they were wiped out some sixty-five million years ago and they, nor anything like them, have ever appeared on the world scene again.

Many people believe that even if life appeared elsewhere in the universe, it would be highly unlikely that anything like human life would develop. In a recent debate with Carl Sagan, a supporter of the SETI project (see Chapter IVd), the biologist Ernst Mayr argued as follows:

> On Earth among millions of lineages and organisms and perhaps fifty billion speciation events, only one led to high intelligence. This makes me believe the utter improbability that, once life gets started anywhere, humanoids will eventually and inevitably appear.
>
> *The Search for Extraterrestrial Intelligence:*
> *Scientific Quest or Hopeful Folly?*
> Planetary Report 16, 1996

Alternatively, we can ask if some catastrophe ever wiped out all advanced life and left only microbes, could we expect life to develop roughly along the same pattern? Stephen Jay Gould[21] answers this in his book, *Life's Grandeur*, as follows:

> The millions of fortuitous steps that make up our own evolutionary history would surely never happen again even in broad outline. The chance that creatures with a self-consciousness would appear again must be effectively nil.

In his book, *Sacred Eyes*, L. Robert Keck[22] divides the development of humankind into three stages or epochs. According to him, in Epoch I, which he called our "childhood stage", we developed physically. This stage ended some 10,000 years ago when humans started to practice agriculture and began to live in permanent settlements. In Epoch II, our "adolescent stage", we developed our mental capacity. This stage, he believes, is now coming to an end with its final achievement, the scientific developments of the last century. He believes that we are now in transition to Epoch III, what he calls our "stage of maturation". In this epoch, we will develop our spiritual capacity which eventually will lead the world to come to some sort of earthly paradise. He is, however, realistic enough to point out that we may never reach this stage, because we may well have destroyed ourselves at the end of Epoch II by the misuse of our scientific discoveries. It is interesting to note that, in his opinion, it is the development of our spiritual capacity which will govern life in the next epoch. Most people would say that there is not much evidence of any great growth in our spiritual capacity, and that the future of humankind will be directed far more by considerations of expediency and economics. John Horgan[23] goes one step further and believes that, although the application of scientific knowledge has given us an awesome power over nature, it still has left us with a society that is plagued by poverty, hatred, violence and disease and with many unanswered questions. We still cannot determine whether the development of the human species was inevitable or a fluke. He contends that scientific knowledge, far from making our lives meaningful, has forced us to confront the pointlessness of existence. We will return to this later in Chapter XI when we consider the importance of humans from a religious point of view.

The history of the universe and the development of human beings is at present considered to have occurred in the following order (see also Figure 3.1).

Table IIIb: *The History of the Universe*

The Event	Years Ago
The origin of the universe – the Big Bang	15,000,000,000
The formation of the solar system	4,000,000,000
The appearance of the first living cells	3,500,000,000
The first algae and bacteria	2,000,000,000
The first land animals and plants	450,000,000
The first mammals	300,000,000
The emergence of the first primates	35,000,000

The emergence of the first anatomically
modern humans:

Homo habilis	1,800,000
Homo erectus	1,500,000
Archaic Homo sapiens – start	400,000
Modern Homo sapiens – start	120,000
Neanderthal	120,000
Modern Homo sapiens reach Europe	40,000
The first human beings with language	50,000
The beginning of agriculture	10,000
The emergence of the written word	5,500

Looking at the table, it is remarkable to see how long it took to advance from the single cell to the first land mammals some 3,000 million years later. The second notable fact is that modern civilized human beings, at least beings who have the capacity to communicate with each other, have been around for such a short time – 50,000 years compared to the 450,000,000 years since the first plants and animals emerged. Because these figures are so difficult to relate to, the age of the universe has often been expressed in terms of the duration of one twenty-four hour day. Doing this, the first living cell appeared about 6:30 in the afternoon; the first mammals appeared half an hour before midnight; the first human-like creature appeared about three minutes before midnight; and modern humans appeared about a third of a second before midnight.

In any case, to the long list of the conditions, as mentioned earlier, that must be met for any life to begin on Earth, we must now add the following requirements for *human life* to develop:

- the emergence of primates with opposable thumbs and walking upright;
- the development of a large brain;
- the development of human consciousness; and
- the capacity to develop language and speech.

We will return to this when we are considering the possibility that life might have developed on other planets in our galaxy or in other galaxies in the universe.

In the last three chapters, no mention has been made of the second law of thermodynamics which, as was pointed out before, states that with time, order will degenerate into complete disorder or chaos. The development of life in general, and of human life in particular, seems to completely contradict this law. In fact, we see greater and greater order appearing during the evolutionary process from single cell to human life. Looking at the whole evolutionary process, it is difficult not to get the impression that the whole development of life on Earth was directed towards the appearance of humankind as the ultimate object of creation. There are simply too many ways that the "development tree of life" could have branched off and ended up in a dead-end to consider that only chance was involved in this process.

For instance, the bees and ants have a social organization reminiscent of our own; the life of the colonies depend entirely on cooperation between the various types of ants and bees in which each type of ant or bee is assigned a very specialized task. Just the same, they seem to be stuck in their present stage of development. In the same vein, perhaps, we could look at the development of dinosaurs: they grew bigger and bigger with time and must have taken an inordinately large percentage of the available food, thereby preventing the normal development of other species. It is now considered that in doing so, they retarded the development of the human species by millions of years. In other words, for humans to be able to eventually evolve, it was necessary for the dinosaurs to disappear first. (Contrary to many cartoons and science fiction stories, dinosaurs and humans did not coexist at any time; the dinosaurs were wiped out some sixty-five million years ago while the first anatomically modern Homo sapiens did not arrive on the scene until two million years ago.)

In summary, the three attributes of humans which made human development possible are: a large brain, language capability and the upright position with opposable thumbs. No doubt, evolution had a great part to play in the development of humans, but the differences between the most intelligent primate and humans are such that there is very little doubt that humans are indeed a very special creation (see also Chapter IIIe entitled, "Evolutionists Versus Creationists"). If humans had developed slowly, say from a chimpanzee, only a slightly larger brain for the first human would have sufficed to give it a dominant position in the animal world, and there would have been no evolutionary pressure to develop larger brains. For instance, the indigenous people of New Guinea and Australia, which I have mentioned before, did not develop what we might call a great civilization; they only used a small part of their brain, nevertheless they dominated their world. This is even more significant because we are told by some scientists that even today we are only using a small part of our brain. So, I believe, it is clear that a process of natural selection and random mutations would not have led to the size of the human brain, simply because there was no reason to have a larger brain for the survival of the species.

The same holds true for our language capability. Primitive societies have language capabilities very similar to our own. Yet for the purpose of the survival of the species, a more limited language capacity would have been sufficient. It is simply not necessary for the survival of the species to be able to write Shakespearean dramas or compose Beethoven's Ninth Symphony. In fact, Jargon Lanai, in an article in the May 1997 issue of *Harper's Magazine*, expresses the opinion that the fundamental process of conversation is one of the great miracles of nature. He goes on to say that two people communicating with each other is an extraordinary phenomenon that so far has defied all attempts to capture it. Communicating with another person, he writes, remains essentially a mystical act.

Considering all this, many people have come to the conclusion that the development of the human being from a single cell was orchestrated and organized by a Guiding Intelligence, which the established religions call God, Allah or Brahman. We see this Intelligence at work in the fine tuning of the laws of nature, in the emergence of life and also now in the emergence of fully conscious human beings.

Just so that we do not get carried away by our own importance in the nature of things, David Suzuki and Holly Dressel[24] point out in their book, *From Naked Ape to Superspecies*, that the human race is not essential for the continued existence of the natural world. On the contrary, the natural world would probably benefit greatly if the human race were to disappear from the surface of the Earth. They contrast this with the importance of the simple and lowly bacteria in the soil who make it possible for things to grow. Without them the soil would not be able to grow the products on which all of nature depends and the natural world would almost certainly change beyond recognition.

IIIe   The Mousetrap Versus the Wagon or Evolutionists Versus Creationists

Ever since Darwin published his book, *The Origin of the Species*, there has been a controversy in the Christian Church of what to believe about the creation of the universe and of humankind. In the Biblical account, as described in the first book of the Bible, humans were created by God as the culmination of a creation sequence, but they were created as complete human beings without any intermediate stages. Using the biblical account, the universe, including us, was created fairly recently, say 6,000 to 10,000 years ago. Bishop Usher in the late 1600s went so far as to calculate from the genealogical records in the Bible that the world was created at 9 A.M. on October 26 in 4004 B.C.E. On the other hand, according to science, the universe was created some fifteen billion years ago; the first living cells appeared somewhere around 3.5 billion years ago, while the first fully human being arrived on the scene some 30,000 to 50,000 years ago.

In contrast, according to Darwin we were created at the end of a very long chain of evolutionary changes from a single-cell organism without a nucleus to organisms with a nucleus and DNA in their cells, and from there through cell splitting and sexual reproduction, and thousands of other intermediate stages, to fully conscious human beings. Darwin identified the driving force behind this continuing evolution as the random mutations of the genetic make-up of the organism followed by a natural selection process. Without these mutations of the DNA, the development of the organism would have stagnated forever at the same level. Of course, these mutations were and are completely random; some mutations increase the viability of the organism and others decrease its viability. It is at this stage that natural selection in the form of survival of the fittest takes over. This natural process ensures that only the most viable mutations survive, thus leading to an ever-increasing complex and viable life form.

At first glance, these two evolution stories appear to be completely irreconcilable and mutually exclusive. However, on closer consideration, they seem to have a number of things in common. In both accounts, human beings appear after the creation of all other inanimate and living things. And the creation sequence is roughly the same in the two accounts. First, the universe was created, then light, then the Earth after water was separated from the land, then fish, plants, land animals and finally Adam and Eve, the first human beings. It is interesting to note that it is possible to interpret verse 20 of the first chapter of Genesis as indicating that life started in the waters:

> Then God commanded, "Let the waters be filled with many kinds of living beings, and let the air be filled with birds… Let the Earth produce all kinds of animal life…" And now (God said) we will make human beings: they will be like us and resemble us.

If we look at the timing in the two creation stories, the date of the creation of a fully conscious human being is not that different in the two stories. As we indicated before, according to science the first human beings arrived some 30,000 to 50,000 years ago, but agriculture did not begin to be practiced until about 10,000 years ago. It is the practice of agriculture that effectively put an end to the nomadic life of our forefathers and made it possible for them to live in settlements. Also it gave them, for the first time in their development, the opportunity to do other things than just hunt for a living. It could, therefore, be argued that the beginning of agriculture, some 10,000 years ago, was in fact the beginning of the first cultured society with people living, more or less, on the same level of development as Adam and Eve did who, according to Genesis, practiced both agriculture and husbandry.

Most Christians today accept that the biblical story of creation is not a lesson in natural history but is a myth, an allegory, that conveys a message to us of far greater importance than a lesson in natural history. As John Polkinghorne[25] recently wrote, "Myth is concerned with conveying truths so deep that only a story can be the appropriate vehicle to explain it." We believe that the message of the biblical creation story is simply that there is a Creator behind the creation of the universe, and that *we are created in the image of that Creator*. Talking about unbelievable stories, the message that we are somewhat like God is probably far more unbelievable than the creation of the universe out of nothing, purely by the will of God. As pointed out before, science today believes that the creation of the universe started from a single point of unknown origin: this is very close, I believe, to saying that the universe was created out of nothing.

One of the clear indications that pure evolution is not the whole story comes from the fact that the fossil record does not show a gradual, steady change over time; rather it shows long periods of stability punctuated by sharp jolts of change – a pattern that has been called "punctuated equilibrium". For instance, the paleontological records show that species of animals which have become extinct were, in their last appearance, very little different from when they first appeared in the fossil records of millions of years before.

No matter what religion we adhere to, the idea of God, the Creator, is always present in some form or another. In most cases this God is so far removed from her creation that it is believed that mere humans cannot possibly have any interaction with that Creator. They believe that if there really is a Creator who made the heavens and Earth, then that God must be so different from them; so high above them in intellectual capacity that it must be impossible for them to understand her, and at best, we can only get a very faint impression of that Creator. But here are the Jews and Christians who believe that God has made herself known to us through the Bible and through Jesus Christ; not only that, they believe that we are created in God's image and are somewhat like her. However, even believing that, it is still very difficult to visualize that Creator who obviously exists in a space/time frame that is entirely different from ours, and who operates on an entirely different level.

As said above, the first chapter of Genesis tells us that, not only are we created by a Creator who guided the evolution of this creation to the eventual appearance of human beings, but also that we are created in her own image. This concept has such a far-reaching effect on all that humanity is, and what it can do, that I have devoted a separate chapter, Chapter XI, to trying to visualize what this means for our long-term future, and what it means about our importance as a species and as individuals.

Today we generally accept as fact that evolution, through random mutations, natural selection and survival of the fittest, was a dominant force in the development of the plant and animal world. As John Polkinghorne[26] writes:

> No reasonable person doubts that natural selection is a component in the history of life, but to believe that it is the sole and totally adequate cause of all that has happened is simply an article of blind faith.

Even the Roman Catholic Church, which has always rejected this idea of evolution, has finally (September 1996) announced that evolution is not necessarily contrary to the teachings of the Church.

What the Christian and other major religions cannot accept is that the human being is just some glorified animal. We know that genetically speaking we are closely related to the apes, but we also know that we are a special creation – a being that is aware of itself and can be aware of the existence of its Creator, and at the same time can have a relationship with that Creator. As we have seen before in this chapter, modern science seems to begin to recognize that humans are a special creation, created at one specific point in time and at one specific place.

Of course, there is a more fundamental objection to evolution as being the principal process in the development of life. This objection centers on the fact that more complex systems are not necessarily more viable. On the contrary, one might argue that they are far more subject to attack and disease than the less complex systems. For instance, bacteria, which are single celled and are the most uncomplicated living creature, have existed almost from the beginning of life, and are still here today much the same as when they first appeared. The question then is, why should there have been a move towards more complex systems. After all, it violates one of the basic laws of nature that everything will become more chaotic with time (the second law of thermodynamics). As someone wrote, "If the meaning of evolution is in adaptation and increasing the chance for survival, as is often claimed, the development of more complex organisms would be meaningless or even a mistake!"

Naturally, not everyone in the Christian Church goes along with the idea that humans evolved through evolution from a single cell into what we are today. There are still a large number of people, generally called "Creationists" as distinct from "Evolutionists", who believe that the biblical account of the creation of the universe as presented in Genesis is a true account in all its detail. For instance, they believe that the geology of the Earth, with all its fossil records, was shaped not by a long period of development but by natural catastrophes such as earthquakes, worldwide floods, and, maybe even, impacts from meteorites. For most people, brought up in this scientific age, it is probably somewhat difficult to believe that there are Creation scientists, as they call themselves, with university degrees in almost every scientific discipline, including chemistry, biology and geology, who believe that the universe, galaxies and all, was created in the not so distant past, say 10,000 years ago, with all the fossils neatly in place in their proper geological strata.

Some of the readers in the U.S.A. will remember the often hard fought battles over what should be taught in the public high schools about the creation of the universe. Sometimes these battles took on a somewhat hilarious aspect such as when someone suggested that the value of pi, which everyone knows is something like 3.146, should be changed in the curriculum to 3.0 on the basis that it is easier to remember; and also because in 2 Chronicles 4:2 it is written that King Solomon owned a basin made with a circumference of three times its diameter. Even today these battles are still continuing as is clear from the recent (summer 1999) decision by the Kansas Board of Education to delete evolution from the state's recommended curriculum and from its standardized texts.

For the true Creationist, the idea that humans evolved directly from animals is repugnant and leads to such statements as: "If man is an evolved animal, then the morals of the barnyard and the jungle are more natural" or "The monkey mythology of Darwin is the cause of permissiveness, promiscuity, pregnancies, abortions, pornography, etc. and proliferation of crimes of all types."

The problem with Creationists, as I see it, is that they only believe in the sudden creation of humans and entirely reject the concept that evolution could have played a part in that creation. On the other hand, very few Evolutionists believe that there was nothing but evolution at work in the evolving universe. Darwin himself had to bring in the idea of mutations – sudden changes in the characteristics of a species – to proceed from one species to the next species in the chain. As a prominent scientist, Stuart Kaufmann,[27] recently wrote: "It is not that Darwin is wrong but he got hold of only part of the truth." One of the reasons for this is that, at the time of Darwin, very little was known about the subatomic structure, nor did anyone have any idea about the almost unbelievable complexity of the living cell. The problem is that with this newly discovered complexity of the cell and of some of the systems that govern life, such as the immune system, no one has ever been able to explain in a detailed scientific fashion how random mutations and natural selection could possibly have built the complex, intricate structures of which life is made.

In *Darwin's Black Box*, Michael Behe describes a number of systems in living things which he calls "irreducibly complex". These are single systems that are composed of several well-matched, interacting parts that contribute to the basic function, and wherein the removal of any one part, or the partial development of any one part, causes the system to effectively cease to function. To illustrate such a system he uses the simple common mousetrap.

Staying with the example of the mousetrap for a minute, let's look briefly at how it works. First, there is the wooden base to which the whole system is attached; then there is the metal hammer which crushes the poor mouse; the device can't work, however, without the spring which causes the hammer to have the force necessary to do its evil deed. The whole system would still not work without a catch and a holding bar which releases the force of the spring and the hammer as soon as the mouse starts on, what is most likely, its last meal. To determine if this system is irreducibly complex, it is necessary to find out if all these components are necessary to make the trap work, or whether there are some parts that can be removed without impeding the effectiveness of the system. Anyone who has ever used a mousetrap knows very well that all the bits and pieces are needed to make it work. For instance, I had a mousetrap the other day in which the staple that holds the frame fastened to the wooden base was loose: the result was that the mouse must have received an awful fright, but it got away with its life. The truth is, a mousetrap is not something which could have slowly evolved from earlier traps that did not have, for instance, a spring to give the hammer its power. In effect, all parts are needed and have to be fully developed to make it work: it could not have appeared on the scene at an intermediate stage that then, through a step-by-step process, evolved into an effective mousetrap. It is clear, I believe, that the contraption in its entirety was conceived by someone with a brain who was plagued by mice eating his corn or messing up his house.

An entirely different process is presented by the evolution of the common wagon or buggy. In the earliest times, when humans wanted to move heavy loads, they used either sleds or rollers made of tree trunks. This worked reasonably well, but using rollers was cumbersome because the rollers had to be continually brought from the back to the front to keep the load moving forward. Somewhere along the line some observant chap must have argued that the system would work better if you put a section of a much larger tree trunk at each end, thereby lifting most of the roller off the ground. The real breakthrough came, however, when someone got the idea to make holes in the center of these larger end-logs; and have the center log penetrate through these holes, thereby getting a fixed axle on which loads could be placed without continually having to move the rollers from the back to the front. Of course, when they started to tie two of these contraptions together, they had the prototype of the wagon and eventually the motor car and they were literally away to the races. Somewhat along these lines, I believe, one of the most important discoveries was made in the history of humankind – the wheel and axle. The process was one of a truly evolutionary nature because each intermediate stage worked well, and the development could have stagnated at each stage forever.

As mentioned before, the Mayans, who lived in Central America until approximately 1300 C.E. had developed a civilization that included observatories to study the movements of the planets; they even had developed enough mathematical skills to calculate the dates of eclipses of the Sun and Moon. Despite this, they never developed the concept of the wheel, other than on toys, and they built their large pyramids without the aid of wheels to transport the heavy stone blocks of which they are made. The point is that, even with a purely evolutionary system, further development can get stalled; what emerges at one place does not necessarily develop elsewhere, even though they start from the same base and even though the intelligence of the people involved is the same.

In *Darwin's Black Box*, Michael Behe describes several biological systems which fall under this category of being irreducibly complex. They are of the "mousetrap" variety; that is to say, it is simply inconceivable that these systems could have developed slowly over time by simple mutations or by natural selection, because anything missing in their make-up would make the whole system inoperative. He describes in detail the workings of the cilium, the hair-like protuberances on some cells that through their whip-like action keep the cell moving. The best-known example of a cilium is probably the tail of the male sperm which keeps it moving in the direction of the female ovum. Other examples, which he describes in detail in his book, are the system which causes blood to coagulate at a cut in the skin; and the immune system which normally prevents us from becoming ill from the millions of bacteria, viruses and germs with which we are bombarded continually (see Chapter V for details of the immune system). Probably, most of our sense organs fall in the same category as well. These systems are all very complex, and it is difficult to see how they could have evolved from less sophisticated systems, since every one of the complex chemical and biological components of these systems are required to make the system work – take one out and the system becomes useless and even counter-productive.

In their book, *Science, Order and Creativity*, the authors David Bohm and David Peat[28] mention the difficulty of creating a bird out of a land animal by small steps or even large mutations. As they write, it is not sufficient to give a bird wings: if it is to fly, its bones must be made lighter while maintaining its strength; its feathers must be aerodynamically adapted; the center of gravity of its body must shift; its breast bones and musculature must develop; and finally, its metabolism must be changed to provide sufficient energy for flight. They make the point that if such changes do not all occur at the same time and in a coordinated fashion, these changes may well be disadvantageous to survival. For instance, a land animal in an in-between stage, say with half-developed wings instead of a pair of legs, would be an easy prey for its predators and this in-between species would not be able to survive long enough to get to the next stage of its development. You might call this an irreducibly complex changeover from land animal to bird.

In principle, this argument is not much different from that introduced by one of Darwin's contemporaries, St. George Mivart,[29] who wrote an essay called "The Incompetence of Natural Selection to Account for the Incipient Stages of Useful Structures". In this essay, he questioned that there could be intermediate stages in the development of what Behe calls irreducibly complex systems. Many people have tried to find some evidence that these intermediate stages, for example of a wing, could be useful in the development of the final product, but none of these explain how the center of gravity of the bird changed with the development of the wing.

In a later paper, Behe[30] mentions that in searching through the literature he has not been able to find one paper that discusses the detailed models of intermediates in the development of complex biological structures. He concludes with the statement:

> It is a shock to us in the twentieth century to discover, from observations science has made, that the fundamental mechanics of life cannot be ascribed to natural selection, and therefore were designed. The theory of undirected evolution is already dead, but the work of science continues.

One last example I personally find very convincing is the transformation through small or large steps of a caterpillar into a butterfly and vice versa. This metamorphosis is such an improbable process that it defies any explanation. It is just impossible, at least for me, to contemplate:

- the spinning of a cocoon;
- the transformation inside the cocoon from a rather drab insect into a beautiful butterfly; and later
- the transformation of the eggs of the butterfly into a caterpillar again;

that all this happened by pure chance through a process of small or even large mutations; what is more, it assumes that all the intermediate stages would have been viable long enough for the next mutation to take place. Obviously, there must have been some nonmaterial force at work that caused nature to change a drab caterpillar into a beautiful butterfly.

Recently, Kenneth Miller,[31] in a book entitled *Finding Darwin's God, A Scientist's Search for Common Ground between God and Evolution*, has argued that both the punctuated equilibrium of Eldredge and Gould[32] and the irreducibly complex theory of Behe are not correct. Miller contends that recent discoveries have shown that there is enough evidence to show that the normal evolutionary process can account for both the punctuated equilibrium and the irreducibly complex systems.

Despite this argument, it is clear to me that pure evolution alone cannot explain the creation of conscious human beings, and that other forces must have been involved which gave direction to that evolving nature. In other words, I believe that there is a design or a plan that has guided the direction of the creation process. This design is most clearly seen at work in the steps leading up to the creation of the first living cells, and in the injections of these irreducibly complex systems into the evolutionary process. In addition, I believe, this design is also clearly evident in the transformation of an ape-like animal into a conscious human being. So, the title "Evolutionists Versus Creationists" is somewhat misleading – it should more correctly have read "Evolution in Creation". The fact seems to be that evolution, without the irreducibly complex systems, simply could not have taken us from the inanimate world to the present state of conscious, thinking human beings. It is interesting to note that Darwin himself wrote that his theory would break down if it could be proven that there were systems which could not evolve through small modifications from a more basic form.

Even Alfred Wallace, a co-discoverer of natural selection with Darwin, pointed out that there were parts in the theory of the human evolving from lower forms which could not be all explained by evolution. For instance, he argued that there was no reason for the human brain to have the capabilities it has for survival. He went so far as to write that if there was no purpose for something then it was not caused by evolution. And, so he believed that there was an "Overruling Intelligence" at work in creation, and that consequently the theory of evolution actually proved the existence of God. This modified story of creation through evolution should go a long way to meet most of the objections of the Creationists. There is clearly some higher force at work that has taken an active part in the creation of the universe and in the creation of human beings. Also humans are clearly not some glorified animals, but they are unique creations who have been given a consciousness, an intelligence, and a free will to make choices.

The question this intelligent being is going to ask is: who or what is this intelligence that planned and directed this creation? To answer this question, Michael Behe uses the amusing allegory of the police discovering a crushed body in a room in which there is a big elephant standing in the middle of that room. A score of detectives are hard at work, with magnifying glasses and other police paraphernalia, looking for clues on the ground trying to discover the identity of the culprit who caused the body to be in such a sorry state; completely ignoring the presence of the elephant. Just so, he argues, we in a similar way run the risk of not recognizing the obvious presence of a designer in the creation of life. As he and others have expressed it:

> To a person who does not feel obliged to restrict his search to intelligent causes, the straightforward conclusion is that many bio-chemical systems were designed – not by laws of nature or by chance or necessity – they were planned… Life on Earth in its most fundamental, in its most critical components, is the product of intelligent activity… Neither science nor philosophy has explained how an irreducibly complex system such as a watch might be produced without a designer. We can confidently conclude that the biological systems, etc. were designed by an intelligent agent just as sure as the mousetrap was designed by an intelligent human being.

All these are "design arguments": one of the better known of the earlier design arguments was first formulated in 1802 by the Reverend William Paley[33] in what became known as the "watchmaker" argument. In his book, *Evidence of the Existence and Attributes of the Deity*, he wrote that if you cross a field and you stumble on a rock you know that it came to be there by accident or by the forces of nature acting on it; if, however, you found a watch at the same place, you would not for a minute think that the same forces of nature had placed that watch there or assembled it at that place. Also, the intricacy of the instrument would clearly indicate that it was assembled by someone for a specific purpose. Similarly he argued, when we look at the complexity of life, you cannot assume that it came to be here purely by the random action of the same laws of nature; instead, you think that someone has designed this life and that it has been created for a specific purpose. See also Fred Hoyle's argument about the impossibility of a 747 assembling itself in a junkyard.

The title of the book by the Reverend Paley inspired Richard Dawkins[34] in 1986 to write a book called *The Blind Watchmaker* in which he firmly rejects the involvement of a Divine Watchmaker in the evolution of human beings. On the contrary, he strongly argues in favor of evolution as the only force that could have generated life out of a random collection of molecules. As could be expected, nowhere in the book is there any reference to spiritual matters: it is all chemistry and chance. As he writes:

> Natural selection has no purpose in mind, the mystery of our existence is solved. (sic) Cumulative selection, by slow and gradual degrees is the explanation, the only workable explanation that has ever been proposed for the existence of life's complex design... The very heart of evolution theory gives it the power to dissolve *astronomical improbabilities* and explain *prodigies of apparent miracle*... The

essence of life is a statistical improbability on a colossal scale. (author's italics)

The answer to all these improbabilities is the random selection process which to Dawkins is the mechanism that guides each step in some particular direction; otherwise, the sequence of steps will careen off in an endless random walk. After making these claims Dawkins goes on the attack and states that bringing in a supernatural power to explain our existence is a kind of lazy way out. He writes:

> To explain the origin of the DNA/protein machine by invoking a supernatural designer is to explain precisely nothing for it leaves unexplained the origin of the Designer. You have to say something like God was always there and if you allow yourself that kind of lazy way out, you might as well say DNA was always there or life was always there and be done with it... If we want to postulate a deity capable of engineering all the organized complexity in the world, either instantaneously or by guiding evolution, that deity must already have been vastly complex in the first place.

I must say, the comment about DNA or life always having been there as an alternative is not a statement that I would have expected to hear from a scientist. He very well knows that this is the very point of the creation story – we all know that we were not always there. And as far as the complexity of the Designer is concerned, every Hindu, Muslim, Jew and Christian will point out that, that is exactly their point of departure. We all believe that this Designer existed before time and space came into being and that this Designer is well capable of guiding the creation of humankind out of essentially nothing.

The same Kenneth Miller, who believes that there is enough evidence to show that continuing evolution can explain all the phenomena of the natural world, believes that God acts through this evolutionary process to impose his/her will on the outcome of that process. According to him, the fact that small changes in the DNA can have such large effects on future generations allows God to influence the eventual outcome of the creation process without having to interfere directly in a major way in that process, and still arrive at the final purpose God has intended for this creation. To quote Miller:[35]

> Fortunately, in scientific terms, God has left Himself plenty of material to work with. To pick just one example, the indeterminate nature of quantum events would allow a clever and subtle God to influence events in ways that are profound, but scientifically undetectable by us.
>
> A God who presides over an evolutionary process is not an impatient, passive observer – the process of continuing creation is woven into the fabric of matter itself. He retains the freedom to act, to reveal himself, to inspire, and to teach. He is the master of chance and time, whose actions, both powerful and subtle, respect the independence of His creation and give human beings the genuine freedom to accept and reject His love.
>
> In the final analysis, God used evolution to set us free.

Much has been written recently about the influence of necessity and contingency on the ongoing evolution of nature in general and human life in particular. Stephen Jay Gould,[36] who has written extensively on the subject, believes that contingency played a large role in this ongoing evolution. Contingency, he defines, as the unpredictable sequence of antecedent states. In other words, evolution did not of necessity follow the path it took; on the contrary, he believes evolution was shaped by continuing small, unpredictable nudges originating from its past. In his words: rewrite the tape of evolution, starting even half a million years ago, and the re-emergence of humankind is very, very unlikely. Similarly, Michael Shermer[37] wrote that we have come to realize that the Newtonian clockwork universe is filled with contingencies, catastrophes, and chaos, making precise predictions of all but the simplest physical systems virtually impossible.

All these scientists seem to agree that the emergence of human life, from the conditions existing even a relatively short time ago, is so unlikely that the fact that we are here is nothing short of a miracle. For Christians, this is just one more proof that there was a Creator active in nature, continually nudging the evolutionary process in the direction that would eventually result in the emergence of humans, who could directly relate to that Creator and in fact become a partner with her in the ongoing evolution of the world.

Of course, knowing that there is, or has been, a designer or planner at work in our creation does not tell us anything about that designer or the intelligence who guided that design or developed that plan. Clearly, identifying the designer is obviously not something that science can do – it is only religion which can throw a light on that. The great contribution of science is that it has found clear indications that there is such a designer and that, as a result, we know today, without the shadow of any doubt, that we are not here just by chance but are here as the result of a carefully worked out plan. In later chapters, we will describe what the various religions have to say about the identity of that designer. For the present, let us just say that, at least in my opinion, looking at all the evidence, it is clear that there is a Guiding Intelligence out there, which has directed the creation process so that the end result would be a fully conscious being with its own intelligence and free will. An intelligence that could produce a painter like Paul Gauguin who could ask questions such as: where do I come from;

who am I; and where am I going?

The finding of Edward Larson[38] of the University of Georgia, who recently duplicated verbatim an investigation carried out in 1916 among biologists, physicists and mathematicians, may be mentioned here. In this survey he asked one thousand scientists whether they believed in the existence of a God who, by the survey's strict definition, "actively communicates with humankind and to whom one may pray in expectation of receiving an answer." The surprising outcome was that of the more than 600 respondents the percentage who answered the question positively had not changed over more than eighty years since the first survey was conducted. Then, as now, 40 per cent of those who replied answered that they did believe in this God. To some extent, I believe this goes to show that the fantastic discoveries of the last eighty years have not turned the scientists away from believing in God: this probably is in contrast to the general public whose belief in a personal God may have substantially decreased over that same time period.

NOTES

[1]Recinos, Adrian, *Popol Vuh, The Sacred Book of the Ancient Quiche Maya*, University of Oklahoma Press, Norman, 1951–1991, pp.81, 83.

[2]Darwin, Charles, *On the Origin of Species by Means of Natural Selection*, John Murray, 1860.

[3]Darling, David, *Deep Time*, Delacorte Press, Bantam, Doubleday, Dell New York, 1989.

[4]Easterbrook, Gregg, *Beside Still Waters, Searching for Meaning in an Age of Doubt*, William Morrow & Co., 1999.

[5]Jonker, Frederik, *Good News for Today, We Are not Alone*, Fairway Press, Lima, Ohio, 1994, p.62.

[6]Ferris, Timothy, *The Whole Shebang, A State-of-the-Universe Report*, Simon and Schuster New York, 1997, p.248.

[7]Bizony, Piers, *Rivers of Mars, Searching for the Cosmic Origin of Life*, Aurum Press Ltd, London, 1997, p.186.

[8]Wheeler, John A., *Mind and Nature*, Harper and Row, San Francisco, 1982.

[9] Behe, Michael, *Darwin's Black Box, The Biochemical Challenge to Evolution*, The Free Press, Simon and Schuster, New York, 1996, p.168.

[10] Franklin, Harold M., *The Way of the Cell*, Oxford University Press, New York, 2001

[11] Davies, Paul, *The Fifth Miracle, The Search for the Origin and Meaning of Life*, Simon and Schuster, New York, 1999, p.95.

[12] Zebrowski Jr., Ernest, *Perils of a Restless Planet, Scientific Perspectives on Natural Disasters*, Cambridge University Press, 1999.

[13] Gould, Stephen, *Rock of Ages, Science and Religion in the Fullness of Life*, Ballantine Publishing Group, New York, 2000.

[14] Alper, Matthew, *The God Part of the Brain, A Scientific Interpretation of Human Spirituality and God*, Rogue Press, Brooklyn, New York, 2000.

[15] Leaky, Richard, *The Origin of Humankind*, Basic Books, Harper Collins Publications, 1994, p.99.

[16] Tattersall, Ian, *Becoming Human, Evolution and Human Uniqueness*, Harcourt, Brace and Co., Orlando, 1998, p.188.

[17] Sykes, Bryan, *The Seven Daughters of Eve, the Science that Reveals our Genetic Ancestry*, W.W. Norton & Co., New York, 2001.

[18] Raymo, Chet, *Skeptics and Believers, The Exhilarating Connection between Science and Religion*, Walker Publishing Co. Ltd, New York, 1998, p.26.

[19] Ornstein, Robert, *The Evolution of Consciousness*, Prentice Hall Press, New York, p.8.

[20] Darling, David, op. cit., 72.

[21] Gould, Stephen Jay, *Life's Grandeur*, Vintage Pockets, 1996.

[22] Keck, Robert L., *Sacred Eyes*, Knowledge Systems, Indianapolis, 1992.

[23] Horgan, John, *The End of Science, Facing the Limits of Knowledge in the Twilight of the Scientific Age*, Addison Wesley Publishing Co., 1996, p.244.

[24] Suzuki, David and Dressel, Holly, *From Naked Ape to Superspecies*, Stoddart Publishing Co. Ltd. Toronto, 1999.

[25] Polkinghorne, John, *Belief in God in an Age of Science*, Yale University Press, 1998, p.96.

[26] Polkinghorne, John, ibid.

[27] Kaufman, Stuart, *At Home in the Universe: The Search for the Laws of Self Organization and Complexity*, Oxford University Press, New York, 1995.

[28] Bohm, David and Peat, David, *Science, Order and Creativity*, Bantam Books, New York, 1987, p.202.

[29] Mivart, St George, "On the Genesis of Species, The Incompetence of Natural Selection to Account for the Incipient Stages of Useful Structures", 1871, *Cahiers Victoriens et Edwardiens*, no. 52, 2000.

[30] Behe, Michael, "Molecular Machines, Experimental Support for the Design Inference", Access Research Network, www.arn.org

[31] Miller, Kenneth R., *Finding Darwin's God, A Scientist's Search for Common Ground between God and Evolution*, Cliff Street Books, Harper Collins, New York, 1999.

[32] Eldredge, Niles and Gould, Stephen J., *Fossils: the Evolution and Extinction of Species*, Princeton University Press, 1997.

[33] Paley, William, *Evidence of the Existence and Attributes of the Deity*, 1803.

[34] Dawkins, Richard, *The Blind Watchmaker*, Oxford University Press, Oxford, 1986, pp.5, 141.

[35] Miller, Kenneth, see note 29, p.241.

[36] Gould, Stephen Jay, *Wonderful Life: The Burgess Shale and the Nature of History*, W. W. Norton, New York, 1989.

[37] Shermer, Michael, *How We Believe, The Search for God in an Age of Science*, W. H. Freeman and Co., New York, 1999.

[38] Larson, Edward, University of Georgia, in an article by Natalie Angier of the *New York Times* service.

Chapter IV
OUR LONG-TERM FUTURE ACCORDING TO SCIENCE

IVa The Future of Human Life on Earth

It is difficult to predict how, and in what way, life on Earth will develop in the time available before the Sun's energy runs out and life here becomes impossible. It is presently estimated that this will occur some 900 million years from now. Considering the very short time in which we have progressed from the stone chip to the computer chip (50,000 years) compared to the time life has existed on Earth (3,500,000,000 years), anything is possible. Unfortunately, in these last 50,000 years, we have, for the first time in human history, also developed a capability to destroy ourselves. We can do it the fast way by a nuclear war or the slower way through the chemical pollution of the atmosphere or even through the genetic manipulation of DNA. This new power of self-destruction gives us humans an awesome responsibility that, so far, we do not seem to have taken all that seriously. In this chapter, we will take a brief look at what may be in store for us in the next millennia. We will also consider the possibility of life regenerating itself on this planet if it were ever completely destroyed by one or more natural or man-made catastrophes.

In the book *The History of Earth* by William Hastermann and Ron Miller,[1] the authors list seven hazards to our existence for which we, the Earth's inhabitants and caretakers, are responsible. There are, in addition to such natural causes as asteroid impacts, the following man-made dangers:

- Foremost of these is, of course, the possibility of a nuclear war breaking out or even a nuclear accident happening at one or more of the hundreds of nuclear power stations which dot the face of the Earth today. It is not only the deaths resulting from the explosion and the radiation afterwards, but there is also the distinct possibility that an explosion of this size would cause sufficient debris to be hurled into the atmosphere to cause a nuclear winter by blocking out the sunlight over a large part of the Earth. At this point in time, spring 2003, there is the additional danger posed by the thousands of nuclear warheads stored at various places in the former USSR. The control by several, now independent, Russian Republics over these potentially lethal systems is extremely lax and there is every possibility that some of these warheads will end up in the wrong hands.
- The greenhouse effect and global warming that are the direct result from the emission of increasing amounts of carbon dioxide. The main culprits here are fossil burning power stations and the cars and trucks which will increase in numbers for the foreseeable future.
- The depletion of our natural resources, mainly by the industrialized countries of the West, which continues at an ever-increasing rate. We have been extremely fortunate so far in that every time we seem to be running out of a commodity we find new resources that make it possible for us to continue on our wasteful ways. But this cannot continue ad infinitum and eventually we will run out of oil and gas. When this happens we will be forced to power our cars and trucks either directly by small atomic engines or, indirectly, by

electricity generated in large power stations and stored in car batteries.
- The damage we are doing to the ozone layer that protects us from the dangerous ultraviolet radiation.
The culprits here are the chlorofluorocarbon chemicals that are used in refrigerants, aerosol sprays and cleaning fluids.
- The danger posed by the storage of hazardous wastes, such as radioactive residues from nuclear power stations. These wastes are accumulating at alarming rates and if they are not stored in earthquake-proof containers they could, over the long haul, cause great damage to the areas surrounding the storage sites.
- The continuing destruction of agricultural land through urban sprawl and desertification, the latter mainly in Africa. It is estimated that, on a worldwide basis, the spread of desert conditions is destroying arable land at the rate of some six million hectares per year (fifteen million acres per year) and that a similar amount of agricultural land is lost each year though urban spread, airports, highways, etc.
- This destruction of agricultural land together with the growth in world population poses one of the major threats to our continued existence. The Earth can only sustain a limited number of people; once we exceed this limit, great political and economic upheavals can be expected. It has been estimated that, in a certain sense, we have already reached this limit; it appears that if all the people in the world living now were to start consuming the same amount of natural resources as the people in the U.S.A. and Canada, the capacity of the agricultural land to meet these demands would be grossly insufficient. In fact, it is estimated that to meet this demand would require the resources of two additional Earth-sized planets.

It is our success in the past to come up with solutions which saved the day that have given us a false sense of security. For instance, the Green Revolution, which made it possible to increase crop yields some three or even fourfold, lulled us all to sleep, because it seemed that the problem was solved for the foreseeable future. Today, however, we are discovering all kinds of adverse effects of the increased use of fertilizers and pesticides that made this "miracle" possible. Thus, we may have come to the end of the road here as well. The other problem with providing enough food for a growing population and a shrinking agricultural base is that, although there may be enough food during normal crop years, the shortages will become first evident during a prolonged drought such as the one that occurred during the Great Depression in the Mid-West. When this happens, it will be too late unless we have stored food during the "seven fat years" for use during the "seven lean years".

The authors of *The History of the Earth* are not alone in this assessment of our future. This is clear from the following examples I used in a previous book *Good News For Today*. Linus Pauling, twice winner of the Nobel Prize for science, said in a recent interview that he is afraid that within the next twenty-five to fifty years there will occur the greatest catastrophe in the history of the world. Nevertheless, he is optimistic in the sense that he expects the human race to survive this catastrophe.

> The looming catastrophe might well result from a world war which could destroy civilization and might well be the end of the human race. Or it might take the form of mass starvation among a world population that has doubled every thirty-five years. Or it might be the result of the collapse of the system on which it depends... I am forced, as I think about what has happened in the world in my life time and as I observe governments in their process of

decision making, to conclude that the coming century is probably going to be one in which the amount of human suffering reaches a maximum.

Alvin Toffler,[2] the author of *Future Shock*, sounds equally pessimistic about the outlook for our society in his recent book, *War and Anti-War*. He points out that it is not only technology that seems to have broken loose, but that many other social processes, such as urban development, violence, ethnic conflicts, and so forth, have run loose as well, and that they defy all our best efforts to guide them. His concern is further deepened by his impression that, while the rate of change seems to be accelerating, there is no evidence of a corresponding acceleration in the rate at which we can respond to these changes. This being so, he believes that we may well be on the threshold of losing all control over our future development and our human destiny.

Hans Küng,[3] one of the best-known modern theologians, expresses similar concerns when he writes in his book, *On Being a Christian*:

> The progress of modern science, medicine, technology, industry, communications, and culture surpasses the boldest fantasies... And yet, this evolution seems still far away from leading us to some sort of paradise and often leads us away from it... The longer we consider the situation the less we can avoid the disturbing observation that something is wrong in this fantastic quantitative and qualitative progress. In a very short time the sense of not being at ease with technical civilization has become universal.

Finally, there is this message from a group calling themselves the Union of Concerned Scientists:

> Human beings and the natural world are on a collision course. Human activities inflict harsh and often irreversible damage to the environment and on critical resources... many may so alter the living world that it will be unable to sustain life in the manner we know.

The adverse way we are affecting the environment is probably best illustrated by Bob Reiss[4] in a recent (2001) book, *The Coming Storm*, in which he points out that in the last eleven years, ten years have been the hottest on record; in five of the ten years the U.S. suffered two of the worst hurricanes of the century, two floods of the century, and one drought of the century. It is obvious from these statistics that, whatever the reason, in the last eleven years the effect of our mismanagement of the environment has begun to show up in a disastrous way in the weather of North America.

The authors of *Science, Order and Creativity*, David Bohm and David Peat,[5] express the belief that what faces humanity is not a continuing cycle of civilizations, such as we have had in the past, but a worldwide annihilation which may destroy the order of nature on which life depends. They think that if we continue on our present path, it would take a very optimistic person to believe that humankind will survive as much as a thousand years, which is, as they point out, only a very short period of time in the life of our planet. They also make it clear that the challenge that faces us today is unique and has never occurred before. They believe that a new kind of creativity is needed, not just in the way we do science, but also in our approach to society and our social consciousness.

As Michio Kaku[6] explains in his book *Hyperspace*, the danger period occurs in the first several hundred years after the dawn of the nuclear age, when a civilization's technological development has far outpaced its social and political maturity in handling regional conflicts. He believes that if we can survive this dangerous era, civilization will have achieved a planetary social structure sufficiently advanced to avoid self-annihilation and a technology powerful enough to avoid an ecological or a natural disaster. However, even then civilization will have difficulty avoiding the ultimate catastrophe – the death of the solar system and later the disintegration of the universe.

Richard Tarna[7] in *The Passion of the Western Mind*, after warning of the danger that humanity may destroy itself through the might of its own technology and science, writes:

> Our moment in history is indeed a pregnant one. As a civilization and as a species we have come to a moment of truth, with the future of the human spirit, and the future of the planet, hanging in the balance. If ever boldness, depth and clarity of vision were called for, for many, it is now.

These quotations present a pretty pessimistic outlook on what lies ahead for our world. Of course, there are others who do not share these somber forecasts about our future. For instance, in a recently published book by the Competitive Enterprise Institute called *Earth Report 2000, Revisiting the True State of the Planet*, the authors argue that many of the environmental problems listed above are under control and that, for instance, the world population will level off, not later than the year 2040, and then will actually decrease. The report claims that one of the elements in making these predictions, which is often not given enough weight, is the fact that greater prosperity and affluence, while increasing the requirement for natural resources, also results in a demand that the supply of these resources be secure and that the environment be protected. They claim that the wellsprings of economic growth are new ideas, designs and recipes. Finally, they conclude that greater affluence and technological sophistication mean an improved natural environment, not a worsening one.

All this may be true; however, the fact remains that these new inventions produce new dangers such as mishaps at atomic energy plants or, more recently, the accidental release of genetically created new viruses against which there is no natural defense. The evaluation of these new threats to our society cannot be left to science or business but must be controlled by ethical considerations and by a set of human values. We will return to this in a later chapter.

IVb The Future of Human Life in the Solar System

As mentioned before, life on Earth is made possible by the energy we receive from the Sun in the form of sunlight. The Sun itself receives this energy from the nuclear reactions within its core that convert hydrogen into helium. Despite the gigantic size of the Sun, there will come a time when the supply of hydrogen runs out and the Earth will lose its source of energy. The results for life on Earth will be disastrous: all living things will die because of the lack of food and later the Sun will increase in size to the extent that it will probably engulf the Earth. In any case, the depletion of the hydrogen in the core of the Sun will spell, once and for all, the end for life on Earth.

The best estimate, of when the hydrogen in the Sun will have sufficiently been depleted for the Sun to die, is somewhere around three to four billion years in the future. In other words, at this point in time, we are approximately halfway through the effective life of our planet (see Figure 3.2). However, long before this stage is reached, the increased luminosity of the Sun during its "dying days" will have heated the Earth and its atmosphere to the extent that vegetation, and therefore human life, will have become impossible. This is expected to occur in about 900 to 1,000 million years.

Considering the inventiveness of the human race, we will want to do something about this. Not that we can possibly stop the demise of the Sun as an energy source, but there are other ways we may be able to continue the existence of life within the universe. If nothing else intervenes, we will have plenty of time to make our plans. Just consider what has happened to our capabilities in the last 50,000 years when we went from "stone chip to computer chip". These technological developments seem to happen at an ever-increasing pace. So with a future of possibly 900 million years ahead of us, it would seem that we should be able to come up with something to continue life, if not on Earth, then somewhere else. That is, of course, if nothing else has interfered, in the meantime, to terminate our existence here on Earth prematurely.

There are, however, a number of major problems with finding ways and means that would allow human life to continue beyond the death of our solar system. The first concern is the limits of what science can do. Recently, a book appeared, written by John Horgan[8] called *The End of Science, Facing the Limits of Knowledge in the Twilight of the Scientific Age*. In this book the author claims that almost every branch of science has come to the end of the road of what can possibly be discovered. This is especially true of the study of the microcosm and the macrocosm. Further expansions of our knowledge in these areas is becoming increasingly expensive and with very little return in terms of our basic understanding of life and our place in the universe. The possible exceptions to this are probably the areas of genetics and genetic engineering and anything that has to do with the mind, including research that investigates the working of the brain and our nervous system.

The other major impediment to our continued, unrelenting scientific progress concerns our inability to solve any of our social and economic problems. It is unconscionable, in some way, that we continue to spend a large percentage of our resources on research and technologies which in the end do very little for the average person, while we have not been able to solve any of the problems of hunger, poverty, crime, drugs and even diseases which affect a large percentage of the world's population. It is clear, that if we do not change our order of priorities, eventually we will end up with social unrest that will prevent all further progress. An example of how this could happen may be found in the history of the Communist regime in Russia. By spending a very large part of their gross national product on armaments, space exploration and other research mainly to keep pace with what the U.S. was doing, they wrecked their economy and caused great poverty and hardship among large segments of their population. Similarly, it has been predicted that if genetic engineering is going to be used to improve the mental capability of some people, the immediate result will be the creation of yet another class of privileged people, which is absolutely the last thing we need. There is also the distinct possibility that this could eventually lead to a revolt against this privileged class.

To continue human life elsewhere, after it has become impossible on Earth, will require immense commitments of money and talents and an unwavering determination. Technically, there is only one way in which this can be achieved and that is by immigration to one of the closest, habitable planets. Since the nearest planet, with an atmosphere that would enable our type of life to exist, is probably at least sixty to eighty light-years away, it would take a very long time to reach this haven, that is, if it exists at all. If, for instance, we were able to accelerate a rocket to one-tenth of the speed of light (the fastest speed so far attained by rockets is 10 to 15 km per second) at 30,000 km per second, it would take up to 1,000 years to reach that place. Someone has calculated that even at this "low" speed, the cost of launching such a venture would be equal to the total present-day Gross Domestic Product of the entire world.

It is clear from this that we have to do something very drastic, both economically and politically, to make interstellar travel possible or to even consider the possibility of colonizing other planets. As explained in Chapter II, there is, quite apart from politics and economics, a theoretical upper limit to the speed we can ever reach, and this will forever limit what is possible and what is not possible in interplanetary travel.

The various scenarios that people have dreamed up all depend heavily on the work of the mathematician, John Von Neumann, who developed the first electronic computer during World War II. He proved mathematically that it is theoretically possible to build robots with the built-in ability to program themselves, repair themselves, and make carbon copies of themselves. By sending thousands of these robots in suitable rockets into space, it is assumed that some of them would eventually land on satellites of stars where they could then start to build small industrial complexes capable of making large numbers of copies of their robotic selves. In this scenario, it is not quite clear where the human being fits in.

Some scientists, such as Frank Tippler[9] in his book *Physics of Immortality*, predict that human colonization of the new planet would take place according to the following scenario. Probes would be sent out to other stellar systems with payloads of self-reproducing universal construction and propulsion systems; the latter would include a system that would slow the rocket down when it reaches its destination, because these sophisticated systems could not survive the impact if the rocket hit the new Earth with an undiminished speed. The whole rocket and associated machinery would be run by robots with human-like intelligence. These probes, once landed safely, would be instructed to search for construction materials, build an industrial complex and then make several hundred copies of themselves, including the propulsion system and the necessary fuel. It is difficult for me to imagine how the robots could locate, mine and refine the minerals they need for this construction program and then build industrial machinery to make the necessary parts. But, that is what some scientists believe will eventually be possible.

The rocket would have human male and female reproductive material on board. Using this material, the robots would cause the sperm to fertilize the female egg and the whole assembly would then be put in an artificial womb, and presto, nine months later there would be the first human being on a faraway satellite of a star. This process would be repeated for some time until there would be enough human beings on this planet to return again to the more normal way of reproduction. Once this new home has been colonized, plans can be started to colonize other satellites in our galaxy. And, of course, as long as you do not mind the time this would take, we can begin to think about colonizing other galaxies. The closest galaxy is about three million light-years away and it would, therefore, take tens of millions of years to reach it.

The whole concept sounds like science fiction and it probably is, but the fact remains that it is being seriously studied. Considering the large amount of time that is theoretically available to develop this concept before we are forced to leave this solar system, it may technically be possible to construct suitable rockets and robots to make these journeys. As pointed out before, the cost of all this would be astronomical and it is doubtful that the human determination will be there to proceed with such an uncertain and costly project. After all, no one living at the time the robots are launched will ever know whether the project will be successful or not. Then there is the question of being able to design mechanical robots with their built-in computers that will operate flawlessly for hundreds of thousands of years. Also, there is the problem of the impact of even the smallest particles that may be floating in space. At these speeds, even a particle the size of a grain of sand would have the effect of a high-speed bullet and would probably make the spaceship inoperable.

Before humankind can even consider entering this interplanetary travel and start an interplanetary civilization, there are a number of hazards the Earth itself has to overcome. Most of these are man-made, but there is one that is not the result of our action and that is the hazard of being hit with a large asteroid similar to the one that caused the demise of the dinosaurs. We know that the Earth, and also the Moon, have been hit repeatedly in the past by similar asteroids: there are half a dozen or so large craters spread across the surface of the Earth which testify that, if time is counted by the millions of years, a recurrence of such a catastrophe is entirely possible.

It has been calculated that we can expect an asteroid that would create a 20 km crater every four million years and a dinosaur-destroying event every 100 to 200 million years. It is hoped that by the time a comet or asteroid is detected coming in our direction, we will have advanced technically far enough to be able to send a rocket with a nuclear capacity to intercept the comet and redirect it away from the Earth and the Earth's atmosphere.

So, the long-term future of the Earth and of the human race is a matter of speculation. The alternatives appear to be:

- The destruction of life on Earth by humankind's own folly.
- The destruction of the Earth by the collision with a large-sized asteroid. The possibility that this will happen in the foreseeable future is very small, because we are talking of an event that probably happens once every three or four million years. Nevertheless, if we are considering time periods that run into millions of years, this must be considered to be a distinct possibility.
- The destruction of life through the natural death of our solar system by the Sun running out of energy. It is expected that our solar system will be running out of energy three or four billion years from now. But, as mentioned before, life on Earth would probably become impossible after "only" 900 million years.
- If, on the other hand, we are able to establish interplanetary societies, human life could possibly survive until the end of the collapse of the universe that will probably not happen for at least another 40 to 100 billion years.
- As we have seen in Chapter III, this ultimate demise of the universe could also happen if the universe continues to expand. This would result in the long run into a very cold and lifeless place. If, on the other hand, there is enough matter in the universe to reverse the expansion and cause the universe to contract, the resulting Big Crunch would also wipe out all life.

Thus, if left to its own, the Earth and human life could flourish theoretically for hundreds of millions and even billions of years; to do that, however, we need to be able to transfer life to other solar systems. The question is what kind of life are we talking about. If life continues that long it certainly will be entirely different from the life we are experiencing now. Almost certainly it would involve creatures that will be more like a combination of a robot and a computer than a human being. Is that what we want? I believe not! It would not be my choice to have life endured in the form of computerized robots. But if that is the choice of the majority of people, we must at some time decide what our priorities are and what we value in life. The sorting out of these priorities and values cannot be left to scientists, but must be decided by society at large, since there will be many philosophical and religious considerations to be taken into account. This makes the practice of any religion and philosophy, which provides the world with values to live by, a basic requirement for the continuation of a meaningful life in the universe.

IVc   Are We Alone in the Universe?

The question, are we alone in the universe or are there other creatures like us living somewhere in the universe, has intrigued humans ever since they became aware of their surroundings and the immense size of the universe. Of course, the interest by the general public has been greatly increased in the last decades by the appearance of a flood of science fiction books, and by the movies and TV programs in which earthlings travel from galaxy to galaxy with the greatest of ease and encounter other hostile civilizations. And then, of course, there is the appearance in the press of stories about alien visits, alien abductions, and the sighting of flying saucers.

Before we consider whether these appearances are in any way real, let us consider what the possibilities are that there are civilizations out there that might be reaching out to us. Just in passing, I must say, however, that if they are out there, and that is a big if, they are behaving in an extraordinarily strange way in making contact with us. I hope that if we are ever able to reach other civilizations that we behave in a more organized and intelligent fashion.

The problem is that we are dealing with such immense numbers. Our galaxy alone contains some 100 billion stars and there are literally billions of galaxies stretching out to the far edges of the universe. Just to make things more confusing, we may also have to consider whether there are other universes somewhere out there, which might operate on completely different principles but still have produced life similar to our own.

If we, for the present, confine ourselves to the part of the universe closest to us, our Milky Way galaxy, the question reduces to, are there stars with planets among these 100 billion stars that have the necessary conditions so that intelligent life, somewhat like our own, could have developed? If there are, the question then is, how far are they ahead of us or how far are they behind us in their development? We must remember that human civilization came into existence only in the last 10,000 years out of a total of 4.5 billion years; furthermore, our ability to send out radio waves, with which it would be possible to communicate with other civilizations, came only in the last 100 years.

Considering that the universe came into being some fifteen billion years ago, it is safe to assume that any life that exists elsewhere is either billions of years ahead of us or billions of years behind us in their development. If they are even thousands of years ahead of us, they should, if they are anything like us, by now have found a way to locate us and contact us. Someone who does not believe that there is extraterrestrial life out there uses precisely this argument. If they are out there, where are they? They should have been able to contact us long ago.

A further consideration is that a good percentage of the stars that are out there are too young to have produced life even if all the conditions for life exist. On the other hand, if the stars on which life developed are too old, the star supporting life on that planet may have burned out, thereby extinguishing any life that may, at one time, have existed there.

The problem is that there are so many stars and there is so much time. In human terms the numbers are almost infinite and so is the time. Infinity is such a strange concept that we cannot really grasp what it is or what is meant by it. But taking our everyday understanding of it, one can argue that with infinite time and an infinite number of stars, anything that is at all possible will happen. This would include the probability that thousands of monkeys typing at random on their typewriters would eventually produce one of Shakespeare's dramas. The possibility that this would happen is indescribably small, but given enough time it will happen. The problem is, of course, that no one will ever be able to find the whole Shakespearean drama between the innumerable completely unintelligible nonsense lines.

Let us take our galaxy for instance; it is reputed to have some 100,000,000,000 stars. If we assume that there are no more than five independent conditions necessary for life to develop and that each condition has a one per cent probability, then at the end of the day, we are left with ten stars on which all the conditions for life are met. For example, if we assume that only one per cent of the stars in our galaxy have satellites, that leaves 1,000,000,000 stars. If we further assume that of these, only one per cent are at the right distance from the star to allow life to exist, we are left with 10,000,000 stars, etc.

So, what are the conditions that we believe must be fulfilled before intelligent, conscious life can develop anywhere? In his book, *Paradigms Lost*, John Casti[10] makes a detailed assessment of the probability that human intelligence is unique in the universe. He asks, "Is there anything special about human beings that really count?" He approaches the question from six different angles:

- The first approach considers the origin of life. Is the particular way in which life arose here on Earth a statistical fluke, unlikely to be repeated anywhere else, or is it an almost inevitable outcome given similar environmental conditions? As pointed out in Chapter IIIc, there are a number of special conditions that must be met for life to be able to develop. After considering these, Casti comes to the conclusion that, if we were ever wiped off the face of the Earth by some catastrophe, the likelihood of life to form again, even in a few billion years, would be very small. His conclusion is yes: not only is human life something special, but so is life in general.

- The second consideration is of a sociobiological nature. He asks: are most human social behavior patterns innate, or are they primarily acquired by means of learning and/or cultural conditioning? Casti's conclusion: maybe, human behavior could very well be special, differing in essentials from that of other living things.

- The third consideration concerns the acquisition of language. The question is: is the human language capability a unique product of the way the human brain and body happen to be put together? His conclusion is yes: the language capability points strongly towards the position that human beings are unique.

- The fourth consideration concerns artificial intelligence. The question is: is there anything unique about our way of thinking or can we duplicate the human cognitive process in a machine? His answer is that he believes that our cognitive capacities are not very special, because it may be possible to construct a thinking machine with these capacities.

- The fifth consideration concerns extraterrestrial intelligence. The question he asks is: as living, intelligent, communicating entities, are we human beings unique in the galaxy? His answer is that we are probably alone, at least in this galaxy, and that we are probably unique in the universe as well.

- The sixth consideration concerns quantum reality. The question he asks is: is the human presence necessary to bring reality into existence? This one is probably the most difficult to understand, but it follows from the quantum theories as briefly described in Chapter II. Some people argue that there is no such thing as an objective physical reality that does not depend on the presence of an observer. Most people, however, will argue that there is indeed a reality independent of the observer. So, Casti's answer to the question is that it is inconclusive.

The end conclusion of Casti is yes: human beings are a very special creature and are unique in the universe.

There are, of course, others who argue that the number of stars and the time available is so large that the universe must be teeming with other life and other intelligent beings. In the end, our choice depends also on how we regard the origin of life from a more philosophical/religious perspective. In Chapter IIId we listed three possibilities:

- If we consider life a miracle or a stupendously improbable accident, then life on Earth can be considered to be unique.
- If we consider life an inevitable outcome of physics and chemistry, then there is probably life elsewhere.
- And, if we consider life to be the result of a divine act, then we can only stand back and say, with God anything is possible.

Before we leave this subject, it may be well to consider the religious and philosophical impact the discovery of life elsewhere in the universe would have on the average person. The impact on the general public would probably be minimal; they have for years now lived with stories about extraterrestrial life in movies and on television that they are probably resigned to the fact that there are other worlds out there.

For the religious people the proof of life elsewhere would probably have a more profound effect. For the Christian the most important question would be: if there are other intelligent beings out there, do they have a concept of God and are they created in the image of God? We certainly cannot, a priori, decide that we are the only children of God. For instance, E. L. Mascall,[11] a philosopher/priest, is quoted in John Davies's book, *Are We Alone?*, as follows:

> The suggestion which I want to make... is that there are no conclusive theological reasons for rejecting the notion that, if there are, in some other part or parts of the universe, rational corporeal beings who have sinned and are in need of redemption, for those beings and for their salvation the Son of God has united (or one day will unite) to his Divine Person their nature, as he has united ours.

What he is saying is that any extraterrestrial beings, if they are out there, could very well relate to God in the same way as we do.

So, if I ever were to encounter a person or intelligence from outer space, my first ten questions would probably be something like these:

- Do you, in your world, have a concept of God as the Creator and Sustainer of the universe?
- Do you have a belief that you are created in God's image with a free will?

- In what way has this God revealed himself to you, and do you have any direct or indirect contact with this Creator?
- Do you in your civilization have any concept of right or wrong? If so, do you consider wrongdoing as a sin against your Creator's will?
- Do you have anything in your history like the figure of Jesus, as a mediator between you and the Creator, someone who showed you the way how life should be lived?
- Does your civilization have concepts such as: soul, mind, body, consciousness or collective unconsciousness?
- Similarly, do you have anything like the concept of love, beauty, compassion, faith or hope?
- Do you experience death, and do you believe in a life hereafter?
- Have you encountered other living, intelligent beings in your journeys through the galaxy?
- Then there would be thousands of technical questions such as how did you get here? Do you have DNA molecules, genes, etc.?

It is clear that if most of the questions regarding God and his relationship with these beings is positive, we should welcome them as brothers or sisters. It should strengthen our faith and greatly encourage people to think more about themselves and this world in religious terms. If, on the other hand, most questions were answered in the negative, it would have a severe impact on the Christian, and probably the Muslim, belief system.

IVd The Search for Extraterrestrial Life

The idea that there could be other worlds out there is certainly not a new one. According to Paul Davies, the ancient Greeks were debating the question and generally accepted the idea that there were indeed other worlds out there in the universe. Later in Rome, the poet and philosopher, Epicurus, wrote: "It is in the highest degree unlikely that this Earth and sky is the only one to have been created."

This interest in people who might possibly be out there has continued unabated through the centuries. So it is no wonder that as soon as it became technically possible to start searching for the existence of other intelligent beings, efforts were made to do so by the powers that had the technical know-how, that is the U.S.S.R. and the U.S.A.

The first attempts that were made were all based on sending spacecraft out to investigate. The first ones, of course, that attracted the greatest attention were the Apollo landings on the Moon. At the time, great precautions were taken to prevent possible hostile bacteria or microbes to be transferred to our Earth. As a consequence, the first astronauts, after safely returning to Earth, spent long hours in decontamination chambers. The samples of rocks they brought back with them showed no signs of life, and it was assumed that life did not and had not in the past existed on the Moon.

Later, in 1976, NASA, the American space agency, landed a Viking space ship on Mars. The rock samples they brought back also did not show any signs of life now existing or having existed in the past. Since Mars is judged to be the only planet in our solar system on which our type of life could possibly exist, it is concluded from these results that we are alone, at least in our solar system. More recently, after very simple life forms were found to exist in deeply situated rocks on Earth, scientists have begun to wonder if similar forms of life could possibly be found to exist buried deep below the surface of the Moon and/or Mars.

In 1973, NASA launched Pioneer 10, the first spacecraft to go beyond our solar system. At this point in time it is "slowly" winding its way through space. It is not expected to arrive at any planet/star combination for the next thousands of years. It carries on board a plaque that has engraved on it some basic data about our Earth and its inhabitants. For instance, it carries a picture of a naked man and a woman; also, there is a picture giving some indication where we are located within the galaxy. Of course, if it ever lands safely anywhere, it will most likely be on a sterile surface such as that of Mars. But, even if it landed on an inhabited planet, it is still highly unlikely that it would be found by inhabitants who would be able to decipher the message and send a response that could be understood by us.

The foregoing attempts to make contact with the possible world out there were all made with spacecraft and rockets. A much cheaper way of doing so is through the use of radio telescopes. The assumption is that if there are intelligent beings out there, some of them at least will be way ahead of us in their development, and they will have been exploring the universe for maybe thousands, or even millions, of years. If they are as advanced as that, they must have sent radio messages which we should be able to pick up with radio telescopes. So, in 1992, NASA launched the SETI program (Search for Extraterrestrial Intelligence) which uses a number of radio telescopes placed around the world. The problem, of course, is that there are so many stars to aim at and so many frequencies on which these messages could have been sent. Even by concentrating on the most likely frequencies and using the latest techniques of computer-controlled search programs, the possibility that they will lock in on the right frequency from the right star or stars is unlikely. However, unlikely success may be, it is the only way to find out and therefore, I believe, worthwhile. The problem with radio messages is that they can only move with the speed of light, so that if we ever make contact, it could take hundreds if not thousands of years for a message sent from Earth to arrive at its destination. This makes for a very slow dialogue and, if the initial message does not contain a lot of information about the life of the extraterrestrial beings, we will remain in the dark for a long time.

All the foregoing discussions and speculations assume that the life we will encounter is somewhat like our own. Considering the advanced state these civilizations must be in, in order to be able to contact us, it is highly unlikely that this is so. I believe that there are at least three possibilities that must be considered:

- If the intelligence we encounter originates from a long dead star, which is a very good possibility, the creature we most likely will encounter will be in the form of a robot that may have lots of information built into it, but it will not be a creature with a soul or consciousness with which we can interact.

- If the intelligence we encounter comes from an active star/planet system, we will probably encounter it first in the form of a robot but one that can put us in contact with the originators of the robot. Communication would be possible but would be extremely slow.

- If the intelligence we encounter is not in the form of a robot or machine, but in the form of an intelligent, self-conscious being, we will still find that this is a "modified" being which has been adapted to survive the long journey from there to here. Most likely, it will have computers implanted in its body to activate or reactivate certain bodily functions. In any case, we would hope that it could put us into contact with the unmodified beings at its home base.

In any event, if we ever make contact with extraterrestrial beings, it will probably be difficult for us to decide whether we are dealing with the equivalent of a human being or with a machine.

In practical terms, the search for extraterrestrial beings is exciting but it is unlikely to have any important impact on our lives today. If they exist, it will take hundreds, if not thousands, of years before we can determine who and what they are. In particular, whether they are anything like what we are now or like what we might be in the future.

For a more detailed discussion of the SETI program and the search for extraterrestrial life, including an evaluation of the many reported sightings of UFOs (unidentified flying objects), see a recent book by Joel Achenbach[12] entitled, *Captured By Aliens, The Search for Life and Truth in a Very Large Universe*. The main title is somewhat misleading in that the author doesn't give much credence to the theory that there are aliens, within striking distance from our planet, who can do any capturing of human beings.

NOTES

[1] Hartmann, William and Miller, Ron, *The History of Earth*, Workman Publishing Co. Inc., 1991.

[2] Toffler, Alvin and Heidi, *War and Anti-War, Survival at the Dawn of the 21st Century*, Little, Brown and Company, Boston, 1993.

[3] Küng, Hans, *On Being a Christian*, Collins, London, 1977, p.39.

[4] Reiss, Bob, *The Coming Storm: Extreme Weather and our Terrifying Future*, Hyperion, New York, 2001.

[5] Bohm, David and Peat, David, *Science, Order and Creativity*, Bantam Books, New York, 1987.

[6] Kaku, Michio, *Hyperspace*, Oxford University Press, Oxford, New York, 1994.

[7] Tarna, Richard, *The Passion of the Western Mind, Understanding the Ideas that Have Shaped our Worldview*, Ballantine Books, Random House, New York, 1991, p.412.

[8] Horgan, John, *The End of Science, Facing the Limits of Knowledge in the Twilight of the Scientific Age*, Addison Wesley Publishing Co, 1996.

[9] Tippler, Frank J., *Physics of Immortality, Modern Cosmology, God and the Resurrection of the Dead*, Doubleday, New York, 1994.

[10] Casti, John, *Paradigms Lost*, William Morrow, New York, 1989.

[11] Mascall, Eric L., "Importance of Being Human", Greenwood Publishing Group Inc., 1974, quoted in John Davies's book, *Are We Alone?*

[12] Achenbach, Joel, *Captured by Aliens, the Search for Life and Truth in a Very Large Universe*, Simon and Schuster, New York, NY, 1999.

Chapter V
THE HUMAN BEING

Va   Introduction

In the previous chapters we have discussed in some detail how life and, in particular, human life came to be, but very little was said about what human beings are and how they function. Just as the ideas about how humans were created have undergone major changes, so has our understanding of what constitutes a human being and how it interacts with its surroundings and its environment. As we found when looking at how life was created, so it is when we look at how our human body and mind function. The complexity and the beauty of the way we function is so astonishing that it is very difficult not to see the mind of an Intelligence behind this creation.

First of all, we should ask ourselves, what constitutes a human being? In its most simple definition we might describe the human being as an assembly of two separate components: a physical body and a spiritual mind which interact with each other on all levels of existence. The physical body we all know too well as we are daily made aware of its strengths and weaknesses – what it can do and what it cannot do. Not so, however, with the spiritual component to our existence. We generally have only a very vague idea what it is and what it can do. Also, there is a great diversity of opinion on how the spiritual component of our being works, what it includes, and how it interacts with the physical component of the human body.

As indicated before, major changes have taken place in our understanding of the physical and spiritual make-up of the human being. To appreciate what these changes mean to our understanding of the spiritual parts of ourselves, I will, in the next pages, use a time frame suggested by Dr. Larry Dossey[1] in his book, *Healing Words*. Dr. Dossey divides the more recent history of our understanding of the interaction between body, mind and soul in three different eras as follows:

- Era I – The era of mechanical, material and physical medicine that dominated medicine from the 1860s to about 1950, and which is still influential today.
- Era II – The era after 1950 when Western medicine started to recognize the healing power the mind can exercise over the physical and mental well-being of the body.
- Era III – The new era in science and medicine in which it is gradually becoming recognized that, outside the mind and the body, there is another component to our existence. It postulates that this new component is not confined by time and space and is therefore eternal.

In the following sections, these three eras in our understanding of the interaction of the body, mind and spiritual components of our being will be used to describe our changing attitudes to, and our knowledge of, what we really are. However, before we go into this in any detail, I believe it will be useful to describe briefly the miraculous way the human body is formed and how it receives, stores and processes the information it obtains from inside and outside the body.

Vb Cells – the Building Blocks of Human Life

Every part of the human body is made up of cells and the things they produce. It is estimated that the human body contains something like sixty trillion (60,000,000,000,000) cells. They vary enormously in function, shape and size: for instance, the nerve cells with their thousands of spikes can be meters long, while the blood cells are round and are only fractions of millimeters in size. Finally, there are small living creatures, such as amoebae, which consist of only one cell.

All these cells, whether animal or plant, have the same basic structure (see Figure 5.1). The outside consists of an incredibly thin membrane which encloses the cell fluid or cytoplasm. In the membrane are tiny pores or openings through which the substances made in the cell can migrate to the outside. Within the cell there exist, in addition to the cell nucleus, a number of different units or organelles each with their own specific task. For our purpose the most important of these are the mitochondria whose main job is to convert energy from one form into another. It is these mitochondria which were mentioned in the previous chapter as being instrumental in establishing the theory that humans descended from one female in Africa because mitochondria are passed on only through the female gender. The shape of the cell is maintained by an internal scaffolding of different types of fibers and struts. If nothing else, the figure shows the incredible complexity of the basic cell, and that is without looking at what is stored in the cell's nucleus.

Amazing as it may seem, most cells in the human body do not have a very long life; they die and are replaced on a regular schedule. It is estimated that each hour in a person's life some 200 billion cells die and are replaced by exact copies of the original through a process called cell splitting. Liver cells, for instance, live on the average only some 500 days, while red blood cells last 120 days and white blood cells have an average lifespan of only 10 to 13 days. The cells that make up our skin are replaced at a rate of some 100,000 per minute; it is said that the dust that accumulates in our houses is made up in a large part by these discarded skin cells. Some cells such as the nerve cells in the brain and in the central nervous system are permanent fixtures: they cannot divide and, if for some reason they are damaged or die, they cannot be replaced, which has rather severe consequences for the effective operation of the central nervous system.

Before leaving the subject of cell splitting, it may be useful to consider the question: if all life is made up of cells that continuously split to form new cells, how did cells arrive on the scene before there were any cells?

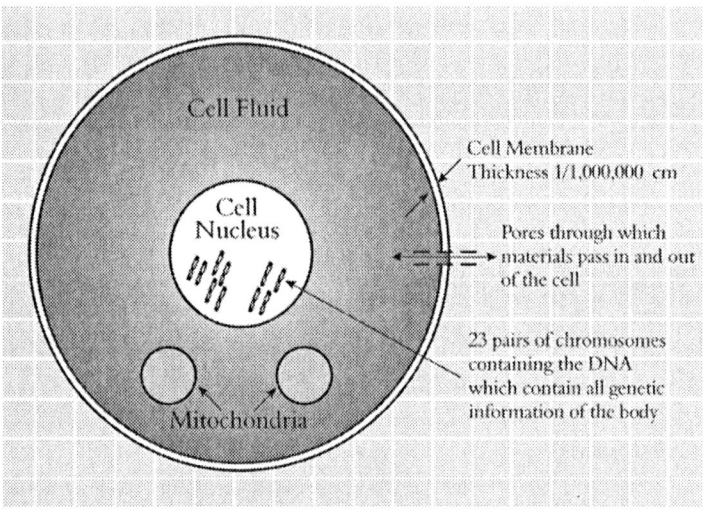

Figure 5.1
A Schematic Cross Section of a Cell
(Source: *The Human Body Explained*)

THE CELL NUCLEUS

The nucleus of each cell in the human body contains two pairs of twenty-three chromosomes or forty-six in total. Among these twenty-three pairs of chromosomes there is one pair that determines the sex of the offspring. The sex chromosomes of the female of the species contain one pair of so-called X chromosomes, while the sex chromosomes of the male contain one X chromosome and one Y chromosome.

When a body cell divides into two cells it also produces another set of chromosomes so that all new cells contain a set of twenty-three pairs of chromosomes. However, when the sex chromosomes divide the chromosome is split through the middle: as a result, the new cells of the female will have again two X chromosomes, but the new cells of the male will have one cell which contains one X chromosome while another cell will contain one Y chromosome. When, at conception, a female egg joins with a male sperm that contains an X chromosome the result will be a female offspring (XX). If, on the other hand, the female egg joins with a male sperm with a Y chromosome the resulting offspring will be male (XY). In the case of the human species, the newly fertilized egg then goes on to organize the production of all the sixty trillion cells in the human body regardless of its sex.

Each chromosome is made up of a very large molecule and its supporting proteins. This molecule, called the DNA (dioxyribo-nucleic-acid), is extremely complex and is so tightly wound inside the nucleus that its total length, when unwound, is in the order of two meters. The almost unbelievable thing is that this molecule, complicated as it may be, contains within its structure all the instructions necessary to build, run and maintain such a complex system as the human body. The molecule itself looks like a twisted ladder in the form of a double spiral or helix. The rungs of this ladder are made up of pairs of molecules which are fairly complicated themselves. These molecules are called bases and the two together are called a base pair. There are four different bases: A (adinine), T (thymine), C (cystosine), and G (guanine). For some reason, A can only pair with T and C can only pair with G, so that a rung of the ladder consists either of the pair AT or CG. The two components of this rung are held together by a hydrogen bond (see Figure 5.2).

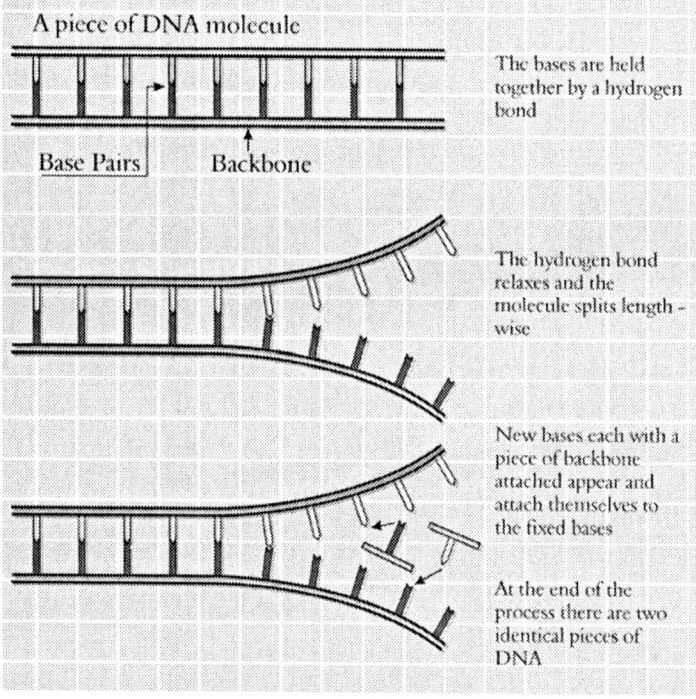

Figure 5.2
Schematic Presentation of the Replication of a DNA Molecule

A pattern of bases along the backbone of the ladder is called a gene. It is these genes that, to some considerable extent, determine the properties and characteristics of the living organism. Human cells are made up of six billion A, C, T, and G molecules (or three billion base pairs) – in other words, the DNA ladder has three billion rungs. The sum of all the DNA information in an organism is known as its genome. To help visualize this enormous amount of information in each cell, it may be helpful to think of each base pair as a word. The genetic information in each cell would then be equivalent to 3,000 books with 1,000 pages and each page containing 1,000 words. In the case of the human cell it was found that among this immense amount of data, there were only 30,000 genes. This is a surprisingly low number since it was originally thought that the human cell might contain as many as 100,000 genes. Even more surprising is the fact that, as reported in the January, 2003 issue of *Discover Magazine*, wheat and rice cells have as many as 50,000 genes each; in other words, 20,000 more than the human cell. Also, there seems to be no relation between the number of base pairs and the number of genes. For instance, the rice cell has 420 million base pairs; while the wheat cell has 16,000 million compared with the human cell which has only 3,000 million base pairs.

In 1989 the US government, in cooperation with other governments, initiated the Human Genome Project. The objective of this project was to identify the sequences of all base pairs that are contained in a cell and to locate the genes hidden in these sequences. The project was expected to be completed by 2005, but the application of computer sequencing techniques greatly accelerated the process so that the first rough draft of the human genome was completed early in 2001. One of the interesting findings of the project was that the genes make up only a small percentage of all the available data. The rest appears, at least for now, to be useless material that seems to have no useful function. Apparently, most illnesses are caused by more than one gene; the problem is then to find the gene or genes that are responsible for each illness among this massive information. Once these genes have been located the challenge will be to find cures for these illnesses. The potential for finding these is certainly there but the full benefit from this work may still be a long way off.

CELL SPLITTING

When a cell divides, each DNA molecule is miraculously split lengthwise over all its three billion base pairs (rungs). Apparently, when this happens the hydrogen bond between the bases breaks and the molecule splits up like a "zipper unzipping". The next miraculous event in this incredible sequence is that somehow each base, left hanging from the backbone, attracts the appropriate mate which just so happens to be floating around in the cell's nucleus. And, it is not only the proper base that so miraculously appears, but the base comes also with the part of the ladder's backbone, so that not only the base but also the backbone is duplicated in this way. Since both the unzipped halves go through the same process, the result is a completely new copy of the original molecule. This process goes on at great speed through all living things. The amazing thing is that this unzipping and zipping of these three billion base pairs is carried out almost flawlessly in the trillion cells in the human body. Remember, 200 billion red blood cells are duplicated in this way everyday of our lives (see also Figure 5.2). The DNA in a chromosome uses another complicated molecule named ribonucleic acid or RNA to transfer instructions to the proteins in the cell which are the actual workhorses in the body that make all these processes happen.

MUTATIONS

These processes of duplication are in the great majority of the cases carried out flawlessly; however, occasionally a mistake is made in the duplication of a cell and if this error occurs in a sex cell the error will be copied into the next generation. This completely random error will then lead to what is called a mutation of an organism. If the mutation results in a better equipped or stronger organism, the mutant may survive and may even take over from the original organism. If, on the other hand, the mutant is not as strong as the original, the mutant will die off quickly (natural selection). Since the process is completely random, the chance that a mutant will be stronger or better equipped than its parent is probably very remote. However, there are still enough of these mutations occurring that, with time, some of these mutations will result in the appearance of new species on the world scene that are, for one reason or another, better able to cope with the challenges of life in the wild than the original ones. Thus the complete random mutation in one of the sex cells of a species, plus the process of natural selection, is thought to be the process by which new species are formed and result in biological evolution. The big question, of course, is whether such completely random processes could have resulted in the creation of such complicated molecules as DNA and RNA or in the equally complicated arrangements of brain cells from the earliest cells that did not even have a nucleus. I personally find that very hard to imagine, even considering that this process has been going on for billions of years.

It is interesting to compare the intricacies of the human cell with the apparent complexity of the world of stars and galaxies. The one operates on the minuscule scale of the cell of which there are trillions in the human body alone, while the other operates on the scale of billions of stars in an almost limitless universe. Looking at it this way, the complexity of the living human cell appears to be infinitely greater than the workings of all the dead matter in the stars and galaxies of the universe taken together.

GENETIC ENGINEERING AND GENE THERAPY

Before leaving the miraculous world of the human cell, I would like to touch briefly upon a rather controversial subject – genetic engineering and its human application gene therapy. These entirely new fields of endeavor were made possible by two discoveries. The first one occurred in 1970 when it was found that there were naturally occurring enzymes in some bacteria whose function it was to destroy foreign DNA that came from invading viruses. These so-called restriction enzymes were found to be able to cut the DNA helix at specific points along the ladder every time they encountered a certain sequence of bases. Since 1970, some 400 of these restriction enzymes have been discovered, each being capable of cutting the helix at different sequences of bases. The second step was the discovery of yet another enzyme, ligase, which has the ability to splice sections of cut DNA together. It was in 1973 that these new discoveries were first used to cut out one piece of DNA from one cell and paste it to a cut section of DNA of another cell. When it was found that these cells were able to reproduce themselves, the age of genetic engineering had started. Eventually this led to the creation of disease resistant plants and later yet to the cloning of animals.

In the new gene therapy, new genes are inserted into the nucleus of sperm, eggs or even embryos. It is believed that in this way some hereditary diseases can possibly be prevented of taking hold in the offspring. Thus, this new type of therapy holds great promise for the curing of many inherited diseases and other illnesses. Unfortunately, the whole field is fraught with great dangers.

THE HUMAN BEING

At this point in time there are some forty types of experimental gene therapy programs in progress around the world in laboratories with varying safety procedures. The danger is that the insertion of foreign DNA into germ cells could have unpredictable repercussions and could lead to cancer and other fatal diseases. Also, a strain of harmful bacteria could possibly escape from a laboratory and attack organisms which have no antibody and therefore no defense against this unnatural, artificial invader. The result could be an almost impossible-to-stop epidemic. In addition, there is the ethical question of how far we should go in changing human characteristics even undesirable ones. Should we try to generate only people with a certain level of intelligence, or only people of one color, or only people with blue eyes, etc.?

It is no wonder then that there have been repeated calls to stop this mad rush into unknown fields and take time out to consider all the consequences before we proceed any further. As Jeremy Rifkin[2] wrote as early as 1983 in his book *Algeny*:

> Once we decide to begin the process of human genetic engineering, there really is no logical place to stop. If diabetes, sickle-cell disease, and cancer are to be cured by altering the genetic makeup of an individual, why not proceed to other "disorders": myopia, color blindness, left-handedness. Indeed what is to preclude a society from deciding that a certain skin color is a disorder.

More recently, late 1999, David Suzuki and Holly Dressel[3] in their book, *From Naked Ape to Superspecies, A Personal Perspective on Humanity and the Global Eco Crisis*, warn about the many dangers of genetic manipulation. Suzuki, who is a geneticist by profession, writes:

> One reason biotechnology is dangerous is its imprecision. For every genetic engineering success there are thousands

and thousands of failures... So, as we move genes from one species to another, we will keep getting unpredictable effects which simply could not have been anticipated.

He sites the example of a biotech firm that has engineered a bacterium that can get rid of farm wastes. When it was finally tested in living soils it caused all plants in the area to die because of an unanticipated reaction between the new bacterium and other microorganisms in the soil. Fortunately, this mistake was caught before the new bacterium was widely used with a potentially disastrous result.

In another recent book, the author Michael Fox[4] paints a frightening picture of what is happening in the field of genetic engineering which he says is being pursued in an ethical vacuum and in secrecy. He writes:

> The integrity and future of creation is threatened more by this new technology than by any other past human invention or activity, including nuclear fission and the development and release of petrochemicals into the environment.

From these and a multitude of similar warnings, it is clear that great caution is needed in these fields of genetic engineering and gene therapy. Not only is there the real problem of accidental release of engineered – unnatural and dangerous – organisms, there is also the big ethical question: are we justified in tinkering with nature, and do we really know what we are doing? For instance, in order to prevent the birth of children with certain handicaps, are we not thereby depriving the world of future geniuses such as Stephen Hawkins and Ludwig von Beethoven?

While acknowledging the dangers associated with the application of these new technologies, some people believe that there is another way of looking at this. The Christian belief has always been that God created humans to be co-creators with him. Following this line of thought, they believe that genetic engineering may be one of the ways humans can participate in that continuing creation process.

One last comment about genes and their ability to determine human behavior: the discovery of genes and their effect on human behavior initially caused some scientists to overreact and state that all our actions are determined by our genetic make-up. It would then be easy to take the next step and say that we are therefore not responsible for our actions and that, in fact, we do not have a free will. While not many people will go so far as that, there is, however, a spirited debate going on about the extent that genes are responsible for our physical and mental characteristics and our behavior. In considering this, it must be remembered that genes themselves do nothing else but produce certain proteins that cause certain complex neurological events to take place.

Any one character trait we may have is shaped by a mixture of different proteins and not by any one specific gene. It is our upbringing, our own will and our environment that will eventually decide what we are and what we will become as humans. At best, genes can present tendencies but they do not dictate action. For instance, it has been found with identical twins that if one is homosexual there is only a fifty per cent chance that the other one will also be. On the other hand, among fraternal twins this chance was found to be only twenty per cent.

In the book *Controlling our Destinies; Historical, Philosophical, Ethical and Theological Perspectives of the Human Genome Project* edited by Philip R. Sloan, the following statement clarifies, I believe, the situation regarding the connection between our genes and our behavior:[5]

> A survey as this highlights the superficiality of any talk which speaks of there being particular genes for particular

> kinds of human behavior. Firstly, behavior is nearly always influenced by complex sets of genes and the link between the immediate output of these genes and human behavior is extremely tenuous – not the least because even the synapsal linkages in the brain are not entirely genetically determined, but depend on the input from learned experiences which creates new ones, and which in the human case, means the input from experiences mediated by human culture.
>
> Also, a human person is not a static entity, but is always in process of becoming – one ought to speak of human becomings rather than human beings.

In the same vein, George Colt and Anne Hollister wrote in an article published in the April 1998 issue of *Life* as follows:

> In any case, if genes are not commands but nudges, we can nudge back. We are the only animal on Earth that can overrule our genes. And we do so constantly – whenever an alcoholic chooses not to drink or an obese person diets... Someone with a propensity for aggression might become an Adolf Hitler, but he might also become a General Patton. We cannot change the genes, but we can change the ways genes express themselves. We can change behavior.

It is this ability to change behavior that makes us responsible for our actions and which places this emphasis on our upbringing: the examples we are given by our parents, teachers, etc. It places the responsibility for our behavior squarely back on our own shoulders and on the shoulders of our caregivers.

Vc   The Human Immune System

The main function of the trillions of cells in the human body is to produce the proteins which are the main building material of the body. However, some of these cells and proteins have as their special function to protect the body against the invasion of viruses, bacteria, fungi, parasites and poisons with which the body comes into contact on an almost ongoing basis. The total of these defenses against the attack by these foreign bodies is called the immune system. It is a system that operates as miraculously as any system in nature. Some of the workings are not clear as of today, but what we do know shows such a fine-tuned operation that is so amazing and effective that it almost defies description. To understand the details requires a thorough knowledge of chemistry; however, the general outline of the system as described in the following pages is, I believe, not difficult to follow and reveals some of the wonders of this system on which our lives depend.

The first line of defense against foreign invaders is the human skin on the exposed parts of the body and the mucous fluids that protect the various body openings such as the mouth, nose, ears, etc. They effectively prevent any viruses and bacteria from entering the bloodstream and doing their destructive work. However, when that skin is pierced or cut in any way, there are two dangers that must be met immediately. First, the loss of large quantities of blood must be prevented. Secondly, the viruses and bacteria that now have free access to the bloodstream must be destroyed before they can penetrate further into the body. The body does this by going all out to close the opening as quickly as possible by the formation of a blood clot that seals off the open area. In the book, *The Human Body Explained*, the authors[6] call the process by which this is achieved another of the body's minor biochemical miracles. They write:

> It may seem so simple – the blood thickens and blocks the flow (of blood) – but it is a complex process which requires as many as thirty-five chemicals to work together

in a precise sequence of steps. This cascade of reactions will in a few minutes patch the hole so that no more blood can escape... After the blood clotting, the wound starts to close and in about twenty-four hours the clot has dried out to form a scab.

Unfortunately, the same clotting process does not take place when blood-sucking insects, such as mosquitoes, fleas and lice, take a drink from our blood supply. By rights, the blood in their stomach should immediately solidify and teach them never to feed on us again. However, over the centuries they have developed inhibitors that prevent this from happening and so they continue with their evil deeds.

In some people the same type of inhibitors effectively prevent blood clotting when the skin is cut, with the result that even minor cuts can lead to heavy loss of blood and even death. Unfortunately, this condition called hemophilia is hereditary and can be passed on from mother to son. The British-Russian royal families are probably the best-known sufferers of this condition.

The foreign invaders that manage to penetrate the human body run up against the defenses organized by the white blood cells of the immune system. There are several lines of defense: if one line cannot hold the enemy in check, the next line of defense is called upon and so on (see also Figure 5.3). The first line of defense is the so-called feeding cells such as the large macrophages, the granulocytes and the monocytes. These cells feed on the invading material mainly by engulfing them and gobbling them up. It is these cells that keep wounds and tissues clean of foreign matter. Some of the bacteria and viruses are immune to attack by the feeding cells; if this happens, the special defense forces are called in consisting of the T-cells, the B-cells and something that is called the complement factor. The complement factor increases the efficiency of the T and B-cells, sometimes by shooting holes in the invaders. As shown in Figure 5.3, the T-cells come in three different types: the helper cells, the killer cells and the suppressor cells. The helper cells detect the invaders even if they are hidden in the body's own cells and call upon the B-cells and the feeder cells to destroy the infected cell. When needed they also call in the help of the suppressor cells to curb the aggression of other cells. The killer cells kill the cells of the body that contain foreign material as indicated by the helper cells. In *The Body Victorious* the author, Nilsson Lennart,[7] describes the other function of the T-cells as follows:

> Every episode in this process also generates T-cells with a particular task; that is to remember for decades, if not for life, the disease-producing substances which invaded the body. The invaders' descriptions are stored in the vast criminal records of the immune system. When a substance matching one of the stored descriptions makes a new appearance, the memory cells see to the swift manufacture of the appropriate antibodies to combat it. The invasion is defeated before it can make us ill. We are immune.

It is the B-cells that actually manufacture the antibodies. There is a specific antibody for each of the millions of different invaders. The antibody itself is a small Y-shaped molecule. At one end it has a structure that fits exactly, like a key in a lock, into the outside of the appropriate invader; it then calls in the complement system to kill the invader through a complicated chemical process. In the end, the macrophages come around and clean up the mess of dead body cells and dead invaders. If the proper antibodies for a virus are not available, modern medicine has found a way by injecting the body with a very small amount of the particular virus – vaccination. This triggers the body to produce the proper antibody for this type of virus, which then is available whenever this type of virus attacks the body

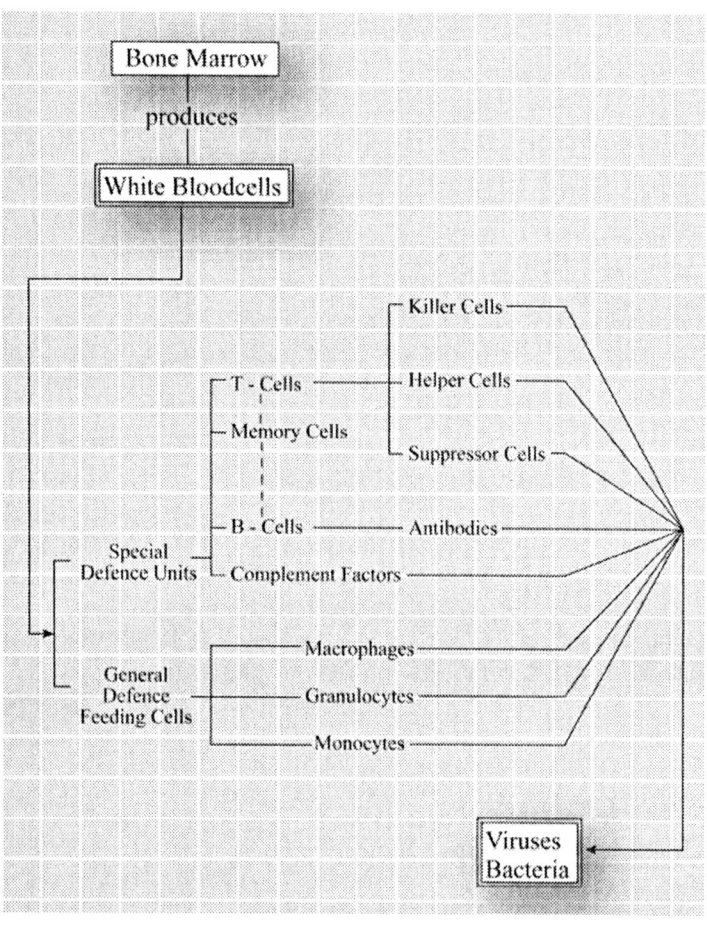

Figure 5.3
A Simplified Diagram of the Operation of the Human Immune System

in the future.

From this very abbreviated exposé, it is clear that for the immune system to work it must be able to do three things:

- First, it must remember its enemies. Once a body has produced an antibody to fight a certain foreign matter, the immune system will continue to produce it so that it is available when the invader shows up again in the bloodstream.
- Second, it must distinguish one invader from the other instantly so that each invading body will be fought by its proper antibody without any waste of time.
- Third, it must recognize its own cells so that it does not destroy these as well.

This "exquisitely precise defense mechanism" is absolutely vital for the well-being of all living creatures. However, occasionally the bacteria and viruses are not killed in time and illness and disease will result. In some cases, the immune system itself is damaged or destroyed. When that happens the person is without defense against all these possible invaders, resulting in the contracting of one disease after another. This condition, AIDS (acquired immune deficiency syndrome), is presently the subject of intense research all over the world: indications are that we may be on the threshold of discovering ways by which we can restore the immune system to its former effectiveness.

The immune system is such a system of precisely interacting sections that it is almost impossible to think that it could have developed purely by chance. It is conceivable that evolution over time could have produced one type of cell of the immune system; say, the killer cells. However, without the active involvement of the helper cells to identify the invading organism, and of the feeding cells to clear up afterwards, the system would have been ineffective; the body would have died anyway and the mutation would have been found not viable. It appears that for the immune system to work almost the entire line-up of dozens of different cells is required. Thus, the creation of an effective immune system by evolution and natural selection would require the mutation of dozens of very special cells to take place at the same time, which would seem to be impossible. Thus, I believe, the immune system is one of these irreducibly complex systems, described in Chapter III, which point to the active involvement of a Guiding Intelligence in the creation of the physical body and of the universe.

Recently, it has been recognized that the immune system should more properly be called a network of interacting components and that the endocrine system, the nervous system, and the immune system all work together and should be seen as a single psychosomatic network (Fritjof Capra[8] in *The Web of Life*). This makes the likelihood that this system was created purely by chance even more remote.

Vd   The Formation of the Human Body

Our physical existence starts with the joining together of the male sperm and the female ovum through what is generally called the sexual act or mating. This mating is a drive built in all living creatures; the difference is that humans appear to be one of the few species which seem to enjoy the experience and engage in the activity entirely independent of the menstrual cycle of the female.

During the mating process as many as 300,000 to 500,000 male sperms enter the female body and, in general, only one of these will penetrate the female egg; that is if there is one available at the time, and in so doing start the process of reproduction. All the other sperms, all containing the same fantastic array of genetic information, will die in a fairly short period of time and all the information they contain is lost. I guess this is the same for plants and trees which every year produce an abundance of seeds of which maybe only one in a million will become a fully grown plant or tree.

After the male sperm and the female egg join together, one of the most amazing and mysterious processes in all of creation begins to take place. The original cells start to divide and keep forming new cells with all the DNA and genes in their proper place. For instance, what starts off as a two-meter-long length of DNA in the original cells ends up as a total length of 100,000 million meters in the new cells, and all, with a few exceptions, are perfect copies of the original DNA. But the most astonishing thing of them all is the fact that, from the original sperm and egg cells, billions of cells of a mind-boggling diversity are produced, each in about the right number. The question then arises, how can so many different cell types come from the same source? How does one cell know to transform itself in a round blood cell, fractions of a millimeter in size, and another to transform itself in a meter-long nerve cell with its surface covered in spikes? Furthermore, how do these cells know where to go in the embryo and in what quantity: the blood cell to the appropriate artery and the nerve cell to the proper set of nerves in the nervous system? The miraculous nature of this process is described by Richard Lewontin,[9] professor of biology at Harvard University, in a book entitled *It Ain't Necessarily So, The Dream of the Human Genome and other Illusions* as follows:

> The nucleus of a cell of the fruit fly has enough DNA to specify the structure of about 5,000 different proteins, and about thirty times that much DNA is available to provide spatial and temporal instructions about when the production of proteins by these genes should be turned on and turned

off. But this is simply too little, by many orders of magnitude, to tell every cell when it should divide, exactly where it should move to next, and what cellular structure it should produce over the entire developmental history of the fly. One needs to imagine an instruction manual that would tell every New Yorker when to get up, where to go, and what to do, hour by hour, day by day, for the next century. There is just not enough DNA to go around.

In the particular case of the formation of the brain, it appears that cells migrate to a specific area in the growing fetus and, once having arrived there, start to mature and differentiate. James Trefil[10] in his book, *Are We Unique?*, compares it to the construction of a large building. First, the foundations are going in, then the steel frame goes up, and then the building is closed in. By this time, the shape of the building is clear from the outside, but it takes months of work to complete the plumbing, the electrical wiring, the heating and ventilating, etc. before the building can be used. Just in this way, Trefil writes, the rough outline of the brain can be seen early in the life of the fetus, but the final details will take months to complete.

All other organs of the body are formed in the same wondrous and miraculous manner. Paul Davies[11] writes in *The Cosmic Blueprint* that in studying the development of the embryo it is hard to resist the impression that there exists somewhere a blueprint, a plan of assembly, which shows in detail where all the different pieces need to go to achieve the intended form. Of course, this does nothing to solve the mystery of the process because we are now going to ask where this blueprint came from and where it is stored. To my mind, the most satisfactory explanation is that our Creator included in nature a set of form-giving fields or "fields of influence" which are part and parcel of the created universe. These fields, as mentioned in Chapter II and first proposed by Rupert Sheldrake, are not material but, at the same time, they are presumed to permeate everything and are the agents through which nature operates to give form not only to the microcosm of atoms and cells but also the macrocosm of stars and galaxies. In our particular case, they are thought to guide the process which eventually results in the creation of a new human being with all its parts in place and all systems functioning, both the bodily as well as the spiritual.

One thing is clear, at least to my mind, and that is this wonderful mysterious process could simply not have evolved through an evolutionary process only. Instead, I believe that the process is guided by a blueprint, or something akin to it, that is embedded in nature by a Guiding Intelligence or Creator.

Ve   Cloning and Stem Cell Research

Before continuing with the description of this marvelous creation of life in general, and human life in particular, I would like to introduce two entirely new techniques that will have a profound effect on the future of our well-being, or even the future of humankind – cloning and stem cell research.

Cloning is the process by which an organism is produced that is identical to another. Because of our new understanding of how cells and genes function, it is now theoretically possible to clone any living organisms, including humans. Cloning was first successfully carried out on a sheep (Dolly) in England in 1996. Since then, a wide variety of other mammals have been successfully cloned. Thus the technique exists for the cloning of humans as well and, in effect, trials may already be under way in some laboratory somewhere in the world. Governments across the world are trying to come to grips with this new development. Up to now, almost all governments are forbidding the creation of human clones because of its many ethical, social and legal problems. For instance, one has to be prepared to answer such questions as: what is the legal status of the clone? Should one be allowed to raise one's own clone? Should one be allowed to clone his parents? Should one be allowed to clone only dead people, etc.? Also, there is the fact that, so far, in the attempts to clone mammals, many unsuccessful attempts have been made before one successful clone is created. What is the status of these unsuccessful or incomplete clones; are they human? Can society be allowed to destroy these creatures? There are millions of other questions that must be answered before most people feel that anything like the cloning of human beings should be undertaken.

A parallel development is taking place in what is called stem cell research. This research has thrown up a host of new names, and because these terms will be used with increasing frequency in the debates that are taking place worldwide on this subject, I am giving a brief description of them below. When the female egg and the male sperm cell first meet, they immediately start to divide into two new cells and these new cells in their turn start to divide to form a cluster of cells. These first cells are called the totipotent stem cells; these cells each have the potential to develop into complete new individuals. After some time, these totipotent cells form a hollow sphere, and within this sphere other stem cells are formed called the pluripotent stem cells. These cells can divide indefinitely and can, under the right circumstances, form all the various tissues and organs in the body, but they cannot form complete individuals like the totipotent cells can. In both cases, the cells are obtained from live embryos that are destroyed in the process of extracting these cells. Another type of stem cell, the multipotent stem cell, can be found in the tissues and organs of the mature body but they can only grow into specific types of cells. They are therefore much more limited in scope. The advantage is that by using these cells, no human embryo is destroyed. The ethical question is then, are we justified in destroying embryos for our research, which, when every thing is said and done, are human beings in the process of being formed? One part of the argument is that some of these embryos are left over from trials for artificial fertilization. The ones that are not being used are eventually destroyed anyway, so the proponents argue, what is the difference?

The potential of the use of stem cells to combat various illnesses and to replace malfunctioning tissues and even organs is staggering. For instance, skin tissue has been created this way and it has been successfully grafted to replace the skin of a burn victim.

So, here we have two completely new ways of combating illnesses and diseases and to increase the human life span – gene therapy and stem cell transplants. Using stem cells it will be possible to eventually grow most of the human organs artificially and implant them in the body, thus eliminating the use of donor organs that are very scarce.

The application of these new techniques is going to have a profound effect on our social structures. For instance, with these new techniques it should be possible to extend the human life span to say 125 or even 150 years. The impact of this extended life span on our social systems will be very severe. Even more frightening is the possibility of people starting to clone for people with exceptional intelligence or artistic ability, or for one particular race or skin color.

For more information about the potential of these new techniques, see two recently published books: *The Shattered Self, The End of Natural Selection* by Pierre Baldi published by the MIT Press and *The Cooperative Gene* by Mark Ridley published by The Free Press, a subsidiary of Simon and Schuster.

All these developments do take nothing away from what was written in the previous section about the miracle of human creation. The fact that all the information to create a complete new human being is contained in one tiny stem cell is as mind-boggling as ever. Also, it must be remembered that, in using these techniques, we are not adding anything new to the creation process; we are just isolating existing stages in the reproduction process and using them in a different way. The basic procedures in the creation process remain the same. The stem cell formed at the moment of fertilization still contains all the information necessary to develop a complete human being.

As indicated before, there is simply not enough DNA in these cells to code the instructions for each individual cell to go to its allocated place in the body at the right time and in the right quantity and then be replaced at the appropriate intervals. It is clear, I believe, that there must be some other process at work, such as the "form-giving fields", mentioned before, to make all this possible. Of course, these "form-giving fields" are just as mysterious as anything else in this area of creation.

Vf   The Central Nervous System

The physical construction of the brain and the operation of the central nervous system have been the object of very intensive research over the last fifty years or so. Much of what has been discovered is mind-boggling in its complexity and, although great strides have been made, there is still much to be discovered. Below follows a brief description of how I understand we experience the inside and outside world through our five senses of seeing, tasting, smelling, hearing and touching. Later we will try to describe how we can experience some of the realities of life through other channels than through these five senses.

First of all, there is our central nervous system consisting of the brain and the spinal cord. The nerves in our body, which are literally everywhere, are all connected, directly or indirectly, to this central nervous system. There are two types of nerves: the ones that bring messages to the central nervous system and through it to the brain, and those who bring messages from the brain through the central nervous system to the muscles and glands of our body and make them act in the appropriate way. The nerves, or neurons as scientists call them, receive their messages from either the external receptors such as the receptors for the five senses, or from the internal receptors which are attached to all internal organs. They let the brain know what is happening throughout the body – when our bladder is full or when our stomach is empty. The brain sorts out these messages, in what would be called today a "central processing unit", and then sends the proper message to the muscle or gland to take the appropriate action (see Figure 5.4).

So far, this looks like a fairly straightforward system but the complexity comes in the details on how this system works: how do the receptors and nerves actually get their message to the brain, and how does the brain process this information?

First, there is the make-up and operation of the nerve or neuron itself. The nerves, like all parts of the human body, are made up of cells; each nerve is one cell with its own nucleus. This nucleus is surrounded by the cell body from which a large number of branches reach out into the area surrounding it. Each of these branches has a large number of sub-branches or spines called "dendrites". For instance, one of the cells in the brain has as many as 120,000 dendrites.

In addition, the body of the nerve cell contains a long fiber called an "axon", which at its end also has a number of branches; each of these branches ends up in what are called "nerve endings". It is through these nerve endings that connections are made with the dentrites of the adjacent nerve cells. Thus, the dentrites provide the input to the cell, and the nerve endings act as the output of the cell by which information is passed on to the next cell. A nerve fiber can be as short as one millimeter and as long as a full meter. Some of the long nerves, such as those that activate the muscles, have only one or two nerve endings, while others have nerve endings along the full length of the fiber, some of them with as many as 330,000 nerve endings per m^3 of fiber (see Figure 5.5).

This is all still relatively simple. The complexity arrives when we learn how the various nerve cells are connected to each other. Remember one cell may have as many as 120,000 dendrites and may be able to communicate with 250,000 other nerves. The result is an unbelievably complex system of interconnected nerves, so that the message, say from a taste sensor, has to find its way through these trillions of interconnections to the central nervous system. The 100 billion nerve cells in the fully developed brain, with its trillions of nerve endings, organize this jumble of messages from, in this case, the taste sensors into the experience of tasting with your palate. It is tempting to compare the system of interconnected cells in the brain with what would be involved in connecting every person, in a city like New York with its tens of millions of inhabitants, with each other. Someone has even calculated that the possible number of ways of connecting these nerve endings is larger than the number of atoms in the universe. As Ian Barbour[12] expresses it, "A higher level of organization and a greater richness of experience occur in a human being than in thousands of lifeless galaxies."

The messages themselves are sent through the system in the form of complex chemical processes or impulses. Each and every message that goes through this system of nerves has to be translated first into what, in computer jargon, we would call today this "machine language". Some nerve cells are able to send impulses at the rate of ten per second, while

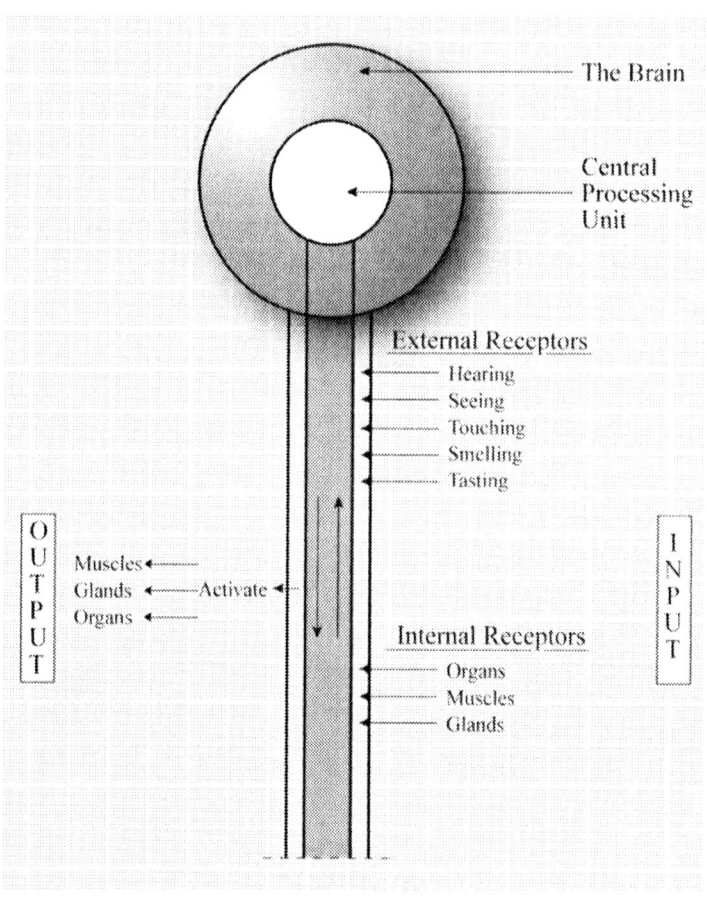

Figure 5.4
Schematic Presentation of the Central Nervous System

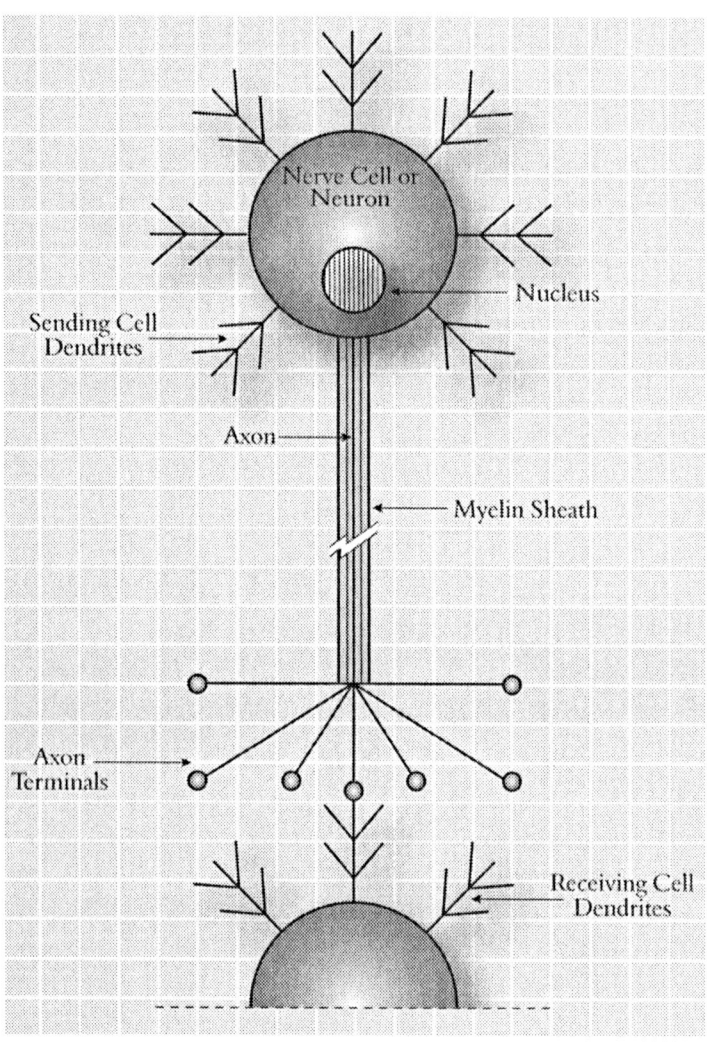

Figure 5.5
A Nerve Cell or Neuron
Source: *The Sciences: An Integrated Approach*

others manage to send as many as 500 impulses per second.

In addition to this immense processing capacity of the brain, it possesses a storage capacity that is equally astonishing. Somehow, all the memories collected during an entire life are stored in this three-pound, jelly-like material. Just think, all the things you have learned in your life are stored there and, for the most part, can be retrieved at will. It has been calculated that the brain can store up to 100 trillion bits of information. In today's parlance, that is equal to the storage capacity of 10 to 20,000 dense compact disks. How the brain stores new information can probably be best described as the making of new interconnections between brain cells each time we learn something new.

It has been argued that, even today, we are not using the total capacity of the brain. Certainly this seems to be true for the storage capacity, since we seem to be able to store more and more information as we age. Whether this is true for the intellectual capacity is debatable: some people argue that it is and believe that, if we would use the entire capacity of the brain, we would be able to understand many things that are a mystery to us today. Others argue that we have reached the limit since close examination of the brain shows that all parts are being utilized. It will be interesting to see how this argument will develop in the future. There is one miraculous capacity of the brain which has been demonstrated repeatedly and that is that humans can function quite well when, for some reason, one section of the brain becomes inoperative. Apparently, the remaining parts are able to adapt themselves to take over some, if not all, of the function of the damaged parts.

The whole process of making even the simplest of body movements consists of a series of actions, feedback, evaluation, and adjustments. For instance, the simple action of turning over a page of this book starts as a burst of electrical nerve activities in the upper part of the brain. The intention to move the page crystallizes as a plan of action for the various parts of the brain that are involved in this simple action. The signals emerge from the base of the brain and flash down the spinal cord and out along the peripheral nerves to the various muscles that must be activated to make this relatively simple move. After the message is received and the muscles, which control the action of your fingers, begin the task of turning the page, there is continuous feedback to the brain where an assessment is made of the results and, if necessary, amending orders are sent out to modify the original instructions. This prevents you from pulling the page too firmly and tearing it, or grasping it too lightly so that it slips out of your fingers. Thus every action of the body, from the smallest to the largest, is a continuous process of action, feedback, evaluation and modified action with instructions going back and forth along the millions of interconnected nerves. All the while, information about past experiences with turning pages, which is stored in the brain, is used to help in choosing the proper corrective actions.

The truly remarkable thing about this brain of ours is that it can differentiate between these millions, if not billions, of messages it receives each second from all over the body. For instance, if we take a walk in the woods, the brain distinguishes between the message from the sensors in our feet which make it possible for us to walk; the smelling sensors which make us smell the woodland; the seeing sensors which make us appreciate the scenery; and the hearing sensors which make us hear the birds. The intriguing thing is that we do not experience these totally different messages in some sort of sequence, but we experience them all at the same time. Truly amazing! As Peter Nathan[13] wrote in his book, *The Nervous System*:

> One of the questions neurology attempts to answer is how do we know what a thing is, how do we collect all sensory impressions

together and combine them to say: There is a white kitten lying curled up on the sofa. How is it that the excitation of one lot of neurons gives us the sensation of something seen, of another lot that of something heard? The straight answer to the straight question is, we do not know.

Before leaving this subject, I would like to describe in lay terms one other magnificently "engineered" transmission system. It is the way the messages are transmitted from the nerve ending of one cell to the dendrites of another cell (see Figure 5.6).

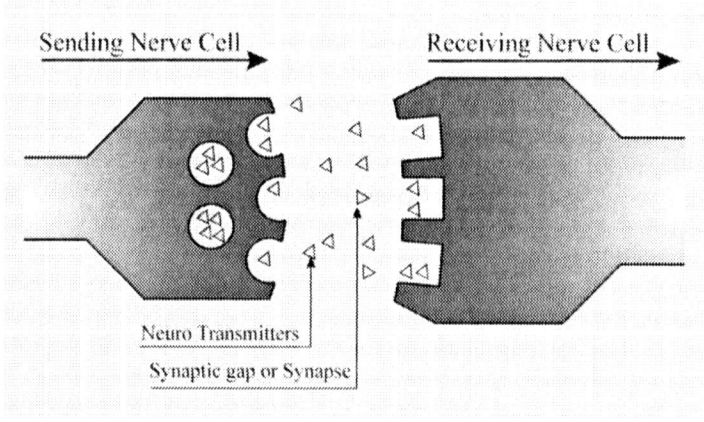

Figure 5.6
A Schematic Presentation of the Synaptic Gap Between Neurons

As shown on this schematic drawing, the two cells do not actually touch each other but are separated by a very small gap called the synapse, or the synaptic gap, where the message from one nerve cell is transmitted to another nerve cell. At this synapse, special molecules called neurotransmitters are released from small sacks, or vesicles, in the nerve endings of the one cell to specially constructed receptors in the receiving cell. The various neurotransmitters fit exactly into the receptors of the receiving cell. This is just a presentation in the form of a diagram of what is happening at each of the millions of synapses in our body; the actual process is far more complicated but is difficult to follow without a thorough understanding of the chemistry involved.

Some nerve cells receive information from only a few other cells but connect to thousands of other nerve cells. Yet others receive information from thousands of other cells but send the messages out to only a few nerve cells. The whole system seems to work almost like magic: it is more complicated than the largest telephone exchange and, at the same time, the sensitivity of the system is truly astonishing. For instance, to quote Mary Kittredge:[14]

> The senses of human beings are not as keen as those of some other animals. A male silkworm moth, for instance, can smell a female moth seven miles away, and some bats find food by emitting high-pitched squeaks, then listening for tiny echoes that bounce off insects. But in some ways the human senses are amazingly perceptive: the skin can feel a touch as light as one-thousandth of an ounce (about the weight of a mosquito); the nose can detect some chemicals in amounts smaller than a trillionth of an ounce; and some people can taste citric acid in concentrations as small as eight parts per million which is about equivalent to a dilution of eight ounces of lemon juice in a million ounces of water.

Of course, the discussion in the previous pages is limited to what we perceive through our five senses. Many people believe that there are other senses in our human make-up: do we not speak of someone having a sixth sense? The most talked about and best known is probably the sense associated with extrasensory perception (ESP) by which people can see things happening elsewhere or see things happening in the future, etc. Most science textbooks tell us that no one has ever been able to prove that these extrasensory events do actually happen. We will return to this later when we discuss other examples of mind over matter such as faith healing, etc.

One of the more interesting phenomena associated with the world of the mind and the senses are the sensation of a phantom limb. Apparently, after someone has an arm or a leg amputated, the person can often still feel pain and other sensations from this amputated limb. Is this a continuing action of the nerve endings in the brain which were originally connected to the nerves in an arm or a leg that is not there anymore, or is there still a "field of influence" associated with this amputated limb (see later in this chapter)? In any case, the pain experienced by the amputee seems to be real enough to that person.

Before leaving the astonishing world of the human sensory system, I would like to just mention one other aspect of our brain and the knowledge stored there for later use. This is the uncanny ability of some animals to recognize certain shapes and sounds at their birth without ever having seen these shapes or heard these sounds before. For instance, many birds, on leaving the egg, seem to know the shape and movement of the predators that may be looking for them. They know the essential outline of a hawk in the sky, and they know instinctively to hide from it. Similarly, a little duckling, when it breaks through the egg, already knows the quacking sound of the mother duck and it will follow no other sound. Clearly, this information was not taught nor is it the result of experience. It simply was implanted in the brain of these animals through the inherited genes before they were born. I don't know whether you can call this a sixth sense, but it surely comes close to it.

Before closing this section, I would like to quote what John Maddox[15] writes in his recent book, *What Remains To Be Discovered*, about the human brain:

...there is only the most shaky understanding of how the human brain engenders mind – the capacity to reflect on past events, to think, and to imagine... The question is simply how a collection of apparently autonomous neurons in the brain can conspire to trigger the response that best matches the self-interest of the body in its own survival. The transduction of a sensory image, stored somewhere in the brain, into neuronal instructions for the muscles of the body to perform the appropriate action will probably be central to the explanation of the workings of the human brain.

Vg The Human Mind, Consciousness and Intelligence

As soon as we leave the purely physical component of the human being and enter into the world of the nonphysical, we run into so many different aspects of this nonphysical world that it is necessary to define precisely what is meant by the various terms and names we will be using. We are all familiar with such words as mind, consciousness and intelligence, but most of us will have difficulty in defining what is exactly meant by these terms. Then there are the others such as the soul, the unconscious, the subconscious, the universal consciousness, the psyche, etc. In order to make sure we all have a similar understanding of these terms, I have used *Webster's Dictionary* to give a definition of these words.

Webster's defines mind as follows:

- that which thinks, perceives, wills – the seat or subject of consciousness;
- the thinking and perceiving part of consciousness, intellect or intelligence;
- all of an individual's conscious experience; and
- the conscious and unconscious together – the psyche.

From this definition it is clear that the mind is very closely linked to consciousness and intelligence and to the processes of thinking, perceiving and willing. It is the mind that perceives or is conscious of the fact that a wrong has been done; it does the thinking about rectifying that wrong and wills the body to take the appropriate action. In *Consilience, The Unity of Knowledge* the author, Edward O. Wilson,[16] writes about the two different understandings of what the mind is as follows:

> Scientists remain unsure about the precise material basis of mind. Some are convinced that conscious experience has unique physical and biological properties that remain to be discovered. A few among them believe that conscious experience is too alien, too complex or both, ever to be comprehended.

Obviously, consciousness or self-awareness is an important aspect of the mind. To make sure there is no misunderstanding about the meaning of the word consciousness, I refer to *Webster's* again, which defines consciousness as follows:

- the state of being conscious;
- awareness of one's own feelings and of what is happening around us; and
- the totality of one's thoughts, feelings and impressions.

Others, like Dr. Scott Peck,[17] believe that consciousness like love, prayer, beauty, etc. are concepts that are too large for a single definition.

Amit Goswami[18] in his book, *The Self-Aware Universe*, talks about a human consciousness that is capable of creativity, love, freedom of choice, extrasensory perception, mystical experiences – a consciousness that dares to form a meaningful and evolving worldview in order to understand its place in the universe. This obviously takes the importance of consciousness one step further in that it allocates to consciousness also the ability to define our place in the universe and, in so doing, to define the importance of the human being in that universe.

John Polkinghorne[19] believes that the emergence of consciousness is the most significant event in the history of the cosmos. He adds:

> As the self-awareness developed, I suppose, that the corresponding spiritual awareness of the presence of God also became part of the experience of these living things.

The third major attribute of the mind according to Webster's definition is intelligence, which is defined as:

- the ability to perceive logical relationships;
- to use one's knowledge to solve problems; and
- to respond appropriately to novel situations.

Summarizing we get the following:

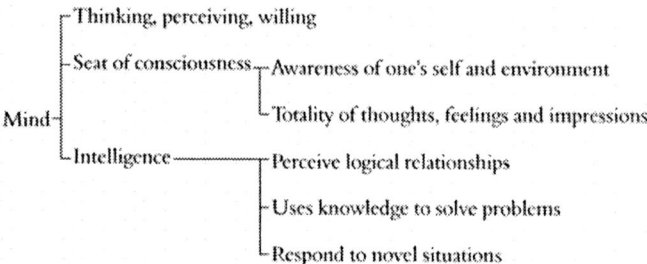

Graph Va
Various Aspects of the Human Mind

Mortimer Adler[20] in *Mind Over Matter* takes the position that intellect is an immaterial component of human nature and is humankind's highest power. Deprived of our intellectual minds we are deprived of our humanity. He goes on to write:

> If we are asked why we attribute any spirit or spirituality to man, only one answer that is rationally supportable is available to us, because we have intellectual powers that cannot be fully explained by the material, corporeal component of our physical make-up.

From our definition of consciousness and intelligence, it is clear that there is a close connection between the two. The question is then, can intelligence and consciousness exist independently of each other? Some scientists, like Paul Davies,[21] believe that the behavior of social animals, such as ants and bees, indicate that they have intelligence without consciousness. Others see consciousness without intelligence in small animals. In any case, they believe that human consciousness can only emerge when life has reached a certain level of complexity. On the other hand, scientists like David Bohm[22] believe that consciousness is not just a product of higher animals, rather they believe that it is written implicitly into all matter, and that matter emerges out of consciousness. He believes that there is mind even down to the quantum level. Thomas Keating,[23] the Roman Catholic priest and writer, believes that the emergence of reason, that is fully reflective self-consciousness, arose around 3000 B.C.E. – he calls it the most dramatic leap in all of human history. It could be argued that the cave paintings, which often included hand prints, would seem to indicate that the human self-consciousness arose much earlier, say around 40,000 years ago.

While most people, when asked, would probably say that intelligence is centered in the brain, many scientists now believe that intelligence of some form or another is present everywhere in the body. For instance, the immune system must have an intelligence of its own because it responds to novel situations and uses inborn knowledge to solve problems associated with attacks on the body, apparently without reference to the brain. Similarly, all cells in the body seem to know what to do under changing sets of circumstances.

As much as we are all aware that we have a mind and are conscious of our environment, it is natural for us to take these qualities for granted as being a necessary part of our existence. Paul Davies[24] believes that consciousness is a fundamental property and a natural consequence of the outworkings of the laws of physics. In April 1966, *Time* magazine devoted a lead article to what it called the "Conscious Mind". In this article, David Chalmers makes some comments which may be relevant here. He writes:

> It seems that God could have created the world physically exactly like this one, atom for atom but with no consciousness at all. For some reason, God chose "to do more work" in order to put consciousness in. After all, consciousness – the existence of pleasure and pain, love and grief – is a fairly central source of life's meaning. For it to have been thrown into the fabric of the universe as a freebie would suggest to some people that the thrower wanted to impart significance. It is always possible that consciousness is not extra, but that it actually does something in the physical world like influence behavior.

It would seem to me that consciousness is not a "freebie" but is a very essential component of our human make-up. However, there are others who believe that in the evolution of the human being consciousness was an accident, a "quirky little by-product of evolution". If life were wiped out, consciousness, according to them, would probably not reoccur. Paul Davies[25] makes the statement:

If we take consciousness seriously we are faced with the conundrum that nobody has succeeded in registering its existence in an experiment. That is to say, the human brain has been much explored and a great deal of its workings is understood, but so far it has not been experimentally demonstrated that consciousness is needed as an additional component of the operation of the brain... Some believe that consciousness is the operation of the brain.

From our point of view, one of the most interesting developments in recent years is the fact that modern physics places mind and consciousness again at center stage. The physicist Eugene Wigner,[26] for instance, holds that quantum results are fixed only when they enter someone's consciousness. He believes that it is not possible to formulate the laws of nature in a fully consistent way without reference to consciousness. It is not surprising then that the involvement of an observer, in both quantum physics and relativity, has been used by some as evidence of the central role played by mind in the creation and operation of the universe.

If we go back to our definition of mind and consciousness, it is difficult to see that life in general, and human life in particular, can survive without consciousness or awareness of its environment. Any animal that hopes to survive, even for a short period of time, must be conscious of the environment in which it exists: it must be aware of the dangers to its existence, its predators, its sexual partners, its food sources, etc. The example, quoted in the previous chapter of the baby chicken, which is aware at birth of the dangers associated with the silhouette of a hawk flying overhead, is a clear indication of the fact that consciousness and awareness of our environment is an inborn quality and is essential to the survival of all animal species, including ourselves. This, of course, does not necessarily mean that these animals possess a sense of self or are self-conscious.

As indicated by the definitions of mind, consciousness and intelligence, all are nonmaterial. We know where the brain is located, but we do not have the faintest idea where we can find the mind or consciousness since they are immaterial and do not occupy a specific place in the body. It is interesting to note that there is a general usage across the world to locate certain aspects of our mind/consciousness in different parts of our body. For instance, we talk about a person with brains (intelligence); we sing about love in our heart; we talk about a brave person having guts or that we have a gut feeling about something; or we cannot stomach something we do not like, etc.

In any case, we are still left with the basic problem of how the immaterial world of mind, consciousness and intelligence can interact with the material world of cells and the brain. They are so different in kind that it is difficult to see how these immaterial aspects of the human being could ever have resulted from the evolution of material things. As James Trefil[27] expresses it:

> Whatever theory of consciousness there is has to explain how to go from a collection of firing neurons to the essential perception of self. The problem of consciousness comes down to asking how a system like the human mind and body could produce the perception of self. How, in other words, can a physical system operating by physical laws produce the experience of self-awareness that we all share. Until you have explained how I come to that central conclusion about my existence, you have not solved the problem of consciousness.

Raymond Moody[28] in his book, *Life After Life*, writes:

> The question at issue here is the mind-body problem. After 2,500 years, Western civilization hasn't gotten any closer to the question of how consciousness is related to

material substance. This is a chronically unresolvable controversy.

Or as Mary Midgley[29] suggests in *Science and Salvation*, if we are looking for cases where mind and matter are conceptually involved together, we might surely expect some mention of the fact that we can move our bodies.

Shimon Malin[30] in his book, *Nature Loves to Hide*, asks the question:

> If the objective, external world is really all there is, then each one of us performs amazing feats of magic all day long. I decide to raise my hand and I raise my hand. How did my decision – a mental event – bring about the physical event of a physical hand moving up?
>
> To solve this riddle philosophers (and others) keep looking for a mind/body interface. But mind is not even a part of the objectivized reality which presumably is all there is. On the one hand, the presence of mind cannot be denied – we know we do experience – and on the other hand, it is nowhere to be found in what we believe to be the real universe.

In summary, I believe it is clear that these immaterial feelings such as beauty, love, etc. and the perception of self are different in kind from the material world. This fundamental difference between the two surely indicates that the one could not have evolved from the other, not even through the largest or longest of evolutionary mutations. The only explanation remaining, to my mind, is that the immaterial aspects of the human being must have been incorporated into the human being as a special creative act of the Mind behind creation. As Richard Swinburn[31] wrote in *The Existence of God*: "Science cannot account for the presence of conscious beings in the world." According to him, something outside the web of physical laws is needed to explain the rise of consciousness. Remember, consciousness includes not only self-awareness but also the whole spectrum of thoughts, feelings, impressions, etc. In a similar vein, John Searle[32] wrote in *The Rediscovery of the Mind*:

> Somehow or another, sentience sprang from pulpy matter, giving matter an inner aspect, but we have no idea how the leap was propelled... One is tempted, however reluctantly, to turn to divine assistance; for only a kind of miracle could produce this from that. It would take a supernatural magician to extract consciousness from matter, even living matter.

Wilder Penfield, the well-known Canadian neurophysiologist, postulated the existence of a center of decision making radically different from the neural network in the brain. He believed that there exists in his words: "A switchboard operator as well as a switchboard." In other words, according to him, there must be a personal involvement of a switchboard operator to make the switchboard operational and to make the system function. John Polkinghorne[33] goes even further when he writes:

> I think that self-consciousness is the most astonishing development in cosmic history. It does suggest to me that the universe is going somewhere and has some meaning and purpose behind it. God is the answer to the question: why is there something rather than nothing?

It is when discussing consciousness and mind that we see most clearly the wide gulf that exists between the purely deterministic-mechanical-chemical explanation of life, and the approach in which a Spiritual Being is thought to have been instrumental in the creation of life. Such books as *The Blind Watchmaker* by Richard Dawkins and *The Web of Life* by Fritjof Capra both promote the idea that life is nothing but a chemical process and that life emerged as the result of complicated chemical processes and systems. Reading these books, there is no mention of anything of a spiritual nature such as love, compassion, beauty, altruism and even consciousness. For instance, according to Capra, mind is not a thing but a process, and the brain is a specific structure through which this process operates. Nothing is being said about the existence of a human soul/spirit or about human values; we are just reiterative computer-like systems and programs. This is in sharp contrast to the world view in which there is a Guiding Intelligence who created the universe and who gave meaning to life, and who also gave humankind values to live by.

As indicated in the introduction to this chapter, we will now briefly review how the thinking about these matters has evolved with time and is still evolving today, using the time frame suggested by Dr. Larry Dossey, starting with Era I.

ERA I: THE HUMAN BEING – A MECHANICAL, MATERIAL AND PHYSICAL MACHINE.

In the purely mechanical world of Era I, that was all there was, a mind and some inbred intelligence. While most people thought that consciousness or awareness was necessary for survival, others doubted that. So, there was only the mind and the body. The whole universe was thought to operate like a machine, and we were told that our body also operated like a machine. The mind was located in the brain and, in effect, was nothing else but an aspect of the mechanical functioning of the brain. It was thought that every cause had a perfectly predictable, invariable effect (see also the chapter on Determinism and Free Will). This led to the belief that if one had a large enough computer, the future course of everything in the universe could be calculated from a given set of starting conditions.

In this scheme of things there was no place for anything that could not be explained by the known laws of nature. There simply was no place in this understanding of nature of anything metaphysical or paranormal, such as a soul and mystical or religious experiences. The human being was considered to be a purely mechanical system consisting of a body and a mind, both of which would disintegrate into nothingness at the death of the body. Even the concept of consciousness was downgraded to a mechanical or chemical process and was considered to be just a by-product of the brain and would, of course, also disintegrate with death. A natural consequence of this understanding of human nature was that the means of interaction and communication between humans, and between humans and their surrounding environment, was understood to be strictly a matter of mechanical processes made possible by the five senses: hearing, seeing, smelling, tasting and feeling (see Figure 5.7).

In this understanding of the human being, the brain/mind was the seat of intelligence and controlled all bodily functions through a nervous system, which was understood to operate on the basis of electrical and chemical impulses, which could reach all parts of the body almost instantaneously.

As far as values were concerned, many thinkers in this era believed that psychiatry and psychology would take over the role that religion had played in establishing a value system humans could live by. The psychiatrist's couch was going to replace the pulpit and the confessional as the new source of moral guidance and spiritual solace for the modern human.

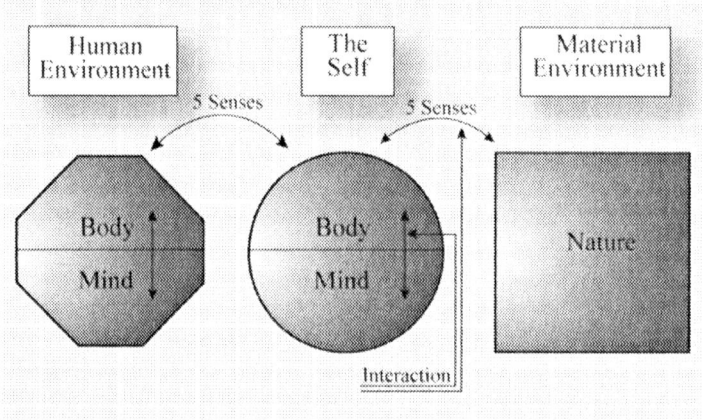

Figure 5.7

The Interpersonal and External Lines of Communications in Era I

As mentioned previously, in this scheme of things there is no real need for a deity; some thought that maybe God was needed to start things off, a sort of first cause, but that was all that was required of the deity in a purely mechanical understanding of the creation of the universe. God became an "Unnecessary Hypothesis". In this way of looking at the universe, there was only one faith, or one belief, that science blindly accepted as being true without any proof of its veracity. That belief, or faith, was that the universe was rational and operated on the basis of rational laws and rules that could be understood by the human intellect. No one asked where this rationality came from in a universe in which everything happened by chance. Surely, no one can expect such an ordered universe to arrive purely by chance. Einstein certainly got that point when he once said that the only thing incomprehensible about the universe was that it could be comprehended.

Fortunately, most people today have discarded this purely mechanistic view of life and acknowledge that there is more to life than a mechanical/chemical process that, purely by chance, has given rise to the existence of human beings. However, as indicated in a previous chapter, there are still some diehards who cling to this materialistic/deterministic point of view. For some, this view is based on the fact that, by stimulating part of the brain, almost all religious and paranormal experiences which people claim to have had can be duplicated. But as I said previously, we can also induce feelings of hot or cold by stimulating specific parts of the brain, but that does not mean that the experience of hot or cold does not exist in real life: this argument is not very convincing and can be safely discarded, especially since no one has actually been able to duplicate these experiences in this way.

ERA II: THE HUMAN BEING – THE BODY/MIND CONNECTION

After the early 1950s, it became increasingly evident that there was more to life than what could be explained by a simple mechanical body and mind concept. The introduction of the various theories of uncertainty, such as were being postulated by quantum mechanics, paved the way for an understanding that life did not operate simply on the basis of cause and predictable effect.

Also, as described in the previous chapter, it was discovered that intelligence exists in all parts and systems of the body, including the immune system. The cells in these body parts seem to know what to do automatically without reference to the brain under a wide variety of circumstances. So, mind, intelligence and consciousness seem to be distributed throughout our bodies. Some scientists go so far as to say that intelligence and consciousness are even found to exist down to the quantum level in the atoms that form our bodies.

Thus, in the last fifty years or so, it has become clear that the sharp distinction between body and mind could not be sustained by the facts. As one writer expressed it, no matter how different they may appear to be, mind and body are both soaked through with intelligence. Also, it was gradually being recognized that the mind can have a very definite and crucial influence on the well-being of the body. Time and time again it has been shown that attitudes, willpower and expressions of love and compassion can, under certain circumstances, affect the recovery of a patient more than the conventional medical intervention of medication and operative procedures. As Dr. Dean Ornish[34] expressed it in his book, *Program for Reversing Heart Disease*, altruism, compassion, and forgiveness – opening your heart – can be powerful means of healing while isolation leads to stress, suffering and illness. Also, simple tests have shown that the practice of meditation can lower blood pressure, improve productivity and decrease health costs.

There are dozens of other experiments in which the health of people was measured against the amount of involvement people had in helping others. These experiments invariably show the considerable influence altruism and meditation have on the health, life span, and general physical and emotional well-being of all people. In one hospital I recently visited, there was a notice in one of the elevators that said that doing volunteer work had proven to increase people's life span.

All these experiments make it clear that there is a spiritual aspect to healing in addition to the standard medical practices. Moreover some experiments which tried to measure the effectiveness of prayer clearly showed that prayer was not just a useless religious practice, but that, if prayer was directed towards healing of a sick person, it could be effective in restoring the person's health. These effects are so strong and well documented that one doctor has predicted that prayer would, before long, become standard procedure in a doctor's office. He went even so far as to say that he could foresee a time when failure to use prayer by a doctor could lead to a malpractice suit (see Chapter IX on the subject of prayer).

As far as psychiatry replacing religion as the source for human values is concerned, it was found to be a complete fallacy. Far from being a neurosis, as Freud claimed, it turned out that there is a strong correlation between faith and mental health and happiness.

At the same time, strictly controlled experiments have shown conclusively that there are humans who can interact with each other without involving the five senses, and that, in fact, there are nonphysical means by which people can communicate with each other. Even the most skeptical person has to admit that such processes as hypnosis, by which one mind influences another mind at close range, and telepathy, by which one person communicates with another person at great distances, do in fact take place; and that this extrasensory capability of the human being must be taken into account when considering the make-up of the human psyche.

Also, it was found that dreams are not always the confused, senseless, jumble of images they appear to be, but that there are dreams that seem to point to a subconscious knowledge of things happening at other places and even of things that will happen in the future.

Eventually, this led to the understanding that maybe the human psyche has another two components to it in addition to the body and the mind: the subconscious and the unconscious. Again to avoid confusion, we will use *Webster's Dictionary* to define what these terms mean in general usage. According to *Webster's*, the subconscious is:

- that which occurs without conscious perception or with only slight perception on the part of the individual; and
- not fully conscious; imperfectly aware.

The unconscious is defined as:

- the sum of all thoughts, memories, impulses, desires, feelings of which the individual is not conscious but which influences his emotions and behavior; and
- the part of one's psyche which comprises repressed material of this nature.

The distinction between the two is not always clear. In our understanding, it is the subconscious which makes it possible, through paranormal channels or extrasensory perception, to communicate with the subconscious and the conscious mind of another individual. Alison Jolly[35] in her book, *Lucy's Legacy*, has this to say about the interaction of the conscious and the unconscious:

> Consciousness is one of the endless mysteries… Although we are baffled, at least for now, about how consciousness works, we are a little clearer about why it works. It is a decision maker for those parts of the mind that need decisions, while many more get on well enough with their unconscious functions. The brain, with or without consciousness, continually deals with the question, "Now what do I do?".

The possible interactions and communications between people and their environment are then seen to take place as shown in Figure 5.8. In addition to showing the various lines of communication between people, the figure also shows that the strict distinction between body and mind has disappeared.

Of course, it is realized that the unconscious plays a large role in our everyday existence: it is responsible for a wide variety of human actions and reactions. It is the area where the sciences of psychology and psychiatry operate, which determines how our subconscious and unconscious leads to

THE HUMAN BEING

behavior that is a danger to both the individual and society at large. In this respect, it is interesting to note that Dr. Scott Peck, who is a psychiatrist himself, goes so far as to say that the unconscious possesses extraordinary knowledge that we are not naturally aware of. It knows who we really are, and it is the unconscious which is wiser than we are in our conscious self.

It is this idea which has led to such practices as transcendental meditation (TM), yoga, and a host of others which all try to establish a communication with our "deeper selves", the subconscious and unconscious. It is here where we are supposed to find out who we really are and what our deepest feelings are. The problem with all these practices is that they tend to be elitist. They require a great deal of sustained effort and willpower which is something that not

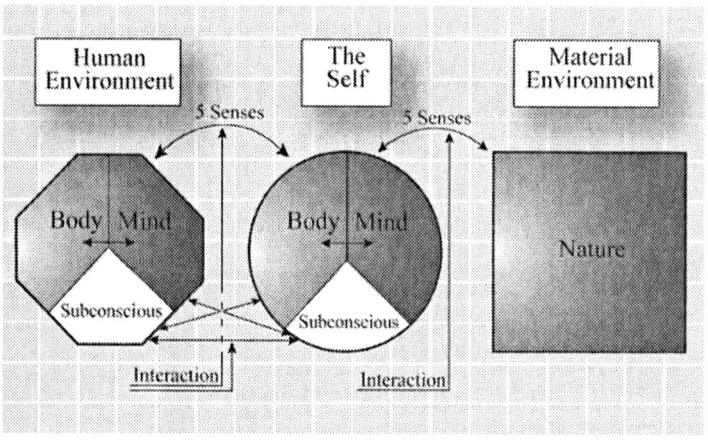

Figure 5.8

The Interpersonal and External Lines of Communication in Era II

every person possesses. While there is no doubt that there is some substance to the idea of the deeper self, it is also true that the majority of people will go through this life never having experienced that part of their being.

ERA III: THE HUMAN BEING – BODY/MIND – NONLOCAL IN SPACE AND TIME

In this era, which for many people is just starting now, there are a number of new insights and developments which occurred more or less independently of each other. First, there is the concept of nonlocality of mind and consciousness in both time and space. We met this concept before in the previous chapter and in discussing some of the effects of quantum mechanics. Secondly, there is the concept that the reality of the physical world may not be as firmly established as we generally think. Thirdly, there is a revival of the old idea of the interconnectedness of all things, at least of all nature. And lastly, there is the idea that much of what we can't understand in the world around us could possibly be explained by introducing the concept of fields of influence.

However, before considering these ideas in any detail, I believe it would be helpful to look into one aspect of the human being that we have hardly touched upon and that is the concept of the human soul. Again, different people have different ideas of what is meant by this word. For instance, the Bible refers time and time again to the human soul, but that has probably very little to do with the way the word is used by many people today. To avoid confusion, we will go back to *Webster's Dictionary* where the word soul is defined as follows:

- an entity which is regarded as being the immortal and spiritual part of the person and, though having no physical and material reality, is credited with the functions of thinking, willing and hence determines all behavior; and

- the moral and emotional nature of humankind.

Because of the overlapping of the functions of the mind, consciousness, the unconscious and the soul, the major functions of all aspects of the human psyche are thus summarized:

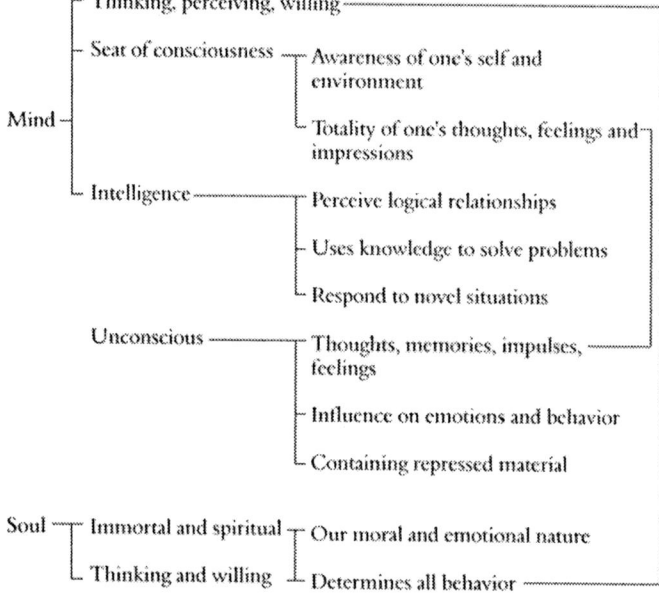

Graph Vb
Major Functions of the Human Psyche

It is clear, from this presentation, that mind and soul have many things in common such as thinking and willing, but it is the soul which is attributed with the capacity to make moral judgments and, finally, to determine the ethical behavior of the human being. The basic facts, on which these judgments must be based, are supplied by all aspects of the mind, including the subconscious. Of course, this makes the functioning of the soul the most important aspect of the human being. In doing so, it clearly defines the position of people who deny that the soul exists.

Recently a number of books have appeared on the subject of the soul, best known among these are the two books by Thomas Moore:[36] *Care of the Soul* and *Soul Mates*. According to Moore, soul cannot be defined; it is a quality that holds body and mind together, which fits fairly well with the descriptions presented in *Webster's Dictionary*. For Moore, it is imperative to have a religion that is intellectually and emotionally satisfying; to take care of the soul is a sacred act. He believes that we know instinctively that the soul has to do with genuineness and depth, and that the soul is revealed in attachments, love and community. Also, according to him, the great malady of the twentieth century, implicated in all our troubles and affecting us individually and socially, is "loss of soul".

In a book by Rupert Sheldrake[37] called *Seven Experiments that Could Change the World*, the author has this to say about the soul:

> The soul is not confined to the head but exists throughout and around the body, it is linked to ancestors, connected with the life of animals, plants, the Earth and the heavens, it can travel out of the body in dreams, in trance and at death and it can communicate with a vast realm of spirits – ancestors, animals, etc.

From the above it is clear that there is considerable confusion over what is actually meant by the word soul. Because of this we will use the word only to indicate the part of the human being which determines its emotional and moral behavior. The religious concept of the immortal soul is assumed to be covered by our immortal consciousness or immortal mind.

THE NONLOCALITY OF MIND AND CONSCIOUSNESS

As indicated in the definitions of mind, consciousness, intelligence and soul, these attributes are not material and are nonlocal. We know where the brain is situated but we have no idea where we can find the mind, consciousness, or the soul. They simply are not associated with any part of our body and are therefore nonlocal. As expressed by Larry Dossey[38] in *Healing Words*:

> The nonlocal nature of consciousness will eventually be recognized by science because of the conclusive evidence affirming it. It will be increasingly recognized that consciousness can do things the brain cannot do. And, no longer will consciousness be considered a by-product of the brain destined to die with the body. It is nonlocal, infinite in space and time, omnipresent and immortal by implication.

Erwin Schrödinger, one of the early proponents of quantum mechanics, came to the conclusion after examining the consequences of these new theories that there was only one alternative and that was that mind and consciousness were really one and the same thing. Mind, he said, is no longer localized in the individual but it is transpersonal, universal, collective, *nonlocal and indestructible*. These opinions of some of the leading scientists of our time direct our attention to the religious aspects of the human existence, its immortality and its relationship with the consciousness of God. We will return to this when we discuss all the inferences of these new ideas on the theological and religious aspects of life. Instead, I would like to recall what the quantum theories have indicated about consciousness and the reality of the existence of the universe.

THE REALITY OF THE PHYSICAL WORLD

You will recall that some of the quantum phenomena seem to indicate that the observer, in the act of observing, changes the quantity that is being observed. This led some scientists to the conclusion that there was no reality outside of our consciousness and that consciousness, human or otherwise, was itself a necessary ingredient of the universe. In his book, *The Self-Aware Universe*, Amit Goswami[39] goes one step further when he states:

> All the above paradoxes are explainable and understandable if we are to give up the precious assumption that there is an objective reality out there, independent of consciousness. It says even more that the universe is self-aware, and that it is consciousness itself that creates the physical world. Consciousness is something transcendental – it is outside of space and time – nonlocal and all pervading. It is the only reality – yet we are able to glimpse it only through the actions that give rise to the material and mental aspects of our observational processes.

Bishop George Berkeley,[40] the archenemy of materialism, phrased it as follows some years ago:

> All the choirs and furniture of Earth, in a word all those bodies which compose the mighty frame of the world, have not any substance without the mind... So long as they are not actually perceived by me or do not exist in my mind, or that of any other created spirit, they must either have no existence at all, or else subsist in the mind of some Eternal Spirit.

This is strong stuff, something that not everyone will readily accept. The author invites us, in fact, to give up the idea of a real world that exists independently of consciousness, not necessarily independent of God's consciousness, but independent of our consciousness. Someone once asked the question: if a tree falls in the forest and there is no one there to hear the crashing sound we normally associate with a tree falling, does the falling tree actually make that crashing sound? In other words, if there is no observer, no human consciousness to record the sound, is the sound still made? If I understand the author rightly, he believes that there is no sound from this falling tree because the sound only becomes real in the act of conscious observation.

In many ways, this philosophy comes close to some of the teachings of the Eastern religions, some of which deny the reality of the universe and believe that life is only an illusion. The major difference between the two is probably that, in the view of consciousness expressed above, consciousness is eternal and indestructible. Of course, this leads to the Christian concept of an immortal soul and to the idea that death is, in fact, a transition to a higher and more all-encompassing consciousness. Or, stated differently, after death we will become aware of a greater reality, a reality that we cannot now grasp because we are limited at present by our capacity to comprehend the reality associated with God, who exists on a plane that we cannot comprehend with our earthly consciousness. Elizabeth Kübler-Ross[41] talks about death as a shedding of the physical body, a transition to a higher state of consciousness where one continues to perceive, to understand, to laugh, and to be able to grow; the only thing you lose is something you don't need anymore – the physical body.

Vh The Interconnectedness of All Nature – The Collective Unconscious

Probably, the most drastic change in our understanding, of what we are and who we are, is slowly taking effect now. It is the result of an increasing awareness that all people are connected with each other through an invisible bond that somehow ties all humanity together. Some people go even further and postulate that not only all of humanity is connected by this bond but that all of nature is connected. Furthermore, it is said that this connectedness is not something that only operates on the basis of the here and now, but that it also ties us to the past and to the future. For instance, anthropologists have often described how widely separated tribes and communities, in different parts of the world and existing at different times, nevertheless have similar myths and religious stories although they do not appear ever to have had any contact with each other. Similarly, it is a fact of life that many discoveries and scientific theories have arisen quite spontaneously in different parts of the world at the same time. In everyday language, we simply say that we believe that "its time had come". This thing which binds us all together was called "The Collective Unconscious" by Dr. Carl Jung many years ago. As he writes:

> In addition to immediate consciousness which is of a thoroughly personal nature and which we believe to be the only empirical psyche, there exists a second psychic system of a collective, universal and impersonal nature which is identical in all individuals. This collective unconscious does not develop individually but is inherited. It consists of pre-existent forms, the arch types, which can only become conscious secondarily and which give definite form to certain psychic content.

Others have called it the "Divine Consciousness" or the "Universal Mind". For the purpose of this discussion, we will call it the collective unconscious. In this view of our psyche, our consciousness is no longer confined to individual minds but is shared by everyone. It includes a kind of collective memory in which individuals participate unconsciously. Dr. Scott Peck[42] writes that this collective unconscious is what makes us inherit the wisdom and experience of our ancestors without ourselves having that personal experience. To quote Jung again:

> In the depth of the unconscious, man is no longer a destined individual but his mind widens out and merges into the mind of mankind – not the conscious mind, but the unconscious mind of mankind where we are all the same. The psyche is no longer confined to individual minds but shared by everyone, it includes a kind of collective memory in which individuals participate unconsciously.

As discussed in the previous chapter, the fact that humans can connect with each other without the benefit of the five senses has been known and acknowledged for a long time; that the human mind can influence plants and animals is something most people will find more difficult to believe. However, a number of strictly controlled scientific experiments at the University of Oregon by Dr. Daniel Benor,[43] the so-called Spindrift experiments, have clearly shown that the human mind can affect the growth of enzymes, bacteria, seedlings and even plants. For a further description of these tests see the chapter on prayer.

This connectedness between humans and nature has been acknowledged by many societies, old and new, across the world. In North America this is probably most keenly felt and appreciated by the native Indian population, who have always felt this close connectedness with all of nature, including the inanimate world. In many Indian communities the hunter will ask the forgiveness of the animal he is about to kill, because he needs it as food for himself and his family. They felt, and still feel in many cases, a real kinship with the animal world and also with the trees and the land upon which they were and are living.

They express this in many of their ceremonies and stories. Chief Seattle is told as having expressed it this way:

> Every part of this earth is sacred to my people. The white man must treat the beasts of this land as his brother. This we know, the earth does not belong to man, man belongs to the earth. All things are connected, like the blood which unites one family. Teach your children that the earth is our mother.

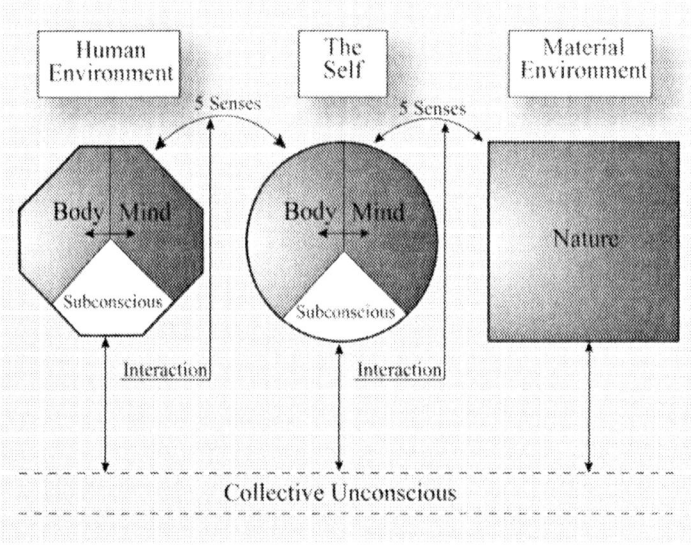

Figure 5.9
The Interpersonal and External Lines of Communication in Era III

The essence of this new paradigm emerging in physics, in general systems theory and in ecology, changes our whole idea of reality with the notion of interconnectedness and understanding of the organic and unified character of the universe.

In Figure 5.9, this interconnectedness is shown

graphically. Each person in the world is shown to be connected with this collective unconscious and, through this, to all other people and to the whole of nature.

Since this collective unconsciousness is assumed to be universal, it cannot be contained within the boundaries of space and time. Shimon Malin puts it this way: "If we adopt the terminology of current cosmology, we can say that it (mind, consciousness) existed before the Big Bang and will continue to exist after the Big Crunch, if there will be one." It is this aspect of this worldview of Era III that will probably be the most controversial and will, no doubt, be the subject of discussion for many years to come.

The reason for this controversy is the assumption that if the collective unconscious is not contained within the boundaries of time and space, then our own consciousness is not bound by these boundaries either and that, in fact, our *consciousness is immortal*. Not only that, but it also means that through this collective unconscious we can also go back and forth in time – in fact, communicate with the past and the future.

If, as argued above, our consciousness (soul) is the immortal part of the human being, then it is maybe logical to take the next step as E. F. Edinger[44] did when he stated that the purpose of human life is to create consciousness, a consciousness that, once created, will live forever.

Strange as this interconnectedness between human beings and nature may seem to many initially, it must be remembered that fundamentally we are all made from the same basic stuff. The atoms of all living and inanimate things are made of exactly the same things: their electrons have the same mass, the same charge and the same spin. Also, the DNA of animals is very similar to that of humans. For instance, the DNA of a chimpanzee differs from that of a human by only 1.1 per cent. Also, it appears that all the cells of our body are renewed or interchanged at regular times, and that atoms which once were part of our body may now be part of other bodies, including animals. No wonder then that there is a certain connectedness between all of creation.

We are, as Paul Brunton[45] expressed it in *The Spiritual Crisis of Man*, like millions of trees which are rooted in one and the same earth. Similarly, millions of human minds are rooted in one and the same Universal Being. Everything and every creature that is in the universe owes its own being to the "Undifferentiated Being" or Mind.

The assumption that we are all connected with this universal consciousness, and that this consciousness is not bounded by time or space, has a number of important consequences for the understanding of ourselves and of our links with the past and the future. To name just a few:

- telepathy – transferring thoughts from mind to mind;
- precognition – the ability to foresee events;
- clairvoyance – being able to see things that are happening elsewhere;
- faith healing – the healing of sickness through prayer;
- bond between pets and their owners; and
- the effects of meditation and contemplation.

Perhaps we should point out that this subconscious connection to other people is not always an unqualified blessing. This interconnectedness between people might possibly explain some of the collective actions of intelligent people that have resulted in some of the worst crimes against humanity, such as the Holocaust and, more recently, ethnic cleansing.

Conclusion

It is obvious, from this chapter that the human being is far from just a material machine driven by evolution and physical and mechanical forces. Also, there are many more components to the human being than previously thought. Elizabeth Kübler-Ross[46] in her book, *On Life After Death*, writes that she sees the human being as consisting of four quadrants: the physical, the emotional, the intellectual and the spiritual. She believes that we were meant to be human beings with all four quadrants working together in harmony and wholeness.

Bohm and Edwards[47] think that the life of human beings has three basic dimensions: the individual, the collective and the cosmic.

The definition which I personally feel expresses the situation most clearly is that contained in the book by Ian Barbour[48] entitled *Religion in an Age of Science* in which he writes:

> In sum, it would be consistent with both the scientific and biblical outlook to understand the person as a multi-level unity who is both a biological organism and responsible self... Some levels we share with all matter, some we share with all living things, some with all animal life, while some seem to be uniquely human.
>
> The person can be represented... as the individual in the unified activity of thinking, willing, feeling, and acting.
>
> In the biblical view, it is this integral being whose whole life is of concern to God.

Taking all this evidence, from particle scientists to psychiatrists together, it is clear that the human being is unique in creation in that it has a consciousness, a self-awareness, that no other creature has. More importantly, it seems to be true that the human being is somehow connected to the universal consciousness and that our consciousness, or soul, is immortal and cannot be destroyed. All these considerations, I believe, point straight to the concept of a Universal Mind, or God, to whom the immortal consciousness of all nature is connected. It was this Mind which created all of nature and to whom all nature will return.

A scientist wrote recently along these lines when he stated that he believed that we are going to understand everything eventually, but that this understanding will require bringing in a realm that we don't understand as yet. We, as he said, are going to have to bring in that extra energy realm, the realm of the spirit and the soul. Personally, I am sure that in the end we will discover a spiritual world that is every bit as real as the physical world. Another scientist put it even stronger when he wrote: "My impression is that the physical world is only a small instant of a much larger context and that reality is primarily unfolding in a nonphysical way." (Whitley Strieber quoted in K. Ring's[49] book, *Heading Towards Omega*.) Finally, I want to quote J.L. Simmons[50] from his book *Future Lives* in which he has this to say about our spiritual nature:

> We are fast approaching a point of incontrovertible, scientific, empirical proof of the spiritual essence of human beings, of life after death, and reincarnation. There is now massive evidence for the spiritual basis of life.

So here we are in the beginning of Era III and already we are talking about physical and nonphysical concepts that were not dreamed of in Era I or even Era II. One thing is clear, the ultimate reality, when and if we ever discover it, will have a much greater spiritual component than we ever dreamed of. In the following chapters, we will try to tie these new concepts of the physical and spiritual world to the concepts of the Christian religion.

I want to end this chapter with a quotation from a noncanonical gospel, "The Gospel of Mary". Unfortunately only small fragments of this gospel have survived. In this gospel the question is asked of Jesus, "Will matter then be utterly destroyed or not?" The Savior replied: "Every nature, every modeled form, every creature exists in and with each other. They will dissolve again into their own proper root. For the nature of matter is dissolved into what belongs to its nature." Whether Jesus actually spoke these words is an interesting speculation. However, the fact that it appeared in as early a document as the Gospel of Mary, which is thought to have been written around the end of the first century, is in itself noteworthy.

NOTES

[1] Dossey, Larry, *Healing Words: The Power of Prayer and the Practice of Medicine*, Harper San Francisco, New York, 1993.

[2] Rifkin, Jeremy, *Algeny*, as quoted in *Genetic Engineering, Progress or Peril*, by Linda Tagliaferro, p.127.

[3] Suzuki, David and Dressel, Holly, *From Naked Ape to Superspecies*, Stoddart Publishing Co. Ltd, Toronto, 1999, p.104.

[4] Fox, Michael W., *Beyond Evolution, The Genetically Altered Future of Plants Animals, the Earth... and Humans*, The Lyons Press, New York, 1999.

[5] *Controlling our Destinies; Historical, Philosophical, Ethical and Theological Perspectives of the Human Genome Project*, ed. P. R. Sloan, University of Notre Dame Press, Notre Dame, Indiana, 2000.

[6] Whitfield, Philip, general editor, *The Human Body Explained, A Guide to Understanding the Incredible Living Machine*, Henry Holt and Company, New York, 1995, p.141.

[7] Lennart, Nilsson, *The Body Victorious*, Delacorte Press, New York, 1987.

[8] Capra, Fritjof, *The Web of Life*, Anchor Books, Doubleday, New York, 1998, pg.282.

[9] Lewontin, Richard, *It Ain't Necessarily So, The Dream of the Human Genome and Other Illusions*, Harvard University Press, Cambridge, Mass., 2000.

[10] Trefil, James S., *Are We Unique?*, John Wiley and Sons Inc., New York, 1997.

[11] Davies, Paul, *The Cosmic Blueprint, New Discoveries in Nature's Ability to Order the Universe*, Simon and Schuster, New York, 1998.

[12] Barbour, Ian, *Religion in an Age of Science*, Harper San Francisco, Harper Collins

Publishers, 1990, p.146.
[13]Nathan, Peter, *The Nervous System*, Oxford University Press, Oxford, 1982.
[14]Kittredge, Mary, *The Senses*, Chelsea House Publishing, New York, 1990.
[15]Maddox, John, *What Remains To Be Discovered*, The Free Press, Simon and Schuster, New York, 1998, pp.276–279.
[16]Wilson, Edward O., *Consilience, The Unity of Knowledge*, Alfred A. Knopf, New York, 1998, p.99.
[17]Peck, M. Scott, *The Road Less Traveled and Beyond, Spiritual Growth in an Age of Anxiety*, Simon and Schuster, New York, 1997.
[18]Goswami, Amit, *The Self-Aware Universe, How Consciousness Creates the Material World*, G. P. Putnam and Sons, New York, 1993.
[19]Polkinghorne, John, *Belief in God in an Age of Science*, Yale University Press, 1998.
[20]Adler, Mortimer J., *Intellect: Mind Over Matter*, Macmillan Publishing Co., New York, 1990, p.xii.
[21]Davies, Paul, *Other Worlds*, Simon and Schuster, New York, 1980.
[22]Bohm, David, *New Age Journal*, September/October, 1989, p.110.
[23]Keating, Thomas, *Invitation to Love*, Elements Inc., Rockport, 1992.
[24]Davies, Paul, *Other Worlds*, Simon and Schuster, New York, 1980.
[25]Davies, Paul, *Other Worlds*, Simon and Schuster, New York, 1980.
[26]Wigner, Eugene, *Symmetries and Reflections*, Indiana University Press, Bloomington, 1967.
[27]Trefil, James, *Are We Unique?*, John Wiley and Sons Inc., New York, 1997, p.182.
[28]Moody, Raymond A., *Life After Life*, Bantam Doubleday Dell Publishers, 1976.
[29]Midgley, Mary, *Science and Salvation, A Modern Myth and its Meaning*, Routledge, Chapman and Hall Inc., New York, 1992, p.176.
[30]Malin, Shimon, *Nature Loves to Hide – Quantum Physics and the Nature of Reality: A Western Perspective*, Oxford University Press, New York, 2001.
[31]Swinburn, Richard, *The Existence of God*, Oxford University Press, Oxford, 1991.
[32]Searle, John, *The Rediscovery of the Mind*, MIT Press, 1994.
[33]Polkinghorne, John, *Belief in God in an Age of Science*, Yale University Press, 1998.
[34]Ornish, Dean, *Program for Reversing Heart Disease*, Ballantine Books, New York, 1990, p.215.
[35]Jolly, Alison, *Lucy's Legacy*, Harvard University Press, Cambridge, Mass, 1999/2000.
[36]Moore Thomas, *Care of the Soul* and *Soul Mates*, Harper Perennial, Harper Collins Publishing, New York, 1992.
[37]Sheldrake, Rupert, *Seven Experiments that Could Change the World*, Berkley Publishing Group, 1996, p.99.
[38]Dossey, Larry, *Healing Words: The Power of Prayer and the Practice of Medicine*, Harper San Francisco, New York, 1993.
[39]Goswami, Amit, *The Self-Aware Universe, How Consciousness Creates the Material World*, G. P. Putnam and Sons, New York, 1993.
[40]Berkeley, Bishop George (1685–1753), *Treatise Concerning the Principles of Human Knowledge*.

[41] Kübler-Ross, Elisabeth, *On Life After Death*, Celestial Arts, Berkeley, CA, 1991.

[42] Peck, M. Scott, *The Road Less Traveled and Beyond, Spiritual Growth in an Age of Anxiety*, Simon and Schuster, New York, 1997.

[43] Benor, Daniel, *Spindrift Experiments*, mentioned in note 1.

[44] Edinger, Edward F., *The Creation of Consciousness, Jung's Myth for Modern Man*, Inner City Books, Toronto, 1984.

[45] Brunton, Paul, *The Spiritual Crisis of Man*, Rider and Co. and S. Weiser Inc., 1970.

[46] Kübler-Ross, Elizabeth, see note 40.

[47] Bohm, David and Edwards, Mark, *Changing Consciousness*, Harper Collins Publishers Inc., New York, 1991.

[48] Barbour, Ian, see note 11.

[49] Ring, Kenneth, *Heading Towards Omega, In Search of the Meaning of Near Death Experiences*, William Morrow and Co., New York, 1985.

[50] Simmons, J. L., *Future Lives, A Future Guide to our Transition Time*, ear & Co. Publishing, Santa Fe, New Mexico, 1990.

Chapter VI
MATERIALISM VERSUS SPIRITUALISM – DETERMINISM VERSUS FREE WILL

Introduction

In the previous chapters, we have followed the evolution of human beings from the single, living cell to the thinking, conscious human beings we are today. In this scenario, there must be a definite point or period in time when our early human predecessors changed from animals, with no self-awareness, to fully conscious human beings who were not only aware of their environment but also of their mortality. Where exactly that dividing line lies is difficult to say. The Neanderthals started burying their dead some 100–150,000 years ago. That action would seem to indicate that they were aware of their mortality and their possible survival in another world.

When Charles Darwin in 1859 proclaimed the message of evolution through random mutations and natural selection, the Western churches violently opposed this theory as being demeaning to humankind and relegating God, at best, to "the winder-up of the clock" or, at worst, to the scrap heap (see also the chapter on Creationists versus Evolutionists). The fact, of course, is that it is hard, if not impossible, to refute the basic ideas of evolution; there are simply too many proofs of "evolution-with-time" staring us in the face. So, while there are still some skirmishes being fought here and there, the great majority of Christians, Jews and Muslims accept the basic fact that evolution played a significant role in the development of nature and that of the human being. Most, however, would make the proviso that there are many steps in the development of human beings which cannot be explained by evolution alone.

So, the battle today is not whether the natural world, and more specifically human life on this planet, evolved over time, but whether humans are just a particularly bright species of animal or whether they are something special and created for a specific purpose. Looking at all the evidence, I find it almost incomprehensible that many people, including some outstanding scientists, still believe that the human being is essentially a bright animal without any special distinction and without any spiritual component. There are a number of different points of view amongst those who believe that humankind did not, in any essential way, evolve beyond the status of an intelligent animal. Because these points of view are still held by many people, even scientists, I am presenting in the following pages a very brief summary of the way they look at the human species.

Materialism – Determinism – Reductionism – Relativism

The first of these philosophies or doctrines is that of materialism. This belief is as old as the onset of the first civilizations. It basically claims that all animals, plants and humans are essentially machines – inanimate machines without any inherent purpose and simply the product of blind chance and natural selection. In particular, they believe that humans are just material molecular assemblies without a spirit or a soul. According to Jacques Monod[1] in *Chance and Necessity*:

Chance is the source of all novelty, all creation in the

biosphere. Anything can be reduced to simple, obvious mechanical interactions. The cell is a machine. The animal is a machine. Man is a machine. There is no soul anywhere.

Francis Crick, a Nobel laureate and co-discoverer of the DNA helix, recently made the statement that he believes that human beings are nothing but neurons – the cells in our brains which trigger all activities of the human body. Compare this with James Jeans'[2] statement, as far back as 1930, when he expressed his impression that the universe begins to look more like a great thought than like a great machine.

Another researcher, Michael Persinger,[3] declares in a recent article that the religious and mystical experiences someone might have had are simply brain artifacts, as he calls them. According to him, he can generate the same emotions to various degrees in a laboratory by stimulating parts of the brain with electrical currents in a sensory deprivation chamber. Melvin Morse,[4] writing on the subject of "near-death experiences" in his book *Closer to the Light*, claims that this is not factual at least for these experiences. He claims that dozens of studies have shown that the lack of oxygen to the brain does not cause the kind of experience as described by the people who have had these near-death experiences. But even if Michael Persinger were right, I am not entirely clear what he is trying to say with this statement. The fact that he can duplicate these phenomena in his laboratory, by doing certain things to the brain, surely does not prove that these are not real phenomena. I am certain that he can stimulate other parts of the brain to give the person, in the isolation chamber, the feeling of cold or heat. Would he then draw the conclusion from this that heat and cold do not exist in the real world, and that hot pokers or cold ice cubes are nothing but artifacts of the brain? I think not.

One of the real dangers to society, created by pure materialism, is that it does away with ethics and the need for moral behavior. True materialists, if they take their convictions to their logical conclusion, should simply live by the concepts of necessity and expediency only. With this philosophical outlook on life, it is completely illogical for us to treat fellow human beings differently from the way we treat animals. Thus, it makes no sense to preserve human life if it is not perfect according to some preset standard. We do away with malformed and sick animals, don't we? So why not do the same with babies who are born with birth defects or with people who need special assistance to survive? As Amit Goswami[5] wrote recently:

> In the world of materialism, where everything is made of matter and where matter is the fundamental reality, in such a world, material needs proliferate and will lead, at best, to a sickening surfeit of material possessions and, at worst, to a world of crime, disease and other ills.

One look at our daily newspapers is enough to show that our materialistic attitude of the last decades has brought us perilously close to this situation.

The second point of view, which is much like the first one, is called determinism. It is exactly the opposite to free will. In its most simple form it states that everything in life is "preordained". Isaac Newton, towards the end of his life, went so far as to say that the universe was like a vast clockwork which God had wound up at the beginning of time and that after that God was not needed anymore. Newton thought that this clockwork operated using its own laws of motion and, that by using these laws, one could calculate the precise position and motion of all particles in the universe in the near and far future. Others took this concept to its final conclusion and stated that all future events, including wars and all human behavior, could be calculated or predicted with mathematical precision if, at a certain point in time, the initial condition of all atomic particles in the universe were known. Michio Kaku[6] points out that, if this theory is taken to the extremes, the determinist believes that he should be able to calculate, again with mathematical precision, what you, your son or daughter will eat in what restaurant ten years from now.

Of course, determinism does away with the concept of God, although some will still tolerate God as the original clock winder who started everything in motion – other than that, God is not needed. Of course, this way of looking at the universe does away entirely with free will. We are all machines, with a wound-up clock inside us, which makes us follow the set pattern forever. In certain ways, this is similar to the predestination dogma of some of the fundamental churches and also of Islam. In its extreme form, this leads to a fatalistic attitude that makes one feel that it is useless to fight disease, hunger or injustice because God willed it so. Anyone who has ever flown in an airplane owned by a fundamental Muslim country will remember the phrase the captain uses when he announces the flight plan – "We will arrive at our destination, at such and such a time, Inshallah – God willing." Even in my own upbringing, I remember that all announcements of time were followed by the letters D.V., Deo Volente, again meaning God willing.

So, some forms of determinism are not strangers to the Christian, Jewish and Muslim faiths. But I believe that it misrepresents some of the basic dogmas of the church. It is our free will which, most of all, is the human attribute that makes us somewhat like God, which is exactly what we are according to Genesis, where it is says that we are made in the image of God. It is our ability to choose freely between good and evil, between accepting God and rejecting her, that makes us different from all God's other creatures in this world. We will return to this later.

By putting these two philosophies together we get what is called material determinism, which simply states that we are machines with a predetermined future and that nothing exists beyond what we perceive with our five senses. Everything in life and in nature can be explained in terms of ordinary physics and chemistry.

With the emergence of quantum mechanics the theory, that everything can be calculated from a set of initial conditions, has become completely untenable simply because Heisenberg's uncertainty principle states that it is theoretically impossible to know all the conditions of an atomic particle at the same time, and that the presence of an observer changes what is being observed. This, of course, makes the philosophy of complete determinism untenable.

Then there is reductionism which states that all structures and phenomena can be reduced to, and completely described by, their components and interactions. There is only one material reality; all things are made of matter and consciousness is a secondary phenomenon. In essence, it is an attempt to explain the higher in terms of the lower, and to reduce the higher to the level of the lower. For example: in biology, all of life is explained in terms of physics and chemistry; in medicine, the body is treated simply as a physical entity without taking into account the power of the spirit and the soul in healing; in sociology, society is reduced to individuals organized by the state, commercialism and capitalism (Bede Griffith[7] in *A New Vision of Reality*). And, as Joel Achenbach[8] writes:

> Reductionism is not all that useful most of the time. Love, for example, may be a function of brain chemistry and animal behaviour shaped by millions of years of evolution, but if you wanted to know more about love you would have better luck talking to a poet than to a biologist.

Finally, there is relativism, which states essentially that moral claims are simply conventions developed by society to regulate social behavior with no ultimate significance. In this type of philosophy, morals and values are simply rules of convenience.

It is my firm belief, that all these theories and philosophies cannot begin to explain some of the most fundamental features of our human existence. George Ellis[9] in his book, *Before the Beginning, Cosmology Explained*, lists five fundamental features of importance relating to human purpose and meaning. All of them relate to human endeavors, which cannot be explained by any of the foregoing theories and philosophies.

First, there is the drive for meaning, which appears to be a universal feature of human life. It manifests itself in the rituals, myths, arts, etc. of all social groups, starting with the earliest civilizations we know of (see also Chapter VII). It is difficult to see how this drive for meaning could possibly be the result of purely physical and chemical processes, or could be the result of evolution and natural selection. In the materialistic/deterministic scenario, the drive for meaning is an unnecessary luxury that adds nothing to the survival of healthy specimens who can propagate the species. Its existence surely cannot be the outcome of some physical and chemical processes.

Harold M Franklin,[10] the author of *The Way of the Cell, Molecules, Organisms and the Order of Life*, writes about his view of life as: "The bedrock of this book is that life is a material phenomenon, grounded in chemistry and physics." Nevertheless, he is looking for meaning and values outside the world of science when he writes:

> The universe revealed by science is under no obligation to be meaningful to mankind, and one can make a strong case that it is in fact utterly indifferent to us.

Then he goes on to say:

> For me, as for most humans past and present, the search for meaning remains unfinished, an aspiration rather than an achievement.
>
> Science, and particularly the narrow focused and reductionist science of the present day, is perceived of denying the world meaning; and without meaning humans cannot live.

For a scientist who believes that life is a purely material phenomenon, the search for meaning outside of science is contradictory. If we insist that there must be a meaning to life, and if science cannot provide it, then there is only one possible answer left: there must be a higher authority or deity who has given that meaning to human life.

Secondly, there is the drive for a source of values that has moral power. There appears to be a universal capacity to recognize high moral qualities, and there seems to exist among all people, including the people in the earliest known civilizations, an equally universal sense of justice. Again, one might ask where does this come from, certainly not from evolution. Natural selection would actually tend to promote those species which are not bothered by values or a sense of justice. On the contrary, natural selection would favor those species which are aggressively self-centered. Is it really reasonable to assume that natural selection and random mutations, acting on the world's population, could select beings for a higher morality? In his book, *The Selfish Gene*, Richard Dawkins[11] argues that there is a certain evolutionary advantage to being altruistic, but we are trying to press the point that we are talking about being altruistic without looking for any advantage to ourselves.

In the book mentioned in the previous paragraph, Frank Harold writes about human values as follows:

Science has little useful to say about good and evil, right and wrong, justice and oppression, and the strange way of the heart.

In the absence of such a transcendent presence (God), many of the premises of civilization lose their historical mooring: that human life is sacred, that we know right from wrong, that we are here to some purpose, and that our lives have a higher meaning... But it is not at all evident that, absent a belief in powers greater than ourselves, a decent and civilized society can be sustained for long.

Again for a scientist who believes only in a material reality, this presents a very pessimistic outlook for the future of our civilization.

Thirdly, Ellis recognizes the drive to search for understanding and truth. It is this search for understanding of nature that fueled the drive for discovery and research that led to the present advances in our science and technology. Apparently, no other species seems to have this drive. True, some animals exhibit a great deal of curiosity but it can hardly be called a drive for understanding and truth. At this point in time, it is possible to see that there is some survival-of-the-species value in the practice of science and technology – that is, if it is properly used. If not, the drive for understanding could easily lead to the destruction of the species by the wrong application of these technological advances. In any case, the search for truth and understanding has been with us long before this search led to our present technological society. Furthermore, the search for truth, quite independent of the search for understanding, is one of the human traits that is quite unique, has no survival value, and is something we all share, whether we are materialists, determinists or reductionists. It is certainly not something that a machine would invent.

The fourth factor Ellis mentions is the propensity of the

human race for hope. Hope for a better future and, in its ultimate sense, the hope for finding a way to conquer death. As Ellis expressed it: "Human beings cannot be adequately understood except in connection with man's unconquerable propensity for hope in the future – it is through hope that men overcome the difficulties of any given here and now". Again, it is difficult to see hope emerging as the end result of purely chemical and physical processes.

Lastly, there is the drive for beauty and decoration. Recent discoveries show that even the earliest humans started to form figurines of clay and began to make exquisite paintings on rock faces with materials which they must have developed over a long period of time. The drive for beauty is obviously the result of a need for self-expression which seems to be present in humans of all ages and in all stages of development. For instance, the primitive tribes of Australia and New Guinea all exhibit a great drive for self-decoration. Again, the drive for beauty is not something that would naturally result from chemical and physical processes or from machine-like creatures. As Wolfhart Pannenberg[12] put it in his book, *Faith and Reality*:

> In all these achievements humankind is both creatively free and appears as a creation of spiritual reality which raises him above and beyond himself. The most decisively creative acts of his spiritual life are the most impressive evidence for this: the creative design of an artist, the sudden discovery of a truth… all that takes hold of us by some kind of inspiration. All such experiences bear witness to the reality of a power, which raises up hearts – the power of the Spirit. When man is most creative, he is most conscious of being grasped by a spiritual power which raises him above himself.

To these five human characteristics of Ellis, I would add the drive for love and compassion. They are somewhat implied in some of Ellis' preceding features, but I believe that the drive for love and compassion is so important in our society that it warrants special mention. Love, in its highest manifestation, takes the form of vicarious love, the sacrifice of one person's life to save the life of another. No one, surely, can deny that this type of love exists; yet it goes against all the concepts of materialism and evolution. Conscious, self-sacrificing love is not compatible with the theory of survival of the fittest; in fact, it is diametrically opposed to those principles. It is recognized that some of the social animals, such as ants and bees, exhibit some of this self-sacrificing behavior when they sacrifice their own lives to defend the colony. However, this appears to be a purely mechanical reaction and the sacrifice is certainly not made as a conscious choice.

There is one more human characteristic I would like to add to this list of fundamental features of human existence and that is the search for meaning through religion. From all the discoveries about the lives of our early ancestors, it is clear that all of these early humans had a profound experience of awe of the holy, and were aware of the existence of something much greater s daily lives; a being who profoundly influenced their lives, and whom they could pray to and make sacrifices to in order for it to look more favorably upon them. I cannot think of any early civilization that did not have this sense of dependency on a higher entity which influenced their lives in a most essential way. Even today, with all our modern technologies, this search for meaning through religion continues unabatedly. There are the "new age" movements, the renewed interests in Eastern religions and Eastern practices such as yoga, etc.

So there we have it. Materialism, determinism and evolution cannot begin to explain some of the most fundamental features and characteristics of the human being. They cannot explain:

- the undeniable existence of the drive for meaning;
- the drive for values, moral principles and justice;
- the search for understanding and truth;
- the hope for a better future;
- the drive for beauty and decoration;
- the drive for love and compassion, and especially the existence of sacrificial love; and
- the search for meaning through religion.

To a degree we are fortunate to live in this day and age during an unprecedented time of scientific discovery and theories, which have, in many ways, proven that the concepts of materialism and determinism can no longer be defended on a scientific basis. First of all there is Einstein's concept of time in which time goes slower if you near the speed of light. Then there is the fact that we cannot know all the properties of an atomic particle at the same time; the fact that in the act of observing we change what is being observed; the fact that such things as light particles can be two things and can be in two places at the same time. There is the feature of nonlocality in which two particles miles apart, and with no connection between them, can interact with each other instantly. And lastly, the final nail in the coffin of determinism, in the subatomic world an action or cause does not always have the same effect; the best that can be said is that there is a certain probability that a defined cause will have a defined effect.

I believe that these theories, which have been proven time and again in laboratories across the world, have once and for all put an end to the philosophies of materialism and determinism. These are not just my beliefs; they are supported by scientists who are far better qualified than me to pronounce judgment on these matters. To quote just a few:

The Bell-Aspect theory of nonlocality is the ultimate challenge to material realism.[13]

We must now acknowledge that the micro world is governed *not* by deterministic laws that precisely regulate the behavior of atoms and their constituents, but by randomness and indeterminacy. (Amit Goswami[14] in *The Self-Aware Universe*)

The calculus of physics has ceased to be deterministic, in the technical sense; it no longer predicts precise outcomes even from ideally defined situations… it made Eddington withdraw his objection to free will. (Donald MacKay[15] in *Brains, Machines and Persons*)

The fact that something can influence something else without any connection and do that instantly changes the perception what is possible in the mind. (Derek Gjertsen[16] in *Science and Philosophy, Present and Past*)

If the materialistic universe can be described as a clock, then a deep suspicion is growing among many scientists that it may be a pocket watch kept in the vest of an intelligence called God. (Sylvia Fraser[17] in *The Quest for the Fourth Monkey*)

Free Will

At several places in this book I have mentioned free will as one of the main attributes of a human being. It is, I believe, the natural consequence of being created in the image of God. It is also one of the most treasured properties of humankind. Nobody, not even the most ardent materialist, wants to think of himself or herself as a zombie, a robot, a creature whose actions are all determined by a bunch of nerve cells, and by the interaction of some subatomic particles that follow the law of cause and effect. A similar argument has arisen recently about the influence of genes over our actions. It is sometimes argued that, since genes determine our physical and emotional make-up, we have no control over our actions, and that we simply do what our genes have preordained us to do. The fact is, however, that the genes do not control our actions; all they do is give us a predisposition to have a certain illness or a certain character trait. In the final analysis it is our internal make-up, our free will if you want, that is influenced by our environment and by the values we are taught, which make us do certain things in a certain way.

That we have a free will is probably best illustrated by the fact that we have a judiciary system which holds us accountable for our actions. Except in cases of mental illness, in which the person is simply incapable of distinguishing right from wrong, a judge will sentence us on the basis that we do have a choice; that we do know what is right or wrong and that we are quite capable of choosing one action over the other. The judiciary system, in all civilized countries, will not accept as valid that it was our genes or an uncontrollable action of some nerve cells which made us do the wrong thing.

In his book, *The Tao is Silent*, the author, Raymond Smullyan,[18] uses a discussion between God and Mortal as a means to highlight some of the essentials of free will. In the beginning of this imaginary discussion, Mortal wants to get rid of his free will. He complains that he did not have a choice, he was not consulted, it was simply foisted on him by God. God then asks him why he does not want to have this ability to make choices. Mortal replies that free will means moral responsibility and that makes it possible for him to do the wrong thing and makes him sin. Without free will he feels that he cannot sin since he is not responsible for his actions.

Later, in the discussion between God and Mortal, God says that he really did not have a choice about giving humans a free will. The writer makes God say: "Did it never occur to you that a sentient being without free will is no more conceivable than a physical object with no gravitational attraction." Free will is not an "extra", it is part and parcel of the very essence of consciousness. A conscious being without free will is simply a metaphysical absurdity. In other words, a creature without free will is simply not a human being.

As Kenneth Miller[19] writes about the freedom God has given his creation:

> He, God, is the master of chance and time, whose actions, both powerful and subtle, respect the independence of His creation and give human beings the genuine freedom to accept or reject His love.

So, if we consider all the evidence I think we can safely say:

- that there is more to life than materialism and that it is the spiritual values which govern human life; and
- that human life is not predetermined or preordained, but that we have a free will which allows us to make our own choices, both good ones and bad ones.

NOTES

[1]Monod, Jacques, *Chance and Necessity*, Vintage Books, 1972.
[2]Jeans, Sir James, *The Mysterious Universe*, Cambridge University Press, Cambridge, 1930, p.186.
[3]Persinger, Michael, quoted in *Equinox*, no.82, August 1995.
[4]Morse, Melvin, *Closer to the Light, Learning from Near-Death Experiences of Children*, Random House Inc., New York, 1991.
[5]Goswami, Amit, *The Self-Aware Universe, How Consciousness Creates the Material*

World, G. P. Putnam and Sons, New York, 1993, p.3.

[6] Kaku, Michio, *Visions, How Science Will Revolutionize the 21st Century*, Doubleday, Dell Publishing Group, New York, 1994.

[7] Griffith, Bede, *A New Vision of Reality*, Templegate Publishers, 1992.

[8] Achenbach, Joel, see Chapter IV, note 12.

[9] Ellis, George, *Before the Beginning, Cosmology Explained*, Boyars/ Bowerdean, London, New York, 1993, p.104.

[10] Franklin, Harold M., *The Way of the Cell, Molecules, Organisms and the Order of Life*, Oxford University Press, New York, 2001.

[11] Dawkins, Richard, *The Selfish Gene*, Oxford University Press, Oxford, 1990.

[12] Pannenberg, Wolfhart, *Faith and Reality*, The Westminster Press, Philadelphia, 1977, p.37.

[13] Goswami, Amit, *The Self-Aware Universe, How Consciousness Creates the Material World*, G. P. Putnam and Sons, New York, 1993, p.139.

[14] Goswami, Amit, *The Self-Aware Universe, How Consciousness Creates the Material World*, G. P. Putnam and Sons, New York, 1993.

[15] MacKay, Donald, *Brains, Machines and Persons*, Collins, London, 1980.

[16] Gjertsen, Derek, *Science and Philosophy, Present and Past*, Penguin Books, London, 1989.

[17] Fraser, Sylvia, *The Quest for the Fourth Monkey*, Firefly Books, 1994, p.24.

[18] Smullyan, Raymond, *The Tao is Silent*, Harper Collins Publishers, New York, 1977.

[19] Miller, Kenneth, *Finding Darwin's God, A Scientist's Search for Common Ground between God and Evolution*, Harper Collins, New York, 1999, p.243.

Part B
Religious Beliefs and Concepts

Chapter VII
RELIGIOUS BELIEFS THROUGH THE AGES

In Chapter III, we have seen how, over a period of some three billion years, life slowly emerged from a single cell creature to full-grown human beings, and how the earliest human-like beings arrived on the scene some 50,000 to 35,000 years ago. These early humans, who had originally emerged from Central Africa, had, by the end of this period, populated almost all the corners of the world from Australia to China to Europe to the Americas.

In his monumental work, *The Story of Civilization*, Will Durant[1] wrote that if we define religion as the worship of supernatural forces, we must observe that although almost all primitive people had some sort of religious practices, there were some, such as a few of the Pygmy tribes in Central Africa, who apparently had no religion or religious ceremonies at all. But, writes Durant, such cases are exceptional and the old belief that religion is universal is substantially correct. He continues with the statement that philosophers are fascinated by the problem of the antiquity and the persistence of religious beliefs. He asks, what are the sources of this indestructible piety of humankind? His answer is that the source of piety for primitive people was the fear of death; he believes that they probably marveled at the phantoms which they saw in their sleep and were struck with terror when they saw in their dreams the figures of those they knew were dead. Such experiences probably convinced early humans that everything had a soul, or a secret life within, which could be separated from the body in illness, sleep or death. It followed from this, they believed, that all things had souls or contained hidden gods. Consequently, anything in nature could become the object of religious worship. Durant even divides these objects of worship into six classes: celestial, terrestrial, sexual, animal, human, and divine. In this chapter, we will follow in a very abbreviated form how these religious concepts and practices slowly emerged during this period from roughly 35,000 years ago to the dawn of the Christian era.

Starting with our earliest known ancestors, the Cro-Magnons who lived some 50,000 to 35,000 years ago, we see from the excavations relating to this period the first signs of the emergence of some sense of a hereafter. This is most clearly shown by the discovery that these early humans apparently buried their dead with some ceremony and placed food and implements in the grave beside the body. They also marked their graves by headstones and animal horns. Considering that they probably needed the food themselves and, that the making of any type of tool must have been a very laborious and time-consuming work, this act would seem to indicate that they thought the departed could very well have a use for these articles in a later life. At the same time, they must have been very much aware that the physical body which they were burying would disintegrate and would have no need for food or implements then and there. So, I believe, it is clear that by this act they demonstrated two things: first, that they believed in some sort of hereafter and secondly, that they cared enough for their dead relatives to go to this length to assure their future well-being. It is of course also possible that they intended these articles to appease the spirits and gods which they thought reigned over the afterlife; or that they tried to appease the spirits of the deceased person so that these spirits would not interfere with the lives of those left behind. The real motive was probably a mixture of these ideas. In some cultures it is even reported that, in order to prevent the possible interference with their own ongoing life, they would remove the body, not through the entrance to the hut, but through a hole they had especially made for this purpose in the side of the dwelling. They would then transport the body three times around the house, so that the spirit of the departed would get confused and would not be able to find the entrance into the house again. In any case, it is clear from these customs that these early humans had a firm belief in a surviving soul or spirit which would continue after death.

Excavations have shown that, even at this early date, the people of that day had a sense of beauty and expressed that in the sculpted figurines of goddesses and paintings of animals. As early as 20,000 years ago, and maybe even earlier, these people painted beautiful pictures of animals in rock caves located in North Africa, Spain and France. There is very little doubt that these paintings were made to assist the painter in the hunt for these animals, their main way of obtaining food for themselves and their offspring. That they were not made for their aesthetic beauty alone is clear from the fact that some of these paintings are hidden in very inaccessible places, not at all conducive to frequent visits by themselves or other members of their tribe to admire their artwork. Also, to make the paint and then paint on uneven rock faces must have taken a lot of effort and skill. So, it can be safely assumed that they believed that by making an image of the animals on which they depended for their survival, they could somehow exert some mastery over that animal.

It is also interesting to note that as early as the year 10,000 B.C.E., or 12,000 years ago, our forefathers had developed distinctive languages and made musical instruments, mainly flutes. It may be assumed that they used their voices to accompany these early musical instruments or, vice versa, that they used these instruments to accompany their singing. Thus, the arts of sculpting, pottery, painting and music developed very early in the human journey from primitive humanoids to our more "sophisticated" modern people.

During much of these early years a thick ice sheet covered most of North America and Northern Europe. So, the people living in those days in Europe had to contend with a much colder climate than we experience today. It is clear from some of the cave paintings that, at a very early date, they covered themselves with animal skins to survive the rigors of the Northern climate. The hunt for animals and the importance of animals in their daily lives became even more pronounced as they provided not only food but also clothing, and later also covering for their teepees and tents. This use of tents made it possible for them to travel further afield for their hunt in that they did not always have to depend on caves for their shelter. It is no wonder that, with this great dependence on the animal world, they began to worship these animals. As we shall see later, there is no animal, from beetles (scarabs) to monkeys to elephants, which has not, at one time or another, been the subject of some type of veneration.

By about 8000 B.C.E. the ice sheet had receded to where it is approximately today. This date, about 10,000 years ago is also considered by many the date of the emergence of the earliest "civilized" human being. It is after this date that human development took place at an unprecedented pace. Somewhere between 8000 and 5000 B.C.E. the most dramatic and far-reaching event in the march of progress took place – the development of agriculture. Without this step, human development would probably have stagnated at a very primitive level, maybe something like that of the Australian aborigines at the time of the discovery of that continent. It is difficult to decide which came first, the domestication of animals, such as sheep and goats, or the tilling of the soil to extract crops of barley and wheat. Of course, the early humans had always gathered fruits and wild grains, but they had never before put seeds in the ground deliberately to harvest a crop later. These developments allowed the transformation of the hunting and nomadic societies into agricultural societies that by their nature were firmly anchored to the land they were farming. As soon as the practice of agriculture became established, we see the rise of the first small permanent settlements that later changed into villages and towns.

Two of the first known larger cities to emerge were Jericho in Palestine and Catal Húyúk in Anatolia, present-day Turkey. Jericho apparently had more than 2,000 inhabitants as early as 8000 B.C.E., and Catal Húyúk counted some 1,000 homes in 6250 B.C.E. with an estimated 6,000 inhabitants. Excavations have shown that the latter practiced a simple form of irrigation, bred cattle, and cultivated three types of wheat as well as barley. They also did a fair amount of trade with neighboring settlements.

These people still buried their dead between, or even in, their houses. Religious practices mainly took the form of adoration of fertility goddesses. These goddesses were, it seems, always depicted as very heavy-set women with enormous buttocks, thighs and breasts. The first appearances of these goddesses occurred well before it became known that the male of the species was also involved in the procreation process. It is clear, however, that the veneration of mother and fertility goddesses went on long after this, since the breeding of cattle requires at least a basic understanding of the procreation process. Since their whole existence depended on the fertility of themselves, of their animals and also of their soil, it is no wonder that they tried to influence this fertility by making images which represented that concept and finally to begin worshipping these images. And so, the people of Cabal Húyúk built shrine rooms between their houses and dedicated these to the supreme fertility goddesses.

It is interesting to see that one of the earliest manifestations of worship, the worship of fertility and mother goddesses, persisted well into the modern era, and was almost universal, at least, in Europe and the Middle East. There was Inana in ancient Sumeria, Ischtar in Babylonia, Isis in Egypt and finally Aphrodite in Greece, spanning some 10,000–12,000 years.

The belief in an afterlife for their relatives and friends led to attempts to contact these people after their deaths, much as many people still try to do today through spirit mediums. However, the methods employed by some of the early rulers were somewhat hard on slaves. It is reported that one ruler communicated with the dear departed by giving the message he wanted to be sent to one of his slaves, and then sent this message on its way by lopping off the head of the messenger. If he later wanted to add to this, he sent another message in the same unorthodox way by another slave.

In the meantime, other developments had taken place that made it possible for the human to increase his mastery over nature (see Figure 3.4). First, there came the practice of irrigation in Mesopotamia around 5000 B.C.E. and the invention of metallurgy shortly thereafter. The next monumental development occurred in Mesopotamia as well – the development of writing. It is thought that this first started as an aid to bookkeeping when they began to trade in herds of animals and other agricultural products. Of course, keeping track of numbers became even more important when the rulers of the day started to collect taxes from their, no doubt, reluctant subjects. So, the first writing appeared as impressions made in clay tablets utilizing symbols both for the product and the quantity transacted. Because these clay tablets were fired in small ovens, they became very durable and made it possible for archeologists to follow the development of writing from simple symbols to more elaborate alphabets later. Bookkeeping may not be the earliest profession, but it ranks up there with the very oldest of professions which was being widely practiced at the same time. The latter was closely linked to religious ceremonies in the early temples when temple prostitution became an honored profession.

With these steps forward, we now enter the era when the first civilizations made their appearances on the world scene. At what time in the development of a society we use the word civilization is rather an arbitrary choice. A fairly widely accepted criterion is that, for a society to be called a civilization, it must have towns with no less than 5,000 inhabitants, use a written language and have ceremonial centers or temples in which some type of religious ceremonies or rites are being performed (see Figure 7.1).

By this definition, probably the earliest civilization was that of the Sumerians which started some time before 3000 B.C.E. in the valley of the Tigris and the Euphrates. This was closely followed by the emergence of the civilization of the Egyptians which started in the Nile Valley around the same time. Next came the early civilizations in the Indus Valley, which started somewhere around the year 2500 B.C.E. This was followed by the first cultures in China which developed in the Yellow River Valley around 1700 B.C.E. This first Chinese civilization is generally called the Shang culture after the Shang dynasty which ruled parts of China from 1750 to 1027 B.C.E.

The earliest civilizations in Europe were those of the Minoans on the island of Crete, which started around 2000 B.C.E. but then suddenly disappeared around 1500 B.C.E. However, before its disappearance, a new civilization had grown up in Greece around the year 1600 B.C.E.: this culture, called the Mycenaean culture, also ended suddenly for no known reason around the year 1100 B.C.E.

In North America, the earliest civilization was that of the Olmecs which started in Mexico around 1000 B.C.E.; it is probably best known for its enormous heads carved out of stone. The Olmec culture blended into that of the Mayan which died out suddenly, again for no apparent reason, around the year 500 C.E. The Civilizations of the Aztecs in Mexico and the Incas in Peru did not arise until around 500 C.E.: both civilizations were brutally terminated by the arrival of the Spanish conquistadors around 1520–1535 C.E.

By putting the development of religions in table form (see Table VIIa), it is easier to see how each civilization went through almost the same developmental pattern. All seem to have started with the idea of a soul or an afterlife, followed by animal veneration, hunting magic, fertility and mother goddesses, veneration of ancestors, worship of kings, worship of city and state gods, and finally the emergence of the present-day major religions.

If we use the arrival of Abraham in Palestine as the beginning of Judaism, it becomes the oldest of the four major religions, starting around the year 2000 B.C.E. This is followed by the earliest manifestations of the Hindu religion in the Indus Valley by about 1500 B.C.E.; Buddhism, which grew out of Hinduism, was started by Siddharta Gautama, the Buddha, probably around the year 510 B.C.E.; and, if we take the resurrection of Jesus Christ as the starting point, Christianity started in the year 33 C.E. Finally Islam is said to have arrived officially with Mohammed's flight from Mecca to Medina in the year 622 C.E.

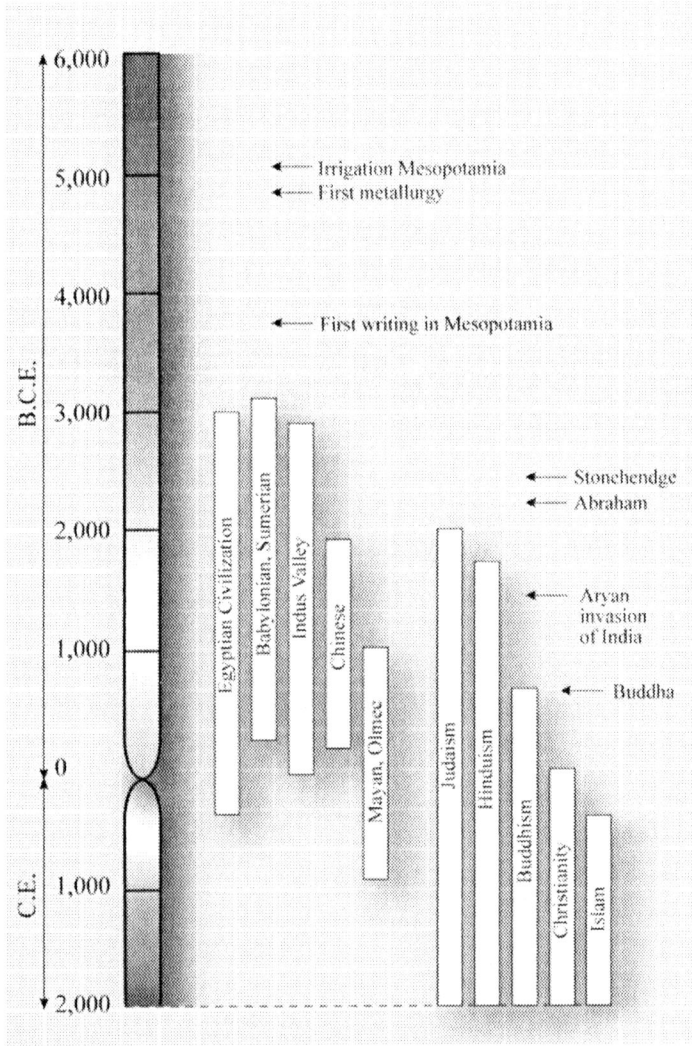

Figure 7.1
The Emergence of the Early Civilizations and the Birth of the Major World Religions

Table VIIa: *Chronology of the Religious and Ceremonial Developments*

To put the religious and ceremonial developments in perspective, I have presented below a brief summary in table form.

PERIOD		LOCATION	RELIGIOUS EXPRESSION
35000	B.C.E.	Middle East	Veneration of animals, dead buried with grave goods
		Europe	Fertility cults, the first goddesses' figurines
15000	B.C.E.	Europe	Cave paintings, hunting magic
8000–5000	B.C.E.	Middle East	Funeral rites, shrine rooms
		Mediterranean	Ancestor worship, mother goddesses, hunting cults
5000–3000	B.C.E.	Mesopotamia	Mother goddesses, city gods living in temples
		Mediterranean	Mother goddesses, fertility cults
		Egypt	Divinity of the pharaohs, animal gods, pyramids
		Europe	Communal burial grounds, ancestor worship
		India	Fertility goddesses, mother goddesses
3000–2000	B.C.E.	Mesopotamia	Lavish temple complexes, ziggurats
		Mediterranean	Fertility goddesses, mother goddesses

		Palestine	Abraham is told by God to move to Palestine
		Europe	Lavish temple complexes, animal sacrifices
		Egypt	Divinity of pharaohs declining, rise of Sun god Re
2000–1000	B.C.E.	Turkey	Hittite fertility gods, storm and Sun gods, 65 deities
		India	Rise of the Hindu gods, first Vedic literature
		Far East	Rise of various divinities, offerings and sacrifices
1000–500	B.C.E.	Mesopotamia	Rise of city gods
		Europe	Olympian pantheon, animal and infant sacrifices
		India	Appearance of Brahma, Upanishads, Buddhism
		Americas	Olmec jaguar worship, funeral cults in N.A.
500–0	B.C.E.	Mesopotamia	Zoroastrianism
		Egypt	Appearance of the gods Isis, Horus and Osiris
		Mediterranean	Appearance of Greek, Phoenician, Etruscan, Roman state gods, human sacrifices, appearance of philosophy as an alternative to religion
		India	Brahmanism develops into Hinduism

		Far East	Philosophical religions such as Confucianism, Taoism
		Americas	Human sacrifices, local gods
33	C.E.	Palestine	Start of Christianity
622	C.E.	Arabia	Start of Islam

One of the astonishing things most of these early civilizations had in common was the construction of large temple complexes. Sometimes, these were accompanied by even larger pyramids (Egypt) and ziggurats (Mesopotamia) as burial places for their rulers. Most of these temples were very large and very elaborate, and the building of them must have consumed a very large part of the GDP (Gross Domestic Product) of these countries. Many were probably built with slave labor, but even so these people had to be fed and housed; furthermore, the way these buildings were made required craftsmen of just about every type, and materials that had to be imported from faraway places. In the Bible there is a detailed description of how King Solomon built the temple in Jerusalem; it includes a long list of the materials and craftsmen he imported from other countries to make a magnificent temple worthy of the God he worshipped.

In some cases, such as the temples and pyramids of the Mayans, these structures were made without the use of wheels or even metal tools. How they built these elaborate structures with their many stone carvings is an utter mystery. Whatever methods were used, it must have been a very laborious process and it must have taken decades, if not centuries, to complete these complexes.

In some sense, this is reminiscent of the churches built in the Middle Ages all over Europe. In the town where I studied, Delft in The Netherlands, the "Old Church" was

RELIGIOUS BELIEFS THROUGH THE AGES

started in the 1200s and the "New Church" was started "shortly" after the completion of the "Old Church" in the 1400s. These churches are masterpieces of architecture and must have cost the equivalent of hundreds of millions of dollars.

Most of these temples and churches were probably built with lots of coercion by the rulers and religious leaders. Nevertheless, the general population must have supported the erection of these elaborate structures as a tribute to the gods they worshipped; otherwise they would probably never have been completed.

Before continuing in the next chapter by tracing the development of the idea of a God, who also created the universe, I would like to end this chapter with a rather lengthy quote from Will Durant in his chapter on "Moral Elements of Civilization".

> The moral functions of religion are to conserve established values, rather than create new ones. Hence a certain tension between religion and society marks the higher stages of every civilization. Religion begins by offering magical aid to harassed and bewildered mankind; it culminates by giving to a people that unity of morals and belief which seems so favorable to statesmanship and art; it ends by fighting suicidal in the lost cause of the past. For as knowledge grows or alters continually, it clashes with mythology and theology, which change with geological leisureliness. Priestly control of arts and letters is then felt as a galling Shaklee or hateful barrier, and intellectual history takes on a "conflict between religion and science". Institutions which were at first in the hands of the clergy, like law and punishment, education and morals, marriage and divorce, tend to escape from ecclesiastical control, and become secular, perhaps profane. The intellectual classes abandon the ancient theology and – after some hesitation – the moral code allied with it; literature and philosophy become anti-clerical. The movement of liberation rises to

an exuberant worship of reason, and falls to a paralyzing disillusionment with every dogma and every idea. Conduct, deprived of its religious supports, deteriorates into epicurean chaos; and life itself, shorn of consoling faith, becomes a burden alike to conscious poverty and to weary wealth. *In the end a society and its religion tend to fall together, like body and soul, in a harmonious death.* Meanwhile among the oppressed another myth arises, gives new form to human hope, new courage to human effort, and after centuries of chaos builds another civilization.

Thus Durant saw the rise and fall of civilizations and religions. Of course, one does not have to agree with him on all points, but there appears to be a lot of truth in it: for instance, his statement that society and religion fall together is one that has proven itself time and time again over the centuries. It is hoped that today's decline in religious practices does not also signify the end of our society or civilization.

NOTES

[1] Durant, Will and Ariel, *The Story of Civilization, Moral Elements of Civilization*, Simon and Schuster Inc., New York, 1935.

Chapter VIII
THE EMERGENCE OF GOD, THE CREATOR

VIIIa God, the Creator in Hinduism

In the previous chapter, we have traced the development of the earliest forms of worship, of fertility and mother goddesses some 20,000 to 30,000 years ago, to the appearance of the first modern concepts of God, the Creator, in India and Palestine 4,000 years ago. In India it was the absolute God, Brahman, who emerged first in the Vedic writings around 3,500 years ago. It should be noted here that Hinduism makes a distinction between Brahman, the Absolute and Brahma, the supreme God. As some writings have it, "There is a variation in the energy of Brahman and the chief energies are known as Brahma, Vishnu and Shiva." To emphasize the difference, the word Brahman is neuter, while the word Brahma is masculine. In the following pages this distinction is not always followed, and there may therefore be some confusion once in a while about whom we are talking.

Brahman is described in the Vedas as the Absolute – it is one and indivisible; it is unchangeable and beyond action and inaction; it is beyond good and evil. It is from Brahman that everything in this world has emerged, and it is the ultimate objective of all Hindus to finally merge with it again. The description of Brahman in one of the early sacred scriptures, the *Bhagavad-Gita*, in a translation by Mohini Chatterji,[1] reads as follows:

I shall declare that which is to be known; knowing which man attains deathlessness, the Supreme Brahman, having no beginning, and said to be neither subject to affirmation nor to negation. (Because He is above all attributes).

His hands and feet are everywhere; everywhere His eyes, heads, and mouths; His ears everywhere in the worlds; enveloping everything He dwells.

Manifested in the operation of all organs and faculties, yet devoid of organs and faculties. Unattached, He supports all, though devoid of attributes, He is the experience of all attributes.

He is the within and without of all beings, moving and stationary. Unrealizable on account of His subtlety; though afar, He is near.

Though undistributed, He appears to dwell as distributed in creatures: the same that which is to be known is the supporter of creatures, is the devourer and producer.

He is the light of lights, is said to be beyond darkness. He is knowledge, that which is to be known and that which is the ultimate end of knowledge, and is seated in the hearts of all.

Thus, the Hindus believe that Brahman is everywhere and in everything. This belief has led to the great reverence by the Hindus of everything living; an attitude which greatly affects everyday life in India even today. It accounts for their vegetarianism; the cows wandering undisturbed in busy streets; the monkeys in the temples, etc.

In Hindu mythology, Brahman manifests itself as the god Brahma, the creator of the universe; as the god Vishnu, the sustainer of the universe; and as the god Shiva who eventually causes the destruction of the universe. Despite this pre-eminence of Brahma as the creator of the universe, it is interesting to note that in the daily life and worship of the Hindu, Brahma plays a very minor role: for instance, there are very few temples dedicated to him as compared with the temples dedicated to Vishnu and Shiva and the thousands of other deities in the Hindu pantheon.

Vishnu, the preserver and sustainer, is considered more to be the god of love and is believed to have taken on a physical form a number of times in the past to overcome evil. So far, it is believed he has appeared nine times, the most important being as Rama, of Ramayana fame, and as Krishna. Shiva, the destroyer is also the god of fertility. In pictorial form he is usually shown as dancing and having four arms. While Shiva is the destroyer, he is also at the same time considered to be the creator, because out of destruction and death comes rebirth and new life.

As said before, the Hindu believes that everything emanates from Brahman but that Brahma was the actual creator. There are a number of creation stories in the Vedas. The following is a passage out of the Hymn of Creation from the Rig Veda.

> At that time there was neither nonexistence nor existence; neither the worlds nor the sky, nor anything that is beyond. What covered everything, and where, and for whose enjoyment? Was there water, unfathomable and deep? Death was not there, nor immortality; no knowledge of night or day. "That One Thing" breathed without air, by its own strength; apart from it, nothing existed. Darkness there was, wrapped in yet more darkness; undistinguished, all this was one water; the incipient lay covered by void. "That One Thing" became creative by the power of its own contemplation. There came upon it, at first, desire which was the primitive seed of the mind, and man of vision, searching in their heart with their intellect, found the link to existence in the nonexistence. There were begetters, there were mighty forces, free action here and energy up yonder… The gods are later than this creative activity; who knows, then, from where this came into being? Where this creation came from, whether one supported it or not. He who was supervising it from the highest heaven, He indeed knows; or He knows not!

From this quotation it is clear that Brahman created the world by his own will and that the gods, presumably Brahma also, came later. While it is not clear from this quote, there are other creation stories which do make it clear that Brahma created the universe from eternally existing material and not from nothing as in the Judeo-Christian tradition.

For most Westerners, the way of describing Brahman and his actions is often very difficult to follow. For instance, the description of Brahman goes continually from affirmation to negation, which leaves the reader hanging in mid-air: "He indeed knows or He knows not; though afar, He is near; though devoid of attributes, He is the experiencer of all attributes; etc."

Thus, Hindus believe that within Brahma is this power to create life, and when this power is exercised it results in the creation of the universe which takes the form of "maya", the material world that we perceive with our senses. In the Hindu's thinking, however, what we perceive with our senses is not necessarily the ultimate reality and so the word maya is often translated as "illusion". But that is misleading. The Hindu would argue that as long as the world appears real and demanding to us, we must accept it as such. In the book, *The World's Great Religions*,[2] this maya is compared with heat arising from a fire: the heat is not the fire and yet it comes from the fire and cannot exist without it. Some Hindu philosophers, while still believing that maya is not a total illusion, nevertheless try to explain the concept of maya by comparing it with a dream. The images that appear in a dream are perfectly real to the dreamer, but only to the dreamer and then only for a short time. I believe this comes very close to saying that the universe and life are an illusion. This is somewhat reminiscent of the modern concepts expressed in some of the quantum theories that the world only exists because it is being observed – it is the observer who gives the universe its reality.

The Hindu belief that the world moves in cycles is another concept in Hinduism which comes close to some modern ideas about the continued existence of the universe. The Hindu believes that at the end of each cycle, fire or water will destroy the universe which will then merge again with Brahman. This process of birth and destruction is believed to go on forever. They believe that each cycle lasts 4,320,000,000 years, which is about the same length of time we believe our solar system has existed. As pointed out in Chapter III, there is a theory in modern scientific thinking that our expanding universe will not necessarily continue to expand forever. If the universe contains less than a minimum amount of matter, the power behind this expansion will eventually run out of steam and make the universe collapse upon itself. It is argued by some that after this happens, the creation story will begin again with the same type of Big Bang that started this universe. The best estimate for the length of this cycle is between 40 and 100 billion years as compared with the Hindu cycle of 4.32 billion years. And while the two figures differ substantially, it is nevertheless interesting to note that Hinduism has thought in terms of cycles of billions of years for a number of millennia.

So, we see Brahman, the Absolute, the Creator of everything giving souls, Atman, to all things which live and breathe. All through this earthly life, this soul is trying to reunite with Brahman in Nirvana. When a soul finally reaches this stage of self-realization, usually after many cycles of reincarnation, it loses its personality and its individuality and the life of the Hindu is over forever. At the same time, Nirvana is also described as a place of unassailable security, of bliss and eternal happiness.

As opposed to the Christian God, Brahman does not speak to humankind; it cannot meet men and women; it transcends all such human activities. Nor does it respond to humans in any personal way: sin does not offend it, and it cannot be said to love us or be angry with us. Thanking and praising it for creating the world would be inappropriate. Thus Brahman is a very distant deity, a deity who has no direct contact with the human being.

Over the centuries, this basic belief has essentially remained the same, despite the fact that literally hundreds of different types of Hinduism have emerged over time: all with their own rituals, their own special deities, and their own temples and places of worship. In recent years, yet other forms of Hinduism have appeared, some of which try to bridge the differences between today's major religions. Some believe that, in more recent times, Brahman has incarnated itself a number of times and that, for instance, Christ and Buddha were incarnations of Brahman. The latest incarnation, they believe, was that of Sri Ramakrishna who lived in the mid-1800s. He taught that all religions are basically the same and are all expressions of the same God. He is said to have practiced various forms of Hinduism, as well as Christianity, Buddhism and Islam, and he claimed to have received visions of God in all these religions.

So, the supreme God of the Hindus remains for us a very shadowy figure. He, or it, created the world and the souls of the people, but life may be as insubstantial as a dream. The highest goal of all living souls is to merge again into its creator and lose all its identity and thus effectively disappear from the world scene.

To conclude this very brief look at Brahman, the supreme God of Hinduism, I would like to use this quote from one of the early Vedic texts:

> Of that Brahman there are two conditions, one possessed of form, the other formless. These decaying and undecaying states exist in all creatures. The undecaying is

the highest Brahman; the decaying is this entire universe. Just as light is diffused from a fire which is confined to one spot, so is this whole universe the diffused energy of the supreme Brahman.

VIIIb God, the Creator, in Judaism, Christianity and Islam

FROM THE CREATION TO ABRAHAM

The emergence of God, the Creator of Judaism and therefore of Christianity, is recorded in the books of the Old Testament which form part of the Christian Bible and the Hebrew Bible, the Tanahk. The difference between them is that the various books which make up the Old Testament are placed in a different order. In both, the Old Testament starts with the book of Genesis. It is in this book that we find the familiar story of the creation of the universe by God virtually out of nothing, and by God's word and divine wish only. Genesis begins as follows:

> In the beginning when God created the universe, the Earth was formless and desolate. The raging ocean that covered everything was engulfed in total darkness, and the power of God was moving over the water. Then God commanded, "Let there be light" – and light appeared. God was pleased with what he saw. Then he separated light from darkness and he named the light "Day" and the darkness "Night". Evening passed and morning came – that was the first day.
>
> On the second day, he created the Earth and sky.
>
> On the third day, he separated the land and the sea and created seed bearing plants and trees.
>
> On the fourth day, he created the Sun, the Moon, and the stars.
>
> On the fifth day, he created the first animals, the fish in the sea and the birds in the sky.
>
> On the sixth day, he created the land animals and

finally he created humans.

Then God said, "And now we will make human beings; they will be like us and resemble us. They will have power over the fish, the birds, and all animals, domestic and wild, large and small." So God created human beings making them to be like himself. Have many children, so that your descendants will live all over the Earth and bring it under their control. I am putting you in charge.

Genesis 1, abbreviated, *Good News Bible*

When looking at this sequence of creation, it is interesting to note how the order of creation is very much like that presently understood by modern science, except for the time that the Sun, Moon and stars appear in this creation story. All that it requires is to interchange the third and fourth day, as it is obvious that they have to come before the arrival of plants and trees. Otherwise, it is almost uncanny how a writer living 2,500 to 2,600 years ago could have gotten so close to the order of creation as we believe it to have evolved.

Today, not very many people believe that the creation story as told in Genesis is the historical account of how the universe and us, humans, were created. Instead we believe that this story of creation is a myth, a legend in which God conveys to us three great truths: first, that God created the universe; second, that we are created in God's image; and third, that God put us in charge of that creation to look after it and preserve it. Later, we will consider what it means for us to have been created in God's image: it gives humans an importance and responsibility that we do not find in other religions. Continuing the story of creation, God gave names to the humans he had created, and called the male, Adam, and the female, Eve. In the beginning, the story goes, they lived in an idyllic state of innocence in the Garden of Eden. However, they soon rebelled against God because they

THE EMERGENCE OF GOD, THE CREATOR

wanted to be like him. As a result they were expelled from their beautiful garden, and they were told that from then on they would eat their food by the sweat of their brow and would give birth to children with pain, and finally that they would eventually die and return to the dust from which they were made.

The story goes on with Adam and Eve having children, Abel and Cain. Soon we have the first murder when Cain becomes jealous of his brother, Abel, and kills him in a fit of rage. Later, the descendants of Adam and Eve behave in a way that is so far removed from what God had intended, that God was sorry he had created humans and he caused a great flood to wipe out most of humanity. Before doing so, God told Noah to build a large ship, "the ark", and to assemble in it all seeds and also pairs of all animals. The flood came and destroyed all humans except those in Noah's ark. Later the flood subsided and Noah and his ark came to rest on Mount Ararat. This mountain is located in Northern Turkey and the summit is almost 17,000 feet above sea level. This, of course, makes the story very suspect, because even with the ice caps of the North and South Pole melting, the water covering the whole Earth could never have reached a height that is anywhere near a mountain top. In any case, the story continues, a new cycle of life started from the seeds and animals Noah had been able to save. God then made a covenant with Noah that he would never again destroy the Earth through floods and as a sign of that covenant God created the rainbow. "As a sign of the promise which I am making to all living beings that I will not destroy the Earth again by a flood." (Genesis 9–11)

While the story of the great flood as depicted in the Bible could never have happened quite as described in Genesis, it is obvious that a great flood did occur at some time which covered most of the land between the Tigris and the Euphrates rivers in present day Iraq. Excavations have shown that underneath the whole of Mesopotamia there exists, at some depth, a thick stratum of mud which could only have been deposited by a prolonged flood. Also, in Sumerian literature there is almost the exact same account of a great flood caused this time by the God Ea, who instructed Utnapishtim to build an ark and save seeds and animals to ensure the continuation of life after the flood subsided. So, I believe, we can safely conclude from this that something like a great flood happened some time in antiquity. The best estimate at present is that it occurred somewhere around 4000 B.C.E. This story of the flood and Noah's ark certainly has fired the imagination of people in all ages. Once in a while, expeditions are still being mounted to try to find the remains of Noah's ark on the slopes of Mount Ararat. I flew over it once and was impressed by its beauty and its snow-covered summit, but from the air it was quite clear that all the water in the world could never have caused a ship to end up near its summit. In *The Bible as History*, Werner Keller[3] points out that there exist some 80,000 publications in seventy-two languages about Noah and the great flood of which 70,000 mention Mount Ararat.

These stories of the creation of the universe and of the great flood were written quite late in the history of the Israelites, probably around 500 to 600 B.C.E. when the Israelites were in exile in Babylon. In any case, well after King David's time and the time of most of the prophets such as Elijah, Isaiah, and Jeremiah. This late appearance of the creation story is the reason that this story of creation and the names of Adam, Eve and Noah are never mentioned again in the rest of the Old Testament. Their importance is that this is the first time God made himself known to the Israelites as the only God and the Creator of everything that exists. So in the history of how God revealed himself to the Israelites, the story of creation should be placed somewhere after the major prophets, instead of at the beginning of the Bible which, of course, is historically correct.

The reason I have gone into some detail with these stories of the creation and the flood is that for the first time we see God emerging as the Creator of the universe, and therefore the God of all people. Secondly, it clearly points to the importance of human beings as having been created in the image of God, somewhat like him. Thirdly, that God has put humankind in charge of that creation and made us responsible for it. Finally, the story of Noah clearly shows that if we go against God's will, the Earth will be put in peril, not maybe as in the case of Noah by a flood, but by conditions we ourselves create by misuse of nuclear power; by pollution of the land, sea and air; and by not stemming the explosive population growth before it is too late. It is interesting to see the renewed interest in the stories of Genesis in recent years. Bill Moyer, the well-known TV commentator, hosted a TV series of ten weekly episodes dealing only with Genesis, and *Time* magazine carried a ten-page story in its October 28, 1996, issue called "Genesis Reconsidered".

After the story of Noah, the book of Genesis continues with a precise genealogy of Noah's descendants. All lived very long lives which decreased with time from Noah's 950 years to Abraham's 175 years. It is with the appearance of Abraham that we come to historical times. It is his appearance that is generally considered the start of the Jewish nation, roughly around 2000 B.C.E.: in other words, 2,000 years after the flood and not the 400 years as may be deduced from the genealogy described in Genesis. The way God revealed himself to the descendants of this Abraham makes up the rest of the Old Testament. In reading it, we must always remember that the Israelites at the time had not heard the creation story as told in Genesis in which

God revealed himself as the Creator of the whole universe. Especially at the beginning, they thought mostly of their God as one among many others.

Up to the point of Abraham's appearance on the world scene, God is not identified with any special people. This changes, however, with the selection of Abraham with whom God made a special covenant and through him with his descendants, the people of Israel. God chose this tribal chief and his descendants to reveal himself over time. He could have selected any other tribe or nation in the Americas, in China, Africa, or Europe, but God didn't and selected this particular people as his own. Of course, looking at the map of the fertile crescent on Figure 8.1, it is clear that God chose a tribe that lived amid nations which were at the cutting edge of civilization and that had highly developed skills of which the ability to write and record history was probably the most important. It was in this central crescent that a number of cultures developed and others could be reached. There were the Persian and Sumerian civilizations to the East; the Greek and later the Roman civilizations to the North and West; the long established civilization of the Egyptians to the South; and the early civilizations of the Indus Valley to the Far East.

The story of Abraham starts with his father, Terah, leaving his home town, Ur, in the south of Mesopotamia, to go to Canaan, the present-day Palestine. However, he did not finish the trip but settled instead in Haran in Southern Turkey. It is here that Abraham first hears God's call:

> Leave your country, your relatives and your father's home and go to a land that I am going to show you. I will give you many descendants, and they will become a great nation. I will bless you and make your name famous, so that you will be a blessing.

THE EMERGENCE OF GOD, THE CREATOR

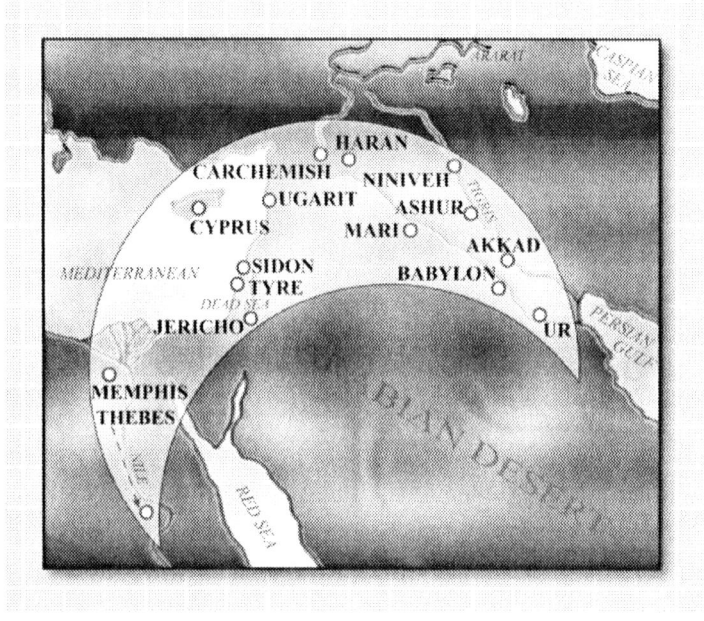

Figure 8.1:
The Fertile Crescent – the Great Centers of Civilization about 2000 B.C.E.
(Source: *The Bible as History*)

I will bless those who bless you,
But I will curse those who curse you.
And through you I will bless all nations.

Genesis 12 – *The Good News Bible*

It is interesting to speculate which God Abraham thought was calling him. Without having heard the creation story of Genesis, there is no indication that Abraham knew or had any previous experience with that God. Of course, living in the southern part of what was then the Sumerian civilization, he must have been very familiar with the gods of the Sumerians. Now, Abraham's wife, Sarah, was barren, which for an Eastern tribal chief must have been a real disappointment and tragedy. So, here is this unknown God promising Abraham that he would become the father of a great nation and that he would become famous. For some reason, Abraham trusted this God to do what he promised and took all his cattle and his whole household on this, probably very dangerous, trip some 600 miles to the south into the land of Canaan, which later became known as Palestine and today is known as Israel. Abraham probably followed the well-established trade routes which led from the North of Mesopotamia to Egypt. He probably did not have to cross any state borders, but he must have passed by a number of city-states such as Damascus. God certainly kept his promise. As we all know, Abraham's descendants are many and can be found all over the world as a distinguished and separate people who follow their own religion. And, as far as Abraham's fame is concerned, there is probably no other person as well-known in the history of the world as he is, even today. This nomadic chief of 4,000 years ago is considered the father of the Jewish faith and thereby of the Christian faith; at the same time, the Muslims consider him the father of their religion. You can't get more famous than that!

Many people consider the history of the descendants of Abraham, the Jewish people, after God made this covenant with Abraham, as the clearest proof that God really does exist. In the 4,000 years which have passed since God made that covenant, the Jews have had a more turbulent and violent history than any other people, yet they are still here today. The descendants of Abraham were enslaved in Egypt for some 450 years; they were sent into exile by the Babylonians for some 100 years; later they were dispersed all around the world. They were persecuted almost everywhere they went: six million of them died in Hitler's concentration camps during World War II. Yet, today they are once more a nation, Israel, at the place God had promised Abraham four millennia ago. Any other group of people, under similar circumstances, would have been assimilated into the general population long ago. Their survival, against all odds, can only be explained as the result of having been chosen as a special people with a special mission.

When Abraham finally settled in what is now the State of Israel, a famine hit the area and Abraham took his entire household to Egypt and later returned when the famine was over. Looking at the map of the Fertile Crescent, it is interesting to note that Abraham during his lifetime traveled from the extreme end of this crescent in Ur to the other extreme end in Egypt. In doing so he came into contact with all the known civilizations and religious practices of the time. When he left Ur in southern Mesopotamia, he left behind the civilization of the Sumerians who worshipped Sun and Moon gods to whom they had dedicated large temple complexes and ziggurats. In Canaan he must have run into the worship of fertility and mother goddesses; while in Egypt he must have seen the pyramids and been confronted with the divinity of the Pharaohs and the worship of the Sun God Re. Yet, as we read in Genesis, Abraham remained true to the God who had commanded him to leave Haran and settle in Canaan.

Although, God had promised him offspring in great numbers, nothing very much happened after that for quite some time. It was his wife Sarah who finally convinced him to take one of her Egyptian maids, Hagar, as a second wife. Abraham did, and Hagar bore him a son whom she called Ishmael. Later on, after God had once again promised him a son, Sarah actually became pregnant and bore a son whom they named Isaac. As could be expected in such a complicated household, it did not take long for quarrels to break out between the two boys and their mothers. In the end, Abraham did a very strange thing: he sent Hagar and his son Ishmael away from their encampment with hardly enough food and supplies to survive in the near desert conditions. After some close calls, Hagar and Ishmael managed to survive: God also promised Hagar that Ishmael would become the father of a large nation. Legends, and the Koran, have it that Ishmael became the father of all the Arabs and thus later became the father of the Muslim faith.

In the meantime, God had made the following covenant with Abraham:

> I will keep my promise to you and to your descendants in future generations as an everlasting covenant. I will be your God and the God of your descendants.
>
> Genesis 17 – *The Good News Bible*

God then told Abraham to circumcise all his male descendants, "as a physical sign that my covenant with you is everlasting." Ever since then, no matter where they went, Jewish male children have always been circumcised. Sometimes this worked greatly to their disadvantage; for instance, during the Nazi period in Germany it was an easy way to verify that someone was indeed Jewish.

It should be noted that, during the later stages of Abraham's life, God identified himself as, "I am the Lord, who brought you out of Ur of the Chaldeans to give you this land to take possession of it," and later as, "I am God Almighty." As said before, the story clearly indicates that Abraham thought of the God revealed to him as one among many others, similar to the gods of the tribes and nations around him.

Eventually, Abraham and his wife died and the story of

God's revelation continues with the story of his descendants, first Isaac and later Jacob, the father of the twelve tribes of Israel.

FROM MOSES TO THE END OF THE OLD TESTAMENT

After the death of Abraham, the covenant between God and Abraham was renewed with his son Isaac and later with Isaac's son, Jacob. Jacob had twelve sons, who later became the fathers of the twelve tribes of Israel. Towards the end of Jacob's life, a severe famine again hit the area and Jacob and his entire family settled in Egypt. They remained there for some 450 years. As they would do again so many times in the future, these Hebrew people did not integrate with the local population but remained separate and did not worship the gods of Egypt, which at that time included the reigning Pharaoh. They prospered in Egypt and grew to be a force to be reckoned with to the extent that the Pharaohs became alarmed at their number and started persecuting them by forcing them into slave labor. They even went so far as demanding that the Israelites kill all their male children.

It was then that a new leader, Moses, arose. Moses was called by God in the "burning bush" incident to go to Pharaoh and tell him that he should let the children of Israel leave for Palestine. But, as the Bible tells it, Moses was not too clear who this God was who was calling him to do such an outrageous thing. So Moses asked God, what am I to say to the Israelites when they ask me who this God is who has ordered me to do this. And God answered:

> I am who I am. You must tell them: "The one who is called I AM has sent me to you." Tell the Israelites that, I, the Lord, the God of their ancestors, the God of Abraham, Isaac and Jacob have sent you to them.
>
> Exodus 3 – *The Good News Bible*

In the original Hebrew text, the name God gave Moses is recorded as YHWH: this seemingly strange, unpronounceable name comes to us this way because the ancient Hebrews did not use vowels in their written word. This leaves us to guess how this name was actually pronounced. Also, the ancient Hebrews thought that God's name was so sacred that no ordinary mortal should use it. In English the name is most often translated as Yahweh or even Jehovah. In any case, it is clear that neither Moses nor the Israelites had a clear idea who the God was who said that his name was YHWH. The meaning of the name has been interpreted in many different ways, most often it has been thought to mean, "I am Who I Am" as used in the quotation above. Some scholars have even suggested that the real meaning is something like, "My name is none of your business, so get on with the job I gave you to do."

In any case, after some persuasive action by God, in the form of pestilences, plagues, etc. Pharaoh eventually let the Israelites go, and they again became the nomadic people they originally were. According to the Bible, they traveled for a period of forty years in what is now the Sinai Peninsula, the Negev Desert and the Kingdom of Jordan. Just before they entered the Promised Land, Palestine, the Lord gave Moses the Ten Commandments on Mount Sinai. Again God identifies himself with the words: "I am the Lord your God who brought you out of Egypt, where you were slaves. You must not worship other Gods but me. Do not bow down to any idol or worship it, because I am the Lord your God and I tolerate no rivals." Note that it does not say, "Do not worship other gods because there are no other gods – I am the only one." Clearly, they still believed that there were many other Gods around and that their God, who now was generally referred to as "Yahweh", was only one of many.

After Moses, Joshua took over as the leader of the

THE EMERGENCE OF GOD, THE CREATOR

Israelites and led them into the Promised Land. Once they had conquered it, the land was divided between the twelve tribes. Joshua then called the people together and repeated all that the Lord had done for them. He then gave them a choice, to serve this God or to serve the gods their ancestors had served in Mesopotamia. The people answered, "We would never leave the Lord to serve other gods." It is quite obvious though that even Joshua believed they had a choice, and that there were other gods whom they could serve and worship. So far, the God revealed to them had many of the characteristics of the major gods they had seen in adjacent countries. He appeared to them first as a warrior God; a God who brought plagues to the Egyptians and who helped them win battles and defeat the armies of the city-states which they wanted to take over. Also, this God was in many ways a cruel God who instructed Joshua to kill all the inhabitants of the lands they were invading. The reason given for this cruelty was that otherwise the Israelites might start to worship some of the idols and gods of the indigenous populations. The Israelites obviously did not do a very good job of this because for many years they had to do battle with the people who had obviously been spared, and many times God had to warn them not to worship the local god Baal or the goddess Asherah.

After the conquest of Canaan, the image of God as a god of war disappeared and the God we know as a personal, compassionate God appeared – this is the God of Psalms 23 and 139.

Psalm 23 is probably the best known and is recited on a great many occasions, especially funerals, all over the world. It reads, in the King James translation, as follows:

> The Lord is my shepherd: I shall not want.
> He makes me to lie down in green pastures:
> He leadeth me beside the still waters.

> He restoreth my soul:
> He leadeth me in the path of righteousness for his name's sake.
> Yeah, though I walk through the valley of the shadow of death,
> I will fear no evil:
> For thou art with me; thy rod and thy staff shall comfort me.
> Thou preparest a table before me in the presence of mine enemies:
> Thou annointest my head with oil; my cup runneth over.
> Surely goodness and mercy shall follow me all the days of my life:
> And I will dwell in the house of the Lord forever.

The idea of a personal God who knows everyone "inside and outside", is most clearly expressed in Psalm 139, probably written by King David some 1,000 years before Christ.

It is quoted here from the New English Bible:

> Lord thou hast examined me and knowest me.
> Thou knowest all, whether I sit or rise up;
> Thou hast discerned my thoughts from afar...
> Where can I escape from your spirit?
> Where can I fly from thy presence?
> If I climb up to heaven, thou art there:
> If I make my bed in hell, again I find thee.
> If I take my flight to the frontiers of the morning
> Or dwell at the limit of the western sea,
> Even there thy hand will meet me
> And thy right hand will hold me fast.

Despite the feelings here expressed by the psalmist, the Bible tells us how God's people time and time again started to worship Baal and Asherah. It is the prophets who are called by God to warn the kings and the people of Israel that they have a covenant with their own God and to mend their ways. Sometimes they do, other times they don't, and God punishes them through the hand of the rulers of the neighboring kingdoms such as the Assyrians and Babylonians.

One of these prophets, Isaiah, who lived around 700 B.C.E., proclaimed, probably for the first time, that their God was not one among many, but was the only one when he wrote:

> The Lord who rules and protects Israel.
> The Lord Almighty has this to say.
> I am the first, the last, the only God;
> There is no other god but me.

In the same chapter, Isaiah takes the next step in God's revelation when he is told to proclaim that this God of Israel is the Creator of all things:

> I am the Lord, your savior.
> I am the Lord, the Creator of all things.
> I alone stretched out the heavens;
> When I made the Earth no one helped me.
>
> I am the one who made the Earth
> And created mankind to live there.
> By my power I stretched out the heavens.
> I control the Sun, the Moon and the stars.
>
> Isaiah 44 and 45 – *The Good News Bible*

All this was proclaimed by Isaiah, some 150 years before the creation story of Genesis was written. So, it is clear that the writer of the first chapters of Genesis was not writing something which came as a big surprise to the Jews of that time. In fact, the basic message of the creation story had been acknowledged by the prophets a long time before. Here for the first time in history, we see God, the God of the Israelites, emerge as the only one and as the Creator of all things. For the Jew, and also for the Muslims, this is such an important part of their religion that the devout Jew and Muslim repeat it daily. For the Jew it is: "Hear, O Israel, your God is one." For the Muslim it is: "There is one God and Mohammed is his prophet."

Later prophets, such as Jeremiah, repeat this acknowledgment of their God as the only one and the Creator of the universe. Jeremiah even has a rather sarcastic thing to say about the other religions being practiced in their area:

> The religions of these people are worthless.
> A tree is cut down in the forest;
> It is carved by the tools of the woodworker and decorated with silver and gold.
> It is fastened down with nails to keep it from falling down.
>
> Such idols are like scarecrows in a field of melons;
> They cannot speak; they have to be carried because they cannot walk.
> Do not be afraid of them: they can cause you no harm, and they can do you no good.
>
> Jeremiah 10 – *The Good News Bible*

Between the first revelation to Abraham and the revelations through the prophets, the perception of God has changed from a tribal warrior god, one among many others, to the one and only God, the Creator of heaven and Earth; a God who is compassionate and close to humans, who has created humankind in his image and has given it responsibility for all of creation. The God who through the Ten Commandments told us how to live and who later told Isaiah to say to the people of Israel:

> Cease to do evil.
> Learn to do good,
> Search for justice,
> Help the oppressed,
> Be just to the orphan,
> Plead for the widow.
>
> Isaiah I:17 – *The Good News Bible*

In trying to understand what God is like, we must remember that we will never be able to fully understand God's nature and God's being. God is a Spirit, who lives or exists on an entirely different plane of existence than we do. In more scientific terms, we might say that God exists in a space with other dimensions than our four-dimensional world. In terms of what we discussed in Chapter II, we might even go so far as to say that God lives in a nonlocal world, nonlocal in both time and space. In other words, he is not bound by time or by space; in his world, time and space simply do not exist.

With this concept of God, it will be clear that we never can or will understand God fully as long as we ourselves are limited by space and time. At best, we will only be able to get glimpses of what God is really like, and even those glimpses will be distorted through our imperfect vision and understanding. In some ways, we are like the four blind men in the Indian fable. The four blind men were walking in the jungle and ran into an elephant. The first one ran into the side of the elephant and said, "Hey, I have run into a wall." The second one who ran into the elephant's leg said, "I don't know about you, but I have run into a tree trunk." The third one who had grasped the tail said, "I have a hold of a thick rope." Finally the fourth man who was feeling the tusks said, "This is crazy, I have got hold of a piece of polished wood." The point is that, although each one was giving a perfect description of what he had experienced, they would never have been able to conjure up the picture of an elephant without someone explaining to them how their individual experiences, although entirely different, fitted perfectly into the image of an elephant.

In some ways, we are like the blind men. We can only experience one aspect at a time of what God really is like. The prophets in the Old Testament certainly showed us some of the aspects of God's nature and being but, for the Christian, it is Jesus Christ who most clearly showed us what God is like as we will see in the next section.

For a more detailed account of the emerging of the concept of God in the history of the Jewish people see *The Gifts of the Jews: How a Tribe of Desert Nomads Changed the Way Everyone Thinks and Feels* by Thomas Cahill.[4] As far as seeing the presence of God in history is concerned, Cahill finds this in the way the Jews developed a whole new way of experiencing reality as he writes:

> The story of Jewish identity across the millennia against impossible odds is a unique miracle of cultural survival. Where are the Sumerians, the Babylonians, the Assyrians today? And though we recognize Egypt and Greece as still belonging to our world, the culture and ethnic stocks of these countries have little continuity with their ancient namesakes. But however miraculous Jewish survival may be, the great miracle is surely that the Jews developed a whole new way of experiencing reality, the only alternative to all ancient worldviews and all ancient religions. *If one is ever to find the finger of God in human affairs, one must find it here.*

For a graphic presentation of the history of the Hebrews see Figure 8.2.

Note: in Cahill's opinion, Judaism gave us the "processive" worldview, a view of the world that had a

THE EMERGENCE OF GOD, THE CREATOR

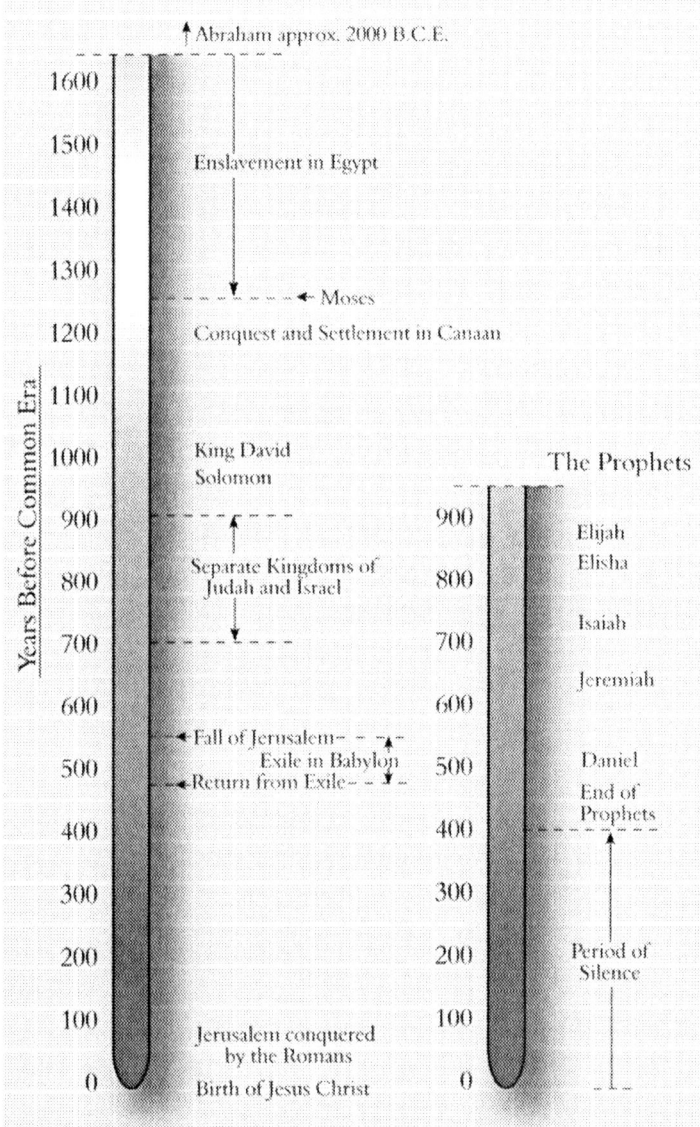

Figure 8.2
The Historical Record of the Hebrews from Abraham to the Birth of Christ

beginning and an end. He contrasts this with the cyclical worldview of the non-Western religions where there is neither a beginning nor an end. He believes that it is only in the processive worldview that concepts such as the Big Bang could have originated.

VIIIc Jesus, the Long-Awaited Messenger of God

All through the Old Testament, God had promised Israel that he would send them a special messenger, someone like a great prophet or king. This leader was visualized as someone especially anointed by God, like the kings of Israel were anointed by the High Priest when they were installed as rulers over Israel. This special messenger was given the name of the *Messiah*, the anointed one of God in Hebrew, or the *Christ* in Greek.

All through their history, the Jews would remind themselves that some day soon the new leader would come who would lead them to national greatness. Of course, this was a lot of wishful thinking since the promise they had received did not refer to an earthly kingdom but to a heavenly one. The Jews kept reminding themselves of this promise during the 400 years between the last great prophet and the birth of Jesus Christ, the Messiah. When Jesus finally was born in very humble circumstances, the majority of the Jews did not accept him as the long-awaited Messiah but rejected him completely. His birth and the accounts of his teachings are recorded in the New Testament. According to these accounts, Jesus was born in a town called Bethlehem at what we now call the beginning of the Christian era. His mother Mary had been told before his birth that he was in effect the long-awaited Messiah, Son of God, and that she was to name him Jesus.

Jesus' father, Joseph, was a carpenter by trade and Jesus probably followed in his footsteps and became a carpenter as well. Although, not directly recorded in the Bible, there are some indications that Joseph died young and that Jesus, as the oldest son, had to support his mother and his younger brothers and sisters. For the first thirty years, Jesus must have led the normal life of an artisan in the village of Nazareth to which the family had returned after a short sojourn in Egypt. Nazareth is located in Galatia, the northern part of Israel and located some 100 km north of Jerusalem.

At the age of thirty, when his brothers were probably old enough to be in a position to take over the family responsibilities, Jesus changed his lifestyle completely and became an itinerant teacher and started to proclaim the message of the Kingdom of God. He soon attracted a band of disciples around him who traveled with him all over the countryside. These disciples were mainly simple fishermen who were so inspired by his message that they left everything and followed him wherever he went. During his travels, he must have visited Jerusalem a number of times during the annual Jewish festivals. Here, he came immediately into conflict with the religious leaders of the day who had made the religion of their forefathers into a legalistic set of rules which had completely hidden the message of love and forgiveness that had been preached by the prophets. Worst of all, he upset the establishment by condemning some of the practices in the temple which brought large financial rewards to the insiders. So, it was not long before the religious leaders tried to silence him. In the end, when that appeared not to be possible by peaceful means, they resorted to violence and sought to kill him. Since they were under Roman rule they had to get this done through the Roman occupiers of their country. So great was their hatred of this most peaceful of all men that they sought the help of the despised and hated Romans. In the end, with some trumped-up charges, they got the

Roman authorities to agree, and Jesus was crucified by Roman soldiers. So died the Messiah, who was proclaimed to be the Son of God, by his disciples at the age of thirty-three, at the urging of the leaders of the official "religion" of that time and by the hand of a foreign military force.

As far as everyone was concerned, this was the end of a rather distasteful episode, the sooner forgotten the better. Then, something strange happened, rumors began to circulate among the people of Jerusalem that this crucified teacher had actually risen from the dead on the Sunday morning, following his death on Friday afternoon, and was actually alive and had appeared to many of his disciples. This resurrection of Jesus on Easter morning is one of the cornerstones of the Christian religion: the Christian believes that, following Jesus, all humans will be resurrected and will continue life in a hereafter in close harmony with God. In fact, we believe that death is not the end but the beginning of a new transformed existence.

What actually happened on that particular Sunday morning will forever remain a mystery. At first the authorities tried to discredit it and many people have questioned the veracity of what happened on that Easter morning. One of the most interesting arguments for the historical truth of the resurrection I have ever read comes from Dr. Principal Hill, as quoted by James Kennedy[5] in his book, *Why I Believe*. In this quotation, Dr. Hill enumerates what we are saying if we do not believe that the disciples were inspired by the resurrection and by the consequent outpouring of God's spirit on them. He writes:

> But if not withstanding every appearance of truth, you suppose the testimony of the apostles to be false, the inexplicable circumstances of glaring absurdity crowd upon you.
>
> You must suppose that twelve men of mean birth, of no

education, living in that humble station which places ambitious views out of their reach and far from their thoughts, without the aid from their estate, formed the noblest scheme which ever entered the mind of men, adopted the most daring means of executing that scheme, and conducted it with such an address as to control the imposture under the semblance of simplicity and virtue.

You must suppose:

- That men guilty of blasphemy and falsehood, united in an attempt the best contrived and which has in fact proved to be most successful for making the world virtuous;
- That they formed this singular enterprise without seeking any advantage to themselves, with an avowed contempt of loss and profit, and with the certain expectation of scorn and persecution;
- That although conscious of one another's villainy, none of them ever thought of providing for his own security by disclosing the fraud, but that amid suffering to the flesh and blood they persevered in their conspiracy to cheat the world into piety, honesty and benevolence.

Truly they who can swallow such suppositions have no title to object to miracles.

This may be a very negative proof; nevertheless it makes it clear that his disciples and followers believed in the resurrection. This is especially important because they had not foreseen this at all. The New Testament describes how Jesus, after his resurrection, remained with them for forty days and nights and then was taken up to heaven and was seen no more in the flesh. Before leaving them, however, Jesus promised his disciples that he would send them a helper – a spirit – which would guide them and tell them what to do.

And so, on the day of Pentecost when the disciples were

in Jerusalem waiting for this helper to arrive, the spirit of God descended on them and they became changed men and women. This fearful band of simple men and women became transformed; they became eloquent and inspired preachers. They stood up to and defied their religious and political leaders and started to travel around the Roman world to spread the message of Jesus. Many of them were killed in the process – some in a manner equally as cruel as the crucifixion of Jesus. But they persevered and others followed in their footsteps. Their message and their way of life was what impressed so many people that, fifty to sixty years after Jesus' death, his message was being proclaimed throughout the Roman Empire from Turkey to North Africa and Southern Europe. Finally in the year 300 C.E., the Roman Emperor, Constantine, made Christianity the official religion of the Roman Empire.

So, you may ask, what is this message which even today has such an influence on people, that hundreds of millions across the world still try to follow that teaching in their daily lives and identify themselves as Christians – that is followers of Jesus Christ?

In the first place, Christians believe that it is Jesus' example, his life when he was alive and living among us, that tells us what God is like:

> Who has seen me has seen the Father. The Father is in me and I am in the Father.
>
> No one has ever seen God. The only Son, who is the same as God and is at the Father's side, he has made him known.
>
> John 1:18 – *The Good News Bible*

So, if we want to know more about God, we should study the New Testament which contains the four accounts of Jesus' life, and the letters the apostles wrote to the young churches they had formed in Asia Minor and Europe. The question then becomes, what did Jesus show us in his life and what did he teach?

First of all, Jesus reconfirmed that God was the Creator of the universe:

> In the beginning, at the time of creation, God made them male and female.
>
> Mark 10:16

> Just as the Father is the source of life, in the same way he has made his Son to be the source of life.
>
> John 5:26

Secondly, Jesus confirms by his own life and death and his teachings that God is love – in fact, God is the personification of love. The best-known statement about that love reads as follows:

> For God so loved the world that he gave his only Son, so that everyone who believes in him may not die but have eternal life.
>
> John 3:16

As a consequence of that love, Jesus urges us to live a life of love ourselves and to love not only God and our fellow human beings, but also our enemies:

> Love the Lord your God with all your heart, with all your soul, and with all your mind, and love your neighbor as you love yourself.
>
> Matthew 22:37

> But now I tell you: love your enemies and pray for those who persecute you, so that you may become the sons of your Father in heaven.
>
> Matthew 5:45

Paul, the apostle, later wrote a whole chapter on that love in his first letter to the Corinthians which contains such well-known passages as:

> I may give away everything I have, and even give up my body to be burned – but if I have no love, this does me no good... Meanwhile, there remains: faith, hope, and love, and the greatest of these is love.
>
> 1 Corinthians 13

Emil Brunner,[6] the Swiss theologian, wrote about this love of God in his book, *Our Faith*:

> God's feeling towards us is infinite love. Fellowship is the one thing he absolutely wants. God created the world in order to share himself. He created us for fellowship.

More recently Robert Keck[7] in his book, *Sacred Eyes*, wrote about this love in yet another way:

> Love is fundamental to everything that is. The suggestion here is that love is the essential energy of the universe.

Thirdly, Jesus' life and teachings confirm what the Psalmist, 600 years before, had told the people of Israel that their God was a very personal God; God knew each one intimately and wanted to have a relationship with each one of them. This closeness to God is one of the distinguishing marks of the Christian and Jewish faiths; no other faith dares even to suggest this. It is probably most clearly expressed in some of the parables Jesus used to tell. These are the parables of the

Lost Coin, the Lost Sheep, the Lost Son, etc.; each one of these tells how God is concerned about losing even one of them and how God will spare no effort to find the lost person:

> For only a penny you can buy two sparrows, yet not one sparrow falls to the ground without your Father's consent. As for you the hairs of your head have been counted. So do not be afraid; you are worth much more than many sparrows!
>
> Matthew 10:29

This personal concern of God is also demonstrated by the open invitation Jesus gave us to pray to God for whatever we need. As an example of a prayer, he gave us "The Lord's Prayer" which includes such mundane requests as:

> Give us today our daily bread… Forgive us our trespasses… Lead us not into temptation…

In other places, Jesus is quoted as saying:

> When you pray and ask for something, believe that you have received it, and you will be given whatever you asked for.
>
> Mark 11:24

> It is God who clothes the wild grass – grass that is here today and gone tomorrow. Won't he be all the more sure to clothe you. Your Father knows that you need all these things even before you ask for them.
>
> Luke 12:28

The last attribute of God that Jesus revealed to us is that God is "just". First, Jesus urges us to be just and forgive people who have wronged us:

> Be compassionate as your Father in heaven is compassionate.
>
> *Luke 6:27*

> Forgive us our trespasses, as we forgive those who trespass against us.
>
> *Matthew 6:12*

At the same time Jesus tells us to obey the laws of Moses and to forget them at our peril:

> Remember that as long as heaven and Earth last, not the least point nor the smallest detail of the law will be done away with.
>
> *Matthew 5:18*

At the end of Jesus' life, he died on the cross as the one who took upon himself our sins and acted as our mediator with God:

> For God did not send his son into the world to be its judge, but to be its savior.
>
> *John 3:16*

As with the emergence of the belief that the God of Israel was the only God and the creator of the universe, so it was with the belief that Jesus was not only the Savior of the people who believe in him but also, in some way, the Savior of all humans. As Paul writes in his letter to Titus:

> You see God's grace has been revealed to save the whole human race.
>
> *Titus 2 – The New Jerusalem Bible*

(All biblical quotes in this chapter, except where indicated, are from The Good News Bible)

NOTES

[1] Chatterji, Mohini, translation of the *Bhagavad-Gita*, Julian Press, New York, 1960.
[2] Various, *The World's Great Religions*, Time Incorporated, New York, 1957.
[3] Keller, Werner, *The Bible as History*, William Morrow and Co., New York, 1956.
[4] Cahill, Thomas, *The Gift of the Jews: How a Tribe of Desert Nomads Changed the Way Everyone Thinks and Feels*, Doubleday, New York, 1998.
[5] Kennedy, James, *Why I Believe*, Word Incorporated, Waco, 1980, pp.111–112.
[6] Brunner, Emil, *Our Faith*, SCM Press, London, 1977, p.39.
[7] Keck, Robert L., *Sacred Eyes*, Knowledge Systems Inc., Indianapolis, 1992, p.5.

Chapter IX
GOD AS REVEALED IN PHENOMENA WE CANNOT PERCEIVE WITH OUR FIVE SENSES

IXa   Introduction

In Part A of this book, we looked briefly at the miraculous ways the universe is put together from the mysterious dance of the subatomic particles to the majestic movements of the stars and galaxies. In Chapter V, we looked at the incredible complexity of life in general and that of human life in particular. We ended the chapter by looking briefly at the relatively new concept of fields of influence which shape the growth and behavior of living things. We followed the human development through the three different eras suggested by Larry Dossey[1] in his book, *Healing Words*. According to him we are now entering Era III, which he describes as the new era in science and medicine in which it is gradually becoming recognized that, outside of the mind and the body, there is another component to our existence which is not confined to time and space and is therefore eternal.

As we mentioned before, this component to our existence is something we do not understand very well because we have not been able to define it precisely or measure it in any way. Unfortunately, in today's scientific society, that means we might as well forget about it or ignore it. However, no matter how hard we may try to do this, there remain a number of phenomena in this world that cannot be explained by the theories of physics: their existence can only be explained by the assumption that there exist other fields or forces which, although not directly measurable, are nevertheless affecting our daily lives. To name just a few:

In the religious sphere:

- There is the often-reported effectiveness of prayer and faith healing.
- There are the miraculous recoveries of people visiting certain shrines and holy places.
- There are the near-death and out-of-body experiences of many people.
- There are the mystical experiences people have reported since the beginning of time.

In the biological sphere:

- There is the ability of the dividing cells after conception to find their exact place in the body and to develop into millions, if not billions, of highly diverse cells – from the cells that make up the eyeball to the entirely different cells that make up the toenail.
- There is the ability of a nonphysical thought to activate muscles and nerves to get a physical action.

In the scientific sphere:

- There is the ability of two particles to be at the same place at the same time; to be two things at the same time; and to influence each other instantly although separated by great distances.
- There is the apparent fact that some natural processes are influenced by the presence of an observer and, even, that they will fail to occur without the presence of an observer.

In the animal world:

- There is the ability of the butterfly to find its way from Northern Canada to Central Mexico. This is an insect which has a brain that is smaller than a pinhead.
- There is the ability of the salmon to find the same spawning ground after having lived in the immensity of the ocean for its entire life.
- There is the ability of cats and dogs to find their owners who have moved across the country and lost their pet on the way.

In the sphere of the paranormal:

- There is the experience of extrasensory perception such as telepathy, clairvoyance, and precognition.
- There is the experience of psychokinesis in which people can move objects without direct contact.

All of this is meant as an introduction to looking at how God is revealing herself through processes and phenomena we cannot perceive through our five senses, and they *cannot* be explained by the presently known laws of nature. Nevertheless, they are both very real to many people including many scientists. They are, in fact, an integral part of a set of processes, forces, energies, fields that govern the operation of the universe and are all of a spiritual nature. At present, we do not understand how they operate since we do not observe them through the use of our five senses. As Carl Jung once said, he never believed that our five senses were capable of perceiving all forms of being. Even William Shakespeare commented that there was more to heaven and Earth than could be understood by Horatio and his fellow human beings.

Since the phenomena we are dealing with are not of a material nature, they must be of a spiritual nature. In this regard it is interesting to note that some scientists have expressed the view that the *new vision* of reality is a *spiritual vision* in its very essence. Or in the words of Robert Keck,[2] who is both a physicist and a theologian, and whom I have quoted before, the spiritual force of love is essential to everything: love, he writes, is the fundamental impulse to life; love is ontological in nature. In other words, love is the most essential and fundamental of all spiritual processes and is the creative force behind nature. The spiritual force of love is the glue that holds the entire universe together.

In her book, *God in All Worlds*, Lucinda Vardey[3] writes in the introduction to Chapter 22 entitled "The Universal Force":

> Over the centuries, a universal force has been revealed to us: through prayer; through miraculous and synchronistic events; through mystical experiences and transformatory episodes, and through the messages received in our bodies and psyches.
>
> God reveals Himself through the invisible energies which are a part of the universe in which we dwell... For the first time in our history, theology is emerging from scientific knowledge. The Universal Force of God eternally creates and renews the face of the Earth, and we are all affected.

So, in this chapter we will look briefly at these revelations of this Universal Force and the invisible energies which Vardey says are part of our universe. We will start off with the subject of prayer and faith healing and then go on to near-death experiences, out-of-body experiences, mystical experiences and finally extrasensory experiences.

IXb The Effect of Religion and Prayer on Health

Someone has said, the sooner we discover that there are spiritual laws which cannot be outwitted, the better for us.

One of these spiritual laws, I believe, is the law which tells us that we can approach our Creator individually in prayer. There is absolutely nothing of a material nature in prayer: there is nothing we can measure, no energy flow, nothing that we can record on the most sensitive of measuring instruments, and therefore a complete non-event for people who still adhere to a purely materialistic view of life. But the evidence that there is more to life than a purely materialistic existence is so overwhelming that it is hard to believe that there are still people who reject the idea that there may be a spiritual component to life. As a consequence they reject the notion that such practices as prayer could possibly be effective, thereby missing out on many things that could be of real help to them in their daily lives.

In this regard, it is interesting to note that despite our increasingly technological world, and despite the decrease in church attendance, and despite the apparent loss of values, the great majority of people in North America still hang on to a belief in God and in the effectiveness of prayer. A survey conducted by the magazine *Newsweek* has shown the following rather astonishing results, as published in their March 31, 1997, issue:

- 87 per cent of the people polled believe that God answers prayer;
- 79 per cent of the people polled believe that God answers prayers for healing;
- 54 per cent of the people polled pray at least once a day; and
- 29 per cent of the people polled pray more than once a day.

These results compare well with a much earlier survey

GOD AS REVEALED IN PHENOMENA

which indicated that some 90 per cent of the people surveyed believed in the existence of a personal God. Also, an article in *Time* magazine in the June 24, 1996, issue, shows that of the 1,000 people polled 82 per cent believed in the healing power of personal prayer; 77 per cent believed that God sometimes intervenes to cure people who have a serious illness. The general interest of people in the subject of healing is also demonstrated by the many home pages on the Internet of people who offer to pray for others with serious illnesses, and the equally large number of people who ask on the Internet to be prayed for by complete strangers.

In a sense, it is truly remarkable that in today's America, where public cynicism seemingly knows no bounds, trust in a personal God seems to persist. It is equally remarkable that such mass circulation magazines such as *Newsweek* and *Time*, and countless newspapers such as *The Wall Street Journal* and *USA Today*, have been publishing lengthy articles on religious subjects, including articles on the healing power of prayer. They obviously are trying to meet a need that the magazines' publishers perceive to be out there among their readers.

For the Christian, prayer is communicating with God. In fact, at its best, it is a two-way communication which operates through the spoken word, the silent word, through our senses and even, maybe, our intuition. In other words it is based on a relationship between God and the human individual and, like any relationship, you don't know in advance how it is going to turn out. You just do it. You make yourself accessible so that you are prepared to receive grace when it comes (Robert Bondi in the *Newsweek* article).

For many people, prayer is simply a presentation of our daily needs: a list of requests to meet the needs of ourselves, our families and our friends. This is certainly an important part of prayer. Jesus, of course, repeatedly urged his followers to petition God for their needs. Many of the miraculous cures he performed occurred only after people had asked him. He even told his followers that their prayers would be heard; on one occasion, he even said, "Ask and it shall be given to you, knock and the door will be opened unto you." By that measure, the latest polls show that millions of Americans are seekers and finders, and the fact that they continue with this practice obviously means that they have found that the door is indeed open to them.

It is probably fair to say that most personal prayers are about our immediate needs, but there is more to prayer than just a presentation of personal requests. When Jesus' disciples asked him how they should pray, he gave them the prayer which has ever since then been known as the "Our Father" or "The Lord's Prayer".

> Our Father which art in heaven,
> Hallowed be thy name.
> Thy Kingdom come.
> Thy will be done in earth, as *it is* in heaven.
> Give us this day our daily bread.
> And forgive us our debts, as we forgive our debtors.
> And lead us not into temptation,
> but deliver us from evil:
> For thine is the kingdom, and the power, and the glory,
> for ever.
> Amen.
>
> Matthew 6:9–13
> *The King James Bible*

Since this is the prayer that Jesus taught us, it may be well to spend sometime analyzing it, so that we may use it as a guide for our own prayers. First of all, it is obvious that Jesus did not mean this to be a cast-in-stone standard prayer that everyone should use on every occasion. Rather, I believe, it is meant to show what is, and what is not, important in our communications with God.

First there is the address acknowledging God's closeness to us by using the father image –

"Our Father who art in heaven,"

followed immediately by the element of praise –

"Hallowed be your name."

– This is followed by the expression of hope for our future –

"Your Kingdom come,"

and by an expression of faith in God's plan for us –

"Your will be done…"

It is only after this that we find the first petition to meet our physical needs –

"Give us this day our daily bread."

It may be significant that only after having asked for our daily sustenance, Jesus asks for the forgiveness of our sins –

"Forgive us our trespasses,"

followed by a request for strength to do the same to others–

"As we forgive those who trespass against us."

The prayer then ends with two requests for not being put in situations which may tempt us to do the wrong thing –

"Lead us not into temptation,"

and to keep us from falling into the clutches of Satan –

"But deliver us from evil."

The last part of the Lord's Prayer is not actually found in the Bible, but was added later and became part of the liturgy of the church and has always been considered as an integral part of this prayer. It is obviously meant as an expression of praise and thanksgiving at the end of the prayer:

"For yours is the kingdom, the power and the glory. Forever and ever. Amen."

As has been pointed out before, Jesus invites us to pray

for our daily needs and earthly concerns. The gospels relate many examples of ordinary concerns that people brought to him, including the following:

- People asked him to cure their sick, both the physically and the mentally ill, and he cured them all provided they came to him in faith. This sickness did not necessarily have to be life-threatening. For instance, he cured Peter's mother-in-law when all she had was a fever.
- His own mother asked him to do something about the wine supply at one of their friend's wedding; and Jesus, in order not to cause the bridal pair embarrassment, changed water into wine.
- Jesus calmed a storm when his disciples, even with him aboard, were afraid that they might sink. When they expressed their concern to him, Jesus calmed the storm.
- When a crowd of people had followed him to an isolated place, where there was no food to be obtained, Jesus took pity on them and fed them.

Looking at these examples of how Jesus is reported to have responded to this wide-ranging list of everyday problems that people brought before him, it is clear that we should not be afraid either to approach God with our own ordinary concerns.

Before we continue, we should make a distinction between the effects of religious beliefs on our mental and physical health, and the more direct effect of how prayer can improve or restore health or at least improve conditions. In the first case, a purely statistical analysis should show if there is any difference between the general health of religious people and nonreligious people.

THE GENERAL EFFECT OF RELIGION ON HEALTH

The results of a number of surveys and special studies have shown that there is indeed a correlation between religious beliefs and general health. Some of these studies are described below.

In *The Faith Factor, An Annotated Bibliography of Clinical Research on Spiritual Subjects*, the authors[4] found that religious factors were involved with increased survival, reduced alcohol use, reduced anxiety, reduced depression and an increased quality of life for patients with cancer and heart disease.

Psychiatrist David Larson[5] started "The National Institute For Health Care Research" which is trying to make health care workers aware of the fact that faith is crucial in the human make-up, and should be taken into account in the treatment of both physical and psychological illnesses. Larson's research has shown that there is a definite correlation between religious beliefs and practices, and health. He is trying to convince people, and especially the medical profession, that, whether or not there is a God, scientific research suggests that religion benefits both bodily and mental health. He attributes this beneficial effect of religion to a mixture of social support, the meaning it gives to life, the sense of alliance with an omnipotent force, and the stress reducing benefits of meditation.

According to the *Time* magazine report, referred to previously, a study at the Dartmouth-Hitchcock Medical Center found that one of the best predictions of survival among 232 heart surgery patients was the degree to which the patients said they drew comfort and strength from religious faith. Those who did not, had more than three times the death rate of those who did.

In the spring of 1999, a course called "Spirituality and Healing in Medicine" was held in the Department of

Continuing Education of the Harvard Medical School and was attended by more than 700 doctors, nurses and other health professionals. Some of the findings dealing with the effect of religious life on health were described as follows:

- A study funded by the U.S. National Institutes of Health showed heart surgery patients assigned chaplains averaged two fewer days in hospital.
- Yale researchers found older adults who frequently attended religious services in 1982 were less physically disabled twelve years later than infrequent attendees, even after adjusting for health and socioeconomic factors.
- Several additional studies make the statistical case for regularly going to church or synagogue to protect against disease and premature death which cannot be explained away by the "clean-living" argument.

A recent article (September 18, 2000) in Toronto's *Globe and Mail* by Ron Csillag bears the headline: "It's official: God is good for your health". In it the author quotes the conclusions of a survey of forty-two studies presented by the American Psychological Association. Simply stated the studies show that regular attendance at one's church, synagogue, mosque, or temple is directly related to longer life. Another study quoted in the article showed that higher religious faith and spirituality were associated with increased coping, greater resilience to stress, a sunnier outlook on life, greater perceived social support and lower levels of anxiety.

The conclusions of all these studies taken together do not leave much doubt that there is indeed a strong correlation between religious faith and general health and that this effect is quite independent of a person's religious affiliation. In the end, the inevitable conclusion is that there is a strong spiritual component to the human existence which influences our health and well-being.

THE DIRECT EFFECT OF PRAYER ON HEALTH AND WELL-BEING

The direct effect of prayer in restoring health, or at least improving the quality of life, is attested to by numerous research projects: some of these investigations have been carried out over very extended periods of time. One study that received a great deal of media attention was that carried out by Dr. Elizabeth Targ in 1996. In this study, forty AIDS patients were divided into two groups of twenty. The one group was prayed for by a group of forty healing practitioners; the other group was not. The participants did not know in which group they were placed. After six months the data was "unblended" and after much scrutiny the results were published in the *Western Journal of Medicine*. The results showed that the subjects not prayed for spent a total of sixty-eight days in hospital and contracted thirty-five AIDS related diseases, while the same figures for the prayed for group were ten days in hospital and thirteen AIDS related diseases. This rather sensational result received much attention at the time. Later the results were questioned because the results could have been influenced by the improvement in AIDS drugs which were introduced during the study.

Dr. Targ continued her studies and in 1997 received funding from the National Institutes of Health's Center for Complementary and Alternative Medicine to examine the efficacy of prayer on patients with a rare form of brain cancer called glioblastoma. Dr. Targ started these studies but, amazing as it may seem, shortly after receiving the grant she was diagnosed with the same rare brain disease. She died from this disease on July 18, 2002. The work on the research grant is being continued by two of her colleagues, Drs. Freinkel and Aston.

At the previously mentioned course at the Harvard Medical School, more than 100 studies were reported making a link between prayer and wellness, putting less emphasis on religious affiliation than on regular spiritual practice. These prayer studies cut across all of the world's major religions.

Another study, now in progress, is the one conducted by Dr. Dale Matthews and involves sixty patients with rheumatoid arthritis. He chose this particular illness because relief of its symptoms can be easily measured. Again the patients were divided into two groups. All patients receive four days of healing prayer through the laying on of hands. In addition, one group receives six months of long-distance intercessory prayer. Although the study is not complete yet, some of the patients have shown what has been called extraordinary short-term results. Both of these experiments are being carried out under the strictest scientific controls. Based on these findings, Dr. Matthews told students at the St. Louis University School of Medicine that the medicine of the future is going to be prayer and Prozac (from the *USA Today* article in the July 25, 1998 issue).

The 1996 article in *Time* magazine mentions the results of a 1988 study carried out by cardiologist Dr. Randolph Byrd. In this study, Dr. Byrd took 393 patients in a coronary care unit and randomly assigned half to be prayed for by born-again Christians. The other half was not prayed for and the patients were not told about this experiment taking place. Dr. Byrd found that the group which was not prayed for was five times as likely to need antibiotics and three times as likely to develop complications compared to those patients who were prayed for. Apparently this experiment has never been replicated, and the methodology has come under criticism. Nevertheless, the results seem to be so conclusive that it is hard to believe that a flawed methodology could negate these results completely.

In his book, *Healing Words*, Dr. Dossey also presents the results of a survey of faith healing experiments conducted by Dr. Daniel Benor. He has summarized the results of 131 controlled trials in tabular form under such headings as:

- healing effects of human physical problems;
- healing effects of subjective sensations such as headaches, anxiety, depression, etc.;
- healing effects on animals and plants; and
- healing effects on enzymes, fungi, yeast and bacteria.

Of the 131 studies, 77 showed results that could not be explained by pure chance with probabilities between one in 100 to five in 100.

Dr. Dossey also discusses the results of the so-called "Spindrift" experiments on the effect of prayer on the germination of seeds and on the growth of molds. The advantage of this type of test is that it removes personal involvement of the subject prayed for, and the results can therefore be measured and expressed in simple statistics showing the degree of correlation between prayer and the effects of prayer on the various plant characteristics being measured. The results of these tests seem to show clearly that there is indeed a strong correlation between prayer and the growth and/or germination of plants. To most of us, it probably sounds heretical that prayer can affect plants. On the other hand, it seems to vindicate those plant lovers who have always claimed that you can talk to your plants and make them grow better. However, when we start taking into account that prayer and mind control may be activated by a field of influence which proceeds from the person doing the praying, the idea may not be as strange as at first thought. Certainly, as compared to some of the latest scientific findings about the behavior of particles on the subatomic level, the results of these tests should not really surprise us. As Dr. Dossey explained it in his book, the central assumption of the "Spindrift" experiments and of his whole book is that:

- All humans have divine attributes and a qualitative oneness with God.
- There is a nonlocal quality of human consciousness.
- Consciousness, like the Divine, is infinite in space and time and is ultimately one.

In some way, the recent discovery that something can influence something else without any connection and can do so instantaneously should change the perception of scientists, and of everyone else for that matter, of what is possible in the area of the mind and consciousness and prayer.

In the Spindrift experiments, prayers were classified in two types: the direct prayer and the indirect prayer. A direct prayer has a specific wish and a specific outcome in mind. The nondirected prayer is simply asking for the best potential of the individual to manifest itself or for the best outcome to happen to that person. The Spindrift Foundation concluded eventually that both types of prayer were beneficial, but the *nondirected prayers* were three to four times more effective.

In addition to the prayer conducted without the direct bodily contact between the one doing the praying and the one prayed for, there is the type of prayer that is accompanied by the "laying on of hands". This practice of "laying on of hands" is actually a very old church practice, but over time it has been replaced, as so many other natural medical practices, by more scientifically oriented methods.

As the name implies, the person or persons who are doing the praying lay their hands on the head of the person prayed for; sometimes the person prayed for assumes a kneeling position. As indicated before, this practice is now being revived in many churches. As with many of these practices, it is difficult to prove how effective it is, but the fact that it is being practiced at all in this scientific age surely indicates that the people receiving this type of prayer, and the people who actually carry it out, must believe that it is successful in reducing illness and promoting well-being.

In addition to these forms of healing, there is the healing resulting from visits to special locations in the world where the mother of Jesus is said to have appeared to some people. There are innumerable testimonies, some very well documented, of people who were cured miraculously at these locations. No doubt an element of prayer is also involved but, in contrast to the normal prayers in which the location is not of importance, these cures only seem to take place at these particular locations. Because, the mother of Jesus is involved, who is especially venerated by the Roman Catholic Church, most of these sightings have and are taking place in predominantly Roman Catholic countries. They include Lourdes in France, Fatima in Portugal, Guadeloupe in Mexico and the most recent one in Madgegory in the former Yugoslavia. Although, I am personally somewhat skeptical that God would choose to make these cures available to people through the Virgin Mary and in special locations only, nevertheless the evidence that something very special has happened and is happening at these locations is overwhelming. For instance, the International Medical Committee, based in Paris, has investigated some 1,300 cases of reported miraculous recoveries in Lourdes between 1948 and 1993 and found at least eighteen cases as "exhibiting an unexplainable, extraordinary phenomenon".

Recently, a very detailed, new chronicle of the Lourdes story has been written by a Jewish historian, Ruth Harris, entitled "Lourdes, Body and Spirit in the Secular Age". As could be expected from a Jewish person who has no special feeling of veneration for Mary, the mother of Jesus, she views the miracle stories of Lourdes with a very skeptical eye.

Considering all the recorded evidence of miraculous cures, she comes to the conclusion that some of these cures cannot be explained away as deceptions. Her opinion of these phenomena is probably best demonstrated in the following passage:

> Rather than seeing the transformations at Lourdes as the effects of suggestion... the cures of Lourdes raise a vision of the "self" as actively engaged and resourceful, able to overcome affliction that all other therapies had failed to alleviate. Such healings deserve to be seen as having something of the "miraculous" about them.

The interesting thing is that there appear to be "healing shrines" that are not associated with the Christian religion and which report similar miraculous experiences.

Another aspect of healing is the increased awareness of our own powers of healing through the power of our own mind and consciousness, and by following certain practices such as meditation. The effectiveness of this type of healing is described in numerous books such as Dr. Bernie Siegel's[6] *Peace, Love and Healing*; Dr. Andrew Weil's[7] *Spontaneous Healing*; and Dr. Deepak Chopra's[8] *Quantum Healing* and *Ageless Body, Timeless Mind*. All these books attest to the power of love and altruism in making people feel well and in improving the quality of life. In his book, *Timeless Healing, The Power and Biology of Belief*, Dr. Herbert Benson[9] makes the point that, in his thirty years of practicing medicine, he has found no healing force more impressive or more universally accessible than the power of individuals to care for and cure themselves.

As could be expected, not all doctors accept these findings. Some are violently opposed to the notion that prayer and religious affiliation could have an effect on health and well-being. Some go so far as stating that to use these results in medical practice could be dangerous to the patient in that it gives them a false sense of security. They accuse the researchers of not using strictly controlled, scientific methods, and that, in addition, they are misinterpreting the facts to fit their beliefs. While this may be true in some cases, the fact remains that, even discounting some of the results, the overwhelming majority of the experiments clearly indicate that prayer and religious affiliation do have a significant positive effect on health and general well-being. One thing seems to be clear, however, and that is that the key element in prayer seems to be love, and that if you remove the feelings of deep compassion, empathy and caring from prayers it does not seem to work.

So, in summary, I believe we can conclude the following from this evidence:

- Personal prayer can be very effective, not only in healing oneself and others but also in improving other conditions mentioned in prayer.
- Group prayer, for people unknown to the people who are doing the praying, can have a marked influence on the well-being of the people prayed for.
- The effectiveness of prayer does not depend upon location or distance, although there is considerable evidence that prayer at some particular shrines can be effective as well.
- People with a deep personal faith are less subject to mental and physical health problems. One reason may be that these people regularly pray for their health; another

may be that their faith in God makes them less subject to anxiety and depression – two sources of ill health which have been accepted as such by all medical practices.
- The human mind and consciousness can, through the principle of mind over matter, cause great improvements in general health and occasionally can affect complete cures.

In *Healing Words*, Dr. Dossey predicts that as the effectiveness of prayer becomes more and more recognized, prayer will become incorporated into the mainstream of medicine. He goes on to say that the use of prayer will become the standard in scientific medical practice. He even goes so far as to predict that in the future it may be considered medical malpractice if prayer is not recommended as an integral part of medical care.

It is interesting to note that, today, more than one third of the medical schools in the U.S. are now offering courses and programs in spirituality and medicine. There is probably no better indication that healing and faith are closely bound together, and that prayer can indeed be effective in improving health, than the slow but steady growth in recognition of this by the academic, and especially the medical world.

Before leaving the subject of prayer, I believe it necessary to touch upon the fact that, of course, not all prayers are answered, or are answered in the way we have asked for. This invariably leads to thinking of God as acting arbitrarily: She intervenes sometimes and not at other times. Marcus Borg,[10] a modern theologian, wrestles with this problem in his book, *The God We Never Knew*. He writes:

> I have no idea how petitionary and intercessory prayer works. I cannot explain it with an interventionist model of God, for to do so implies that God decides to respond to

some requests and not to others. I cannot reconcile such a notion of God with collective brutalities such as the Holocaust and the often arbitrary character of private tragedy. I cannot believe that God could have stopped the Holocaust but chose not to, just as I cannot believe that God responds to some prayers for healing and protection but not to others. Yet I am convinced that paranormal things happen, even though I cannot imagine an explanation. And so, though I don't think of God as an Interventionist, I still make requests of God. It seems to be a natural part of the relationship to do so, just as it feels like a way of caring for people.

So, in the end, we must confess with Borg that we don't know how prayer works. We don't know why God intervenes sometimes and not in others. We do know, however, that it works often enough for a large percentage of the population to keep praying and placing their concerns before God, accepting the fact that God may not act on their requests. We, at the same time, know that God has given us a free will and that God cannot intervene every time we do something wrong without taking that free will away from us.

The conclusion of all these studies taken together does not leave much doubt that there is indeed a strong correlation between religious faith and general health and that this effect is quite independent of a person's religious affiliation. In the end, the inevitable conclusion is that there is a strong spiritual component to the human existence which influences our health and well-being.

IXc Out-of-Body Experiences and Near-Death Experiences

OUT-OF-BODY EXPERIENCES

Both the out-of-body experiences (OBE) and the near-death

experiences (NDE) have only recently received the attention they deserve. Although both have been mentioned in world literature since the beginning of time, it is only in the last twenty to thirty years that these subjects have been the object of scientific inquiry and have been acknowledged as true human experiences. How we look at these experiences has a profound influence on how we see the human condition and how we view the connection between the human body and the human mind. In some ways, it also touches upon the subject of life after death.

One of the earliest writers and researchers on these subjects, Dr. Elisabeth Kübler-Ross,[11] wrote a revolutionary book in 1969 called *On Death and Dying*. This was followed in 1975 by Dr. Raymond Moody's[12] book, *Life After Life*, which went into great detail about these experiences. Since then the study of OBEs and NDEs has skyrocketed with dozens of books and scientific articles appearing annually and with the recent creation of the International Association of Near-Death Studies (IANDS) (www.iands.org). As could be expected in our modern society, the Internet is flooded with OBE and NDE stories; some of them providing very detailed descriptions of the person's experience which is often followed by the equally detailed descriptions of how the experience affected the person's spiritual life.

So, what then are these two phenomena which have stirred the imagination of so many people? First, the OBEs. Persons who have had an out-of-body experience characteristically believe that they have, voluntary or involuntary, left their bodies and were projected some distance above their physical bodies. They remain consciously aware of what is going on around them, and they are able to observe their bodies and their immediate surroundings even though their physical bodies are in a state of unconsciousness. While in this state they generally experience a feeling of lightness and general detachment and calm. Often the experience happens during an operation when the person is under anesthetics and unconscious. There are literally hundreds of cases documented when the patient, on recovery, can tell the doctors and nurses, who were present at the operation, exactly what they did and what they said to each other during the operation.

Of course, the first reports were met with disbelief and even ridicule by people who could not accept the fact that it was possible for the spiritual body to become separated from the physical body or, for that matter, could not believe that there does exist a spiritual body as distinct from the physical body. Dr. Kübler-Ross decided to, as she called it, "calm the critics and prove once and for all that out-of-body experiences are real and that the mind can be separated from the body." To do this she used people who were blind and who had not had any light perception for at least ten years. Those of this group who had an out-of-body experience and came back were able to describe in great detail the colors of the clothes and the jewelry the persons present at the operation were wearing, thereby proving that in the out-of-body state they regained their sight and were able to see. On returning to their physical bodies they, of course, lost their sight again. It is no wonder that many found it hard to come back to their physical state. In any case, as Kübler-Ross wrote, these statements refer to facts which cannot be invented and the test is repeatable at any time.

One of the interesting things about the OBEs is that people who had lost limbs in an accident or were blinded did not have any of these handicaps when they were in this spiritual body. It was only when they returned to their physical bodies that they again had these handicaps. They all seem to perceive that they have spiritual bodies, without any blemishes during this state; although, at the same time, they can see their physical bodies with all their flaws on the hospital bed. In any case it appears that people in the spiritual body can see and hear but apparently they cannot touch or smell or taste, so that only two of the five senses seem to operate in this spiritual body.

It appears that some people can enter this stage of separation of body and mind at will. They claim that when they are in that state they are not constrained by time and space; they feel that they can move instantly from one place to another and that they can observe what is going on but cannot influence it. Among the many well-known people who have reported to have had such experiences are a number of famous writers, including Hemingway, Tolstoy, Dostoevsky, Tennyson, Edgar Alan Poe, D. H. Lawrence and others. It appears that the experience is not limited to just a few people, as was originally thought; on the contrary, recent studies seem to indicate that as many as ten per cent of the population has had an out-of-body experience at one time or another.

In his book, *Parapsychology, Philosophy and Spirituality, A Postmodern Exploration*, David Griffen[13] gives a list of the common features of an OBE. He included in this list:

- the feeling of being outside the body;
- the conviction that the experience was real;
- a greatly altered emotional state;
- the absence of pain;
- normal or better than normal visual perception;
- description of facts and situations as they actually happened; and
- similarity and universality, etc.

He concludes his investigation of OBEs as follows:

OBEs, while not providing direct evidence of life after death as such, do provide strong evidence that the self can exist, feel, perceive, think, decide, and even sometimes influence other actualities while apart from the physical body. OBEs thereby provide strong evidence against the primary assumption behind the rejection of belief in life after death.

An American professor of psychology, Dr. Dean Shiels,[14] actually analyzed over a thousand reports from people in some seventy non-Western cultures who had had an out-of-body experience. He apparently had expected to find distinct ethnic variations, yet he found exactly the opposite. So universal was the nature of the recorded experiences that, in the end, he had to conclude that the phenomenon had to be genuine. I believe with Dr. Shiels (and David Griffen) that: "There is such an overwhelming body of evidence that these experiences are real, that I have to come to the conclusion that body and mind are separable and that humans have both a spiritual body and a physical body." (D. Shiels in a 1978 article in the *Journal of the Society for Psychical Research* entitled "A Cross-Cultural Study of Belief in Out-of-the-Body Experiences.")

NEAR-DEATH EXPERIENCES

The near-death experience is exactly what the term implies: it is an experience some people have when they are so near death that there are no vital life signs left, yet the body recovers after some time. People who have undergone this experience describe a great many and varied experiences while in this close-to-death state. Among these are a feeling of peace and quiet; feeling oneself out of one's body like an OBE; going through a dark tunnel; meeting others who have died before; meeting one or more "Beings of Light"; undergoing a review of one's life; reaching a border or limit beyond which one cannot go; coming back; seeing life differently; and having entirely new views of death. In the book, *The Case for Heaven*, Mally Cox-Chapman[15] has made a composite story of what a person experiencing this phenomenon might see, hear and experience. I have changed it to the second person singular to make it more dramatic:

> You have been in a near fatal car accident or heart attack. The medical staff cannot find any signs of life. Suddenly you hear an uncomfortable noise or loud ringing or buzzing and you realize that you are lifting out of your physical body. You may hover over your physical body watching resuscitation attempts or watching loved ones grieving. You may try, to no avail, to communicate with those below you or assure them that you are fine. Pain is gone. At the same time you feel yourself moving rapidly through a long, dark tunnel.
>
> On the other side of the tunnel you take some time to get your bearings. You notice that the nature of your body has changed, but the change does not feel alarming. You may find yourself in a gray mist or in a beautiful pastoral setting. Soon others come to meet and to help you. You see relatives and friends that have long been dead. A loving, warm being dressed in long white robes begins to communicate with you by telepathy. You are asked to review your life and are shown a panoramic, instantaneous playback of your life. You then approach a barrier or a border – it may be a stream, a fence, a stone wall – that you intuitively know is the limit between earthly life and the next life. You must make the choice about whether to stay or go back to Earth.* Having never felt such love, joy, and acceptance before, you yearn to stay but realize that your job on Earth is not yet complete.** The time for your death has not yet come. As soon as you make that decision you are instantly back in your body.
>
> Later, you try to tell someone close to you, but no one seems to understand. When ridiculed, you learn to keep quiet about your experience. Still, the experience transforms

your life. You now believe that love and learning are the only things that matter. You completely and totally lose your fear of death and are convinced that you will participate in an afterlife.

★ In some cases, it is a person who tells you that you must go back to Earth because your work there is not yet finished.
★★ As someone described it: "The most depressed, the most severe anxiety I have ever had was at the moment I realized I must return to this Earth."

It should be remembered that the above is a composite description of a NDE and includes all the different elements that people have experienced. Not all people have experienced all these elements, but all, with very few exceptions, have felt the feeling of great peace, love and joy surrounding them after they emerged from the dark tunnel. All the investigators of the NDE have come to the conclusion that it does not matter in which way a person approaches death, be it through illness, accident, or suicide. Nor did a person's previous religious faith make the experience more or less likely to occur, since religious and nonreligious people had NDEs in roughly equal numbers.

Again, as with the out-of-body experiences, the near-death experience has been felt by far more people than originally thought. It is presently thought that in America alone more than eight million people have had this experience. Dr. Kübler-Ross and her associates have, in the last twenty-five years, interviewed some 20,000 people from across the world who have had the experience. They interviewed people with different racial and cultural backgrounds, from Muslims to Eskimos, and from the ages of two to ninety. All these people reported to have had virtually the same experience with some deviations mainly due to cultural influences. For instance, Muslims tended to equate the Being of Light with Mohammed, while Buddhists tended to associate it with Buddha, and Christians with Jesus. Many called it the Spirit of Love, though the experience was far from impersonal. That this experience is not just a recent one is clearly shown in a painting by Hieronymus Bosch (1460–1516) which depicts departing souls being led by angels through a dark tunnel to a bright light at its end.

In any case, it changed Kübler-Ross from a person who had no belief in an afterlife to one who firmly believes that these are not coincidences or hallucinations, but a clear indication that some part of us survives in an afterlife.

BAD OR NEGATIVE NEAR-DEATH EXPERIENCES

While by far the greatest majority of near-death experiences are of the positive kind with the feeling of being surrounded by great love and joy, there are some people who have had near-death experiences that are frightening and terrifying. Two researchers in the U.S., Dr. Bruce Greyson, head of psychiatry at the University of Connecticut, and Nancy Bush, president of the International Association of Near-Death Studies, have made a more detailed study of these frightening or negative NDEs. They found that there appears to be more than one type of negative experience. Apparently, some feel themselves thrown into an empty void, while others go from a frightening experience to a more blissful one. In their investigations they were able to find only fifty people who had had these negative experiences out of thousands of cases they had access to. One problem with the negative NDE is, no doubt, the fact that people who have gone through this are less likely to want to talk about it than people who have had the more positive experience. Thus the figures quoted above may not be all that meaningful. In any case, as Greyson and Bush point out, there is, at this point in time, not enough information available to make any firm conclusions about the nature and aftereffects of negative NDEs.

One thing seems to be clear, however, and that is that there is more than one type of NDE and not all are loving experiences. Of course, the frightening or negative experiences of some people raise the question whether there is such a thing as a hell as opposed to the heaven experienced by those people who had a positive experience. I doubt that near-death experiences will ever be able to give a definitive answer to that question. The thing to remember, however, is that both positive and negative near-death experiences confirm that there is a mind distinct from the physical body and that these can be separated from each other even in this life.

THE AFTEREFFECTS OF A POSITIVE NEAR-DEATH EXPERIENCE

It is generally acknowledged that people who have had a NDE are changed people when they recover. The main reason for this appears to be that they are convinced that they have experienced a glimpse of life after death, and that they will return there some day and take part in this afterlife. A firm conviction like that cannot fail to have a profound influence on their outlook on life and death and how they behave in their earthly existence. All reports indicate that they have entirely lost their fear of death and actually look forward to regaining the state of being they experienced during their NDE, which is not all that surprising since a great number of them had not really wanted to return to their earthly existence.

Dr. Peter Fenwick of the Institute of Psychiatry in London, England, reported recently in the English scientific journal *Resuscitation* on the near-death experiences of sixty-three survivors of cardiac arrests at the Southampton General Hospital. He writes:

> ...the collected data is the first medical evidence that proves the mind can continue to exist after the body is clinically dead, and that a form of afterlife is now scientifically explainable. Those who return all report that they have been changed. Those who were religious found their faith renewed. Those who had no faith acquired at least a belief in some form of afterlife.

The general consensus seems to be that people who were atheists became religious or at least became believers; while people who had been firm believers and supporters of one church, afterwards had much less interest in attending their church. As some expressed it, "I just don't have that feeling anymore that the church is the only place where God is. I have this feeling that he is everywhere." Someone else expressed it this way, "The basic thing that has changed is that now I know the things people say but don't believe, namely that 'God is love'. There is nothing exclusive about God whatsoever."

Generally the people, who have had near-death experiences, after their recovery tend to have a greater interest in spiritual values and lifestyles: they become more tolerant towards other people; they have a greater interest in acquiring knowledge; and they have a greater desire to be of service and to help others. These changed attitudes do not make them saints, but they do seem to actively seek opportunities for spiritual growth.

Dr. Michael Sabon,[16] in *Recollections of Death*, reports on his study of the long-term aftereffects of a NDE. He followed a number of people who had had NDEs and re-interviewed the subjects and their families over a period of years to see whether they had changed their stories at all. He found that even after all those years, they felt as strongly about it and were as convinced that it actually occurred as they were right after the experience. They were no longer afraid of dying and they did not mourn the death of loved ones as they were convinced that death was a pleasant experience.

Other researchers,[17] who have studied the aftereffects of NDEs, found that the aftereffects are so transformative and life-potentiating that they not only change the people involved, but also other people who interact with them and even those who simply read or hear their stories.

While much of this is very positive, there is a negative side to having had this near-death experience. The main reason for this seems to be that these people feel sort of set apart by the experience they have had. Also, they have to deal with the fact that their wives, partners or friends have not had this experience and may not be able or willing to make the lifestyle changes they are making. This has, in some cases, led to divorce and alienation from their friends. In general, however, it appears that the experience has greatly enriched their lives and made them seek to enrich the lives of others as well.

OBJECTIONS TO AND REJECTIONS OF THE NEAR-DEATH AND OUT-OF-BODY EXPERIENCES

The acceptance of the NDEs and OBEs as facts implies that there is a strong spiritual component to human life and that the spiritual body and the physical body can be separated. This, of course, is unacceptable to all people who label themselves as materialists and who do not believe that there is a spiritual component to life. These people will generally accept that there are people who have these experiences, but they cannot accept the logical explanation that these experiences are representative of what an afterlife is like. They have and still are looking at arguments to disqualify these conclusions. Among the attempts to disqualify the conclusions from a medical point of view are the following:

- The people who had these experiences were not actually dead because they recovered. Therefore, while not detectable, the brain and the nervous system must have continued to function. The phenomena they encountered must therefore have a perfectly natural cause, such as hallucinations, dreams, etc.
- The near-death state results in a reduced flow of oxygen to the brain which is well-known to cause hallucinations. This argument has now been completely refuted simply because dozens of experiments have shown that lack of oxygen does not cause anything like out-of-body experiences.
- The NDE is caused by a dysfunctional temporal lobe, or an imbalance in neurotransmitters, or simply in an abnormal functioning of the brain.
- The effect is caused by the administration of painkillers and narcotic drugs. This can be quickly discounted by the fact that many people who have experienced the NDE did not receive any drugs whatsoever before they had this experience.
- The experience is the result of a rare medical condition called autoscopy in which people see mirror images of themselves. This condition occurs mainly in schizophrenic patients. The fact is, however, that very few of the people who had the near-death experience were suffering from schizophrenia, and this argument can therefore also safely be discarded.

In addition to those medical arguments there are some more general objections, including the following:

- These people are simply making up these stories and are expecting a reward for their efforts.
- They are fantasy fulfilling, religious, and cultural expectations.

- It is an unconscious, psychological defense against the dread of death.
- They are simply dreams.

Looking at these arguments, it is obvious that the subscribers to these arguments are clutching at straws. As Geoff Viney[18] writes in his book, *Surviving Death, Evidence of the Afterlife*:

> For my money, the doubters are wasting their time – none of these explanations, whether taken individually or collectively, can account for the sheer consistency and similarities of these recollections.

And later:

> The fact remains that there exists a truly staggering body of documentary evidence to support the notion that the human mind and the human body are not inseparable. To write off such evidence wholesale, as some rationalists attempt to do, is an act of intellectual dishonesty.

FINAL CONCLUSIONS CONCERNING THE OBEs AND THE NDEs

I believe, with many others, that all the evidence points to the fact that the OBEs and the NDEs are real experiences. To my mind this is not only obvious from the messages the people who have had these experiences bring back, but also from the way the lives of these people have changed. The experiment of Kübler-Ross with blind people who could, after they had an OBE, describe in detail the clothes, etc. of the operating staff, I find most convincing and illuminating.

The out-of-body experience proves to my mind decisively that the mind and body can be separated and that there is therefore a spiritual component to the human being. The near-death experience, I believe, shows clearly that there is a life after death and that there is something, which we call heaven, to which the soul returns after death. Combined, these phenomena clearly indicate, at least to me, that there is a Spiritual Being which we call God who has created both the Earth and the heaven and to whom we return at the end of our lives. I want to close this section with another quotation from Geoff Viney as follows:

> Along with many other paranormal investigators, I have grown steadily convinced that the idea of human life ending in oblivion at the moment of death makes as much sense as the theory that the world is flat. And I say this not on the basis of a prayerful revelation or blind faith, but after years of carefully assessing the various phenomena and their possible cause.

One of the more interesting things about the OBE and NDE is that the people who have researched this subject may start out as skeptics but later turn into believers. This is probably as good an indication of the truth behind these phenomena as we can ever hope to get.

IXd Mystical Experiences

Mystical experiences have been recorded from the earliest times and by all major religions. In 1902, William James[19] published a book called *The Varieties of Religious Experiences* with the subtitle *A Study of Human Nature*. In this book, James describes hundreds of mystical experiences people have had over the ages. The book was reissued in 1985 and is still often quoted by modern authors. William James was a psychologist who later became a philosopher; he taught at Harvard for over thirty-five years. The experiences he is writing about cover a wide field of different emotions and feelings; generally they include an awareness of God's presence and a feeling of closeness to the godhead.

Following are some excerpts from the hundreds of similar statements contained in the book:

> I never before so clearly felt the Spirit of God in me and around me. The whole room seemed to be full of God.
>
> I did not seek Him, but felt the perfect unison of my spirit with His.
>
> God surrounds me like a physical atmosphere. He is closer to me than my own breath.

James lists four typical characteristics of mystical experiences:

- Ineffability – the experience defies expression and no adequate report of its contents can be given in words.
- Noetic quality – the people who experience them feel that they are in a state of knowledge, insight, illumination, and revelation.

The other two qualities are less clearly marked but they are usually present.

- Transience – the mystical states cannot be maintained for long.
- Passivity – the mystic feels as if his own will is in abeyance, and indeed sometimes he feels as if he were grasped and held by a superior power.

Probably one of the best known of all mystical experiences ever recorded is that of the apostle Paul on the road to Damascus. Paul, who was known as Saul before he became a Christian, began as a persecutor of the newly formed Christian communities but changed overnight when he had the experience of meeting Christ, as it were, in person.

When he had this experience he was actually on his way to arrest some Christians who had fled to Damascus. As recorded in the New Testament in "The Acts of the Apostles" this is what happened:

> On his way to Damascus to arrest Christians in that city, suddenly a light from the sky flashed around him. He fell to the ground and heard a voice saying to him, "Saul, Saul! Why are you persecuting me?" "Who are you Lord?" he asked. "I am Jesus, whom you are persecuting," the voice answered. "But get up and go into the city, where you will be told what you must do."
>
> *The Good News Bible*

As said before, mystical experiences have been recorded in all ages and in all religions. Again, some may be faked, but by far the greatest majority is recorded by ordinary people who would not receive any benefit from disclosing their experiences. Actually, some of them are recorded by well-known people who have been recognized through the ages as being straightforward, saintly people such as Teresa of Avila, Meister Eckhart, Hildegard of Bingen, and many others.

Today, like almost every other human experience, the place to find descriptions of recent mystical experiences is on the Internet. There are now several organizations which record and analyze these experiences. For instance, there is the Exceptional Human Experience Network (EHEN) (www.ehen.org.) It advertises itself as an educational, research and information resource dedicated to the study of all types of psychical, mystical, death-related encounters, and enhanced experiences. They call these experiences exceptional because they believe that these experiences don't fit the Western scientific materialistic worldview. Instead, they see them as potential seeds for personal and spiritual growth. Some relevant statements at their website are:

> Our view is that all exceptional human experiences are indications that the entire universe is sacred.
>
> It seems to us that exceptional human experiences are leading us first toward a more integrated sense of self. Second, they are leading us toward a sense of oneness with other humans, other life forms, and the Earth itself.

The organization has collected hundreds of its findings in books and other publications.

The importance of the research of this and other similar organizations is that they prove that these experiences are not something that happened in the past to some particularly saintly people, but that they are occurring regularly to very common people today as well, some who have a religious background, others who have not.

Recently, a paper was presented at the conference "Towards a Science of Consciousness" under the title of "What Does Mysticism Have to Teach Us about Consciousness?" by Robert Forman.[20] After investigating several recorded experiences, he concludes that mysticism is not an artifact of any one culture but is something closer to an experience that is reasonably common and available in a variety of cultural contexts. He further concludes that mysticism suggests a definite distinction between consciousness and the brain and that awareness may have a nonlocal, quasi-spatial character much like a field.

He ends his article with this statement:

> In the absence of compelling reasons to deny the suggestions of their reports, we would be wise to seriously examine the direction towards which the finger of mysticism points. If the validity of knowledge is indeed governed, as we like to claim, by the tests of evidence, openness and clarity, then we should not be too quick to throw out the baby swimming in the bathwater of mysticism.

It is, I believe, clear from the foregoing that mysticism and mystical experiences occur as much today as they did in the past. They are clearly of a spiritual nature and could not possibly be explained from a purely materialistic point of view; instead they support a more spiritual interpretation of reality.

Recently several studies have been carried out to determine what happens in the brain when we have spiritual experiences or engage in religious practices such as prayer or meditation. Of course, with modern equipment it is relatively easy to pinpoint the areas in the brain that are activated when we pray or meditate. The point is that these studies show something that we have always known intuitively, namely that, of course, the brain must of necessity be involved if we have any experience, including a spiritual one. And, of course, it is our spiritual sensations which cause these brain activities and not the other way around. As a researcher in this area, Dr. Andrew Newberg, expresses it:

> The fact that spiritual experiences can be associated with distinct neural activity does not necessarily mean that such experiences are mere neurological illusions. It is no safer to say that spiritual urges and sensations are *caused* by brain activity than it is to say that the neurological changes through which we experience the pleasure of eating an apple cause the apple to exist.

See also the article in the May 7, 2001 issue of *Newsweek* entitled "Religion and the Brain" by Sharon Begley.

IXe Parapsychological Phenomena

Like the mystical experiences, parapsychological phenomena have been recorded since the beginning of time and by all cultures. As I wrote before, the acceptance of these phenomena as being factual suffers from the fact that the whole field is riddled with fraud. There are simply too many people who think that parapsychological phenomena can be easily faked and that, for instance, the human tendency to want to know more about loved ones who have departed can be easily exploited by unscrupulous people. It is therefore often very difficult, when studying these phenomena, to separate fact from fiction. Despite this, there are simply too many well-controlled tests and exercises described in the literature to enable us to simply dismiss all these experiences out of hand. Also, to use a metaphor suggested by William James, it takes only one white crow to prove that not all crows are black. In other words, it takes only one proven case to show that these parapsychological phenomena are indeed factual and real, and it is not necessary to debunk all the false claims to prove the opposite.

In his book *Parapsychology, Philosophy and Spirituality*, David Griffen[21] distinguishes between three types of paranormal phenomena: Extrasensory Perception (ESP), Psychokinesis (PK) and Mediums.

Extrasensory perception: he describes as events or occurrences in which the human consciousness receives messages or influences without the use of the five senses. There are three main forms of ESP as follows: *telepathy*, the ability to receive influences from other minds without the use of the five senses; *clairvoyance*, the ability to perceive things that are not in sight and cannot be seen; *precognition*, the ability to perceive events, conditions etc. before they occur.

Psychokinesis: the ability to influence physical objects by thought processes only.

Mediumship: the ability by which some people seem to be able to transfer messages from people who are dead.

The reason we have such difficulty in accepting these

phenomena as possibly being true is that they do not fit into our modern worldview, which is still basically of a mechanistic and materialistic nature and which does not make allowances for such things as spiritual forces.

Griffen lists a number of "white crows" in his book, which he believes demonstrate the validity of these phenomena; among them he mentions:

- the testimony of a large number of credible people;
- the demonstration of paranormal capacities on a regular and repeatable basis;
- paranormal phenomena of a spontaneous nature have been repeatedly reported in various places and throughout all recorded time; and
- paranormal effects that have been repeatedly produced in laboratory experiments at recognized scientific institutions.

In this regard he mentions that, in the last four or five years, the conduct of these experiments has been improved so much that he believes that the case for ESP is now infinitely stronger.

Griffen concludes:

The evidence for the genuineness of interactions that are now called paranormal points to the need for a postmodern philosophy. On the one hand, we have overwhelming evidence that influence at a distance to and from minds does occur. We have testimony from every period of history and from every culture, including the testimony of various religious saints whose integrity is otherwise undoubted. We have a one-hundred-year tradition of often rigorous, scientific investigations that has validated the reality of these phenomena time and time again.

Or as psychiatrists Shaun Josh and Colin Ross wrote in the *Journal of Nervous and Mental Diseases*:

> Paranormal experiences are so common in the general population that no theory of normal psychology or psychopathology which does not take them into account can be comprehensive.

The writers of *Love Beyond Life* add to this:

> This is a welcome change from the not-too-distant past, when anyone admitting to such experiences was declared hysterical, prone to hallucinations, or worse.

MEDIUMSHIP AND AFTER-DEATH COMMUNICATIONS

Mediumship is the ability of some people to transfer messages from dead people to their living relatives. But mediums are not necessary as an intermediary between the living and the dead. The literature is filled with accounts of people who feel that they have been in contact with a person who died fairly recently, either through a dream or through direct communication with a person who materialized right in front of them. In the book *Love Beyond Life*, the writers Joel Martin and Patricia Romanowski[22] describe hundreds of these occurrences. They define after-death communications as any contact between a living person and the consciousness, spirit, or soul of the so-called dead. They go on to describe the various phenomena as follows:

> From beyond the veil of life, our deceased loved ones may assume many different roles: messengers, guardians, protectors, comforters. They may pass on vague, general warnings and advice, or they may actually appear to us and intervene to avert tragedy. They may predict the future accurately or reveal to us elements of our past or their own

that we could not have known any other way. Whatever happens, they offer us a chance to heal – from grief, from pain, from loss.

The problem with these phenomena is that there are so many fakes and so many inconsistencies and anomalies. For instance, one could ask if there is this way of the dead communicating with us, why are there not more of them? Why does my deceased father, mother, son or daughter who were close to me in this life, why do they not communicate with me? Why did I not receive a warning from my closest deceased relative when I was in danger? And so on. The questions are legion.

Then, of course, there is the question of the state-of-being of the deceased who does the communicating. Is he/she in heaven, or in an intermediate place? Most apparitions do not give any indication of their state-of-being, although all of them, or at least the majority, seem to indicate that they are all right and that the persons they are communicating with should not worry about them. Also, in most cases, the apparition or the spirit that is being observed does not seem to have the physical impairments that they had when they were alive. This they have in common with the people who have near-death or out-of-body experiences who also, during this stage, do not have any of the impairments they have in real life.

Some have suggested that when we die, our soul or essence survives in the form of energy. It is now generally accepted that all matter is, in fact, an alternative form of energy. And energy can generate electromagnetic fields which can influence events and processes at great distances. If this is so, it is possible to postulate that all paranormal phenomena are simply forms of energy fields which interact in some form. Of course, this is, so far, pure speculation. We may never know the real process by which these phenomena are generated.

In closing this section, I quote Richard S. Broughton,[23] who in his book, *Parapsychology: The Controversial Science*, wrote as follows:

> Occasionally, you will hear some scientific pundit proclaim there is no evidence for parapsychological phenomena, therefore parapsychology is a pseudo-science with no subject matter to study. That is patent nonsense. For over 2,000 years people have been reporting a class of human experiences – the kind commonly called psychic – and for almost as long, scholars and scientists have been trying to understand them. Two millennia of human experience *is* subject matter.

As I wrote in Chapter V, the postmodern assumption that we are all connected with this universal consciousness, and that consciousness is not bound by time and space, has a number of important consequences for understanding ourselves and our link with the past and the future. As regards the paranormal phenomena described in this section, the interconnectedness of all things can possibly explain some of these phenomena.

Without going into greater detail, it is clear that some of these phenomena are real and that there exist more than one "white crow" to prove the reality of at least some of these phenomena. If this is so, it is a clear indication that we are not mechanical automatons, but that we have a spiritual component to our existence which does not cease to exist when we die and which has powers that we are only now beginning to recognize.

NOTES

[1]Dossey, Larry, *Healing Words, The Power of Prayer and the Practice of Medicine*, Harper San Francisco, New York, 1993.

[2] Keck, Robert L., *Sacred Eyes*, Knowledge Systems Inc., Indianapolis, 1992, p.157.

[3] Vardey, Lucinda, *God in All Worlds, An Anthology of Contemporary Spiritual Writing*, Vintage Canada, Random House, Toronto, 1996, p.796.

[4] *The Faith Factor, An Annotated Bibliography of Clinical Research on Spiritual Subjects*, quoted in *Timeless Healing, The Power and Biology of Belief* by Herbert Benson, Simon and Schuster, New York, 1996.

[5] Larson, David, "The National Institute for Health Care Research", article in the *International Journal of Psychiatry in Medicine*, issue 8/18.

[6] Siegel, Bernie, *Peace, Love and Healing*, Harper and Row, New York, 1989.

[7] Weil, Andrew, *Spontaneous Healing, How to Discover and Enhance Your Body's Natural Ability to Maintain and Heal Itself*, Ballantine Books, 1996.

[8] Chopra, Deepak, *Quantum Healing, Ageless Body, Timeless Mind*, Crown Publishing Group, 1993.

[9] Benson, Herbert, *Timeless Healing, The Power and Biology of Belief*, Simon and Schuster, New York, 1996.

[10] Borg, Marcus, *The God We Never Knew*, Harper Collins Publishers, New York, 1997, p.124.

[11] Kübler-Ross, Elisabeth, *On Death and Dying*, Macmillan Publishing, New York, 1969.

[12] Moody, Raymond, *Life After Life*, Bantam, Doubleday Dell Publishers, 1975.

[13] Griffen, David, *Parapsychology, Philosophy, and Spirituality, A Postmodern Exploration*, State University of New York, Albany, 1997.

[14] Shiels, Dean, "A Cross-Cultural Study of Belief in Out-of-the-Body Experiences", *Journal of the Society for Psychical Research*, 1978.

[15] Cox-Chapman, Mally, *The Case for Heaven, Near-Death Experiences as Evidence of the Afterlife*, G. P. Putnam and Sons, New York, 1995.

[16] Sabon, Michael, *Recollections of Death*, Harper and Row, New York, 1982.

[17] Viney, Geoff, *Surviving Death, Evidence of the Afterlife*, St Martin's Press, 1993.

[18] Viney, Geoff, ibid.

[19] James, William, *The Varieties of Religious Experiences*, Penguin Books, London, 1902.

[20] Forman, Robert, "What Does Mysticism Have to Teach Us about Consciousness?", Conference Towards a Science of Consciousness.

[21] Griffen, David, see note 13.

[22] Martin, Joel and Romanowski, Patricia, *Love Beyond Life*, Harper Collins Publishers, New York, 1997.

[23] Broughton, Richard S., *Parapsychology: The Controversial Science*, Ballantine Books, New York, 1991.

Chapter X
GOD AS REVEALED IN THE CREATION AND PRESERVATION OF THE UNIVERSE

Xa   Introduction

The question we have to ask ourselves is, how do these new theories and discoveries affect or relate to the main beliefs of the world religions and, in particular, how do they relate to the Christian belief in God, the Creator of the universe? At the outset, we must remember that religion is a matter of faith, hope and love and as such does not need any scientific insight or defense to make it real for the believer. However, for those with inquiring minds, it is not always possible to separate religious and scientific considerations entirely: to them it is not only a matter of faith but also a matter that needs to be approached from an intellectual point of view. After all, God created humans with a mind and an ability to use that mind to look for answers to the questions of human existence. Furthermore, I believe, we also have a duty to use these God-given faculties to help others to appreciate the beauty of God's creation.

So, we look around us to see where we can find God's hand at work in the universe. After all, if God created the universe, in all its stunning complexities, it would seem impossible for God to have done so without revealing a divine presence in the way the universe is put together and how it operates. In this chapter then, we look at where we can see the hand of God in the creation and maintenance of this universe, making use of the scientific discoveries made in the last decades and described in the previous chapters.

According to the Apostle Paul in his letter to the Romans, all we have to do to see God in the world around us is to use the eyes of reason:

> For what can be known about God is perfectly plain to them, since God has made it plain to them: ever since the creation of the world, the invisible existence of God and his everlasting power have been clearly seen by *the mind's understanding of created things*.
>
> Romans, Chapter 1, verses 19 and 20,
> *The Good News Bible*

and in the letter to the Hebrews:

> And it is after all only by faith that our minds accept as fact that the whole scheme of time and space was designed by God – that the world we can see is operating on principles that are invisible.
>
> Letter to the Hebrews, Chapter 11, verse 3,
> J. B. Phillips translation

As a result of these and similar statements in the Bible, the church for centuries has made a clear distinction between *natural theology* and *revealed theology*. In the previous chapters, we have seen something of how God revealed himself in the scriptures and in particular through Jesus Christ, whom Christians believe to be his Son. In this chapter, we will be looking at how the divine presence is revealed through nature.

The old Greeks had an argument which said that where there is order there must be a mind, and because there is order in the universe then it naturally follows that there is a mind beyond the mind of humans. With this argument we arrive straight away at God. "To look outward upon the world is to come face to face with God." (*The Daily Bible, the Gospel of John*, by William Barclay[1])

In the long history of the Christian Church a number of similar arguments have been used trying to prove the existence of God, the Creator, and to prove that the universe did not just come about by pure chance. While I will not use these propositions as such in this book, a number of the arguments I will be developing are closely related to some of their underlying principles. For this reason I will briefly mention some of them here.

First, there is the so-called *Ontological Argument*. Ontology refers to what lies at the essence of existence. The argument is of a rather philosophical nature and is not all that easy to follow. In its most simple form it is based on the fact that we have an idea of perfection in our mind. At the same time, there is nothing in the natural world that we can conceive that is greater than God; and since God embodies perfection, God must exist.

The second argument is called the *Cosmological Argument*. Within the context of this argument there are a number of approaches one can take. The easiest way to demonstrate this proof is through the idea of cause and effect. From the human perspective every cause has an effect. For instance, the fact that you are here (effect) is caused by the fact that your parents lived together and caused you to be born and, going back further, that your grandparents lived together in the same way. Therefore, the argument is that by going back far enough in time, you must come to the very first cause which (or who) started the ball rolling. This first cause is then called God.

The third argument is called the *Teleological or Design Argument*. It is based on the idea that if you found a complicated and intricate piece of machinery clicking away on a deserted island, you would not think that it had assembled itself there by pure chance. How could luck or accident account for the coming together of a number of complicated interlocking parts? Most likely, you would conclude that someone has put this intricate piece of machinery there. Furthermore, since it is still working, you will conclude that there is someone who is maintaining it as well. In the same way, this argument postulates that when we find these unbelievably complex and purposeful living organisms here on Earth there can be only one explanation for their existence, namely that there must have been a Master Designer or Intelligence at work who carefully assembled these organisms. Over the years, this argument was refuted and lost most of its champions, both in theological and scientific circles. However, in recent years the argument has been given new life and has gained new prominence. This time, however, the most convincing arguments originate with the scientists and not the theologians and philosophers, as was the case with earlier versions. Variants of this argument will be used extensively in the following pages.

The fourth argument is called the *Moral Argument*. This argument is based on the fact that humans have moral values. This sense of values is not something that could have come from a mechanistic, material universe. Since, almost all civilizations have a sense of right and wrong, it follows that there is a Supreme Being who must have incorporated this sensitivity for "the good" in the human psyche.

Before we start our own journey through nature to see where we can find the evidence of God's existence, I would like to remind the readers that, I believe, we are all created in the image of God, which, at the very least, must mean that we can think and reason and can detect the order in nature as designed by God. With this capacity to reason we should be able to see God's hand in the way the universe is put together and how it operates. Also, it is clear, I believe, that God has put us in charge of that creation; this in turn must mean that God has given us the capacity to understand at least some aspects of his master plan. No earthly creator would put someone in charge of something he has created without giving that person at least some idea of how his creation works and how it should be maintained.

In evaluating the various arguments presented in the following pages, we must be careful not to fall into the trap of using every phenomenon we cannot explain (yet) as proof of God's involvement in the design of the universe. This "God of the Gaps" will lose credibility every time a discovery is made that provides an explanation for this phenomenon. The Creator we are looking for in these arguments is a God who is directly involved in a positive and continuing way in his creation. In the following pages I will try to demonstrate that this God was there right at the beginning of the universe, and that this God is here right now at this point in the development of our universe.

Reviewing these arguments, we must remember that we have only two basic choices about the presence of God in the universe: either the universe was created by the most incredible luck or chance, or it was created by a Master Designer or Guiding Intelligence/Mind who created it according to a set design. With the first choice, the creation of the universe and the reason for its existence will forever remain a mystery and beyond our comprehension. With the second choice, the creation of the universe and the reason for it become the subject of the world's religions and philosophies which at that point must take over from science.

In some ways, the arguments that I will be using in the following pages for the existence of this Guiding Intelligence are of the negative type in that they demonstrate that nature could not have evolved in the way it did by pure chance and that, therefore, there must have been a Master Designer or Guiding Intelligence at work in the creation of the universe. Other arguments are all related to the fact that more and more scientists have come to accept the fact that there is a spiritual component to nature and that there is more to life than a purely physical existence. An entirely mechanical concept of nature simply cannot begin to explain the more recent discoveries in physics, medicine, psychology, etc. The point I am trying to make is that this spiritual component to life could not have evolved from a mechanical, evolutionary process, and that it requires the concept of a Spiritual Power in the universe to explain its presence in nature.

In evaluating the strength of these arguments I have used two levels of certainty, which are, of course, highly subjective. They are respectively:

- Level 1: No other explanation possible – the observed phenomena can only be explained, I believe, by the active involvement of a Guiding Intelligence or Master Designer in the creation and preservation of the universe.
- Level 2: Strongly suggests involvement of a Guiding Intelligence – the observed phenomena strongly suggest that this is the case; but there may be explanations forthcoming later based on physical laws that have not yet been formulated.

In evaluating these arguments, we might use the criteria proposed by George Ellis[2] in his book, *Before the Beginning, Cosmology Explained*, for the selection of a satisfactory explanation of the facts from amongst the many alternatives. What he called "primary candidates" for these criteria are:

- simplicity;
- beauty;
- prediction and verifiability; and
- overall explanatory power and unity of explanation.

Of course, the arguments on the following pages do not always meet all these criteria, but most, I believe, meet at least three out of the four.

The Christian, the Jew and the Muslim looking at the evidence of God's presence in nature start off with the conviction that God is real and that God created the universe and maintains it as well. It is, therefore, far easier for them to see God's hand in the creation and preservation of the universe than for the non-Christian, non-Jew or non-Muslim who do not have such a starting point. So, I have summarized the areas where I see the hand of God most clearly according to the two levels of certainty as defined in the previous page. Finally, the various arguments are presented in tabular form at the end of this chapter.

Xb   The First Level of Certainty – No Other Explanation Possible

NO. 1 – THE BEGINNING OF THE UNIVERSE (Aa) (CHAPTER IIB)

[The letters behind each argument refer to the numbering of these arguments at the end of this chapter. The chapter shown in brackets below the argument refers to the chapter where the main reasoning behind the argument is developed.]

It is now general accepted in science that:

- The universe did have a distinct beginning some twelve to fifteen billion years ago.
- The universe was essentially created out of nothing.

- Time, space and all matter, together with the laws of nature, were created at this time.
- Matter was created in the form of the most basic particles that eventually evolved into atoms and molecules.

Accepting these statements as fact, I believe, means almost automatically that the creation of the universe must have involved a Guiding Intelligence or Master Designer. Who or what else could have possibly started a universe on its way that had such an unbelievable potential, a potential that led from the tiniest superstrings or quarks to fully conscious human beings.

Some scientists argue that it was a quantum fluctuation that started the process. But if there was no matter, no space and no time before the Big Bang, where does this quantum fluctuation come from and what was fluctuating? Are quantum mechanics and quantum fluctuations outside the realm of nature and, therefore, not created? The answer, at least to my mind, is very clear: quantum mechanics may be weird and wonderful, but it is just as much a part of creation as any of the other elements of nature, and it is an integral part of the grand design of the universe.

I believe that, no matter what explanation is offered for the creation of the universe, eventually we will always come to a full stop when we try to explain where this first matter or where this first law of nature came from. Thus, I believe, there is no alternative – there simply is no other choice but to accept the fact that some Guiding Intelligence, existing beyond time and space, created the universe.

NO. 2 – HUMANS APPEAR TO BE THE CROWNING RESULT OF CREATION (Ac) (CHAPTER II)

There is no doubt, looking at how over time more and more complex systems evolved, that human beings are the most complex and intricate creatures in the solar system and probably in the universe. All this in defiance of the second law of thermodynamics which says that the universe, in the long run, will become more and more chaotic. On the other hand, Heisenberg's uncertainty principle states that the act of observing subatomic particles changes what is being observed. This has led some scientists to write that the universe must be such as to admit the creation of observers in it at some stage. In other words, the whole universe was created in such a way that eventually humans would emerge. This, of course, puts humans right back at the center of the universe. Some scientists have even gone further and have postulated that the whole universe is only real if there exists an intelligence to observe the universe. It is argued that without the observer reality may not exist. Since, as far as we know, outside the Creator himself, human beings are the only fully conscious observers in the known universe, it is argued that the existence of humans is considered crucial to the reality or definition of the universe.

In Chapter II we quoted John Wheeler as saying: "The entire universe exists because someone is watching it: everything right back to the Big Bang, some fifteen billion years ago, remained undefined until it was noticed." In the same chapter, we find Amit Goswami taking the final step when he writes: "We are the center of the universe because we are its meaning."

In many ways, this new view of humanity's importance coincides with what the major religions tell us about the centrality of the human being in creation. Following our argument, if we are indeed the meaning of, or the reason for, the creation of the universe, then there must have been a Guiding Intelligence involved in that creation who planned it that way.

I realize that there are people who think that placing

humans at the center of the universe, and even going as far as claiming that humans are the meaning of the universe, is very presumptuous on our part. The question is then, if not humans, who or what then is the meaning of this very complicated and involved creation. In this solar system I simply cannot see any creature other than humans filling this role. Thus, whether we like it or not, it appears that humans are the culmination of the long creation process, at least in this solar system. What there is in the cosmos beyond our solar system that could possibly give the universe its meaning, we do not know at present and probably will never know. For the present, we can only assume that we are it.

NO. 3 – THE VALUES OF THE BASIC CONSTANTS THAT DETERMINE THE OPERATION OF THE UNIVERSE (Ba) (CHAPTER IIC)

Recent discoveries have shown that the operation of our universe is governed by four basic forces and by a number of laws of nature that between them contain something like fifteen constants. Some of these constants are well-known: they include the speed of light, the gravitational constant, the charge of an electron, etc.; others are more obscure and are only familiar to specialists in the various disciplines of physics. The intriguing fact about these constants is that even the slightest change in any of them leads to an unstable universe and therefore makes life, as we experience it, impossible. In the words of Trinh Xuan Thuan:

> Life as we know it would not have the slightest chance of emerging in any universe that was the least bit different from our own. All the model universes would be sterile and devoid of consciousness. The numerical parameters do not suffer *any* modification.

In a world that is determined entirely by chance and not by

a Guiding Intelligence, a sustainable universe could have been achieved only by allowing for the creation of literally trillions of other universes, all with slightly different values of these constants. Some of these universes would have been able to survive, but they could not have led to the creation of life; others would have collapsed almost immediately. Our universe would then be the end result of a long list of trials and errors until a universe was created that could lead to the development of life. To accept this process, you must also accept the fact that something in the nature of the universe kept creating these new universes with slightly different constants until ours came along. That is not too far from admitting that even under this scenario, there must have been a guiding hand at work who kept adjusting the value of these constants until eventually, after trillions of trials and errors, a set of values turned up that led to a stable universe with conditions suitable for the emergence of life.

I believe that the only acceptable explanation for us being here must be that there was indeed a Guiding Intelligence at work in the creation of the universe; and that it was this Intelligence who created the laws of nature, including the constants, right at the beginning of the creation process and in such a way that life, and ultimately human life, could develop.

NO. 4 – THE EXISTENCE OF THE IRREDUCIBLY COMPLEX SYSTEMS IN LIVING THINGS (Ca) (CHAPTER IIIe)

Irreducibly complex systems are systems that could not possibly have developed through evolution from previous stages because all parts are needed for it to function; take away one of its parts, or have one part that is still evolving or is not yet fully formed, and it will not work and is not viable. The standard example used by Michael Behe, one of the earliest proponents of this concept, is that of the ordinary mousetrap. Take one of the components of the trap away and it will not function. Thus a mousetrap could never have developed by small intermediate steps from a more basic mouse-catching device.

In nature there are many of these irreducibly complex systems, systems that could not have developed gradually simply because any intermediate steps would make them unworkable. The literature contains many examples of such systems; most of them, however, require too much detailed knowledge of the subject to use as an example here. Some of the easier to understand include the workings of our immune system and the transformation of a land animal to a flying bird. The example that I personally find most persuasive is that of the metamorphosis of a drab caterpillar into a beautiful butterfly. Surely, this almost mystical change cannot possibly have been the result of small evolutionary steps starting from either the caterpillar or the butterfly; any intermediate step in its development would simply not have been viable.

The fact that our bodies, and all living things, are riddled with these irreducibly complex systems simply proves, to my mind, that some agency, or intelligence, must have been at work to put these systems in place, bypassing temporarily the normal evolutionary processes. Darwin himself once wrote that his theory would break down if it could be proven that there were systems that could *not* evolve through *small* modifications from a more basic form. Well, here we are! We believe that we can prove that there are dozens of these systems, which could not possibly have evolved from more basic intermediate forms.

The only explanation I can see for the existence of these systems must be that a Guiding Intelligence was at work and intervened in the normal evolutionary process to put these irreducibly complex systems in place, which are so essential to the proper functioning of all living beings. The only alternative is that the creation of these systems was due to very large and complicated single steps in the evolutionary process. In their turn, these steps must have been subject to some basic law of nature, maybe in the form of organizing fields. These fields must have been put there at the beginning of creation by some Intelligence; it certainly could not have been pure chance that caused these large evolutionary steps to happen. So, even using this explanation we come back to the involvement of a Creative Spirit or Intelligence in the development of living things.

NO. 5 – THE COMPLEXITY OF THE HUMAN CELL – THE FACT THAT BILLIONS OF DIFFERENT CELLS ARE MADE FROM THE ORIGINAL TWO CELLS AND THEN FIND THEIR RIGHT PLACE IN THE HUMAN BODY (CB) (CHAPTER V)

The living cell is such an unbelievably complex structure that it defies any speculation that it was pure chance which made all these elements come together in exactly the right place and in the right sequence. Not only is the cell itself an extremely complex structure, but the cell nucleus is even more astonishingly complicated with its DNA and RNA molecules. These molecules are made up of millions of strands of proteins which in themselves are very complicated molecules. Someone has calculated the probability that the atoms in these proteins would assemble themselves into these complicated molecules by chance. His conclusion was that the odds that these chains of molecules would form by chance was so small that it was impossible to express in meaningful terms. The fact that these DNA and RNA molecules contain thousands of these proteins, in a pattern that is equally complicated, makes the probability that this would happen by pure chance even more unlikely. Not only are these molecules extremely complex, but so is the way they propagate by splitting along their length and then miraculously finding the exact bits and pieces to make a complete copy of the original strand. This happens millions of times in all of the millions of cells in the human body and, in most cases, without any major mistakes or errors.

Finally, in all of nature there is no more miraculous process than the one by which the female egg and the male sperm manage to form thousands of different cells. These cells vary in size from the round, one-millimeter diameter blood cells to the one-meter long, spiky nerve cells. The real miracle is that all these different cells are then dispatched in about the right numbers to the right place in the body. The fingernail cells to the right fingernail and the blood cells to the right artery in the blood circulation system. Somehow this fantastic process must be encoded in some way in the original two cells. Think of all the instructions necessary to make this happen. Even if each atom in these two original cells could each contain one instruction, there would not be enough atoms available in these two cells by a couple of magnitudes. This whole process of the evolution of life from two cells is so miraculous that it is difficult not to see the hand of a Superior Intelligence in the way life was formed and maintained.

NO. 6 – THE FACT THAT HUMANS ARE BORN WITH A CONSCIOUSNESS WHICH IS IMMORTAL (DA) (CHAPTERS VF AND VG)

The human consciousness has two different aspects to it. Firstly, there is the feeling of self-awareness, the sense of our surroundings and of our body's mortality. Secondly, there is the consciousness which expresses itself in the emotions of love, anger, joy, sadness and the appreciation of beauty, justice, etc. and all these influence our human behavior. It is this consciousness which comes closest to the concept of a human soul: like the soul it is believed that human consciousness is immortal and cannot be destroyed once created. Because of its immaterial nature, it can obviously not have been the result of material, evolutionary changes in the brain. Anyone who believes in the purely mechanical/chemical origin of life must explain how nature could have made the jump from a collection of firing neurons to the perception of self and the emotions of love and beauty. Dr. Dossey, whom I quoted in Chapter V, believes that science will eventually recognize the nonlocal nature of consciousness and that it will no longer be considered a by-product of the brain which will die with the body. As he writes, "It is nonlocal, infinite in space and time, omnipresent and immortal by implication."

NO.7 – THE FACT THAT OUR IMMATERIAL MIND CAN CONTROL MATERIAL EVENTS (DB) (CHAPTER VG)

It is now generally accepted that there is both a spiritual and a material component to human life, and that we have a consciousness that is fundamentally different from that of animals. In particular, we believe that we have a mind that can control physical properties. For instance, our entire life is controlled by actions that are generated from nonphysical thoughts, feelings, desires, etc. My willpower to finish this sentence, which is nonmaterial, results in me tapping out the appropriate words on this keyboard, which is a very material action indeed. So, unless we are willing to admit that thoughts, feelings, desires, hopes, love, etc. are physical phenomena, we must admit that we also have a nonphysical component to our existence. At the same time, it must be clear that a nonphysical component to life could never have resulted from purely physical developments of the body. John Searle[3] writes in *The Rediscovery of the Mind*:

> Somehow or another, sentience sprang from pulpy matter, giving matter an inner aspect, but we have no idea how this

leap was propelled... One is tempted, however reluctantly, to turn to divine assistance: for only a kind of miracle could produce this from that. It would take a supernatural magician to extract consciousness from matter, even living matter.

I believe that sums up the argument pretty neatly. Only a supernatural Intelligence could have produced such things as love, hope and all other spiritual components of our consciousness from material components.

NO. 8 – THE EXISTENCE OF OUR FREE WILL (DC)
(CHAPTER VI)

There are people who believe that there is no such thing as a free will: they believe that all their actions have been predetermined by their atomic and subatomic make-up. The programmed action of nerve cells is what they believe governs their lives. On the other hand, most people believe that their daily experience shows that they do have a free will; that they can make a choice between good and evil; between making a right turn or a left turn at the next intersection, etc. Imagine for a moment what the absence of a free will would do to our behavior and to the operation of our society. Without a free will, you can do the most horrifying things without feeling any regret or remorse; after all, it was your neurons that were programmed to make you do those things. Consequently, without free will we lose all moral responsibility for our actions and our judicial system could not operate under these conditions. But we do have a judicial system which is based on the assumption that we do have a free will and that we are responsible for our actions. So, I believe, it is quite clear that society at large decided a long time ago that humans do have a free will and are responsible for what they are doing.

Recent discoveries have clearly shown that cause and effect are not necessarily always the same, but that at best there is only a possibility that a certain cause will have a certain effect. This simple fact has forever, I believe, done away with determinism which states that our lives are completely predetermined and that we simply are nothing else but a clockwork that is running down.

In the *Tao is Silent*, in the discussion between God and Mortal, the writer makes God say,

> Free will is not an extra, it is part and parcel of the very essence of consciousness. A conscious being without free will is simply a metaphysical absurdity.

Since free will is a nonmaterial concept, that could never have developed through a process of evolution and mutation of some physical aspects of the human being, it must have been put there by this Intelligence which oversaw the creation of the entire universe, including the development of human beings who are free to make their own choices.

NO.9 – THE OUT-OF-BODY EXPERIENCE OF A GREAT MANY PEOPLE (Fa) (CHAPTER IXC)

Recent studies have shown that the out-of-body experience is not as rare as originally assumed and has actually been experienced by as much as ten per cent of the population. People have this experience mostly when, for one reason or another, they are unconscious; for example, during an operation. They tell that they are suddenly becoming aware of occupying a *spiritual* body quite distinct from their *physical* body, and that they can actually observe that physical body and what is being done to it. During this stage, their spiritual body is without blemishes: for instance, people who have lost a leg see themselves with that leg in place during their out-of-body experience. Later when they return to their physical body, they can describe in great detail what went on in the operating room, what people were wearing and what they were saying to each other. The most impressive evidence of the reality of this experience comes from people who have been blind for many years, yet when they have an out-of-body experience, they can describe in detail the people in the operating room and what they were wearing, etc.

The interesting thing is that people from all cultures and religions report to have had the same experience. As described in Chapter IX, Dr. Shiels has analyzed over a thousand reports from people in some seventy different non-Western cultures who have had these out-of-body experiences. In the end, he did not find any distinct differences in the experience of these diverse, ethnic groups. Thus this type of experience seems to be universal and to cross all cultures and religions.

I believe, the experience of all these people clearly demonstrates that:

- There exists a spiritual body or mind.
- This spiritual body can be separated from the physical body and thus has the capacity to survive death.

NO. 10 – THE ODDS THAT LIFE COULD HAVE DEVELOPED SPONTANEOUSLY ANYWHERE (I) (CHAPTER III)

As we have seen time and time again in the previous chapters, the odds against life developing spontaneously anywhere in the universe are enormous. In fact, so enormous that it is virtually certain that there must have been some type of planning and guidance involved in the long evolution from the basic particles that were created at the beginning of time to the fully conscious human beings of today. In the following pages, I have described the conditions that must be met during the various stages of evolution so that human consciousness could develop:

a. conditions necessary for the formation of a stable universe;
b. physical conditions our planet must meet to make the creation of life possible;
c. cells to be created out of essentially dead matter and to make these cells replicate; and
d. conditions needed to have human consciousness develop from the most basic living cells.

a – The creation of a stable universe

- It is believed that our universe was created some twelve to fifteen billion years ago with, what is now generally called, the Big Bang. Since it is further believed that time, space and all basic matter were formed at that time, it is, in principle, impossible for us to go back in time before the Big Bang and to find out what led up to this event and to explain why it happened. It is simply a miracle that cannot be explained in terms of physical laws. There is not even a probability that can be attached to this event – it just occurred. In the end, we have no other recourse than to accept that creation was an act of a Creative Force existing beyond time and space.

- Given the fact that all matter, in some form or another, was created at the time of the Big Bang, it does not naturally follow that further development would lead to a stable universe. On the contrary, it appears that the likelihood that a stable universe would be formed from this primordial material is extremely remote. The main reason for this is that laws of nature, which were also established at the time of creation, contain some fifteen constants that must have precisely the value they have for the universe to exist at all. The chance that fifteen independent constants would have these precise values, just by chance, is so remote that it can be effectively discarded.

- It is now understood that at the time of the Big Bang a number of subatomic particles were formed that eventually arranged themselves to form hydrogen and helium atoms. This is one of the points in time when the creation process could have easily stalled. It appears that to produce heavier elements from these two types of atoms requires temperatures and pressures that can only be found in stars that are ready to explode; even then the conditions for this to happen are so remote that it made Fred Hoyle exclaim that it made him believe in the involvement of a Creator in this process.

b – The physical conditions our planet must meet to make the creation of life possible

- The range of temperatures in which life, as we know it, can operate is extremely narrow; for the sake of argument let us say it is 150 degrees. This is very small compared with the temperatures that occur in the universe where temperatures go from a low of absolute zero to a high of millions of degrees Centigrade. So for life to be possible in the universe, it must be at a location where this small temperature variance can be maintained indefinitely. This condition exists only at satellites of stars that circulate around their star in a near circular orbit and at a very specific distance from that star. If the planet gets too far from its star everything will freeze, and if it gets too close everything will fry. Also, a suitable planet must have an orbital speed, a rotational speed and a certain tilt all within very close limits. For a planet to meet all these conditions is extremely unlikely, even considering that there are billions of stars in our galaxy.

- Our solar system contains a multitude of meteors and asteroids whose path regularly intersect the orbit of our planet. Occasionally, these collide with the planets circling the Sun. On Earth, with its water and wind erosion, the impact craters are fairly quickly obliterated. But on the Moon where there is no effective erosion, the marks of hundreds of collisions are clearly visible. It is believed that the large outside planets, Jupiter and Neptune, because of their size regularly intercept most of these large and small chunks of matter before they can cause harm to our planet. Without these large "protective" planets we would be regularly bombarded by these meteors and asteroids; thus, wiping out large percentages of the flora and fauna every time they strike. So, the existence of these large outer planets is one other condition a planet must meet for life to be able to develop uninterruptedly.

- There is one other condition for life to exist at all on any given planet, a condition which exists on Earth but which we put at risk through our disregard of the environment. This requirement is that there must be a certain thickness of an ozone layer that protects the Earth from the deadly ultraviolet radiation from the Sun. Without this layer remaining in place, we will eventually be unable to exist as we do now and have to live underground or something like it. Also, life on this planet is only possible because of the absence of deadly gases such as methane and ammonia which are found in abundance on some of the other planets.

In summary, the conditions for the existence of a planet on which life can develop are so many and varied that it begs the question, how did this all come about and what Intelligence is behind the existence of a planet that meets all these unlikely conditions?

c – Conditions required to make it possible for living cells to be created out of essentially dead matter and to make these cells replicate

- For life to evolve anywhere, there must first of all be an abundant supply of the chemicals which make up the raw material of all living things, such as carbon, hydrogen, oxygen, etc. In addition, the amount of free oxygen must lie within strict limits: if there is too much, everything will burn; if there is too little, nothing will burn.

- Somehow, a cell must be formed from these basic chemicals: first without a nucleus and then later with a nucleus which contains the unbelievably complex DNA and RNA molecules. The information contained in these molecules, in the form of genes, determines to a large extent how the body will develop.

- The original male and female cell must contain enough information to guide the production of thousands of different cells and to direct these new cells to their proper location in the body. It has been calculated that if each atom in the original cells contained one instruction there would not be nearly enough atoms to contain all the information required. It has been postulated that there must be some sort of "form-giving field" that is an essential component of the original male and female cells. These fields would be immaterial and could not possibly be created by accident from material substances.

- The random errors in the duplication of the DNA molecule (mutations) must somehow be directed towards the formation of more and more complicated organisms, eventually leading to the emergence of human beings. This is the more surprising since the more complex an organism is the more it is subject to attack and extinction. For instance, the one-celled creatures which were formed billions of years ago are still thriving today while most of the more complicated organisms formed after them have mostly become extinct.

The whole process of the evolution of life is so miraculous that it is difficult not to see the hand of a Superior Intelligence in the way life was formed and is still maintained.

d – Conditions needed to have human consciousness develop from the most basic living cells

- Even after the formation or creation of living cells leading to the emergence of living animals and plants, the creation of a fully conscious human being is as mysterious as any of the previous steps in its evolvement. For instance, it is believed that during the evolution of life on Earth, there were some fifty billion speciation events, that is events when a new species was developed. Only one of these events led to the creation of a fully conscious human being. It has been postulated that if life on this planet was ever reduced to that of microbes again, the chance that human beings would be created again is absolutely nil.

- Even if all life on Earth was reduced to the existence of the large primates, the possibility that consciousness would emerge again by itself is extremely remote. Consciousness with its spiritual components such as love, intellect, beauty, compassion, etc. simply cannot be created from material entities. As someone said, consciousness is not some peripheral add-on to the brain but is an essential component of human life. Without it we are simply not human. How it got here is simply not explainable in scientific terms.

This whole sequence of events is so improbable: the chance that this would happen, even over the long time available, is so small that it makes far more sense to assume that there was a Guiding Intelligence which caused this sequence of events to happen according to a basic plan. To use Fred

Hoyle's words, the chance that this would happen is about the same as a Boeing 747 airplane spontaneously assembling itself when a whirlwind hits a junkyard.

Xc The Second Level of Certainty – Strongly Suggests the Involvement of a Guiding Intelligence

With the background of these arguments, which I have assigned the first level of certainty, let us now look somewhat closer at the other places in nature where we see the operation of this Guiding Intelligence at work. This second set of arguments may not be as clear-cut as the first set, but they are nevertheless sufficiently persuasive to decide, using Jim Holt's words, that we are here because of a deliberate, supernatural design.

NO. 1 – THE NEW EVIDENCE THAT HUMANS MAY HAVE DESCENDED FROM ONE PROTOTYPE MOTHER (Ab) (CHAPTER III)

For a long time, it was believed that human beings evolved at different times at different locations from different prototypes. In other words, the evolution of humans was thought to have occurred not as a single event but that it occurred at different places from different initial conditions probably leading to the formation of different races. Thus the rise of human beings could have happened following different evolutionary paths starting from a variety of predecessors.

All this changed in recent years, when the research of the genetic make-up of the various races and groups around the world proved that the earliest humans (Homo sapiens) were created as one distinct evolutionary event in Africa, and that all humans can trace their origins back to one woman living in Africa some 150,000 years ago. This creature was so different from its predecessors that normal evolution and mutations cannot begin to explain the sudden appearance of this fully conscious and intelligent being. It is difficult to see, at this point in time, how this could have happened without the deliberate intervention of a Master Designer or Intelligence. However, further anthropological research may lead to other conclusions. It is, therefore, necessary to keep an open mind. For the present, these findings would seem to confirm the contention of all the major religions that humans are a separate creation, set apart and distinct from the other living creatures.

NO. 2 – THE MATHEMATICAL SIMPLICITY AND BEAUTY OF THE LAWS OF NATURE THAT GOVERN THE OPERATIONS OF THE UNIVERSE (Bb) (CHAPTER IIb, IIc)

The argument for the existence of a Guiding Intelligence behind the simplicity and beauty of the laws of nature is almost as compelling as the argument based on the fact that the value of the fifteen universal constants must be exactly right for a stable universe to emerge. In addition, there is the fact that there are only four forces of nature which govern the entire operation of the universe. In my opinion, it is difficult to believe that chance is the "mastermind" behind creating a universe that has only four basic forces, which guide the operation and behavior not only of the minuscule subatomic particles but also of the immense assembly of galaxies and stars. Not only that, these laws of nature appear to be the only things in the universe that are not subject to change: in other words, they are eternal. Again, I believe, there is a clear indication of an Intelligence behind the wonderful simplicity of these universal laws. However, once having accepted a Designer in the setting of the values of the fifteen universal constants, it may be inevitable that there needs to be only four forces to make the system work. So, the simplicity of the laws of nature may not constitute an independent argument for the existence of this Intelligence, but it is, nevertheless, a strong indication that there is more to nature than pure chance.

In addition to this simplicity, there is the fact that mathematics can be used to describe these natural laws so accurately. It may be thought that mathematics is simply a human invention, but that does not explain why it is so effective in describing nature in all its complexity. To quote Eugene Wagner again: "The unreasonable effectiveness of mathematics in uncovering the structure of the physical world is a kind of a hint of the presence of a Creator given to us creatures who are made in the divine image."

NO. 3 – THE INTRICATE OPERATION OF THE HUMAN BRAIN AND NERVOUS SYSTEM (Cc) (CHAPTER Ve)

The human brain is such an astonishingly complicated assembly of interacting nerves that it is difficult to imagine that it came into being through a slow evolutionary process. We know that the size of the brain of the earliest hominids was only one-third to one-quarter of the size of the brain of a modern human being. So, it is clear that evolution had a real part to play in the development of the human brain. Recognizing this, however, does not take anything away from the mystery of this wonderful assembly of nerves that makes us remember things, makes us aware of our surroundings, and gives us the capacity to perceive concepts and work out solutions to complicated problems. The fact that the size of the human brain increased with the further development of the human being poses the question of why the size of the brain kept increasing long before our forefathers had any immediate need for it. It may be conceivable to some that the human brain developed slowly over the ages; however, there is no explanation for the fact that early humans had brains with potentials that were not used for thousands of years. It is as if there was a Creative

Force involved that foresaw the need, in the far future, for a brain that could invent calculus, could build electronic computers, could write Shakespearean dramas and could compose Beethoven symphonies. At the time that this capacity was built into the brain there was no need whatsoever to have a brain of that capacity to survive as a species. There must, therefore, have been something more involved in the creation of the brain such as a Creative Force which carefully planned it this way.

As far as the animal brain is concerned, it may be useful to consider what Martin Gardner[4] recently wrote in a book, *Did Adam and Eve Have a Navel?*: "The brain of an earthworm is more complicated than a lifeless galaxy."

NO. 4 – THE LANGUAGE CAPABILITY OF HUMANS WHICH FAR EXCEEDS THAT NECESSARY FOR SURVIVAL (Cd) (CHAPTER IIID)

One of the most important abilities of the human being is the capacity to communicate with each other through the spoken word. This capability seems to be universal for all humans whether they lived in the Stone Age or live in today's highly developed technological society. For the simple survival of the species this special capability was obviously not necessary; however, it was essential for the growth of human beings into the cultured being of today for whom communication is an absolute necessity. As James Jargon Lanai wrote in the May 1997 issue of *Harper's Magazine*:

> I think that the fundamental process of conversation is one of the great miracles of nature, that two people can communicate with each other is an extraordinary phenomenon that has so far defied all attempts to capture it. Communicating with another person remains an essential mystical act.

It is clear that most animals have means of communicating with each other in ways we do not understand, but there is nothing in the animal world that compares with the human language skills. I believe that the language capacity is one of the most marvelous gifts that a Benevolent Creator could have bestowed on us, in that it makes it possible for humans to express verbally their love and affection for each other and for their Creator. Also, a language capability is an essential condition for the development of culture and technology.

No. 5 – The Human Search for Values, Beauty and Understanding (Dd) (Chapter VI)

It is an unmistakable fact that people, from the most primitive to the most sophisticated, all share some of the same fundamental aspects of life such as the search for values, for beauty, for understanding, for justice, etc. For instance, ever since conscious human beings first emerged, they have expressed their sense of appreciation of beauty through the creation of such art forms as paintings, carvings, pottery, etc. As Pannenberg[5] wrote:

> All such expressions bear witness to the reality of a power, which raises up hearts – the power of the Spirit. When man is most creative, he is most conscious of being grasped by a spiritual power which raises him above himself.

I believe that all this is a clear indication that we are not just made up of neurons and atoms, but that there is a spiritual component to our existence as well. In the battle for the "survival of the fittest" it is not necessary that we can appreciate the beauty of the Ninth Symphony of Beethoven or the statue of the Venus de Milo. For our survival as a species it is not helpful to discover how the universe is put together, or to have compassion for other people. On the contrary, from a purely materialistic point of view, both are unnecessary and wasteful and counter-productive activities. I believe it requires the creative involvement of a Guiding Intelligence to have incorporated all these fundamental features into our human psyche. They certainly are not there as the result of the evolution of the material component of life.

NO. 6 – THE EXISTENCE OF INTUITION AND EXTRASENSORY PERCEPTION (De) (CHAPTERS V AND IX)

There are a great many phenomena which are being experienced by the average human being that are not transmitted to us through the five senses of feeling, seeing, hearing, smelling and tasting. One of these is intuition, a phenomenon that most people have experienced in their lives at one time or another. Someone "knows" suddenly that someone close to him or her is in danger or is dying. The experiences are legion. The obvious conclusion is that information can be conveyed to us through other channels than through the five senses.

There is also the fact that some people have dreams which seem to point to a subconscious knowledge of things that are happening or have happened in other places; sometimes even of things that will happen in the future. Then there is the practice of hypnosis by which one person conveys messages to another person, also without using the five senses.

There is telepathy by which one person transfers thoughts to another person, sometimes over great distances. Finally, there are all the other elements of ESP such as precognition (the ability to foresee events), and clairvoyance (the ability to see things that are happening elsewhere). The point is that these phenomena have been recorded from time immemorial and in every area of the world and in every civilization, both primitive and highly developed.

The problem with these phenomena is that they are

extremely difficult to confirm. So far, none of them appear to have been confirmed as factual by rigorously controlled tests. The point is, however, that the experience is so universal that it is unwise to discard all of them as being clever deceptions, which no doubt many of them are; but, if only a minute percentage of them are true, it proves that there is a spiritual component to the human existence which operates outside the normal physical body. Someone even suggested that physics would never be complete until it can account for extrasensory perception and telekinesis (Brian Josephson, physicist and Nobel laureate).

NO. 7 – THE POWER OF THE HUMAN MIND TO CONTROL PHYSICAL AND PSYCHOLOGICAL PROCESSES (Df)
(CHAPTER IXB)

In recent years there has been a virtual flood of books by medical doctors about self-healing. They all report results of self-healing that border on the miraculous. Some of them use such practices as yoga, meditation, etc. as the medium through which the healing is affected. In all cases, however, it is acknowledged that, in the end, it is the human mind that affects healing. Others maintain that it is the body itself which is the greatest healer of them all. Some go so far as to say that all cells have their own intelligence and that mind is present in every cell of the human body. In the end, I believe that this built-in intelligence is a clear indication of the influence of the nonmaterial spirit over the material body. Another example of the power of the human mind to influence bodily functions and health is the proven fact that altruism and related activities have a profound effect on the general health of the caregiver. For instance, it was found that people who did not do volunteer work were much more likely to die during the study period as compared with people who did volunteer work at least once or twice a week. So, I believe it is clear that we are spiritual beings who can use our own spiritual gifts to work for ourselves and for others. As Paul Davies wrote, "We are spiritual beings becoming aware of our spiritual essence." I believe that this nonmaterial spiritual force can only have been created as a purposeful act by a Creative Force that exists beyond our material world.

NO. 8 – THE MANY TESTIMONIES TO THE EFFECTIVENESS OF PRAYER (Ea) (CHAPTER IXB)

Prayer is essentially a two-way communication between the individual and God. For the Christians, Jesus not only gave us an example of prayer but also prayed often to God in the presence of his disciples. Following this example, Christians have for 2,000 years followed his example and prayed to God for their most immediate needs. In particular, they have prayed for their sick and dying. The literature of the last 2,000 years is literally filled with accounts of cures that appear to have been the result of prayer. Even to this day, every Sunday morning in thousands of churches across the world, prayers are offered for peace and for the healing of the sick. At special shrines where the mother of Jesus is said to have appeared, people seem to be receiving miraculous healing, many of them attested to by testimonies of independent observers. Also, there are hundreds of charismatic church services held every week where people receive healing through the laying on of hands or through other rituals. All this goes a long way to explain why people in need continue to pray in this science-oriented world even though, in many cases, they may not be particularly religious. Dr. Larry Dossey has even suggested that prayer may become a standard practice in the physician's office. This power of prayer in helping to cure people is starting to become recognized by the academic world to the extent that one third of the medical schools in the U.S.A. now offer courses and programs in spirituality and healing. In any case, the effectiveness of prayer is, I believe, a strong indication of the reality of a Spirit who is in touch with humankind. Skeptics, of course, will not accept that this healing is the result of prayer and will argue that any healing that does occur is the result of the placebo effect or would have occurred anyway. This argument is, of course, difficult to disprove and is the reason why the effectiveness of prayer was not included among the first category of certainty.

NO. 9 – THE RESULTS OF SCIENTIFICALLY CONTROLLED EXPERIMENTS ON THE EFFECTIVENESS OF PRAYER (Eb) (CHAPTER IXB)

Because of the aforementioned difficulty to prove the effectiveness of prayer, there is now a movement afoot to try to prove its effectiveness by experiment. At present, there are a number of scientifically controlled tests in progress which try to measure the effectiveness of prayer. In general, these experiments have shown that prayer has indeed a positive effect on the well-being of the people prayed for. Many of these tests are still ongoing and the final results may take years before they become generally known. However, so far these tests have shown that the effectiveness is not affected by distance or location. What is even more interesting is that it appears that the people who are being prayed for do not necessarily have to be aware of this fact for this type of prayer to be effective. If this can be substantiated, it would rule out the explanation that the positive results of prayer might be the result of a placebo effect. Of course, there remains the standard argument that these healings would have taken place anyway, and that the intervention of a Healing Spirit is therefore not necessary to explain the healing that took place. In any case, it is clear that until we get some more confirmation from these tests about the effectiveness of prayer, most people who are not religious will not be convinced of the existence of a Healing Spirit who is directly involved in the lives of people.

NO. 10 – THE NEAR-DEATH EXPERIENCE (NDE) OF MANY PEOPLE (Fb) (CHAPTER IXc)

Many people who have been clinically dead have reported that during this period they underwent a wonderful experience: they all report that they went through a tunnel into a space of light where they felt surrounded by an all-encompassing love and beauty. Some of them report to have encountered the source of this light. Dr. Kübler-Ross, who first brought this phenomenon to the attention of the general public, together with her associates interviewed over the years some 20,000 people all over the world. They report that all had, more or less, the same experience and that it was the same for people of all religions, cultures, racial backgrounds and ages.

Some critics claim that this does not prove anything about the reality of an afterlife because the people did not actually die. They claim that the same effects can be artificially created by manipulating the brain and depriving it of oxygen. This argument, however, has been discounted in recent years due to the fact that no one has been able to actually do this and generate feelings of peace, love and well-being in this way. For the Christian, the interesting point is that these experiences were the same for people of all religions. Also, while most people who had this experience did not suddenly become religious, most changed their lifestyle and became more considerate and were never again afraid to die. This last point is probably the most convincing evidence; the people who had this experience consider what they experienced as real.

It is, of course, true that these people did not actually die; and their experience may, therefore, not have any significance as far as proving that there is an afterlife. However, both the near-death experience and the out-of-body experience would seem to indicate that there exists a human spiritual body independent of the physical body which can be separated from that body.

NO. 11 – THE UNIVERSAL FEELING OF INTERCONNECTEDNESS, THE COLLECTIVE UNCONSCIOUS (Fc) (CHAPTER IXH)

There is a strong feeling in the world today about the interconnectedness of all things in nature, which is probably something most clearly expressed by the native Indians of North America. Dr. Carl Jung called this the collective unconscious. This collective unconscious is assumed to be shared by everyone, and everyone participates in it unconsciously. It is proclaimed to be universal and not limited by time or space. In fact, it is thought to be immortal.

This concept of the immortal collective unconscious is closely linked to what the Christian would call the spiritual body, or immortal soul, which is also thought to survive after the death of the physical body. This human soul, which, although it has no physical or material reality, nevertheless is credited with the functions of thinking, willing, etc. and is believed to determine to a large extent how we behave.

The important point is that many physicists, medical doctors, psychologists and scientists in general are now talking about an immortal aspect to the human being. The Christian concept of the resurrection of the body and soul, and Jung's concept of a collective unconscious that is immortal may be far apart, but both consider that the physical death of a person is not the end of the person's consciousness. Erwin Schrödinger, one of the fathers of quantum mechanics, goes so far as to suggest that mind and consciousness are the same thing. Mind, he said, is no longer localized in the individual, but is transpersonal, universal, collective, nonlocal and indestructible.

Again, these theories and feelings do not directly point to the existence of a Creative Spirit, but they do point to a general acceptance of the fact that there is an immortal component to the human being. This immortality, I believe, implies the existence of a deity who is part of, and has created, this immortality.

NO. 12 – EINSTEIN'S THEORIES OF RELATIVITY (GA) (CHAPTER IIC)

The theories of Einstein have profoundly affected our appreciation of what nature is and how it operates. The simple fact that he proved that matter and energy are essentially the same caused a great change in the appreciation of nature. After all, we know what matter is, we can feel it and work with it, but energy is of a much less substantial nature – you cannot hold it in your hand and, what it really is, is difficult to describe; we know that it can perform work and as such we can experience its effects, but it is almost nonmaterial.

Secondly, the fact that time is not a fixed thing, but depends on such factors as the speed of the observer and the proximity of a large mass, must be somewhat unsettling for the dyed-in-the-wool determinist. Also, it appears that space is not the three-dimensional space we are experiencing but that there is a fourth dimension – time – and that we live in a space-time continuum. Furthermore, this space-time continuum is thought to be curved which makes everything that much more difficult to comprehend. When time and space are no longer the solid concepts we once imagined, how can we continue to think that the universe is made up of solid building blocks and that the future course of our lives and that of the universe is fixed and predetermined.

NO. 13 – QUANTUM MECHANICS (GB)

One of the more difficult scientific concepts to understand, and which has had a profound influence on the thinking of the last fifty years, is the theory of quantum mechanics.

There are many aspects of this theory that go against our most treasured concepts of how things ought to work. Only the repeated assurances of scientists of repute, who have experimentally proven that these phenomena exist, have made outsiders reluctantly accept them as fact. Assuming therefore that these findings are factual, they certainly go a long way in proving that materialism and determinism are not tenable any longer and that there are forces at work in the universe which are of a spiritual nature. The quantum phenomena that I am referring to include the following:

- Atomic particles can take the form of a particle or of a wave, and they can be in two places at the same time.
- Some particles seem to be able to sense what is going to happen to them in the future.
- You cannot measure two properties of a particle at the same time.
- The observer, in the act of observing, changes what is being observed.
- The same causes do not always result in the same effects; there is only a probability that they will do so.

Of course, the fact that a particular cause will always have the same effect is one of the cornerstones of materialistic determinism. It is this assumption that makes the adherents of this theory state that they can predict the future of all things given enough data, and that everything is predetermined and therefore there is no free will. In *The Quest for the Fourth Monkey*, Sylvia Fraser writes: "The two foundations of twentieth century physics – quantum physics and relativity theory – both force us to see the world very much in the way a Hindu, Buddhist or Taoist sees it." I would add to that – the way the Christian, Jew, or Muslim sees it.

NO. 14 – SHELDRAKE'S FIELDS OF INFLUENCE (GD) (CHAPTER IIB)

The existence of fields of influence, as suggested by Rupert Sheldrake, could, in principle, solve many of the completely mysterious facts of nature. According to this theory, space everywhere is filled with these fields which are invisible and not measurable and therefore nonmaterial. It is thought that these morphogenetic, or form-giving, fields give shape to almost everything in the universe, including particles, cells, stars and galaxies. For instance, it is believed that the growth and assembly of the human body from the original egg and sperm is directed by these "form-giving" fields. These fields are assumed to be inherited by each one of us at birth in the same way we inherit genes from our parents. The fact that these fields are apparently nonmaterial throws an entirely new light on the essence of nature. The whole movement of science in the last decades seems to go more in the direction of acknowledging the existence of a spiritual component to life in addition to the material component. These morphic fields are a prime example of this trend, because, if these fields are nonmaterial, they must be of a spiritual nature. This certainly reinforces the idea that if science does not start to think about nature in a more spiritual way, there will shortly be no more science because further breakthroughs in scientific thinking must take the spiritual aspects of life into account if it is to advance. Let me stress at this point that the existence of these form-giving fields is a theory only, and their existence will be difficult, or maybe even impossible, to prove. The great attraction of this theory is, of course, that, in principle, it can explain many things in nature that are not explainable in any other way; and that it can be understood by anyone who has ever seen a demonstration of the existence of magnetic fields or, for that matter, has seen flocks of birds or schools of fish turn as if connected by invisible strings. In the case of the birds and fish, they do not only turn as if bound together, they also all move to a destination that is, in many cases, thousands of miles away.

NO. 15 – THE BELL-ASPECT EXPERIMENT – NONLOCALITY (GC) (CHAPTER IIB)

This experiment demonstrates that one particle can influence another particle separated from it by great distances and that it can do so instantaneously. The experiments proving this rather mind-boggling conclusion have been repeated in several laboratories across the world. Up to recently, it was thought that no information could travel faster than the speed of light and here we have information traveling at an infinite speed. Also, up to recently, we thought that for one entity to interact with another there must be some connection between them, but here there is no such thing. This, more than any other theory, has led to the notion of nonlocality of both time and space. It is argued that these immediate interconnections do not only play a role in the behavior of atomic and subatomic particles, but that they underlie all events of everyday life and that these nonlocal connections are there because *reality itself is nonlocal in space and time*.

This theory, of course, suggests that many phenomena we thought of previously as being extrasensory perceptions are in fact a normal outcome of the way nature operates. For instance, intuition, telepathy and most other expressions of extrasensory perception are, by this way of thinking, nothing more than a natural result of this nonlocality of space and time.

In any case, the theory suggests that we live in a far more complicated world than previously assumed, and that we must change our way of thinking drastically especially when it comes to a materialistic view of the universe.

NO. 16 – THE TESTIMONY OF HISTORY (H) (CHAPTERS VII AND VIII)

The history of the world shows that from the very beginning when the early humans became fully conscious, rational beings, they began to worship some sort of Supreme Being – that is, someone or something which controlled their lives and was outside their own worldly existence. Even today, with all our sciences and with our technical achievements, most people still believe in the existence of some mysterious Supreme Being or Spirit which is outside their sphere of understanding. The point is that there is obviously an ingrained tendency for humans to believe in something outside of themselves, something much larger that is influencing their lives in an essential way. Almost all the major religions believe that this outside force actually was responsible for the creation of the universe. The fact that, even today, there are still billions of followers of these religions across the world must tell something about the reality of the deities they believe in. Their beliefs are not all the same, but the persistence of these beliefs over the ages says something about the possibility that these believers are correct and that there is a deity in charge of this world. The experience of billions of believers cannot be put aside as simply being superstition and wishful thinking. The fact that today science seems to support the idea of a spiritual component to life and nature will assure, I think, that this ancient belief in a Spiritual Power at work in the universe will not disappear. On the contrary, it is entirely possible that, with time, when all the findings described in this chapter become more universally accepted, this belief will lead to a resurgence of interest in spiritual things and, ultimately, in the acceptance of the existence of a Creator God.

Another example of where history can possibly be used

as an indication of the involvement of God in the history of this world may be the survival of the Jewish nation. The Jews have been persecuted like no other race or nation in the world. After World War II, the survival of the Jews and the establishment of a Jewish nation was only predicted by the most optimistic Jews. Yet here we are fifty-five years later, the State of Israel is very much alive and looks like it is here to stay. The only way, I believe, this can be explained is by accepting the fact that they are a special people, chosen by God for a special task. Almost any other group of people, subjected to the same persecutions over a period of 2,000 years, would have disappeared a long time ago.

Xd   Conclusions

In the previous pages, I have listed some twenty-six arguments for the existence of a Guiding Intelligence or Creator God who was directly involved in the creation of the universe and who is still active in its operation today. The first ten arguments are so persuasive that, in my view, there is simply no other explanation possible. There are another sixteen arguments which, I believe, strongly suggest that this is the case; however, there may be other explanations possible providing an equally persuasive argument for the existence of the observed phenomena. As I said before, these judgments are, of course, highly subjective; others who have studied these arguments have come up with quite different evaluations. The fact is, however, *that all these arguments taken together*, to my mind, *present overwhelming evidence of the existence of a Creator God, Guiding Intelligence or Master Designer*.

In the end, every one of us has to make his own choice; we either accept the worldview of such scientists as Francis Crick who expressed his belief this way:

> The astonishing hypothesis is that you, your joys and your sorrows, your memories and your ambitions, your sense of personal identity and free will, are in fact no more than the behavior of a vast assembly of nerve cells and the associated molecules.

Or, we believe that the observations and the arguments for the existence of a Guiding Intelligence, presented in the previous pages, offer sufficient proof that there is such a Guiding Intelligence and that this Intelligence or Spirit is at work in the world today. Scientists from different disciplines have come to similar conclusions: Albert Einstein, probably the best-known scientist of this century, wrote:

> Everyone who is seriously involved in the pursuit of science becomes convinced that a Spirit is manifest in the laws of the universe, a Spirit vastly superior to that of man.

In the same vein, George Elise writes:

> Comparing the different possibilities, it is difficult to avoid the conclusion that the design concept is one of the most satisfying overall approaches when broadly conceived, necessarily taking us outside the strictly scientific area.

Rupert Sheldrake writes:

> Thus the view of nature without God must include a creative unitary spirit that includes the entire cosmos and unites the polarities and dualities found throughout the natural realm. But that is not far removed from views of nature with God.

Anna Wise[6] writes:

> It is through that subconscious and unconscious realm that we make our strongest spiritual connection. A leap of faith

occurs that allows us to fully and truly believe in some form of divine order of the universe, some form of power greater than ourselves.

Even the *Wall Street Journal*, which is not usually the place where we look for spiritual guidance, recently published an article in which Jim Holt, after reviewing a list of books linking science and religion, wrote the following:

> As far as contemporary science can tell, nearly everything about the universe, its knack for self organization; its fine-tuned potency to bring about galaxies, life, consciousness; its sheer existence; is vastly improbable. This would seem to suggest that we are here because of a deliberate, supernatural design.

Trinh Xuan Thuan, as quoted in Chapter II, writes:

> For myself, I am prepared to bet on the existence of a supreme being... Finally, betting on chance implies nonsense and despair. Why not then bet rather on sense and hope.

Finally, a quote from the Internet: Robert John Johnson, founder of The Center for Theology and the Natural Sciences, expresses the view that these new discoveries have led to humankind rediscovering its place in the universe. As he writes in *Bridging Science and Religion*:[7]

> Ours then is a universe in which we once again have a place, and for which we can speak to and for a cosmic destiny. Once again, perhaps for the first time in three centuries, we humans are finding ourselves at home in the universe. We are able once again to speak of the numinous quality of the universe, to understand the joy and sorrow of all mortal life as part of an overarching cosmic story, and therein to detect the connection between all of nature and its divine source known to us through the self-revelation of God.

I, personally, believe with these scientists that it is almost impossible today to think of the creation of the cosmos without the involvement of a Guiding Intelligence which the Christians call God, the Muslims call Allah, and the Hindus call Brahman. So, I invite you with Trinh Xuan Thuan to bet on the existence of a Supreme Being and thereby bet on sense and hope, and with Robert Johnson to feel once again at home in this universe.

TABLE Xa
The Areas in Nature Where We See a Creator's Presence Most Clearly

LEVEL OF CERTAINTY

    Level 1 –   There is No Other Explanation Possible
    Level 2 –   Strongly Suggests the Involvement of a Guiding Intelligence

	Level
A – <u>The creation of the universe and human's position in it</u>	
(a) Science confirms that there was a definite beginning to the universe; this requires a Designer or Intelligence to start that creation.	1
(b) There seems to be new scientific evidence that humans were created as a distinct evolutionary event from one prototype mother in Africa.	2
(c) The emergence of fully conscious human beings appears to be the final objective of creation.	1
B – <u>The orderliness in which the universe is put together points to the involvement of an intelligence in its design</u>	
(a) The fact that there are fifteen constants which must have precisely the value they have to make life possible.	1

(b) The mathematical simplicity of the laws of nature that govern the operation of the universe and the fact that these laws are valid all through the universe and do not seem to change with time. | 2

C – <u>The incredible complexity of life which could not have been the result of pure chance</u>

(a) The fact that evolution cannot explain the existence of irreducibly complex systems, such as the human immune system. | 1

(b) The complexity of the human cell and the fact that all the billions of different cells are created from the two original cells, and that somehow they find their right place in the body and in the right numbers. | 1

(c) The intricate operation of the human brain and nervous system; its size compared to what is needed for survival of the species. | 2

(d) The language capability of humans which is not essential for the survival of the species. | 2

D – <u>The fact that there is a spiritual component to human existence</u>

(a) The fact that humans possess a consciousness which is immortal and which cannot possibly have been created by physical forces and processes. | 1

(b) The fact that nonmaterial thoughts can cause material actions. | 1

(c) The fact that humans have a free will to choose between good and evil. | 1

(d) The fact that humans have a drive for values, beauty and justice. | 2

(e) The existence of intuition and extrasensory perception. | 2

(f) The power of the human mind over mental and physical processes. | 2

E – <u>The proven effectiveness of prayer</u>
(a) The many testimonies to the effectiveness of prayer. — 2
(b) The results of scientifically controlled experiments on the effectiveness of prayer. — 2

F – <u>The spiritual body that is immortal</u>
(a) The out-of-body experiences of many people. — 1
(b) The near-death experiences of many people who were clinically dead. — 2
(c) The feeling of interconnectedness of all things – the collective unconscious. — 2

G – <u>Some of the latest scientific findings which seem to point to the involvement of an Intelligence in the operation of the Universe</u>
(a) Einstein's theories of relativity, time, space, matter, mass and energy. — 2
(b) Quantum Mechanics which includes such unlikely propositions as: — 2
- Atomic particles can be a particle or a wave or both.
- There is no certainty, only a possibility, that a given cause will have a certain effect.
- Some particles seem to be able to sense the future.
- Subatomic particles can be at two places at the same time.
- You cannot measure two properties of a particle at the same time.
- Observation changes the properties of what is being observed.

(c) Sheldrake's theory of fields of influence which are thought to be active in many aspects of the creation and maintenance of life and which are considered to be nonmaterial. — 2

(d) The Bell-Aspect experiments which allows two particles to interact instantaneously without any discernible way of communication between them although they may be large distances apart. | 2

H – <u>The evidence from history</u>

The history of the world, the march of progress, and the almost universal belief in a Deity strongly suggests that there is indeed a Spiritual Power involved in the operation of the universe. | 2

I – <u>The odds</u>

The chance that life in any form would accidentally develop from inanimate molecules, and that this life would then lead to the creation of conscious human beings. | 1

NOTES

[1] Barclay, William, *The Daily Bible, The Gospel of John*, Welch Publishing Co. Ltd, Burlington, ON, 1995.

[2] Ellis, George, *Before the Beginning, Cosmology Explained*, Boyars/Bowerdean, London, New York, 1993.

[3] Searle, John, *The Rediscovery of the Mind*, MIT Press, 1994.

[4] Gardner, Martin, *Did Adam and Eve Have a Navel?*, W. W. Norton &Co., New York, NY, 2000.

[5] Pannenberg, Wolfhart, *Faith and Reality*, The Westminster Press, Philadelphia, 1977, p.37.

[6] Wise, Anna, *The High Performance Mind*, Putnam Publishing, New York, 1997.

[7] Johnson, Robert John, *Bridging Science and Religion, Why It Must Be Done*, The Center for Theology and the Natural Sciences, Internet article.

Chapter XI
THE MEANING OF LIFE – WHERE ARE WE GOING?

XIa   Introduction

If we accept the arguments of the previous chapters that there is a Master Designer or Guiding Intelligence at work in the universe, and that there is a strong spiritual component to nature, we will look at life and the purpose of life in an entirely different light. Of course, the fact that we recognize the hand of a Guiding Intelligence behind creation, and see a strong spiritual force at work in nature, does not say anything about the nature of that Intelligence. For the purpose of this book, however, we will equate that Intelligence with the God of the Christian religion. Others can, with equal justification, equate that Intelligence with Yahweh, Allah or Brahman.

So, what is changed by accepting the existence of a Guiding Intelligence and by equating that Intelligence with the God of the Christian religion? I believe that it changes our response to the following basic questions about life in a most essential way:

- Who are we?
- Why are we here?
- What is the meaning of life?
- What is my own importance in the scheme of things?
- What are my responsibilities?

- How should my acceptance of God affect the way I live my life?
- What is my final destiny?

Without believing in any religion, and accepting the theory that we arrived here by pure chance, the answers to these questions are very simple indeed.

- Who are we? We are simply a mechanical system that operates on the basis of the interaction of millions of nerve cells.
- Why are we here? Just a lucky run of circumstances!
- What is the meaning of life? There is none.
- What is our importance in this scheme of things? Nil, nothing.
- How should we live? Live it up; tomorrow we may not be here.
- What are my responsibilities? To look after myself.
- What is our final destiny? Total oblivion.

In the next pages, we will look at these questions from the Christian point of view. Not surprisingly, the answers to these basic questions are entirely different if we believe in God as the Creator of the universe and have faith in him to have a final destiny planned for us.

XIb Who Are We?

The answer to this question is basically very simple: we are God's children, created not by chance but purposefully by God and for a special reason. What is more, we believe that God created us in his own image. As strange and presumptuous as this may sound, we believe that we are somewhat like God. The reason for this belief is that we are repeatedly told in the first chapter of Genesis that we are created in God's image. In this way of thinking, it does not matter how we were created, by a long process of evolution or by a sudden creation. The fact is that, when we became truly conscious human beings, we were somewhat like God. Now, personally, I find God, the Creator, hard to visualize, especially now that we must begin to think of God as existing beyond time and space. In some way, this concept puts God further away as being even more different from us than we could have imagined previously. On the other hand, it puts God closer to us in that, if he is not bound by space or time, he can be near to every one of us at any time and at any place.

Someone has asked the question that if we believe the Genesis story to be a myth, and not a factual account of creation, what validity does the assertion have that we are created in God's image. The answer lies in what we believe a myth to be. In the way it is used here, a myth is a story that contains a truth that cannot be properly conveyed in any other way. A factual account of the creation story for an audience living some 2,600 years ago would have been completely incomprehensible to them and would therefore have been useless.

From the Bible, we know certain things about God that may help us to understand what it means to be somewhat like him. For instance, to be like God must, I believe, include the following:

- We can think and reason like God can, but unlike the rest of creation. Thus, the fact that we have been able to unravel some of the mysteries of the macro and micro cosmos – in short, do science – is one of these qualities that are a result of being somewhat like God.
- We can distinguish between good and evil, like God can, but again unlike the rest of creation. The world would be a very sorry place indeed if we were not able to make

that distinction and, although we do not always use that capacity, it still guides the operation of our society.
- We have a free will which gives us the ability to make choices, to choose between good and evil; again not like any other creature. This is probably the most distinguishing mark of humanity as it gives us dignity in that we are not slaves to a mechanical or spiritual system, but we are free to make our own choices.
- We can respond to God and can communicate with God; in particular, we can respond to God's love and to the love of other people. Being somewhat like God places us on a level that makes it possible for us to communicate with God and to reciprocate God's love and respond to the love of other people.
- We can create, maybe not create something from nothing like God can, but nevertheless create. As we will see later, this creativity gives us the heavy responsibility to look after God's creation, including the other animals and the environment in which we all live.

In short, being somewhat like God means, I believe, that at least we can do the following:

- We can think.
- We can distinguish between good and evil.
- We have a free will and we can make choices.
- We can respond to God.
- We can communicate with God.
- We can create somewhat like God.

Having created us with these special gifts and abilities, it is clear that we were created for a special purpose, which leads us to the next question.

XIc   Why Are We Here?

The reason we are here and the purpose of our existence is probably most clearly expressed by the Swiss theologian, Emil Brunner,[1] in his book, *Our Faith*, when he wrote:

> God's feeling for us is infinite love. Fellowship is the one thing he absolutely wants. God created the world in order to share himself. He created us for fellowship.

This same feeling is expressed in the assertion of the Eastern Orthodox Church which states:

> The world was created from nothing by the sole will of God – this is its origin. It was created in order to participate in the fullness of the divine life – this is its vocation.

Of course, these are very strong statements to make. For one thing, they imply that the whole universe was created just so that, in one of the millions of galaxies, a star would emerge with a satellite which was positioned in such a way that human life could develop. Sometimes we become overwhelmed by this concept of billions of stars having been created just so that we could emerge. But we can look at this in a slightly different way that is less intimidating. The universe may be complex, but after all it is all dead matter (as far as we know today), and is therefore not nearly as complex as any one of the trillion cells of which all living matter is composed. Just looking at a nerve cell, its DNA, its system of interconnections and its connection to the brain, makes one dizzy. In many ways, I find that far more impressive than all the galaxies together whirling around in the universe in a way that seems to have no discernible purpose at all.

The other side of the statement that God created us for companionship, which is hard to understand and can only be accepted on faith, is the presumption that God is not self-sufficient and wants companionship. To understand this it may be helpful to think of the other quality of God which is that he is the personification of love. Recent scientific discoveries have made some people proclaim that the glue, which holds everything together in the universe, is love. It is thought to be *the* binding ingredient that holds not only atoms but also galaxies together. Thus the force of love is equated with the four operational forces in the universe. Personally, I find this somewhat difficult to comprehend, and I look forward to further clarification of this concept.

In any case, we believe the reason we are here is that God wanted us here as his companions. This, of course, gives humans an importance they would not have under any other scheme of things and far beyond what we could reasonably expect. This concept of being God's companions made the theologian Marcus Borg[2] proclaim that the central issue of Christian life is not believing in God, or believing in the Bible or Christian tradition; rather, he writes: "The Christian's life is about entering into a relationship with God."

XId   The Meaning of Life and Our Importance in the Scheme of Things

Thus the meaning of life is that we are the present and the future companions of God and that we, humans, are the centerpiece of creation. It is interesting to note, in this context, that science itself has been putting humans again in that same position based on the theory that without human observers the universe may not really exist in a material sense. Physicist Eugene Wigner[3] expresses it this way:

> The conscious mind is firmly placed in the center of the universe, for consciousness now influences events. The observer determines that what is observed.

In the same vein, we quoted Amit Goswami[4] in Chapter II as follows:

> We are the center of the universe because we are its meaning.

Of course, this is not the same as our belief that we are central to creation because of God's wish to have companions. Both of these concepts have of course their own difficulties. As was pointed out before, the Christian concept has the problem that it is difficult to visualize God as needing companionship. On the other hand, the scientific view has the problem that humans' importance rests on their function as observers, as a consciousness that, through the fact of being aware, gives substance to nature and to the entire cosmos.

In either case, this concept of the importance of human life changes our view and our evaluation of the worth of human life in general. In both views, the importance of human life is that humans are conscious beings who in the one case can respond to God's love, and in the other case can be aware of its surrounding nature. In both cases, the question is not how important we are in human terms; what role we played in history; what we invented or discovered; how much money we made; what battles we won; etc. On the contrary, we are important by simply being human and by being able to respond to God's love and by having the conscious awareness of the nature that surrounds us.

This sense of importance is entirely independent of how smart we are, how rich we are, what talents we have, etc. Psychiatrists and psychologists tell us that a very large percentage of their clients come to them because of their feelings of purposelessness, meaninglessness and alienation from a world that seems without purpose. If these patients could accept the view of their importance as described above, they would be able to change their opinions of themselves and could possibly heal themselves. It is clear that a person's importance is not measured by human values but by the fact that God has chosen us as his companions. The human being with the severest physical and mental disabilities is as important in this scheme of things as Einstein or any other great achiever. All of us are here because God wanted us to be here, and no one is more important than the other in God's eyes. What is more, we all have the same responsibilities and same ultimate destiny.

XIe Our Responsibilities and Tasks During Life on Earth

The fact that we are put on this Earth for a special purpose brings with it a number of obligations that we can never forget. It starts right there at the beginning of the Bible in the myth of the creation story. After God had created Adam, he tells him and by implication us:

> Have many children, so that your descendants will live all over the Earth and bring it under their control. I am putting you in charge of the fish, the birds and the wild animals.
>
> Genesis 1:28
> *Good News Bible*

The environmental movement should have started right then and there but it did not, and since then we have come perilously close to polluting the world beyond repair. It is clear from this passage that we are God's hands and feet and that God acts today mainly through us, people like you and me. This has probably never been more clearly expressed than by Teresa of Avila, a Roman Catholic nun, who lived in Spain from 1525 to 1582, when she wrote:

> Christ has no body now on Earth but yours: yours are the only hands with which he can do his work, yours are the only feet with which he can go about the world, yours are the only eyes through which his compassion can shine forth upon a troubled world. Christ has no body now on Earth but yours.

When God led the Israelites out of Egypt, he gave them, and through them to us, a set of rules to live by. These rules, the Ten Commandments, are still as valid and relevant as when they first were written. In fact, these rules are still the cornerstone of the justice system of a large part of the world's population. But these rules are mostly of a negative type as they tell us what not to do. When Jesus was asked how people should live, he condensed these commands into a more positive set of rules. He said:

> You shall love the Lord your God with all your heart, with all your soul, with all your mind and you shall love your neighbor as yourself. Everything in the law and the prophets hangs on these two commandments.
>
> Matthew 22, The New English Bible

The challenge that has faced the world, ever since Jesus made this statement, is to interpret this command for the situations and conditions we find ourselves in at any given point in time.

When we look around us, it is quite obvious that we have not done a very good job of it. Bede Griffith[5] in his book, *A New Vision of Reality*, warns us that the conflicts of the present world do not merely derive from human failings or miscalculations. He contends that there has been a reversal of values and a spiritual breakdown which has brought into play forces beyond the material and the human. Similarly, E.F. Schumacher[6] writes that the modern experiment to live without religion has failed. He asks the question: "Can we rely on it that a turning around will be accomplished by enough people quickly enough to save the modern world?"

It is evident, from these and other writers, that there is a certain urgency in reversing the trend of living without the old, generally accepted values. As far as I can see, we will need all the wisdom we can muster to decide on such issues as genetic engineering, cloning, nuclear proliferation and to solve such old issues as population control, hunger and poverty. Also, the gap between the rich and the poor, instead of closing, is actually widening. Added to this, we now have the danger that with the introduction of personal computers and the Internet in our daily lives, a large group of people will become increasingly alienated from the mainstream because they are mentally or economically not able to participate in these new developments. If these problems are not addressed in time, they may lead to political and economic unrest of a magnitude which the world has not seen before.

I believe that we in the industrialized world should give careful consideration of what our values are and what our priorities are. Someone has suggested that if our objective is to do the most good for the most people, then we should ask ourselves if we are justified in spending large amounts of money and brain power on finding cures for illnesses that affect only a very small percentage of the world's population; while at the same time billions of people still live in extreme poverty and die of hunger and malnutrition and from illnesses that are curable, but for which there is no money to affect the cure.

So, I believe it is clear that, if we accept the fact that God is the Creator of the universe and that he has given us the responsibility to look after that creation, then as Christians we have the task to ensure that our society behaves or is directed towards a future in which:

- Hunger and demeaning poverty are eliminated around the world.
- The population is controlled to sustainable levels.
- War is eliminated as a means of settling disputes.
- Ethnic cleansing is eliminated as a means of settling racial and religious boundaries.
- Violence and crime at the personal level is stopped.
- Further pollution of the Earth is stopped and polluted areas are reclaimed.
- Further developments in genetic engineering are carefully scrutinized and monitored.
- Proliferation of nuclear weapons is stopped and existing stockpiles are eliminated.
- Most important of all, the trend is reversed that sees humans as intelligent animals only, without a soul or spiritual values, and in which the brain is considered to be analogous to a computer and human actions are considered only as the firing of millions of nerve cells in the brain.

I believe that, as custodians of the Earth, we have no other choice but to attempt to restore values on both the personal and national levels. Hopefully we will be able to change the direction in which we are going before it is too late and before, for a large part of the world population, life becomes untenable.

XIf   What Is Our Final Destiny?

If we are here because God wanted us to be here as his companions, then it makes sense that there is a life after this one that is eternal. After all, this life is short, and God certainly cannot have meant to have fellowship with people who are here today and gone tomorrow. Thus, it is reasonable to believe in an existence beyond this one, and that the ultimate meaning of our lives lies not so much in our existence in this world but in that of the world to come. It is only when we enter this new world that we will finally know what the meaning of our existence on Earth was and what it will be in the future. One can legitimately ask that if our long-term future is in another existence in close communion with God, why did we not enter into that world directly without going through this earthly existence? We simply do not know.

As we have seen, the idea that something like a soul or a spirit can survive the disintegration of the body is very old and pretty well disseminated across all religions and civilizations. For the Christian, this takes on the form of the soul reuniting with God in the hereafter, presumably also in some type of physical existence that is beyond time and space. If this is true, it is even more difficult to attempt to understand what this life will be like. I believe, we can be sure of one thing; it will be beyond our wildest dreams and way beyond what we can imagine.

In closing, I would like to quote Nicholas Beale[7] when he writes:

> In my view, there exists a loving ultimate Creator, and it is my contention that this view performs better when subjected to the normal scientific and philosophical tests than its negation. I don't think the opposite is impossible, just very unlikely.

NOTES

[1]Brunner, Emil, *Our Faith*, SCM Press, London, 1977, p.39.
[2]Borg, Marcus, *The God We Never Knew*, Harper Collins Publishers, New York, 1997.
[3]Wigner, Eugene, *Symmetries and Reflections*, Indiana University Press, Bloomington, 1967.
[4]Goswami, Amit, *The Self-Aware Universe*, G. P. Putnam and Sons, New York, 1993, p.141.

[5] Griffith, Bede, *A New Vision of Reality*, Templegate Publishers, 1992.
[6] Schumacher E. F., *A Guide for the Perplexed*, Harper Collins Publishers Inc., New York, 1977.
[7] Beale, Nicholas, *The Anthropic Principle*, Star Course Discussion Page, www.starcourse.org

Chapter XII
WHEN AND HOW DOES GOD ACT OR INTERACT IN CREATION?

In the previous chapters, I have tried to lay down what I think are sound foundations for the belief that there exists a Creator God who was directly involved in the creation of the universe some fifteen billion years ago, and who is still involved in the continuing development of that creation. Christians generally believe that this Creator's ultimate objective was the emergence of conscious human beings who could interact in a meaningful way with that Creator. The question we are asking now is: when and how did and does this God interject herself in this creation process, and how did she ensure that the ultimate objective would be reached?

As we have seen, modern science has come to believe that quantum uncertainties and indeterminism play a significant role in the operation of the universe. How then could God, after having introduced these uncertainties into creation, ensure that her ultimate goal would be reached? Did God let out a sigh of relief when humans finally arrived on the scene, fifteen billion years after she had started the universe on its way with the Big Bang?

As said before, it is difficult to believe that the Big Bang was a spontaneous creation out of nothing, or that the Big Bang was created by a quantum fluctuation. One might ask the question: fluctuation of what? And is this quantum fluctuation, if that is what God used, not part and parcel of creation itself? Most scientists, I think, will accept the fact that with this Creation not only matter but also time and space were created. Thus, before the Big Bang there was neither time nor space – only God was there. Thus God exists beyond time and space, and neither time nor space offer any constraint to God, not at the beginning of time or now. Thus, when we are talking about time in the billions of years and about space in the billions of light years, they may seem formidable to us, but in God's perception their magnitudes must be completely irrelevant.

It is now generally accepted that the universe started some fifteen billion years ago. During much of this time, after this event, our solar system did not even exist and the universe contained only the two lightest elements: helium and hydrogen. It was only after the first star collapsed that heavier elements were formed under the influence of the enormous pressures and temperatures which occurred during the final stages of the collapsing star. These heavier atoms were dispersed throughout the universe and made their appearance on the adjacent galaxies some eight billion years after the Big Bang. Only after these heavier atoms, including carbon atoms, reached our solar system was it possible that sufficiently complicated molecules could be generated here that could eventually lead to the emergence of life. After the arrival of these heavy atoms it took another three to four billion years for the first forms of life to appear. In other words, during the first eleven to twelve billion years of the existence of the universe, it consisted only out of atoms and molecules which formed oceans, rocks and land, but there were no plants, no fish and no land animals anywhere. The only thing that made the continuous existence of this empty universe possible was the four laws or forces of nature and the exact values of the constants of nature. As we have seen, even the slightest variations in any of these laws and constants would have resulted in an unstable universe and the continued existence of even this empty universe would have been impossible.

Considering this state of the universe, it seems reasonable to assume that after the initial creation at time zero, and after God had put in place the exact values of the constants and the laws of nature, God did not actually involve herself, in any significant way, in the fortunes of creation for a period of some eight billion years. After this, the first time God interjected herself in the creation process was probably her involvement in the collapse of the first stars and in guiding the heavy elements to other stars, and eventually to our solar system. This dispersal of heavy atoms is so crucial to the further development of the universe that it is difficult to see this happen without a Creator's direct or indirect involvement. It almost looks as if God looked at her creation and saw that it was stuck in place and was going nowhere unless something drastic was done to set it on its way again.

After the arrival of the heavy atoms, further development of the cosmos was probably inevitable and God may not have been involved again until the creation of life some three or four billion years later. The introduction of life at that time changed everything. The creation of life, we believe, was a deliberate act of God. Up to that time, the universe had consisted basically of only one component – matter and energy – which Einstein proved to be interchangeable. With the introduction of the first life forms, we now have to add another basic component, namely information. The introduction of information in the ongoing evolution of our world added a complete new element to its basic components. This was not simply a change in degree but it was a fundamental change in kind; something that could not be classified as a further natural development of more complex molecular structures. Instead, the addition of information to the evolutionary process changed this process in a fundamental way, in that the existence and propagation of any life form came to depend on the information stored in the DNA and genes of that life form. As Holmes Roston[1] writes:

> What is the most adequate account of the origin of the genetic information? In the course of evolutionary history, one would be disturbed to find matter or energy spontaneously created – but here is information floating in from nowhere. For the lack of a better explanation, the usual term here is simply to conclude that nature is self-organizing. Perhaps a more plausible explanation is that, complementing the self-organizing, there is a Ground of Information, also known as God.

Basically, the involvement of God in the creation of the universe and in the ultimate emergence of conscious human beings can be visualized in a number of different ways. As far as I can see, there are four distinct possibilities (see Figure 12.1):

1. After setting the universe on its way with the Big Bang, God did not interject herself again in its further development; the eventual arrival of humans on the scene was left to chance and was purely accidental.
2. All information necessary for the development of human beings was already contained in the laws, forces and elements that were created at the time of the Big Bang.
3. After the Big Bang, and before the arrival of the earliest life forms, God's involvement was limited to seeing that the heavy elements were formed and to the creation of self-organizing features in the cell structure which would lead without any further divine intervention to the emergence of human beings.
4. After the Big Bang, and after the creation of the heavy atoms, which made it possible for life to evolve, God

was involved in the further development of the universe on an almost continuing basis, always ensuring that the path of development led to the emergence of conscious human beings.

In the first case, considering the prevalence of quantum uncertainties, the emergence of human life was not at all a foregone conclusion. This is where God would have let out that sigh of relief, when humans finally appeared on the scene. I believe we can safely disregard this possibility. The chances that humans would have finally emerged without any further guidance in that direction are nil. Also, it does not make much sense that God would not have involved herself anymore after having started creation on its way at the time of the Big Bang and then leaving everything to chance thereafter.

In the second case, if the initial material included all the information necessary for the creation of the entire cosmos, including human beings, it is difficult to see where all this fantastic amount of information could have been stored. As far as we know, immediately after the Big Bang there was nothing else than the initial basic subatomic particles in the form of quarks or superstrings and the fundamental laws of nature which governed their behavior. It is difficult to see how these basic particles could contain any information at all. For the storage of information it is necessary to have long strings of atoms and molecules such as the genes in the DNA. The particles created at the beginning of the universe were just that; a multitude of single entities which do not appear to have the capability to store information of any kind.

In the third case, it is assumed that God used an enormous amount (by our standards) of creative planning and introduced this plan in the earliest life forms as self-organizing capabilities. In this scenario, the evolvement of human life would go along a smooth path; one development following the other according to this carefully prepared plan. The information necessary for the execution of this is assumed to be inscribed in the DNA of living matter. Thus, the development of the cosmos is as stated in the weak anthropic principle which postulates that we are here because the universe has been so designed. If this were the way evolution was used by God, there would not be any gaps in the fossil record, as one step logically followed the other.

In the fourth scenario, God, after having started the evolutionary process on its way, intervenes only when it appears that this process does not lead in the desired direction. Howard Van Till[2] calls this "episodic creationism" which he describes as:

> The belief that the formation of certain physical structures and life forms, now found in creation, was accomplished by occasional episodes of extraordinary divine action in which God imposed those structures and forms on matter.

In the same vein, Kenneth Miller, who was mentioned in Chapter III, believes that God acts to shape the world according to God's will through the quantum uncertainties and the evolutionary process. Through these, he believes, God influences the appearance of mutations, activates individual neurons in the brain, causes the survival of individual cells and organisms, etc. In other words, God acts in nature through many subtle ways that are not discernable by humans, but nevertheless guide the evolving nature in the direction she has chosen.

Thus, from our human point of seeing things, God's divine action is mostly not discernible as such, and it will always be difficult to distinguish between God's intervention and pure chance. On a larger scale, for instance, the destruction of the dinosaurs by the impact of a large meteor some sixty-five million years ago could be attributed to nothing more than an accident; on the other hand, it could be one of God's periodic interventions to make sure of the emergence of humans. The reason for considering this possibility is that it is now believed that, if the dinosaurs had continued to dominate the landscape, the chance of humans being able to emerge would have been very small. Thus, the emergence of these very large animals could be considered to be an example of evolution having taken a wrong turn and requiring divine intervention to rectify the situation.

There is however another possible scenario somewhere between the direct miraculous intervention of God and pure chance. Douglas Hallman[3] calls this "an extraordinary coincidence of a beneficial nature" in which God's intervention in nature is of the kind in which God sets all the conditions that lead to what appears to be a miracle or pure chance. For instance, some years ago, a canoe came too close to the Niagara Falls and the canoe and its occupant went over the brink. It was acclaimed a miracle that the boy was saved. First of all, the boy was thrown free from the water surface instead of being swept with the current deep under the plunging water. Secondly, he landed in the water at a place where a sightseeing boat was passing by just at that time. If the boy had not been thrown free, or if the boat had not been there at just that time, or if nobody had spotted the boy in the water, he would not have survived the ordeal. Hallman argues that God did not cause a miracle to happen; she worked her will through a number of extraordinary coincidences of a beneficial nature that brought all the conditions into play which saved the boy and which had the same effect as a direct intervention.

Of course, God could have used any one of these processes or others to gain the final desired result.

Personally, I believe that the last process using "episodic creationism" fits the facts best. These include the following:

- The fossil record shows that there are gaps in the development of the species. In particular, in the final development of humans the record shows that early humans had all the capacity to develop into today's modern beings. In other words, if we were able to take a baby from an early human mother and educate it along with today's children, it would be able to participate in today's technological environment and become, for instance, a computer programmer. It can be argued that if there had been a gradual development in human perception there should be people of an intermediate stage still around, because even a partially developed human being would be better equipped to survive than its animal neighbors. From this, I believe, we can conclude that the early humans were a special creation not directly related to earlier life forms.

- The second law of thermodynamics seems to preclude the development of more complex life forms from less complex forms, including the development of life from inanimate matter. It may be that only "episodic creationism" may be able to overcome these hurdles to the creation of higher life forms.

- In Chapter III, we have noted the existence of a number of irreducibly complex systems. These are systems that cannot possibly have developed from less complicated systems because none of the intermediate systems would have been viable. I believe that only the occasional intervention of a Creator could have overcome these obstacles to the ongoing development of nature.

WHEN AND HOW DOES GOD ACT IN CREATION?

Up until now, God's involvement with creation was completely impersonal and was limited to seeing that her objectives were met and that humans finally did emerge from this long process of evolution. I believe that God's involvement changed again radically some 6,000 to 10,000 years ago, when God made herself known to a Semitic tribe, the Israelites, as the Creator of the universe, and became actively involved in the individual, personal lives of the members of that tribe. How this involvement slowly emerged over the history of that tribe is told in detail in the Old Testament of the Bible. The thing to note is that this involvement is so recent that it is impossible to show it as a distinctive time period on the graph in Figure 12.1. At best, this period of 10,000 years would appear as having the width of a razor blade cut just before "today".

Of course, our understanding of the evolution of the last 6,000 years is highly colored by the fact that this book is written from a Christian perspective. Up to this point in time, the story of evolution is probably acceptable to most religions; however, with the appearance of God to the Israelites as a chosen people, there is an obvious choice God made to the apparent exclusion of all other people. Other religions will naturally see this differently and point to their own revelations of God, the Creator.

Using the Old Testament, it is clear that, as in the distant past, humans did not evolve the way God had planned, and humans did not become the perfect creatures that God had planned. And, as in the past, God set forth to rectify the situation. However, God's involvement took an entirely different form this time. For instance, one could see God's intervention in the story of the Great Flood. This story seems to be fairly universal and modern excavations have shown that there was indeed at some time in antiquity such a flood. It is entirely possible that God saw her Creation go in the wrong direction and, as it were, started with a new set of people.

Later, God injected herself in human history in a personal way with the birth, 2,000 years ago, of Jesus of Nazareth. Some Christians believe that God herself took on a human form and that, in fact, Jesus was divine and an integral part of the Trinity of Father, Son and Holy Spirit. Other Christians believe that Jesus never made that claim. However, all agree that Jesus was a special messenger sent by God to be a mediator between God and humankind, to show humankind how to live in "God's way", and to become reconciled with its Creator.

For Christians, it is through faith that we see God's involvement in our lives. After all, millions of prayers are offered daily for God to actively intervene in our lives in a positive way. So today, after fifteen billion years, we can see God active in the lives of people. But again as in the past that involvement is often hidden behind chance. In fact God's activity in this world can mostly only be discerned by people who believe in God as their Creator. Sometimes, we can maybe get a glimpse of that involvement by looking at the lives of certain people who have lived clearly in God's way – such as the lives of Francis of Assisi or Mother Teresa and many others.

In summary then we have the following possible interventions of the Creator in the ongoing process of creation:

- The act of creating the first basic elementary particles out of nothing, together with the creation of time and space, and the introduction of the laws of nature, some fifteen billion years ago.
- The creation, and the dispersal throughout the universe, of the heavy atoms which were formed in the collapsing stars and which are essential for the ongoing evolution of nature, some 6.5 billion years ago.
- The creation of a complicated information system

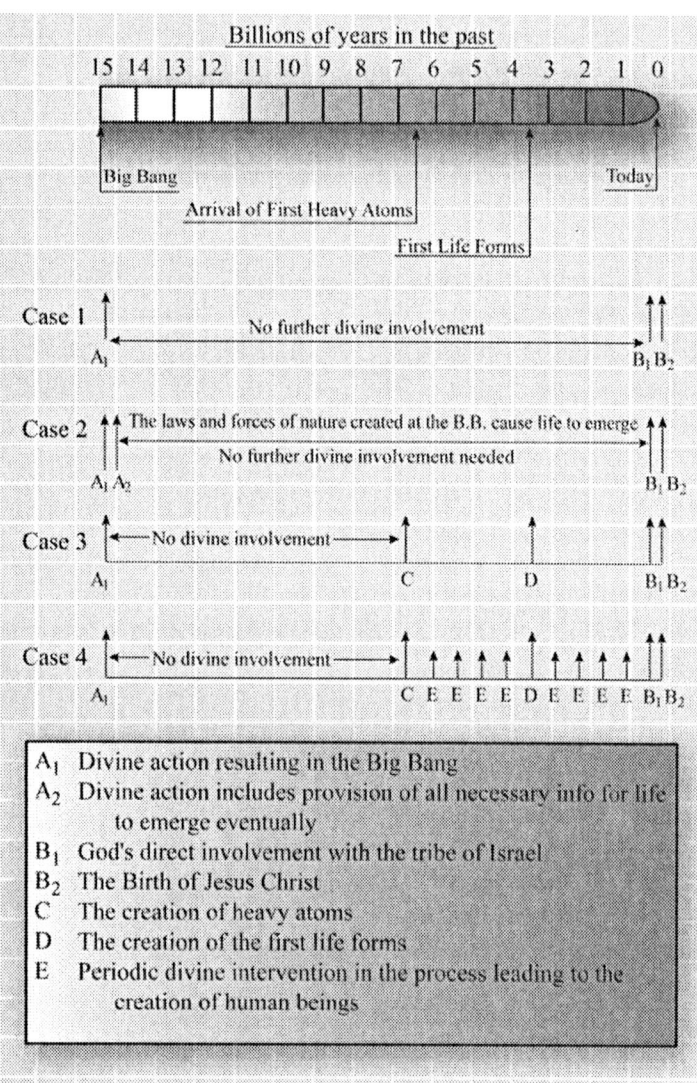

Figure 12.1
Places Where God's Direct Intervention in Creation May Be Discerned

which guides the development of more complex living systems, or possibly the creation of a self-organizing capacity within the basic elements of nature, some 3.5 billion years ago.

- The occasional intervention in the ongoing evolution of the universe. These interventions are mostly blocked from our view by the possibility that blind chance could have led to the same results.

- The involvement, starting some 6,000 to 10,000 years ago, of God in the lives of the Israelites, when for the first time God became involved in the personal lives of individual people.

- The appearance of Jesus Christ, some 2,000 years ago, who, as the special messenger of God, showed humankind how to live and who reconciled us with God after humans had not lived up to God's expectations.

As Christians, we of course believe that God's intervention in the universe, and in particular in human life, did not stop there but is still ongoing and will continue until God's purpose for the creation of the universe is accomplished.

NOTES

[1] Roston, Holmes, "Evolutionary History and Divine Presence", *Theology Today*, Vol. 55 no. 3, October 1998.
[2] Van Till, Howard, "The Creation: Intelligently Designed or Optimally Equipped", *Theology Today*, Vol. 55, no. 3, October 1998.
[3] Hallman, Douglas, *Perspectives*, Private Bible Commentaries.

Appendix I
SOME BASIC PHYSICS

As indicated in the introduction, the chapters on the new scientific findings will be easier to understand with some basic knowledge of the physics involved. This section will explain in simple terms some of the theories and concepts which are integral to how we understand the universe to function today. Of course, by the very nature of this book, the various theories and discoveries can be dealt with only in a cursory way; sufficiently, however, to give an appreciation of the importance of these findings and how they affect both our lives and our understanding of the workings of the universe. The reader who is interested in a more elaborate treatment of these subjects, still in layman's terms, is referred to a book entitled *The Ascent of Science* by the British-born, Israeli scientist, Brian Silver.[1]

This section of the appendix is divided into two sub-sections: the first deals with the microcosm of atoms and molecules, while the second section deals with the macrocosm, the world of stars and galaxies.

The Microcosm

Some of the earliest attempts of humankind to describe nature was in terms of four basic elements: earth, water, air and fire. Our forefathers believed that everything they saw in nature was made up of a mixture of these four elements. As the Greek philosopher Plato stated it:

> All heavenly bodies, all plants, all animals, etc. are created out of these four elements – not from any action of mind, or any gods or by any art – but by the action of chance and of the forces arising out of certain inherent affinities among the natural bodies.

This view was still generally accepted up to the later Middle Ages and is depicted in many of the graphic presentations of what people believed the cosmos to be like at that time (see Figure A.1). Long before this, however, around 400 B.C.E. a Greek philosopher, Democritus, put forth the idea that all matter was composed of invisible, indestructible, small particles which move in infinite space. He believed that it was the movements, collisions and alignments of these particles, which he called atoms, which made the material world. These atoms were thought to be too small to be observed and were considered to be solid and indivisible. This theory was not based on any physical evidence but was pure speculation on the part of its proponents. It was effectively ignored for many centuries and only began to gain acceptance with the birth of modern science at the end of the nineteenth century when it was discovered that nature was indeed made up of very small entities which, after the early Greeks, were called "atoms".

It turned out, however, that these atoms were not indivisible or indestructible but could be split into two components: a nucleus and one or more electrons circling around this nucleus. The electrons were found to have a negative electric charge while the nucleus had a positive electric charge. Since particles with an opposite charge attract each other, there is a force needed to keep the electron from crashing into the nucleus. The force that keeps the two separated is called the electromagnetic force, one of the four fundamental forces which govern the entire operation of the universe.

Long before this discovery, humankind had identified a number of basic elements such as gold, iron, copper, etc. With the discovery of the atomic substructure, it was now possible to describe the differences between these elements in terms of their nucleus and the number of electrons in the atom of that element. For instance, the lightest atom – hydrogen – has only one electron circling around its nucleus and has been given an atomic weight of 1.0 while the heaviest naturally occurring atom, uranium, has some 92 electrons per atom and has an atomic weight of 238.0. It was found that, while the nuclei of the various atoms are different, all electrons in the universe are exactly the same regardless of which atom they are attached to or whether they are located in one of the farthest away stars or here on Earth; they all have exactly the same mass and the same electric charge. It was further found that they move around the nucleus in a number of fixed orbits and that each of these orbits can only accommodate a fixed number of electrons. It should be noted here that this model of the atom is not necessarily the latest one, but it is the easiest to understand and describes the action and interaction between the various atomic components with sufficient accuracy for our purpose.

Not long after the discovery that the atom consisted of a nucleus and electrons, it was found that the nucleus itself could be split in more elementary particles, namely protons which carry a positive charge and neutrons which have no charge. Since each proton has a positive charge, two or more protons in a nucleus repel each other. So, for the nucleus to stay together a force is needed to hold the protons in place and, since the protons are tightly packed together, the repulsing force is very strong. Consequently, the force to counteract this force must be very strong as well. It was later discovered that this force is the strongest of the four forces of nature and is therefore called the strong nuclear force (see also Figure A.2).

SOME BASIC PHYSICS

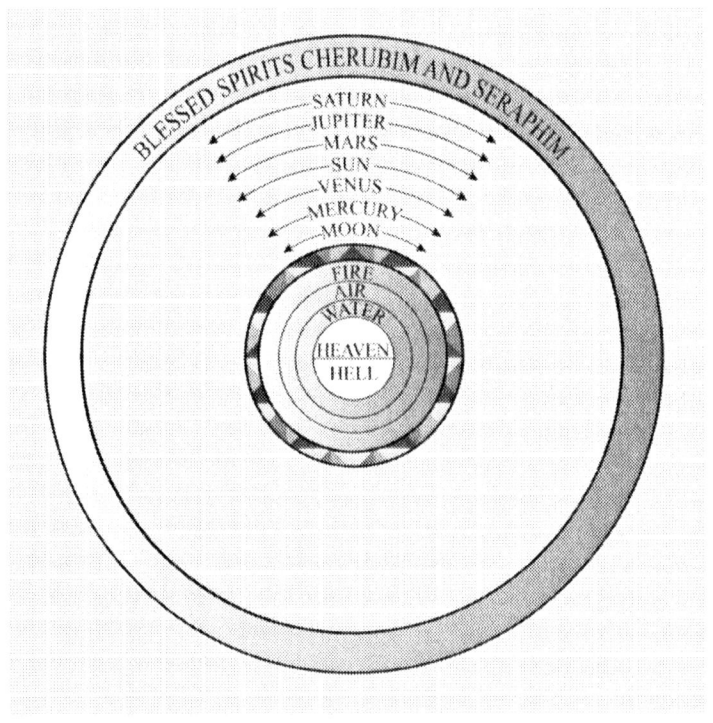

At the center, Earth is divided into heaven and hell.
The elements of water, air and fire surround the earth.
Moving outward concentrically are the spheres containing the seven planets, the
Moon and the Sun, as well as the "Twelve Orders of the Blessed Spirit," the
Cherubim and Seraphim. From a German Manuscript dated c.1450.

Figure A.1
The Geocentric Universe in Europe in the Middle Ages

One of the great mysteries of the atomic world is that not only the electrons but also the protons and neutrons were found to be exactly the same for all elements; the only difference between the elements is therefore the number of electrons, protons and neutrons in each atom. Furthermore, since the neutron has no electrical charge, there must be the same number of protons and electrons in each atom to make the atom itself neutral. As a result of this, all matter known to us is made up of various combinations of these three subatomic particles. Thus it is theoretically possible to create one carbon atom from three helium atoms. It is this process that made carbon-based life possible.

As was mentioned before, the electron is the only particle in the atom that cannot be divided into smaller particles. The protons and neutrons in the nucleus, on the other hand, were found to consist of a number of even smaller particles called quarks. Whether these quarks can yet be divided in even more elementary particles remains to be seen. The problem is that it is possible to prove the existence of these particles only by constructing very large atom smashers, which each cost billions of dollars. In this time of fiscal constraints, it is difficult to justify the expense of these machines when there is no demonstrable benefit other than expanding our knowledge about the subatomic world. In line with this, the American Congress canceled the construction of the super collider, which was already under construction, the sole purpose of which was to probe deeper into the atomic structure. So, it is entirely possible that as far as progress in experimental particle physics is concerned, we have come to the end of the road, at least for the foreseeable future. That is not to say that purely theoretical work on particle physics cannot proceed. For that, the only thing that is needed is an inquiring mind, imagination and a thorough knowledge of physics and mathematics. The prime example of this is Stephen Hawkins who is almost completely paralyzed and can communicate only through a computer; nevertheless, he is able to remain at the cutting edge of theoretical physics and cosmology and he continues to generate new ideas and new concepts.

A more recent hypothesis based entirely on theoretical and mathematical constructs is the superstring theory. These superstrings are considered to be the absolute smallest building blocks of the universe: they are thought to be millions of times smaller than even the quarks which themselves are not of a very robust size. In essence, these superstrings are considered to be very small loops of energy. Because the whole concept is so difficult to grasp, some scientists think it may be years before the concept is fully understood. On the other hand, there are those who think that this theory can explain just about everything. According to Michio Kaku[2] and Brian Greene,[3] the superstring theory will eventually be able to make it possible to formulate an unified theory of everything, a goal that has been hotly pursued, so far without success, by many scientists, beginning with Einstein. It has been calculated that, if ever we want to prove the superstring theory experimentally, we need to build a particle accelerator roughly the size of our entire solar system! It appears, therefore, that we will have to accept this theory for the time being on blind faith. This has led Sheldon Glashow[4] to write: "For the first time since the Dark Ages, we can see how our noble research may end with faith replacing science once more".

Martin Gardner[5] in his book, *Did Adam and Eve Have a Navel?*, has this to say about superstrings:

> What are superstrings made of? As far as anyone knows they are not made of anything. They are pure mathematical constructs. If superstrings are the end of the line, then everything that exists in the universe seems to be made of nothing, yet somehow it manages to exist. Many famous scientists believe that the universe has bottomless levels. As soon as one level is penetrated, a trapdoor opens to a hitherto unsuspected sub-basement.

SOME BASIC PHYSICS

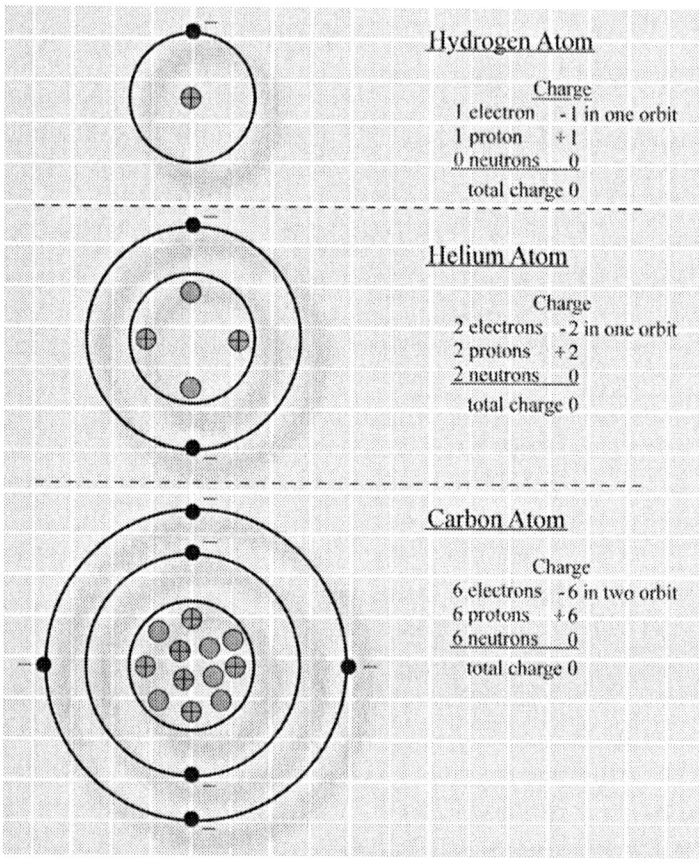

Notes:

1- Since positive and negative charges attract, a force is needed to prevent the negatively charged electrons from crashing into the positively charged nucleus: this is the Electromagnetic Force.

2- Since positively charged particles repel each other, a force is needed to prevent the protons in the nucleus from separating: this is the strong nuclear force.

Figure A.2

The Classical Model of the Atomic Structure of Hydrogen, Helium and Carbon

In all this, we must remember that all these quarks and superstrings exist only for the briefest of moments after a forced unnatural collision in a particle accelerator. The only real, naturally occurring, permanent particles are the proton, the neutron and the electron.

It is necessary to mention two other particles that play an important role in the way the universe works at the level of both the microcosm and the macrocosm. First, there is the photon which is a particle that carries the electromagnetic force. It is supposed to have no mass when at rest but it does have a small amount of energy. The photon is envisaged, for instance, as the carrier of light and therefore moves at the speed of light. (As was pointed out before, light can move in two modes and manifests itself, at the same time, as a wave and a particle.) The other particle is the graviton, which is envisaged as carrying the gravitational force. So far, I believe, its existence has not been experimentally proven; it is just a mental construct to explain how gravity can act on everything that has mass.

Before leaving the world of subatomic particles, I want to briefly mention the concept of particles that have the same mass as normal particles but have an opposite charge. The existence of these particles, called antimatter, has been demonstrated in the laboratory where they have a very short life, because as soon as they meet up with a normal particle the two will annihilate each other in a burst of energy. It is believed that antimatter does not exist naturally in the universe. Here on Earth, it can only be created as the result of particle collisions in high energy colliders used in the study of the basic structure of the subatomic world. Some people have speculated that there may exist other universes, outside ours, which consist entirely of antimatter.

To get some idea of the sizes of these particles, the following model is often used: if you blow up the nucleus of a helium atom to the size of a baseball then, on the same scale, the electron will be the size of a ping-pong ball circling the nucleus at a distance of four kilometers from the nucleus. From this it is clear that the atom, and therefore all matter, consists 99.99 per cent of empty space. In other words the wooden chair or, for that matter, the metal chair you are sitting on is almost entirely made up of empty space and has very little real substance. The reason we can sit on the chair, or construct things from metal and wood, is that these atoms are so small that trillions would fit in a cubic millimeter and so they give the appearance of a solid material. It is similar to viewing a forest from a distance. From far enough away it looks solid and quite impenetrable; however, when we get closer we may discover that the trees are spaced at quite a distance apart. The solid impenetrable appearance came from the fact that the forest is deep and that there are thousands of trees situated behind and between the trees that make up the outer edge. The actual size of an electron is 10^{-18} meters, while the proton and the neutron each measure 2.10^{-15} meters. In other words, the electron is about 2,000 times smaller than the neutron and proton. This is exceedingly small for a particle that plays such an important role in the way nature operates.

The way we often experience atoms in our daily lives is in the form of molecules made up of two or more atoms. For instance water, the most common molecule without which life is impossible, consists of two atoms of hydrogen and one atom of oxygen. The interesting thing about these molecules is that once their atoms are bound together, the resulting molecule has none of the qualities of the original atoms. For instance, ordinary table salt, which is used in about every meal we eat, is made up of sodium and chlorine. Both of these elements are such strong poisons that, if we consumed them separately, we would probably not survive the experience; once bound together in a molecule though, they become the salt of the earth. Molecules are formed when two or more atoms come so close together that the outer electrons of one atom begin to feel the attractive force of the nucleus of the other atom. Depending then on the space available in the fixed orbits of these atoms, this attractive force will bind the two atoms together and the two atoms will begin to act as one molecule.

Molecules can vary in size from the simple ones such as water to the most complicated forms of DNA molecules which contain literally millions of atoms. It is these complicated molecules, mostly made up of carbon, oxygen, nitrogen, phosphorus and sulfur, which are basic to the existence of all life. The DNA molecules in our body, for instance, are grouped together in units called chromosomes which are stored in the nucleus of all the cells of our body. It is these cells which are the basic building blocks of all living things, animals as well as plants. Certain short sequences in this DNA molecule form the genes which to some extent determine the physical and mental make-up of the human individual. For further details on cells and DNA see Chapter V.

So the sequence from the most basic elementary particles to the living organisms is:

- Quarks (maybe superstrings)
- Subatomic particles such as electrons, protons and neutrons
- Atoms
- Molecules
- DNA – Genes
- Chromosomes
- Cells
- Animals and plants

In all of this, we must remember that the atom and its subatomic particles are constructs of our mind. No one has ever seen an atom. What is more, according to present-day theories we cannot even know what an atom really is. We can only know what it is like and what the properties are that we experience. The standard model of an atom with a nucleus in the center and electrons circling around it is just that, a model that fits the facts as we know them today. As a matter of fact, the theoretical physicists now view all atomic sub-particles as manifestations of fields, or as they say "bunched-up fields". This concept is even more difficult to understand for the lay person than the classical model: I only mention it here because, as we will see later, there are now theories stating that almost everything in the universe is governed by fields of influence. These fields are considered to be nonmaterial, but nevertheless control much of what is happening in the universe on both the macro and micro levels. Others, such as Fritjof Capra,[6] talk about subatomic particles not as things, but as interconnections among things, or as a set of relationships that reach outward to other things.

Shimon Malin[7] in his book, *Nature Loves to Hide*, writes: "The universe is an immense network of experiences and potentialities for experiences, influencing each other." And it is not only the scientists who talk in this vein. The founder of Process Theology, Alfred Whitehead, goes even further when he postulates that all objects can best be described as experiences rather than concrete facts. He writes that the universe and all its constituents are alive and that "atoms of reality are throbs of experience".

All this seems to indicate that our understanding of reality as being made up of material hard units of matter must be drastically revised. Matter seems to have been replaced by such immaterial concepts as bunched-up fields, sets of relationships, mental constructs, and throbs of experience. These concepts, once they have been generally accepted, will have a decisive influence on how we see the universe and how we fit in it. For one thing it does completely away with materialism and seems to confirm that the universe and our world are far more spiritual in nature than ever thought even by the various religions, with the possible exception of Hinduism. Brian Silver seems to have come to the same conclusion when he writes: "At this point, reality is rapidly running through our fingers. What is left? A universe that is a maelstrom of interacting fields."

Before leaving the world of the microcosms, we should briefly mention a phenomenon that plays a very important part in our daily lives – the electromagnetic spectrum. As was mentioned before, the protons and electrons carry electrical charges; these electrical charges are the source of three fundamental aspects of nature – electricity, magnetism and light. Oscillations in these electrical charges create waves of electromagnetic energies that spread out in all directions at the speed of light and in a wide band of frequencies and energies. On the one side of the spectrum are the gamma rays with a very small wavelength 3.10^{-16} meters and a frequency of 10^{24} cycles per second. On the other side of the spectrum are the long waves with a wavelength of 3.10^6 meters and a frequency of only 100 cycles per second. In between these lie the X rays, ultraviolet light, visible light, infrared light, microwaves, short and long radio waves, etc. Light, as we know it, occupies a very narrow range of this wide spectrum. It varies from violet at a wavelength of 4.10^{-7} meters to red with a wavelength of 7.10^{-7} meters. One of the more important aspects of this wave spectrum of light is that when a light source moves in relation to the observer, the frequency of the light shifts. If the light source moves farther away from the observer the wavelength becomes longer, the frequency becomes shorter, and the spectrum moves to the red end – the so-called red shift. If the light source moves in the direction of the observer, the wavelength becomes shorter, the frequency becomes larger, and the light shifts to the violet end of the spectrum. This effect, named after its discoverer, Doppler, is the same effect we experience when a source of sound approaches us; when it moves towards us, the sound has a higher pitch compared to when it has passed us and is receding.

The Macrocosm

As soon as our ancient ancestors became conscious human beings, aware of their surroundings, they began to follow the movement of the objects they noticed in the sky. Day and night followed each other like clockwork with the movement of the Sun across the sky. The seasons of winter, spring, summer and autumn followed each other in a similar regular pattern. It was quite obvious to them that the Earth was the center of everything they observed; the Sun and the Moon seemed to circle around the Earth and were there clearly for the benefit of our ancestors.

Of course, they thought the Earth was flat. There was nothing to indicate that this was not so, that is, until a gentleman, named Eratostenos, proved them to be wrong. The way he came to this conclusion is, I believe, one of the milestones in the progression of scientific thought, and one of the most interesting ones as well, because he based his conclusion on experiment and observation and not on purely deductive reasoning and speculation, which was then the generally accepted way of "discovering" things about the natural world. Eratostenos, who lived in Alexandria around the year 250 B.C.E., heard from someone that in Syene in the South of Egypt, on June 21 at midday, a vertical stick did not cast a shadow. Fortunately for the future of cosmology, he did not just accept this tidbit of information at face value but decided to see if this was also true in Alexandria. He found that this was not so and that a vertical stick continued to cast a shadow on that date. Eratostenos deduced from this that the Earth could not be flat but must be round. He went so far as to calculate the diameter of the round Earth by measuring the angle by which the Sun rays struck the Earth, and by measuring the distance between Syene and Alexandria. The surprising thing is that his calculations were amazingly accurate considering the data he had to work with.

The idea that the Earth was round, and not flat, changed the way people envisioned the universe. Naturally, it was difficult to accept at first that there could be people living, as it were, upside down at the opposite side of the round Earth. This was especially difficult to understand since there was then no known force which could keep people from falling off the other side of the Earth. Eventually the idea of a round Earth became generally accepted, and a number of models were proposed which fitted this round Earth in with what was being observed in the sky. The most generally accepted model was that of Ptolemy who lived around 150 C.E. in Greece. He envisaged a cosmos with the Earth as its center with the Sun and the planets moving around the Earth in concentric circular paths. This model held until the development of the telescope in the seventeenth century, which made it possible to look deeper into the universe and make more accurate measurements of the movements of the planets.

By the late 1600s, it was quite clear that what was being observed in the sky could only be explained if it was assumed that the Earth circled around the Sun and not the other way around. This, of course, was revolutionary thinking and it took a while for it to become generally accepted. The Christian Church especially had a difficult time accepting it; had not Joshua asked the Lord to stop the

Sun on its journey around the Earth so that he could continue to pursue his fleeing enemies. The problem, of course, was that if the Earth was not the center of the universe, then humans were most likely not the center and purpose of creation either. Today some postmodern thinkers have put humans right back again into the center of the universe. In fact, it is believed by many today that we are the purpose of the universe's existence, and that the universe is only real unless there are living, conscious beings, such as humans, able to observe it.

While the existence of most of the planets has been known for many centuries, the increasing power of the telescope has made it possible to get a better picture of the relative sizes of these planets and of the relative distances between these planets and the Sun. Table Aa presents some of the details concerning these planets. They are arranged in increasing distance from the Sun, and for easy comparison, their mass and distance from the Sun is given in multiples of the Earth's mass and the Earth's distance to the Sun.

Table Aa: *Relative Distance Between the Planets and the Sun*

	Distance From the Sun	Mass	Average Surface Temperature in Centigrade
Mercury	0.38	0.055	+ 120
Venus	0.72	0.815	+ 460
Earth	1.00	1.00	+ 16
Mars	1.5	0.107	− 55
Jupiter	5.2	317.83	− 149
Saturn	9.5	95.16	− 178
Uranus	19.2	14.54	− 214
Neptune	30.1	17.15	− 214
Pluto	39.5	0.002	− 240

It is clear from this table that our Earth is puny compared

with such giants as Jupiter and Saturn, and that the temperatures on the other planets are either too high or too low for any type of life, as we know it, to exist.

As it turned out, the Sun is not something very special either as became obvious when more and more became known about the vastness of the cosmos with the aid of more powerful telescopes. In fact, it was found that the Sun was only one of billions of stars in an agglomeration of stars called the Milky Way, which we can observe at night as a misty, white streak across the sky. The distance between these stars (suns) turned out to be so large that it became almost impossible to express it in multiples of kilometers, and so the light-year was invented to measure large distances. A light-year is not a measurement of time but of distance: it is the distance that light travels in a period of one year. This is, of course, a very large distance since light travels at a speed of 300,000 kilometers per second. This is so fast that a photon of light can travel around the Earth seven times in one second. A light-year is thus equivalent to a distance of 9,000,000,000,000 kilometers. Using this measure of distance, we find that the closest star to our solar system, Alpha Centaur, is 4.3 light-years away from us.

Also, it was found that the Milky Way is not the only agglomeration of stars in the universe; when some of the faint specs of light in the night sky were closely examined by ever more powerful telescopes, it turned out that the sky was filled with these clusters of stars called galaxies. Each of these galaxies was found to contain billions of stars and at distances of billions of light-years from the Earth. Examining the spectrum of light that reaches us from these remote locations, it was found that they all had this red shift in their spectrum indicating that these galaxies are moving away from us at great speeds.

Our galaxy turns out to be a flat-lying, spiral structure with a diameter of 100,000 light-years and with our solar system located some 35,000 light-years from its center. While these seem to be phenomenally large numbers, it was soon discovered that this was nothing compared to the size of the observable universe which is estimated to have a diameter of some 10 billion light-years and to contain billions of galaxies. The launching of the Hubble telescope in 1990, and its subsequent repair in 1993, gave us for the first time the opportunity to see the outer edges of the universe some 12.2 billion light-years away, which means we are seeing that part of the universe as it was 12.2 billion years ago, which is fairly close in time to the beginning of the universe that is presently estimated to have taken place fifteen billion years ago.

One of the more intriguing discoveries of recent years are the "black holes" which seem to exist in every galaxy we can observe. A black hole is a region of such immense mass, and hence such powerful gravity, that nothing, not even light, can escape its clutches. Their existence can, therefore, only be inferred by the effect they have on the stars and galaxies that are close to them. From these observations, it appears that a black hole can have a mass equivalent to as much as that of three to five billion stars, and that it swallows up matter at the rate equivalent to one million stars a year. What happens to all of this matter after it is swallowed up is still a mystery. One thing to remember in all of this is that a large part of the galaxies consist, not of solid matter, but of dust and gas; furthermore, it is believed that there is a very large amount of dark matter which cannot be seen and which may make up as much as 90 to 99 per cent of the total mass of the universe.

So our Sun and our Earth are nothing very spectacular in the universe. We have, however, one thing that makes our Sun stand out: our solar system of nine satellites, also called planets, circling the Sun. Recently, a number of observations have been made of faraway stars which seem to indicate that these stars also have planets. The importance of the existence of these satellites is that they can create the conditions which make life possible. All stars are basically the same as our Sun in that they convert their matter into radiant energy at unbelievably high temperatures, and they are therefore not very hospitable to life of any form. The satellites which do not generate their own radiant energy are potentially more hospitable to life. They receive light and energy from their star by radiation. Life can only evolve on these satellites if there is a specific distance between the star and its satellite. The satellite must receive just the right amount of light and energy to initiate growth and sustain life. However, for that to be possible they have to be at exactly the right distance from the star and circle that star in a near circular orbit.

If, for instance, our Earth were only slightly closer to the Sun, the temperature on Earth would rise to make life, as we know it, completely impossible. Similarly, if the Earth were to be slightly farther removed from the Sun, the temperature would drop to such an extent that life would be equally impossible. So, it is no surprise that of the nine satellites of the Sun only one, our Earth, can sustain life. Recently, it has been argued that there is one more requirement for a planet to be able to sustain life. This argument is based on the belief that the two largest planets, Jupiter and Saturn, because of their large mass, attract and absorb most of the comets which enter the solar system before they can continue their journey through space and crash into one of the other planets. It is argued that without such large planets to catch these comets, life on other planets would be difficult to sustain because of the frequent impacts of these comets. Also it is entirely possible that these comets, which contain a large amount of ice, would actually flood the planet and thus prevent life from developing.

At the time of writing (spring 2003), a total of fifty stars have been identified which exhibit signs that they may have satellites. These satellites, however, appear to have very strange orbits. Most of them appear to be far too close to their star to make life possible; others have very large elliptical orbits which means that sometimes they are too close and, at other times, too far from their star to make it possible for life to exist on those planets. Most of the stars with planets are located between forty to sixty light-years from our solar system; although recently the star, Epsilon Eridani, which is located only ten light-years from us was found to have a Jupiter-sized planet. Some scientists have speculated that the closest star, which could possibly have satellites that might be habitable, is at least sixty light-years away. That is so far that a light signal or radio signal that left the Earth in 1943 will only be arriving there now. In looking at this, it must be remembered that none of these satellites can actually be observed; the only evidence we have of their existence is a slight "wobble" in the star's position in the sky.

To get some idea of the sizes we are talking about when discussing the microcosm and the macrocosm, I have taken some figures from the book, *The Natural History of the Universe*, by Colin A. Ronan.[8] Because these figures are either very large or very small they are normally expressed in a notation by which figures are given as multiples of 10. In this way 100 becomes 10 times 10 or 10^2, and 1/1000 becomes 1/10 times 1/10 times 1/10 or 10^{-3}. The speed of light in that notation then becomes 3.10^5 km/sec or 3.10^8 m/sec; a light-year in this notation becomes 9.10^{15} meters long. The figures below are expressed in multiples of the size of a human being. To convert to meters multiply the indicated figures by a factor of 2.

Table Ab: *Size of a Human Being in Comparison to Other Measured Quantities*

Quantity	Size
Quarks	10^{-24}
Atoms and molecules	10^{-11} to 10^{-7}
Viruses	10^{-8} to 10^{-6}
Visible light wavelength	10^{-7} to 10^{-6}
Protozoa, the simplest living creatures	10^{-4}
Human beings	10^{0}
Diameter of the Earth	10^{+7}
Diameter of the solar system	10^{+13}
Size of an average galaxy	10^{+20}
Size of the observable universe	10^{+26}

Thus, the size of a human being is about midway between the size of the largest and the smallest measured quantity in the universe, that is if these measurements are expressed on a logarithmic scale: –24 compared with +26.

NOTES

[1] Silver, Brian, *The Ascent of Science*, Oxford University Press, New York, Oxford, 1998.

[2] Kaku, Michio, *Hyperspace*, Oxford University Press, New York, Oxford, 1994.

[3] Greene, Brian, *The Elegant Universe, Superstring's Hidden Dimensions and the Quest for the Ultimate Theory*, W. W. Norton and Co., New York, 1999.

[4] Glashow, Sheldon Lee, *The Death of Science*, University Press of America, London, 1992.

[5] Gardner, Martin, *Did Adam and Eve Have a Navel?*, W. W. Norton and Co., New York, NY, 2000.

[6] Capra, Fritjof, *The Web of Life*, Anchor Books, Doubleday, New York, 1996, p.30.

[7] Malin, Shimon, *Nature Loves to Hide, Quantum Physics and the Nature of Reality, A Western Perspective*, Oxford University Press, New York, 2001.

[8] Ronan, Colin A., *The Natural History of the Universe, From the Big Bang to the End of Time*, Macmillan Publishing Company, New York, 1991.

BIBLIOGRAPHY

Achenbach, Joel, *Captured by Aliens, the Search for Life and Truth in a Very Large Universe*, Simon and Schuster, New York, NY, 1999

Adler, Mortimer J., *Intellect: Mind Over Matter*, Macmillan Publishing Co., New York, 1990, p.xii

Alper, Matthew, *The God Part of the Brain, A Scientific Interpretation of Human Spirituality and God*, Rogue Press, Brooklyn, New York, 2000

Barbour, Ian, *Religion in an Age of Science*, Harper San Francisco, Harper Collins Publishers, 1990, p.146

Barclay, William, *The Daily Bible, The Gospel of John*, Welch Publishing Co. Ltd, Burlington, ON, 1995

Barrow, John and Tippler, Frank J., *The Anthropic Cosmological Principle*, Clarendon Press Oxford University Press, Oxford, 1986, p.31

Behe, Michael, *Darwin's Black Box, The Biochemical Challenge to Evolution*, The Free Press, Simon and Schuster, New York, 1996, p.168

Benor, Daniel, *Spindrift Experiments*, mentioned in Larry Dossey's book *Healing Words*

Benson, Herbert, *Timeless Healing, The Power and Biology of Belief*, Simon and Schuster, New York, 1996

——, Herbert, *The Faith Factor, An Annotated Bibliography of Clinical Research on Spiritual Subjects*, quoted in *Timeless Healing, The Power and Biology of Belief*, Simon and Schuster, New York, 1996

Berkeley, Bishop George, 1685–1753, *Treatise Concerning the Principles of Human Knowledge*, 1709

Bizony, Piers, *Rivers of Mars, Searching for the Cosmic Origin of Life*, Aurum Press Ltd, London, 1997, p.186

Bohm, David and Edwards, Mark, *Changing Consciousness*, Harper Collins Publishers Inc., New York, 1991

——, David and Peat, David, *Science, Order and Creativity*, Bantam Books, New York, 1987, p.202

——, David, *New Age Journal*, September/October, 1989, p.110

——, David, quoted in *Schroder's Kittens*, p.159

Bohr, Niels, *Atomic Theory And The Description of Nature*, Cambridge University Press, 1934

Borg, Marcus, *The God We Never Knew*, Harper Collins Publishers, New York, 1997, p.124

Broughton, Richard S., *Parapsychology: The Controversial Science*, Ballantine Books, New York, 1991

Brown Taylor, Barbara, *The Luminous Web, Essays on Science and Religion*, Cowley Publications, Boston, 2000

Brunner, Emil, *Our Faith*, SCM Press, London, 1977, p.39

Brunton, Paul, *The Spiritual Crisis of Man*, Rider and Co. and S. Weiser Inc., 1970

Cahill, Thomas, *The Gift of the Jews: How a Tribe of Desert Nomads Changed the Way Everyone Thinks and Feels*, Doubleday, New York, 1998

Capra, Fritjof, *The Web of Life*, Anchor Books, Doubleday, New York, 1998, pp.30, 282

Casti, John, *Paradigms Lost*, William Morrow, New York, 1989

Chatterji, Mohini, translation of the *Bhagavad-Gita*, Julian Press, New York, 1960

Chopra, Deepak, *Quantum Healing, Ageless Body, Timeless Mind*, Crown Publishing Group, 1993

Cox-Chapman, Mally, *The Case for Heaven, Near-Death Experiences as Evidence of the Afterlife*, G. P. Putnam and Sons, New York, 1995

Cramer, John G., *Review of Modern Physics*, Vol. 58, 1986, p.647

Crosswell, Ken, *Planet Quest, The Epic Discovery of Alien Solar Systems*, Harcourt Brace & Co, 1998, p.247

Darling, David, *Deep Time*, Delacorte Press, Bantam, Doubleday, Dell, New York, 1989, pp.115, 172

Darwin, Charles, *On the Origin of Species by Means of Natural Selection*, John Murray, 1860

Davies, Paul, *Other Worlds*, Simon and Schuster, New York, 1980

——, Paul, *The Cosmic Blue Print, New Discoveries in Nature's Ability to Order the Universe*, Simon and Schuster, New York, 1988, p.203

——, Paul, *The Fifth Miracle, The Search for the Origin and Meaning of Life*, Simon and Schuster, New York, 1999, p.95

Dawkins, Richard, *The Blind Watchmaker*, Oxford University Press, Oxford, 1986, pp.5, 141

——, Richard, *The Selfish Gene*, Oxford University Press, Oxford, 1990

Dossey, Larry, *Healing Words, The Power of Prayer and the Practice of Medicine*, Harper San Francisco, New York, 1993

Durant, Will and Ariel, *The Story of Civilization, Moral Elements of Civilization*, Simon and Schuster Inc., New York, 1935

Dyson, Freeman, *Disturbing the Universe*, Harper and Row, New York, 1979, p.250

Easterbrook, Gregg, *Beside Still Waters, Searching for Meaning in an Age of Doubt*, William Morrow & Co., 1999

Edinger, Edward F., *The Creation of Consciousness, Jung's Myth for Modern Man*, Inner City Books, Toronto, 1984

Eldredge, Niles and Gould, Stephen J., *Fossils: the Evolution and Extinction of Species*, Princeton University Press, 1997

Ellis, George, *Before the Beginning of Time, Cosmology Explained*, Boyars/Bowerdean, London, 1993, p.104

Ferris, Timothy, *The Whole Shebang, A State-of-the-Universe Report*, Simon and Schuster New York, 1997, p.248

Forman, Robert, "What Does Mysticism Have to Teach Us about Consciousness?", Conference Towards a Science of Consciousness

Fox, Michael W., *Beyond Evolution, The Genetically Altered Future of Plants Animals, the Earth… and Humans*, The Lyons Press, New York, 1999

Franklin, Harold, *The Way of the Cell, Molecules, Organisms and the Order of Life*, Oxford University Press, New York, 2001

Fraser, Sylvia, *The Quest for the Fourth Monkey*, Firefly Books, 1994, p.24

Gardner, Martin, *Did Adam and Eve Have a Navel?*, W. W. Norton and Co., New York, NY, 2000

Gjertsen, Derek, *Science and Philosophy, Present and Past*, Penguin Books, London, 1989

Glashow, Sheldon Lee, *The Death of Science*, University Press of America, London, 1992

Goswami, Amit, *The Self-Aware Universe, How Consciousness Creates the Material World*, G. P. Putnam & Sons, New York, 1993, pp. 3, 9, 139, 141

Gould, Stephen Jay, *Life's Grandeur*, Vintage Pockets, 1996

——, Stephen Jay, *Wonderful Life: The Burgess Shale and the Nature of History*, W. W. Norton, New York, 1989

——, Stephen, *Rock of Ages, Science and Religion in the Fullness of Life*, Ballantine Publishing Group, New York, 2000

Greene, Brian, *The Elegant Universe, Superstring's Hidden Dimensions and the Quest for the Ultimate Theory*, W. W. Norton and Co., New York, 1999

Gribben, John, *Schroder's Kittens and the Search for Reality*, Little, Brown and Co., Boston, 1995, pp. 140, 142

Griffen, David, *Parapsychology, Philosophy, and Spirituality, A Postmodern Exploration*, State University of New York, Albany, 1997

Griffith, Bede, *A New Vision of Reality*, Templegate Publishers, 1992

Hallman, Douglas, *Perspectives*, Private Bible Commentaries, St. Davids United Church, St Davids, Ontario, 2002

Hartmann, William and Miller, Ron, *The History of Earth*, Workman Publishing Co. Inc., 1991

Horgan, John, *The End of Science, Facing the Limits of Knowledge in the Twilight of the Scientific Age*, Addison Wesley Publishing Co., 1996, p.244

Hoyle, Fred, quoted in *Science and Philosophy*

James, William, *The Varieties of Religious Experiences*, Penguin Books, London, 1902

Jeans, Sir James, *The Mysterious Universe*, Cambridge University Press, Cambridge, 1930, p.186

Johnson, Robert John, *Bridging Science and Religion, Why It Must Be Done*, The Center for Theology and the Natural Sciences, Internet article www.ctns.org

Jolly, Alison, *Lucy's Legacy*, Harvard University Press, Cambridge, Mass, 1999/2000

Jonker, Frederik, *Good News for Today, We Are not Alone*, Fairway Press, Lima, Ohio, 1994, p.62

Kaku, Michio, *Hyperspace*, Oxford University Press, New York, Oxford, 1994

——, Michio, *Visions, How Science Will Revolutionize the 21st Century*, Doubleday, Dell Publishing Group, New York, 1994

Kaufman, Stuart, *At Home in the Universe: The Search for the Laws of Self Organization and Complexity*, Oxford University Press, New York, 1995

Keating, Thomas, *Invitation to Love*, Elements Inc., Rockport, 1992

Keck, Robert L., *Sacred Eyes*, Knowledge Systems Inc., Indianapolis, 1992, pp.5, 157

Keller, Werner, *The Bible as History*, William Morrow and Co., New York, 1956

Kennedy, James, *Why I Believe*, Word Incorporated, Waco, 1980, pp.111–112

Kittredge, Mary, *The Senses*, Chelsea House Publishing, New York, 1990

Kübler-Ross, Elisabeth, *On Death and Dying*, Macmillan Publishing, New York, 1969

——, Elisabeth, *On Life After Death*, Celestial Arts, Berkeley, CA, 1991

Küng, Hans, *On Being a Christian*, Collins, London, 1977, p.39

Larson, David, "The National Institute for Health Care Research", *International Journal of Psychiatry in Medicine*, issue 8/18

Larson, Edward, University of Georgia, in an article by Natalie Angier of the *New York Times* service

Leaky, Richard, *The Origin of Humankind*, Basic Books, Harper Collins Publications, 1994, p.99

Lennart, Nilsson, *The Body Victorious*, Delacorte Press, New York, 1987

Lewontin, Richard, *It Ain't Necessarily So, The Dream of the Human Genome and Other Illusions*, Harvard University Press, Cambridge, Mass., 2000

MacKay, Donald, *Brains, Machines and Persons*, Collins, London, 1980

Maddox, John, *What Remains To Be Discovered*, The Free Press, Simon and Schuster, New York, 1998, pp.276–279, 312

Malin, Shimon, *Nature Loves to Hide, Quantum Physics and the Nature of Reality, A Western Perspective*, Oxford University Press, New York, 2001

Martin, Joel and Romanowski, Patricia, *Love Beyond Life*, Harper Collins Publishers, New York, 1997

Mascall, Eric L., "Importance of Being Human", Greenwood Publishing Group Inc., 1974, quoted in John Davies's book, *Are We Alone?*

Midgley, Mary, *Science and Salvation, A Modern Myth and its Meaning*, Routledge, Chapman and Hall Inc., New York, 1992, p.176

Miller, Kenneth R., *Finding Darwin's God, A Scientist's Search for Common Ground between God and Evolution*, Cliff Street Books, Harper Collins, New York, 1999, pp. 241, 243

Mivart, St George, "On the Genesis of Species, The Incompetence of Natural Selection to Account for the Incipient Stages of Useful Structures", 1871, *Cahiers Victoriens et Edwardiens*, no. 52, 2000

Monod, Jacques, *Chance and Necessity*, Vintage Books, 1972

Moody, Raymond A., *Life After Life*, Bantam Doubleday Dell Publishers, 1976

Moore Thomas, *Care of the Soul* and *Soul Mates*, Harper Perennial, Harper Collins Publishing, New York, 1992

Morse, Melvin, *Closer to the Light, Learning from Near-Death Experiences of Children*, Random House Inc., New York, 1991

Nathan, Peter, *The Nervous System*, Oxford University Press, Oxford, 1982

Ornish, Dean, *Program for Reversing Heart Disease*, Ballantine Books, New York, 1990, p.215

Ornstein, Robert, *The Evolution of Consciousness*, Prentice Hall Press, New York, p.8

Paley, William, *Evidence of the Existence and Attributes of the Deity*, 1803

Pannenberg, Wolfhart, *Faith and Reality*, The Westminster Press, Philadelphia, 1977, p.37

Peck, M. Scott, *The Road Less Traveled and Beyond, Spiritual Growth in an Age of Anxiety*, Simon and Schuster, New York, 1997

Persinger, Michael, quoted in *Equinox*, no.82, August 1995

Polkinghorne, John, *Belief in God in an Age of Science*, Yale University Press, 1998, p.96

Raymo, Chet, *Skeptics and Believers, The Exhilarating Connection between Science and Religion*, Walker Publishing Co. Ltd, New York, 1998, p.26

Recinos, Adrian, *Popol Vuh, The Sacred Book of the Ancient Quiche Maya*, University of Oklahoma Press, Norman, 1951–1991, pp.81, 83

Reiss, Bob, *The Coming Storm: Extreme Weather and our Terrifying Future*, Hyperion, New York, 2001

Rifkin, Jeremy, *Algeny*, as quoted in *Genetic Engineering, Progress or Peril*, by Linda Tagliaferro, p.127

Ring, Kenneth, *Heading Towards Omega, In Search of the Meaning of Near Death Experiences*, William Morrow and Co., New York, 1985

Ronan, Colin A., *The Natural History of the Universe, From the Big Bang to the End of Time*, Macmillan Publishing Company, New York, 1991

Roston, Holmes, "Evolutionary History and Divine Presence", *Theology Today*, Vol. 55 no. 3, October 1998

Sabon, Michael, *Recollections of Death*, Harper and Row, New York, 1982

Schumacher E. F., *A Guide for the Perplexed*, Harper Collins Publishers Inc., New York, 1977

Searle, John, *The Rediscovery of the Mind*, MIT Press, 1994

Sheldrake, Rupert, *Seven Experiments that Could Change the World*, Berkley Publishing Group, 1996, p.99

——, Rupert, *The Rebirth of Nature, Science and God*, Bantam Books, New York, 1991

Shermer, Michael, *How We Believe, The Search for God in an Age of Science*, W. H. Freeman & Co, New York, 1999

Shiels, Dean, "A Cross-Cultural Study of Belief in Out-of-the-Body Experiences", *Journal of the Society for Psychical Research*, 1978

Siegel, Bernie, *Peace, Love and Healing*, Harper and Row, New York, 1989

Silver, Brian L., *The Ascent of Science*, Oxford University Press, New York, Oxford, 1998

Sloan, Philip R., ed., *Controlling our Destinies; Historical, Philosophical, Ethical and Theological Perspectives of the Human Genome Project*, University of Notre Dame Press, Notre Dame, Indiana, 2000

Smullyan, Raymond, *The Tao is Silent*, Harper Collins Publishers, New York, 1977

Suzuki, David and Dressel, Holly, *From Naked Ape to Superspecies*, Stoddart Publishing Co. Ltd, Toronto, 1999, p.104

Swinburn, Richard, *The Existence of God*, Oxford University Press, Oxford, 1991

Sykes, Bryan, *The Seven Daughters of Eve – The Science that Reveals our Genetic Ancestry*, W.W. Norton & Co., New York, 2001

Tarna, Richard, *Passions of the Western Mind, Understanding the Ideas that Have Shaped our Worldview*, Ballantine Books, New York, 1991, pp. 397, 412

Tattersall, Ian, *Becoming Human, Evolution and Human Uniqueness*, Harcourt, Brace and Co., Orlando, 1998, p.188

Thuan Trinh Xuan, *The Secret Melody, and Man Created the Universe*, Oxford University Press, New York, 1995, p.229

Tippler, Frank J., *Physics of Immortality, Modern Cosmology, God and the Resurrection of the Dead*, Doubleday, New York, 1994

Toffler, Alvin and Heidi, *War and Anti-War, Survival at the Dawn of the 21st Century*, Little, Brown and Company, Boston, 1993

Trefil, James S., *Are We Unique?*, John Wiley and Sons Inc., New York, 1997

——, James S., *The Moment of Creation – Big Bang Physics*, Charles Scribner and Sons, New York, 1983, pp. 182, 222–223

Van Till, Howard, "The Creation: Intelligently Designed or Optimally Equipped", *Theology Today*, Vol. 55, no. 3, October 1998

Vardey, Lucinda, *God in All Worlds, An Anthology of Contemporary Spiritual Writing*, Vintage Canada, Random House, Toronto, 1996, p.796

Various, *The World's Great Religions*, Time Incorporated, New York, 1957

Viney, Geoff, *Surviving Death, Evidence of the Afterlife*, St Martin's Press, 1993

Weil, Andrew, *Spontaneous Healing, How to Discover and Enhance Your Body's Natural Ability to Maintain and Heal Itself*, Ballantine Books, 1996

Wheeler, John A, quoted in *Schroder's Kittens*, p.142

——, John A., *Mind and Nature*, Harper and Row, San Francisco, 1982

Whitfield, Philip, general editor, *The Human Body Explained, A Guide to Understanding the Incredible Living Machine*, Henry Holt and Company, New York, 1995, p.141

Wigner, Eugene, *Symmetries and Reflections*, Indiana University Press, Bloomington, 1967
Wilson, Edward O., *Consilience, The Unity of Knowledge*, Alfred A. Knopf, New York, 1998, p.99
Wise, Anna, *The High Performance Mind*, Putnam Publishing, New York, 1997
Wynn, Charles and Wiggins, Anita, *The Five Biggest Ideas in Science*, John Wiley and Sons, New York, 1993
Zebrowski Jr., Ernest, *Perils of a Restless Planet, Scientific Perspectives on Natural Disasters*, Cambridge University Press, 1999

INTERNET

Beale, Nicholas, *The Anthropic Principle*, Star Course Discussion Page, www.starcourse.org
Behe, Michael, "Molecular Machines, Experimental Support for the Design Inference", Access Research Network, www.arn.org
Johnson, Robert John, *Bridging Science and Religion, Why It Must Be Done*, The Center for Theology and the Natural Sciences, Internet article, www.ctns.org

INDEX

A

abortion, 20
Abraham and Sarah, 296
  covenant, 298
  founder of religion, 296
  travels, 297
Achenbach, Joel, 175
Adler, Mortimer, 218
AIDS, 196
Allah, 23, 130
  Muslim prayer, 304
anthropic principle, 77
  participatory, 78
  strong, 78
  weak, 78
antimatter, 20
arguments for the existence of God
  cosmological, 366
  moral, 367
  ontological, 366
  teleogical, design, 366
artificial, 168
  extraterrestrial, 169
artificial intelligence, 168
Aspect, Alain, 46, 402
asteroid impacts, 103–4, 163
atoms, 42
  subatomic particles, 43, 68
Aztecs, 121, 276

B

Barbour, Ian, 205, 244
Barclay, William, 366
Barrow, John, 74
bases, base pairs
  adinine, 182
  cystosine, 182
  guanine, 182
  thymine, 182
Beale, Nicholas, 424
Behe, Michael, 98, 137, 139, 140, 376
Bell, J. S., 46, 402
Benor, Daniel, 333
Benson, Herbert, 336
Berkeley, Bishop George, 44, 237
Big Bang, 68, 86, 373, 429
Big Crunch, 34, 164
Bizony, Piers, 91
black holes, 457
Bohm, David, 47, 140, 156, 218, 244
Bohr, Niels, 31, 40–42, 45
Bondi, Robert, 325
Borg, Marcus, 338, 418
Bosch, Hieronymus, 346
Brahman, 23, 130, 283
brain, emergence and capacity, 113

Broughton, Richard, 361
Brown Taylor, Barbara, 57, 81
Brunner, Emil, 315, 417
Brunton, Paul, 243
Buddhism, 276, 279
  Siddharta Gautama, 276
Butterfly Effect, 55
Byrd, Randolph, 332

C

Cahill, Thomas, 306
Cambrian Explosion, 102
Capra, Fritjof, 197, 224, 450
carbon atom, 444
Carter, Brandon, 78
Casti, John, 167
Catal Húyúk, 273
cells
  human, 178–90
  nucleus, 179, 181
  organelles, 179
  splitting, 179, 184–86
  T and B-cells, 193
Chalmers, David, 219
Chaos Theory, 57
Chatterji, Mohini, 283
Chopra, Deepak, 336
Christianity, 26, 288, 289
chromosomes, 181
civilizations
  Maya, 82, 120
  Mesopotamia, 120
Civilizations
  Aztecs, 121, 276
  Chinese, 278
  Egyptian, 278
  Greek, 278
  Incan, 278
  Indus Valley, 278
  Mayan, 82, 120, 280
  Mesopotamian, 120, 280
  Minoan, 278
  Olmec, 276, 279
  Sumerian, 275
Colt, George, 190
comets, 458
Confessio Belgico, vii
consciousness, 115, 378–81
  collective unconscious, 53, 238–40, 398–99
  divine, 239
  subconsciousness, 214
  unconsciousness, 214
  universal, 25
constants of nature, 74, 427
Copernicus, 21
Cox-Chapman, Mally, 344
creation of life, 96–106
creation stories, 82
Creationists, 82, 135, 249
Crick, Francis, 251, 405
Cro-Magnon, 107, 270
Croswell, Ken, 79
Csillag, Ron, 330
cytoplasm, 179

D

dark matter, 457
Darling, David, 50, 76, 85, 116
Darwin, Charles, 21, 83, 130, 139
Davies, Paul, 44, 102, 170, 199, 218, 219, 395
Dawkins, Richard, 144, 224

de Bres, Guido, vii, 23
Democritus, 441
determinism, 249, 250–55
dinosaurs, 103
DNA molecules, 98, 111, 181, 449
Doppler effect, 452
Dose, Klaus, 98
Dossey, Larry, 178, 224, 236, 320, 332, 338, 379
Dressel, Holly, 130, 187
Durant, Will, 269, 281
Dyer, Gwynne, 112
Dyson, Freeman, 76

E

Easterbrook, Gregg, 87
Eastern Orthodox Church, 417
Ediacaran, 102
Edinger, E. F., 242
Einstein, Albert, 34, 45, 69, 226, 410
  general theory of relativity, 38, 399–400
  special theory of relativity, 34, 399
Eldredge, Niles, 141
electricity, 51
electromagnetic force, 66
electromagnetic spectrum, 451
electrons, 41
Ellis, George, 40, 70, 75, 256, 369
entropy, 32
Epicurus, 172
episodic creation, 431

Eratostenos, 452
euthanasia, 20
evolution, 128
evolutionists, 130
Exceptional Human Experience Network, 355
extra terrestrial intelligence, 172
extraordinary coincidences of a beneficial nature, 432
extrasensory perception (ESP), 212, 322, 358, 403
  clairvoyance, 322, 358
  mediumship, 358
  precognition, 322, 358
  psychokinesis, 322, 358
  telepathy, 322, 358

F

Fenwick, Peter, 347
Ferris, Timothy, 90
fertile crescent, 294
fertility goddesses, 273, 278
fields of influence, 51, 52, 53, 233, 401, 450
  form-giving, morphogenetic, 53, 402
forces of nature
  electromagnetic, 66, 67, 441
  gravity, 66, 67
  nuclear, strong, 37, 66, 67
  nuclear, weak, 66, 67
  relative strength, 67
  universal, 323
Forman, Robert, 356
Fox, Michael, 188
fractals, 58

Francis of Assisi, 435
Franklin, Harold, 99, 256, 257
free will, 75, 249, 380–81, 416
fundamental constants of nature, 72, 390

G

galaxies, 456
Gardner, Martin, 391, 445
Gauguin, Paul, 147
Gautama, Siddharta, 276
gender of God, 28
genes, 53, 182
  gene therapy, 186–90
  genetic engineering, 186–90
  genetic manipulation, 106
Genesis, 83, 132, 289, 293, 415, 420
  King David, 292
geocentric view of the universe, 443
Gjertsen, Derek, 47, 77, 262
Glashow, 460
Glashow, Sheldon, 445
God's intervention in creation, 426
Goswami, Amit, 44, 216, 237, 252, 262, 373, 418
Gould, Stephen Jay, 106, 125, 141
gravity, 39, 67
  gravitation, 39
Green Revolution, 154
Greene, Brian, 445

Greyson, Bruce, 346
Gribben, John, 43, 47, 48
Griffen, David, 342, 343, 358
Griffith, Bede, 254, 421
Guido de Bres, vii, 23

H

Hallman, Douglas, 432
Harper's Magazine, 129, 392
Harris, Ruth, 335
Harvard Medical School, 329
Hastermann, William, 151
Hawkins, Stephen, 444
heat death of universe, 33
Heisenberg, Werner, 43, 254, 373
helium, atoms, 86
hemophilia, 192
Hill, Principal, 311
Hindu religion, 62, 276, 279, 283
  Atman, 287
  Bhagavad-Gita, 283
  Brahma, Brahman, Vishnu, Shiva, 283, 284
  cycles in the universe, 287
  Krishna, Rama (Yana), 285
  Nirvana, 85, 287
  Sri Ramakrishna, 288
Hollister, Anne, 190
Holocaust, 22
Holt, Jim, 389, 406
Homo archaic, 107
Homo erectus, 107, 114, 127

Homo habilus, 107, 114, 126
Homo sapiens, 71, 107
Horgan, John, 126, 159
Hoyle, Fred, 77, 91, 101
Hubble telescope, 86, 457
human ancestry
    Mitochondrial Eve Hypothesis, 111
    Multiregional Model, 111
    Out-of-Africa Model, 108, 111
human drives for purpose and meaning, 256–57
    for beauty and decoration, 259
    for love and compassion, 259–60
    for meaning, for source of values, 257–58
    for religion, 260
    for understanding and truth, for hope, 258–59
human genome, 198

I

immune system, 190–97
    feeding cells, macrophages, 192
    granulocytes, monocytes, 192
    T and B-cells, 193
information as building block, 98, 445
intelligence, 247
interconnectedness, universal, 398
Internet, 19

irreducibly complex, 137, 375–78
Islam, 280

J

James, William, 353
Jean, Sir James, 71
Jericho, 273
Jesus Christ, Christianity, 306
    death and resurrection, 310
    Messiah, 311
    Pentecost, 312
Johnson, Robert John, 407
Jolly, Alison, 230
Jonker, Frederik, 148
Josephson, Brian, 394
Judaism, 26, 276, 307
    Genesis, 289
        Abraham, Noah, 293
        Moses, 299
        YHWH, 300
Jung, Carl, 239, 322, 398

K

Kaku, Michio, 66, 156, 253
Kaufmann, Stuart, 136
Keating, Thomas, 218
Keck, Robert, 125, 315, 323
    adolescent stage, 125
    childhood stage, 125
    stage of maturation, 125
Keller, Werner, 292
Kennedy, James, 311
Kistrakowsky, Vera, 77
Kittredge, Mary, 212

Koch curve, 59, 61
Kübler-Ross, Elizabeth, 238, 244, 340, 341, 345, 352
Küng, Hans, 155

L

Lanai, Jargon, 129, 392
language development, 118–19, 392
　acquisition, 168
　written, 119
Larson, David, 329
Larson, Edward, 148
laws of nature, 68, 390
　of conservation of energy, 32
　of thermodynamics, 33, 128
Leaky, Richard, 108
Lewontin, Richard, 198
life
　conditions for, 100
　human life, 126–28
　origin, 97–99
Life magazine, 190
light years, 68
Lourdes, 335

M

MacKay, Donald, 262
macro cosmos, 25
Maddox, John, 71, 214
magnetic field
　magnetism, 52
many-world theory, 63
Martin, Joel, 360

Mascall, E, 170
Matthews, Dale, 332
Maya, 82, 120
Mayr, Ernst, 125
metabolism, 96
meteors, 385
micro cosmos, 25
microwave background, 87
Midgley, Mary, 222
Miller, Kenneth, 141, 145, 264, 431
Miller, Ron, 151
Miller, Stanley, 97
mind, defined, 213, 214–38, 392–95
mitochondria, 179
　Mitochondrial Eve Hypothesis, 111
Mivart, St. George, 140
molecules, 33
Monod, Jacques, 250
Moody, Raymond, 222, 340
Moore, Thomas, 235
morphic resonance, 54
Morse, Melvin, 251
Mother Teresa, 435
Moyer, Bill, 293
multi-regional model, 108
mutations, 116, 184–86
mystical experiences, 353–57

N

NASA, 105, 172
Nathan, Peter, 210
National Institute of Standards and

Technology, 46
Nature magazine, 111
Neanderthal, 107, 127
near-death experiences, 248, 251, 339, 397–98
  after effects, 347–49
  aftereffects, 347–49
  negative experiences, 346–47
  objections and rejections, 349
nerve, central nervous system, 198
  spines, dendrites, axon, 204
neurons, 204, 442
neurotransmitters, 211
Newsweek magazine, 79, 324
Newton, Isaac, 21, 252
Nirvana, 85

O

Occam's razor, 70
organelles, 179
Ornish, Dean, 228
Ornstein, Robert, 115
Out of Africa Model, 108, 389
out of body experiences, 339–43, 381–82

P

Paley, Reverend William, 144
Pannenberg, Wolfhart, 259, 393
parallel universes, 73
Parapsychology, 358
Paul, Apostle, 315, 354, 365
Pauling, Linus, 154
Peat, David, 140, 156
Peck, Scott, 215, 231, 240
Penfield, Wilder, 223
Penrose, Roger, 71
Persinger, Michael, 251
pilot wave, 47
planets, 39
Plato, 440
Polkinghorne, John, 132, 134, 217, 223
Popol Vuh, 82
prayer, 316
  effectiveness, 323–39, 395–97
  nondirected, 334
  The Lord's Prayer, 326
processive worldview, 309
protons, 54
psychokinesis, 322, 358
Ptolemy, 453
punctuated equilibrium, 133, 141

Q

quantum theory, mechanics, 20, 40–42, 400–401
  fluctuations, 75, 372
  leaps, jumps, 41
  reality, 169
quarks, 64, 444

R

Raymo, Chet, 115

receptors, 204
reductionism, 250–55
relativism, 250–55
relativity, theories, 34–37
religion and health, 323–39
Rifkin, Jeremy, 187
Ring, Ken, 245
RNA, 99, 184
Romanowski, Patricia, 360
Ronan, Colin, 44, 459
Ross, Colin, 359
Roston, Holmes, 429

S

Sabon, Michael, 348
Sagan, Carl, 125
Schumacher, E, 421
Scientific American, 71
Searle, John, 223, 379
Seattle, Chief, 241
self reproduction, 96
self-awareness, 215
self-similarity, 58
sequence of events in the life of the universe, 96
SETI program, 125, 173, 175
Sheldrake, Rupert, 51, 199, 235, 401
Shermer, Michael, 24, 147
Shiels, Dean, 343, 382
Siegel, Bernie, 336
Silver, Brian, 40, 48, 77, 440
Smullyan, Raymond, 263
soul, 178
space-time continuum, 61

spectrum, 451
speed of light, 35
spindrift experiments, 240, 333
spiritualism, 249
Steady State theory, 88
Strieber, Whitley, 245
strong nuclear force, 72, 442
subconscious, 229
Sumerian, 274, 275
super novae, 91
superstrings, 66, 445
Suzuki, David, 130, 187
Swinburn, Richard, 223
Sykes, Bryan, 112
synapse, synaptic gap, 211

T

Tarna, Richard, 45
Tattersall, Ian, 108
Tayon, Edward, 90
Teresa of Avila, 355
theology, revealed, natural, 365
theory of everything, 66, 445
Time magazine, 219, 293, 325, 329
Tippler, Frank, 74, 161
Toffler, Alvin, 155
Townes, Charles, 79
transcendental meditation, 231
Trefil, James, 76, 199, 221
Trinh Xuan Thuan, 72, 76, 374, 407

U

uncertainty principle, 20, 43
unconscious, collective, 53, 398–99
Unified Theory of Everything, 66, 445
Union of Concerned Scientists, 155
universal consciousness, 214
uranium, 442
Usher, Bishop, 131

V

Van Till, Howard, 431
Vardey, Lucinda, 323
vesicles, 211
Viney, Geoff, 351
viruses, 191
Von Neumann, John, 161

W

Wallace, Douglas, 111
weak nuclear force, 66
Weil, Andrew, 336
Wheeler, John, 78, 93, 373
Wiggins, Anita, 43
Wigner, Eugene, 44, 71, 220, 418
Wilson, Allen, 111
Wilson, Edward O., 215
Wineland, David, 46
Wise, Anna, 406
worm holes, 63
Wynn, Charles, 43

Y

yoga, 231

Z

Zebrowski, Ernest, 105

Printed in the United States
18089LVS00001B/34-51